Integrated Treatment of Child Sexual Abuse

INTEGRATED TREATMENT OF CHILD SEXUAL ABUSE

A Treatment and Training Manual

Henry Giarretto

Science and Behavior Books, Inc.
Palo Alto, California

Library of Congress Card Number 81-86-712

ISBN 0-8314-0061-7

Edited by Rain Blockley
Interior design by Bill Yenne
Cover design by Bill Yenne
Printed by Haddon Craftsmen

This publication was made possible, in part, by grant number 90-C-1754 from the National Center on Child Abuse and Neglect, Children's Bureau, Administration for Children, Youth and Families, Office of Human Development Services, U.S. Department of Health and Human Services.

Proceeds from the sale of this book, as well as the author's royalties, are contributed to Parents United, Daughters and Sons United, and Adults Molested as Children United.

Contents

Foreword

by Robert S. Spitzer, M.D.

Hank Giarretto likes to introduce me at Parents United meetings as the man who started the Incest Project and who tried to hire his wife, Anna Einfeld Giarretto, to run it. Since Anna was too busy, Hank says I had to settle for him. At the time, I did prefer Anna. Through a one-way mirror, I had seen her work with a family and liked her style. Hank was unknown to me, and I was concerned that a man might inherit overwhelming negative transferences from all sides.

It didn't work out that way. If anything, Hank has been seen as a kindly, youngish grandfather type. He has a quiet charisma that was not apparent to me at first but which has been essential for the development and spread of the program. And after a year or so, Anna was able to join the program. They have been a most effective pair and a wonderful support for each other. I have heard Anna refer to the project as "raising a second family." Hank is the apparent leader, the administrator; Anna, the nurturing teacher and therapist. And yet they can easily switch roles if the occasion demands.

It's fun for me to look back on my first thoughts about the project and see what we have learned. I was the consulting psychiatrist at Juvenile Hall in San Jose when a marriage counselor in private practice asked me to see a family. The father had served his time for incest—a year in county jail. The father and mother had entered couple therapy and had improved their communication and relationship greatly. Their daughter, the incest victim, joined therapy, confronted her father, and over time developed a trusting relationship with him. The other children also joined therapy. They all came in to see me and it was clear this family could now talk openly.

But the judge had given an order that the father could not return home until after the youngest child had reached her majority. As it was, the father frequently visited his family at home, and they were afraid of getting caught. They had the expense of two residences. And they all wanted to be together. They wanted a letter from me to the judge saying it was safe for the father to return home.

I felt very comfortable about writing a strong recommendation. No counseling had been ordered; this family had done it on their own and had grown. Everyone had learned to talk and confront in this family.

But when the daughter recounted her story, I had been stunned at how the system had added to her trauma, i.e., the interrogation by the police, placement in the Children's Shelter, separation from her parents, cross-examination in court, and the resentment and misunderstanding of her siblings. I then talked to other people about their experience in treating incest, sought out some more cases, and became convinced that our previous method of handling it was about as bad as it could be. I suspected judges sent the fathers to jail because no one had set up an alternate program and could offer a way to realistically protect the family.

Just about that time, Eunice Peterson spoke to me about setting up a program for the treatment of incest perhaps similar to the parents' groups that she had helped start for battered children. As we talked, it became apparent to me that we needed someone who would be able to work with the families from the first contact with the system, when they needed help the most. To reduce red tape and territorial disputes, I felt it should be someone from outside the county system. I decided to hire someone myself on an experimental basis until we had enough evidence to be able to get a grant. Hank agreed to work part time, and almost from the beginning he was overwhelmed by referrals. I remember probation officers stopping me to say, "This guy Giarretto is something else." They liked his informal, practical manner and the way he made himself accessible to them, and morale had improved because of his effectiveness.

We usually recommended to the judge that the father be treated in the community. I had been taught in medical school and psychiatric residency that incest was rare and the perpetrator severely disturbed. In most of our cases, however, the father did not seem so disturbed. He usually functioned well in other areas of his life, the incest had gone on for years, and he had good reason to believe he could continue to get away with it.

An initial hypothesis I had was that incest required secrecy. The family could not talk about it openly and allow it to continue. I felt confident that family therapy and/or multiple-family therapy and/or group therapy for the girls would prevent reoccurence, since the father would know he would be caught again.

The case load was soon much too large for me to supervise. However, it didn't seem to matter because in a relatively short period of time, Hank had more experience in treating incest than I had—or, for that matter, probably more than anyone in the country.

In retrospect, it seems to me that it is fortunate that we were always understaffed. This made it essential that clients help each other and led to Parents United. It also led to a strong volunteer component of people who knew they were making a significant contribution.

I also did not foresee the degree to which the large group would prove helpful. In certain ways, large groups do something ordinary group family or individual therapy cannot achieve, perhaps by identification with a larger entity. This is evident at meetings of Parents United, and Hank, Anna, Ellie et al. have been able to capture the same spirit in the training sessions. Trainees from Calfornia, other states, and increasingly from other countries leave with the enthusiasm and wherewithal to establish their own programs. This book should facilitate that process.

Preface

The purpose of this manual is to help workers in child protective services, mental health, law enforcement, and associated agencies to establish programs similar to the Child Sexual Abuse Treatment Program (CSATP) of Santa Clara County, California. This CSATP has provided comprehensive, community-based services to more cases of familial and extrafamilial child molestation than any other single organization. The training project, funded originally by a California state grant and presently by a federal grant, has resulted in the establishment of sixty-five centers all based on the CSATP model.

A CSATP becomes effective to the degree that its staff is able to integrate the interventions of human service agencies, the criminal justice system, trained community volunteers, and members of the program's self-help component. Although a sufficiently integrated, operational CSATP will develop gradually and will involve quite a few people, only two or three trained workers are required to start one and to guide its development. The CSATPs now functioning were begun, typically, by one or two employees of child protective services and a mental health worker who were trained at the Santa Clara County project.

This manual will be useful to all people involved in the treatment of sexually abused children and their families. Of course, the manual alone cannot engender learning equivalent to the actual training course, which permits the personal participation of trainees in the ongoing functions of the CSATP. Workers in the field who wish to form a CSATP in their communities as quickly and productively as possible are advised to apply for admission to the national training project by contacting the training coordinator, Chuck Juliano (National Child Sexual Abuse Treatment Training Project, P. O. Box 952, San Jose, CA 95108 or call 408-280-5055).

Acknowledgments

The information in this publication reflects the experiences of the many individuals who have contributed to the development of the Child Sexual Abuse Treatment Program (CSATP) and its training projects. The most important contributors to this ten-year-old effort have been the members of Parents United and Daughters and Sons United, to whom this publication is dedicated. Key leaders in the growth of Parents United include: Marge, Sharon, and Nora, who were the first mothers to help one another and incoming mothers and who became the charter members of the organization; Tom, the first father to join the group, who currently serves as the national coordinator for Parents United and who is certainly the one member who has provided the most protracted and valuable service to the organization; Peggie and Art, who in more recent years have led many of the activities of Parents United, including its vital crisis-intervention and public-information functions and who, with Tom, form the nucleus of the outreach team that helps the formation of new chapters; Kathy and Jo, who recently joined the staff to take on respectively the tasks of office manager and secretary; and Sharon, the charter member who continues to spearhead the development of Parents United; Vickie M., who coordinates our spouse violence project; Niki, who promotes the special interest of adults molested as children; and Maria, who fills the difficult role of receptionist for the PU/DSU counseling center.

Major credit for the progress of Daughters and Sons United must be given to Cindy DeNoyer-Greer, Vicki Imabori, and Diane Goza, and to DSU members Debby, Terry, Cletus, Kathy, Joanna, and Cheryl. These individuals continue to refine and augment the activities of the local model chapter of the DSU and to assist similar groups elsewhere.

The professionals principally responsible for the CSATP are: Eunice Peterson, section supervisor, and Bob Spitzer, consulting psychiatrist, of the Juvenile Probation Department, both of whom recognized the problem and took action and who continue to bolster the overall effort; Hank Giarretto, who with Anna Einfeld-Giarretto initiated and guided the humanistic approach and continue to improve the treatment model and direct the training projects; and Dorothy Ross of the Juvenile Probation Department and Vicki Imabori, who composed the CSATP staff (with Giarretto) until late 1976. Ross and Imabori persist in their respective roles as program coordinator and as administrator of special projects in the current treatment and training projects.

In early 1977, the following individuals— who had previously provided long-term voluntary services—joined the staff officially: Bob Carroll of the Juvenile Probation Department was program administrator for the California treatment and training project and currently supervises the Department's CSATP and takes an important part in the national training project; Chuck Juliano, the training coordinator for the California project, who now performs as administrator for the national training project; Bee Brown and Ellie Breslin, former interns, are staff-counselors and training specialists who remain with the staff to take on the many tasks associated with counselor-trainer functions; Elizabeth Cobey— our legal consultant, fund-raiser, and general trouble-shooter—is responsible for similar functions in the current projects. Elizabeth is the author of appendix 4D, "Parents United Guidelines to Confidentiality."

The CSATP would be less effective—and indeed, would have a different character—were it not for the volunteered services of a large cadre of administrative and counseling interns. The staff of the CSATP is immensely grateful to these volunteers for their invaluable contributions to the treatment and training projects. All cannot be mentioned individually, but special thanks are due to Jane Lewis, Wayne Littrell, Anne Riley, Barbara Berns, Terry Williams and Richard Reinhardt, who have served unstintingly for several years; and to Bernice Lynch and Leona Tockey, who also after lengthy service as interns recently joined the staff as counselor-trainers.

The constructive impact of the program on sexually abused children and their families would not have developed without the cooperation or at least forbearance of the criminal justice system. The CSATP was spawned within the Juvenile Probation Department headed by Richard Bothman, and it was directly nurtured by numerous probation officers. Among the most active were the officers mentioned previously and those who recently were added to the staff of the department's CSATP: Steve Baron, Laura Costello, Phil Giambrone (who helped to start Parents United), Paul Jordan, Anne Myers, and Nancy Tadlock.

The vital support of the San Jose Police Department was in large part fostered by Sgt. Gene Brown. He was the first police officer to recognize the potential benefits of the program, to initiate investigative methods that complemented the objectives of the program, and to promote persistently the advantages of the approach to police jurisdictions throughout the nation. Brown helped form and presently supervises the San Jose Police Department's Sexual Assault Investigation Unit. The personnel of the unit are responsible for the critical first phase of the family's passage through the criminal justice system, and several members of the unit participate in the training. The staff of the CSATP is also grateful to Police Chief Joseph McNamara, Lt. Arthur Knopf, District Attorney Louis Bergna, and to the many judges and other officials of

the criminal justice system who endorse the CSATP. Among the judges who support the CSATP, special mention is due to California Superior Court Judge Leonard Edwards, whose views are clearly expressed in appendix 4A, "Dealing with Parent and Child in Serious Abuse Cases."

The dissemination of the CSATP model to other communities in the nation was initiated by John Vasconcellos, assemblyman of the California state legislature. He wrote the law that established the California training project and which eventually paved the way for the national project. The gratitude of the staff is due to Assemblyman Vasconcellos and to his assistant Brian Kahn for their extraordinary efforts in getting the law passed.

The potential value of this manual to the profession was perceived by Kee MacFarlane of the National Center on Child Abuse and Neglect. She also served as project officer for the federal grant and more than fulfilled her duties in this regard by participating in the initial design of the manual and by contributing her knowledge of the field and her editorial skills.

Particular gratitude is owed to Mona Smith and John Daniel, who were deeply involved in the early planning of this manual. Finally, Ellie Breslin must be singled out as a major contributor to Part II and as the author of appendix 1, "Counseling Methods and Techniques."

Abbreviations

CJS	Criminal justice system
CPS	Child Protective Services
CSATP	Child Sexual Abuse Treatment Program
DSU	Daughters and Sons United
JPD	Juvenile Probation Department

JPO	Juvenile probation officer
MDSO	Mentally disordered sex offender
OR	Own Recognizance
PU	Parents United, Inc.
SAIU	Sexual Assault Investigation Unit (Santa Clara County, California)

Introduction

History of the CSATP Training Project

The Child Sexual Abuse Treatment Program

In 1971, members of the Juvenile Probation Department (JPD) of Santa Clara County, California, decided that the case management of sexually abused children and their families needed to be drastically improved. The department's consulting psychiatrist asked a family counselor to volunteer his services for a pilot effort of eighty hours spread over ten weeks. Clients were counseled on-site at the JPD, and a close collaboration ensued between the counselor and the probation officers. Counseling was based on the principles and methods of humanistic psychology, emphasizing treatment for the victim and the mother. But it was soon discovered, particularly in father–daughter incest cases, that the victims' interests were best served if the mother, father, and the rest of the family were included in the counseling plan.

The pilot effort proved successful and in time developed into what is now known as the Child Sexual Abuse Treatment Program (CSATP). The CSATP has grown substantially over the years: the referral rate has jumped from thirty families in 1971 to over seven hundred families in 1980; the program is known nationwide for its success in resocializing sexually abusive families and in training other communities to set up similar programs.

The success of a CSATP depends on the effective interaction of its professional,

volunteer, and self-help components. However, it is the self-help component, Parents United and Daughters and Sons United (PU/DSU), that assumes the pivotal position in a CSATP and contributes most heavily to the resocialization of clients.

California State Assembly Bill 2288.*

In May 1975, California Assemblyman John Vasconcellos introduced a bill requiring the state Department of Health to establish a demonstration and training center for the prevention of the sexual abuse of children. Many of the goals and functions stated in the proposed bill were modeled on the original goals and functions of the CSATP in Santa Clara County:

1. To provide counseling and practical assistance by on-site professionals to sexually abused children and their families, particularly to victims of incest;

2. To hasten, where in the interests of the child, the process of reconstitution of the family and marriage;

3. To marshal and coordinate the services of all agencies responsible for the sexually abused child and his or her family, as well as other resources to ensure comprehensive, systematic case management;

4. To employ a model that fosters self-managed growth (rather than a medical model based on curing disease) and avoids static theories and methods;

5. to respond to individual physical, emotional, and social needs of clients so that supportive services are individually tailored and applied as long as necessary;

6. to facilitate the expansion and autonomy of self-help groups and to provide training to the members in such areas as co-counseling,

*California Legislature, 1975–76 Regular Session, Assembly Bill 2288, Sacramento, CA.

self-management, intrafamily communication techniques, and locating community resources; and

7. to inform the public at large and professional agencies about the existence and supportive approach of the program with the aim of encouraging victims and offenders to seek the services of the program voluntarily.

Assembly Bill 2288 also proposed that this center should go beyond serving the needs of its own immediate community. The bill provided that the center should motivate and train other communities in the state to start similar programs of their own. The bill directed the center to develop "informational and training materials and seminars to enable emulation or adaptation of the program by other communities, emphasizing the program's stress on cooperation and coordination with all appropriate elements of the criminal justice system and law enforcement system."

AB 2288 was passed on the Assembly floor by a vote of sixty-six to one. It was approved unanimously by the state Senate and was signed into law by Governor Jerry Brown at the end of the session, October 1975. The designation "Demonstration and Training Center" was awarded to the Child Sexual Abuse Treatment Program in Santa Clara County.

The Training Program

In compliance with AB 2288, members of the CSATP in Santa Clara County developed a two-week course to train members of agencies holding jurisdiction over cases of child sexual abuse. The trainees are given an intensive course in the nature of child sexual abuse (incest in particular) and how the CSATP copes with it. They are taught a number of humanistic counseling techniques and they sit in on staff meetings, learn how to handle various administrative problems, attend meetings of PU/DSU, and assist in actual counseling sessions with incestuous families. In sum, they are influenced through intimate contact with the staff and clients to internalize the philosophy and methods and to implement them in their own communities.

The training course is followed up with continual support by an outreach unit of the CSATP. Members of the professional staff and Parents United are always available for

consultation and for troubleshooting visits as the new programs develop.

Full funding became available (through AB 2288) in February 1977, and the first two-week course was conducted in April 1977. The project was refunded by the state in 1978; that funding ended in June 1979. By July 1979, there were twenty-two new CSATPs throughout the state of California in various stages of development, all begun primarily by child protective service workers and other agency personnel trained at the CSATP Training Project in Santa Clara County. All of the new programs have formed chapters of Parents United and Daughters and Sons United, some more advanced than others.

Work on a federal grant application to establish a national training project started in October 1979; the first course for that project was begun on January 28, 1980.

How Trainees Are Selected

When a county makes contact with the CSATP in Santa Clara County and expresses interest in the CSATP approach to the problems of child sexual abuse, they are first sent a package of literature about the program, the problem of incest and child molestation, the CSATP's humanistic approach to the treatment of this problem, and the curriculum of the two-week course. People from the interested county's responsible agency—usually Child Protective Services—are invited to come to San Jose to observe the program in action, to talk with the counselors, interns, and administrations of the program, to attend a meeting of Parents United, or to participate in the first three days of the training program. Often personnel of the training project visit the interested county to promote the CSATP model. Finally, arrangements are made for a group of trainees to come to San Jose for the two-week training course.

Counties and communities interested in developing their own CSATPs must carefully select the people they send to the training course. Integral to the program is strong personal dedication by a central person who will serve as program coordinator: someone who will act as a liaison between the family and other community resources, guide the family through criminal justice proceedings, and orchestrate the entire reconstructive process. In counties with limited staffs, this person should also have counseling experience.

It is important for the person who will act as principal coordinator/counselor and for all the trainees to be chosen for their open-minded and life-process-oriented attitudes. The training course is not just an academic exercise or sensitivity training retreat; it will consist of practical and methodical training in the real work the trainees will be doing in their own communities. Thus, trainees must be genuinely interested in starting child sexual abuse programs, must be assigned that responsibility by their supervisors, and must be prepared to devote a great deal of energy to the task—not only during the training course but also in the months and years to come.

As mentioned above, some people attend the course for only the first three days. This group might include supervisors or other individuals with decision-making responsibilities from agencies that have expressed interest in the CSATP and want to find out more about this approach before committing their energy and resources to forming a program of their own. Also, there are usually several short-term trainees among the people from the county being formally trained. These might be supervisors, police, probation officers, district attorney deputies, therapists—in short, the various people in the community who will intervene in child sexual abuse cases in one way or another and are linked to the central treatment process.

The rest of the trainees are those who will be involved directly with the treatment of client families. They will be the ones who set up the new CSATP in their county or community. They will be directing the development of the CSATP and doing the basic counseling. These trainees remain for the full two-week course.

Goals of the CSATP Training Program

The CSATP training project was originally developed to help communities throughout the state of California establish their own programs for the treatment of child sexual abuse. Its primary purpose is to teach agency people the skills and techniques that have proved effective for the Santa Clara County CSATP in dealing with the problems of incest and child sexual abuse. The training course offers basic instruction on the philosophy and methods of humanistic psychology, particularly as they are applied to this sensitive area.

More importantly, the course gives the trainees instruction and practice in individual, family, and group counseling, cooperating with the other professionals in their county, techniques for productive case management, identifying and using private and official county resources usually available for troubled families, relating to the general public on the volatile subject of incest, and in general in the obstacles they are likely to face while establishing a child sexual abuse treatment program based on the Santa Clara model. At the end of the two weeks, trainees should anticipate the challenges ahead of them and should have a realistic plan and the preliminary skills for facing those challenges.

The CSATP training course uses the lecture mode sparingly. Films and other audio-visual aids are employed and the trainees are given talks with the opportunity to confer with offenders, victims, mothers, counselors, and administrators. But again, the greater percentage of time spent in the training course is devoted to practical learning experience. Trainees sit in on actual individual and group counseling sessions, administrative meetings, and meetings of Parents United and Daughters and Sons United. The concept of people helping people is internalized by the trainees by real-world experience. By the end of the course, trainees usually begin to interact cooperatively and to prepare for their future work in their community.

They are reminded frequently, however, not to feel overwhelmed by the Santa Clara County CSATP; they are seeing a system that took ten years to develop. Their own tasks, when they return to their jobs, will be simpler, and they will be helped in devising a plan of action suited to each of their communities on the last day of the course.

The whole issue of incest is controversial and disturbing, even for the seasoned child protection worker. Humanistic concepts can be simply stated, and they make good sense intellectually, but they are difficult to master such that they can be applied consistently in true-world situations. Coping with sexually abusive families in a humanistic way is easy to explain but difficult to do.

The sine qua non of the humanistic attitude is self-knowledge, and, therefore, the teaching of skills for self-exploration is an essential goal of the CSATP training program. Using experiential learning techniques, the trainees begin to probe their subconscious feelings concerning human sexuality and incest. They learn to identify past related experiences in their own families which are usually repressed and to discuss them openly. In learning to express their feelings, they ultimately discover that they have found a powerful method for developing a humanistic attitude toward themselves, their co-workers, their clients, and other important people in their lives.

How to Use This Manual

Part I gives the history, principles, and general methodology of the Child Sexual Abuse Treatment Program of Santa Clara County. It is recommended that this be read thoroughly as a foundation for Part II, which describes in detail the two-week course conducted by the training project of the Santa Clara County CSATP. Each of the ten units represents a day of the course; each unit is divided into modules and activities for satisfying specific goals and objectives.

Supplementary material such as talks by CSATP trainers or suggested talks by other trainers, explicit instructions on the exercises used in the training sessions, forms, and schedules accompany the appropriate modules. Additional resources can be found in the appendices.

Some readers will find that some of the units in this manual are more appropriate or important than others for the needs of their particular communities. Users of this manual are advised to read the entire book before making use of whatever they find most appropriate for their specific purposes. All communities should feel free to copy the Santa Clara County model exactly or to modify it as they see fit.

In modifying the training course, however, trainers should note that those who have been through the training program in Santa Clara County have found the experiential sessions and exercises to be the most valuable. Any child sexual abuse treatment and/or training program should emphasize the value of working together, self-knowledge, and the irrefutable rule that only through continual practice can the principles and methods of humanistic psychology be internalized.

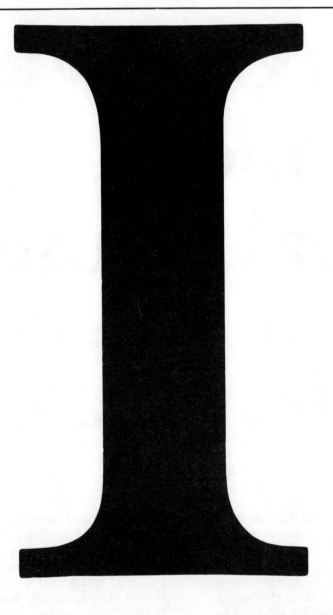

I

The CSATP's History and Background

1. An Overview of Child Sexual Abuse

The sexual exploitation of children by adults remains a serious and widespread problem. Indications are strong that the majority of child sexual abuse crimes are never reported to the authorities. During the past decade, only a handful of programs were begun for the purpose of treating the victims and their families. Once the programs became known to the public, all experienced sharp increases in referral rates. The number of treatment programs throughout the country has increased moderately in the last two or three years. A recent survey by MacFarlane of the National Center on Child Abuse and Neglect resulted in the identification of over 200 such programs, of which 65 are directly based on the CSATP model. It can be safely assumed, however, that only a fraction of the actual cases of child sexual abuse are referred to these few programs, leaving the nation's needs met only meagerly.

Definitions

The commonly used phrase "child sexual abuse" suggest the sexual exploitation of a child by an older, more mature person. The relationship is considered exploitive if the partners were obviously mismatched in psychosocial maturity: that is, if the two persons involved were not equally capable of negotiating a mutually beneficial sexual partnership.

Professionals in the field as well as the public at large are generally in agreement about the meaning of child sexual abuse. However, the phrase and its commonly accepted meaning are disputed by a few members of that amorphous population known as the intelligentsia, who suggest that the phrase incites excessive alarm over the problem and that this undue reaction is the main cause of the trauma to the child and his or her family. A very few critics of the phrase and its commonly accepted definition take the extreme view that children might profit from early sexual indoctrination by responsible adults.

State penal codes reflect concern over child sexual abuse but differ significantly in their legal definitions of the problem and in the penalties to offenders. For example, the definitions of common legal jargon such as "child molestation," "carnal abuse of a child," and "impairing the morals of a minor" vary from state to state. Nor do the laws agree exactly as to the "age of consent" or to the age difference between the partners which, when exceeded, makes one a victim and the other an offender.[1]

Great disparity also exists in state laws regarding incest. For example, the legal codes of some states specify that the partners must be blood-related before the crimes can be prosecuted under the incest laws. In other states, consanguinity is not necessary for legal intervention, and acts are incestuous even if the partners are only contractually related: for example, the sexual abuse of a child by a stepparent or stepsibling.[2]

[1]Donald E. J. MacNamara and Edward Sagarin, *Sex, Crime and the Law* (New York: The Free Press, 1977).
[2]Kee MacFarlane, "Sexual Abuse of Children" in J. R. Chapman and M. Gates, eds., *The Victimization of Children* (Beverly Hills: Sage Publications, 1978).

The CSATP is concerned, of course, over the lack of uniformity in the laws and their unpredictable implementation by the criminal justice system. The training staff includes a legal consultant and a module of the training course is based on her input. The public education effort of Parents United is intended to influence both lay and professional elements in the community to take a more temperate, more productive stance toward familial and extrafamilial child sexual abuse. The personnel of all CSATPs should study their state penal codes and try to get their legislators to improve them.

These efforts, however, will at best produce results in the future and have little to do with the primary task of a CSATP counselor, which is to provide immediate humanistic treatment to the child and her family. Humanistic treatment implies individualized treatment. For the counselor, the best and certainly the most useful "definition" of child sexual abuse can be found in the child and members of her family during the initial counseling sessions. The way the counselor draws forth and interprets the child's personal experiences (as well as those of family members) constitutes the key initial step in a successful counseling plan for the family.

The majority of the cases referred to the CSATP in Santa Clara County have been cases of father–daughter (stepfathers and other paternal figures are included in this category) incest. Father–daughter incest also seems to be the most frequent form of child sexual abuse nationwide. In 1953, Kinsey reported findings indicating that 25 percent of American adult women were molested as children. More than half of the offenders were close friends or relatives, and of this number, 45 percent were fathers.[3]

The Effects of Untreated Incest

A father–daughter incestuous relationship imposes severe stresses on the structure of the family in our society. All family members usually suffer conflict and confusion; this is particularly true for the daughter, who is at an age when her developing sexuality requires clear and reassuring guidance. Family roles become blurred, and the victim does not know how to relate to her father, mother, or her siblings.

Among the adolescents who are referred to the CSATP for treatment, almost all confide various forms of self-punishing behavior, including truancy, heavy drug use, and promiscuity. It is important to stress that this self-punishing behavior existed prior to the report of the incest.

The assumption that similar problems afflict those girls whose victimization goes unreported is supported by the hundreds of letters received by the CSATP from women molested as children whose cases were not reported. According to Masters and Johnson:

> The victim suffers from the experience itself, which occasionally causes physical damage and frequently results in psychological damage; and she (or he) also eventually suffers the loss of her sense of security and of her own personal worth. In fact, a long-continued, guilt-ridden repression of the feelings generated by incest may eventually affect every aspect of her life.[4]

Hard data concerning the personal and social price paid for the societal neglect of children who are being sexually molested are beginning to accumulate through recent studies. Weber cites Burnstine's report that nearly all the girls residing at Chapin Hall, a residential program for disturbed and homeless children, have been sexually abused. Many of these girls are runaways from sexually abusive families. In the same article, Weber also noted that in treating more than five hundred adolescent children for drug addiction, Silverson found that about 70 percent were molested in their own homes.[5] Densen-Gerber, director of Odyssey House (a project that provides homes in several states for drug-abusive young adults) interviewed 118 female residents for their sexual history and found that 44 percent of them had experienced incest as children.[6]

Repressed fear, shame, and guilt usually have psychosomatic consequences, and it is not

[3]A. C. Kinsey et al., *Sexual Behavior in the Human Female* (Philadelphia: Saunders, 1953), pp. 104–27.

[4]William H. Masters and Virginia E. Johnson, "Incest: The Ultimate Sexual Taboo," *Redbook* Magazine, April 1976, pp. 54–58.
[5]Ellen Weber, "Incest: Sexual Abuse Begins at Home," *Ms.* Magazine, April 1977, p. 64.
[6]Jean Bernard and J. Densen-Gerber, *Incest as a Causative Factor in Antisocial Behavior* (New York: Odyssey Institute, 1975).

surprising to find that many women who were abused as children are sexually dysfunctional. Baisden discovered that an inordinately high percentage of women who were unable to enjoy sex in any form had been sexually exploited as children. In questioning a group of 160 women whom he was treating for sexual dysfunction, Baisden found that 90 percent had been molested during childhood, 22.5 percent by fathers or stepfathers.[7] The varieties of sexual dysfunction preceded by childhood molestation range from frigidity to nymphomania and the general inability to develop intimate relationships.

When the incestuous relationship is reported to the authorities, the traditional reactions usually aggravate the problems of the family. The court process often further victimizes the victim, who may already have been removed from her mother, home, and family and placed in a children's shelter. She is then expected to recount the incident in agonizing and embarrassing detail to the police department, the prosecuting attorney's office, and again in court before a host of unfamiliar faces, as well as in front of the accused, her father.

The judicial system, which purports to protect juvenile offenders from as much courtroom trauma as possible, curiously has made little such effort on behalf of child victims of sexual abuse. As Stevens and Berliner have stated, "If child molesters are prosecuted, child victims must endure the same processes as adult victims do, without benefit of special procedures or protection."[8]

Father–daughter incest has damaging effects on the entire family. The victims, mothers, father-offenders, and other children are devastated by the harsh reaction of the community. (Incest laws are inconsistent from state to state, but they are consistently punitive.) The members of the family are totally unprepared for the emotional and practical problems they meet. The marriage, poor to begin with, frequently goes bankrupt and ends in divorce, and the family is fragmented. There is certainly no single cause of incest or child sexual abuse. Incest can be regarded as a symptom of a dysfunctional family: a family headed by parents who are unable to develop a satisfying marital relationship and who cannot cooperate effectively as parents.

[7]M. J. Baisden, *The World of Rosaphrenia: The Sexual Psychology of the Female* (Sacramento, CA: Allied Research Society, 1971).

[8]Doris Stevens and Lucy Berliner, "Special Techniques for Child Witnesses" (Washington, DC: Center for Women Policy Studies, n.d.), p. 2.

2. History of the CSATP

In mid-1971, a pilot project was started to offer counseling to sexually abused children and their families in Santa Clara County. Most of the child sexual abuse cases referred to the project were cases of intrafamily sexual molestation—usually father–daughter incest. Because of the relatively large number of such cases (around thirty a year during the early 1970s) and because there was no other coordinated system of case management, the pilot project was continued and eventually grew into what is now known as the Child Sexual Abuse Treatment Program (CSATP). To understand the origin of this innovative resource, it is necessary first to look at the situation as it existed just before the project was formed.

The Problem

The population of Santa Clara County, California, in 1970 was approximately one million (322,870 households). The median educational level was quite high: 12.6 years. The population was 76.8 percent white, 17.5 percent hispanic, 4 percent oriental, 1.7 percent black and 1 percent other races. The county's economy before the Second World War had been primarily agricultural; by 1970, it was strongly based in the electronics, aerospace, research-and-development, and data-processing industries.

Along with this meteoric rise in industry had come a similar rise in population, and much of the county that had once been farmland and orchards was now given over to middle-income housing developments. The average household in Santa Clara County earned over thirteen thousand dollars a year, the highest median income of any metropolitan community in California. The county's main population center was and is the city of San Jose (population: 561,382).

No reliable statistics exist on the incidence of incest or of child abuse in general in Santa Clara County before 1971. Although the county was receiving around thirty referrals a year of cases involving sexual abuse of children, this figure did not include other cases in the juvenile justice system such as the so-called "beyond control" girls, many of whom, as it turned out, also were victims of incest. Despite the fact that the thirty reported cases a year in no way reflected the true number of ongoing cases, it was considered quite high in relation to the generally accepted estimate of one or two cases per million. (S. Kirson Weinberg had arrived at this estimate in 1955, citing 203 court cases over the period 1907–1938.[1] Other studies had substantiated Weinberg's figure, and it was regarded as the best statistic available.)

The reason that the CSATP was formed, however, was not so much the high number of child sexual abuse cases. More immediately pressing was the problem of how these cases were being handled by the criminal justice system at that time. Most often, the traditional tactics of law enforcement further aggravated the family's already deeply troubled state. The criminal justice system relied primarily on two devices: separation and punishment. It seemed that the courts' primary interest in the child had to do with what testimony she could give toward the conviction of the alleged perpetrator. In incest cases particularly, the whole family became entangled in the process of retribution. The damage to the family and the marriage was often irreparable.

In short, traditional community intervention added to the child-victim's fear, shame, guilt, and confusion, often ruined the father's career as well as his self-respect, and usually led to

[1]S. Kirson Weinberg, *Incest Behavior* (New York: Citadel Press, 1955), p. 36.

the break-up of the entire family. With these alarming consequences to be expected, it is no wonder that most families would not risk the danger of reporting their incestuous situation and did not receive the help and therapy they desperately needed.

In Santa Clara County, the Juvenile Probation Department (JPD) is the mandated reporting agency for child abuse cases; Child Protective Services is the agency usually responsible for this function elsewhere. The help the JPD offered was fragmented and complicated by bureaucracy, with the result that the already dysfunctional family dynamics were subjected to additional trauma.

The victim and her family were referred to one of the counseling agencies scattered over the county. Many clients resisted treatment because it was made so difficult for them. There were complicated eligibility requirements and long waiting lists. A counselor usually was assigned to a case on the basis of availability, rather than on the basis of training and skill. In fact, rather than receiving counseling, the client was often subjected to many diagnostic tests that would later be used in court.

Even when counseling was provided, there was little cooperation between mental health workers and probation officers. The supervising probation officer usually lacked the information, resources, and authority for proper case management. This poor management of reported cases of incest and child sexual abuse was not unique to Santa Clara County. In fact, it is a situation that still prevails in most communities throughout the United States.

The CSATP Is Started

In 1971, Eunice Peterson, supervisor of the Dependent/Placement section of the Juvenile Probation Department, and Robert S. Spitzer, M.D., the consulting psychiatrist for the JPD, contacted Hank Giarretto concerning the establishment of a pilot effort. Giarretto, a licensed marriage and family counselor, would provide counseling to sexually abused children and their families for a trial period of eighty hours spread over eight weeks. At the end of this period, the pilot program would be evaluated by Spitzer, Giarretto, and Peterson to determine if it should be continued. The initial ground rules of the pilot program were: the clients would be counseled on-site at the

Juvenile Probation Department; the program would emphasize conjoint family therapy as developed by Virginia Satir; and the therapeutic approach would follow a growth model predicated on humanistic psychology.

Early Objectives

To provide immediate on-site counseling. The first objective of the pilot program was to provide counseling to sexually abused children and their families as soon as possible after their referral to the JPD. Consequently it was decided that clients would be counseled at the JPD, where the counselor could be readily available to them, rather than at his private office. It also was hoped that having the counselor there would help destigmatize the JPD, so that it could be regarded as an agency where people could get help rather than punitive treatment. It was anticipated that having the counselor on hand would facilitate communication and coordination among all those persons responsible for the cases.

By the time the pilot program had completed its eight weeks, Giarretto found that he was inextricably involved with many clients. It was apparent that each client required far more time than the traditional weekly hour. In addition to the hour devoted to counseling, for example, Giarretto had to spend an equal or greater amount of time consulting with juvenile and adult probation officers, police, lawyers, school teachers, and rehabilitation officers. All of this work could not be handled by Giarretto alone, especially since he had to continue his practice to supplement his income. Most of the clients could not afford to pay for the counseling, even when the fee was based on a sliding scale. They had already suffered sudden financial setbacks as a result of exposure (bail bonds, legal fees, separate housing for the father, and juvenile hall fees, for example). It was clear that the program had to be expanded in order to be fully effective.

To marshal and coordinate available services. It also became apparent during the pilot program that counseling alone was not enough; the family required a great deal of practical assistance to help them through this troubled period. They needed help in locating community resources for such pressing needs as housing, employment, financial advice, and legal assistance. This effort required close collaboration between the counselor and the juvenile probation officer responsible for the case—another advantage of the counselor's working on-site at the JPD.

To hasten reconstitution of the family. It was decided at the outset that the counseling program would emphasize conjoint family therapy since incest was a family problem. However, it soon became clear that conjoint family therapy was inappropriate for the early stages of the incestuous family's crisis. The families were badly fragmented as a result of the incest and the dysfunctional family dynamics that preceded it; they were further fragmented by the trauma that accompanied the disclosure of their secret to civil authorities. If a daughter reported an incestuous situation with her father without consulting her mother, she usually was not ready to face her mother, or her father, nor was the wife ready to confront her child or her husband. Thus, it was decided that the child, father, and mother had to be treated separately before family therapy would work.

The pilot program of eight weeks had already proved effective with the families involved, and Spitzer, Giarretto, and Peterson had no difficulty in deciding that it should be continued and expanded. In time it became known as the Child Sexual Abuse Treatment Program. It soon captured the attention of the criminal justice system, the media, and the general public. The CSATP helped awaken these groups to the realities of child sexual abuse in our society. The program's growing reputation was based on several factors: it was the first program of its kind; it was providing counseling and support to more incestuous families than any other public agency in the country; it was winning the cooperation of both public and private agencies; and it was becoming an effective resource for the criminal justice system.

3. Treatment Philosophy of the CSATP

The Child Sexual Abuse Treatment Program does not rely heavily on the traditional methods of psychotherapy or behavior modification. Just as the traditional tactics of the criminal justice system are inappropriate for cases of intrafamily sexual abuse, so are the medical treatment models based on the curing of disease. Generally speaking, the CSATP counseling procedure does not probe the traumas of the past to "cure" mental afflictions, nor does it employ behavior modification to "desensitize" maladaptive behavior.

The goals of the CSATP's humanistic approach are to enable self-awareness and self-management, rather than the curing of mental illness. What clients can expect from their participation in the CSATP is a growing ability to monitor and direct their own life processes and to become socially responsible members of society.

Humanistic Psychology

A neglect of the inner needs of its citizens is the price American society has had to pay for its preoccupation with material goods and competitive individualism. A few Western psychologists sounded early warnings of this defect in Western culture and in particular of the reductionistic view of man held by behavioristic psychology. Among these writers were Jung, Adler, Gurdjieff, Allport, Horney, Goldstein, May, Fromm, Buber, Assagioli, Rogers, and Maslow—who are essentially "self-theory" psychologists. The role of the self as the center of the personality is an elusive concept, one that becomes tangible and internalized more by practice of the techniques of self-awareness than by reading the theoretical explorations. The latter should, of course, not be ignored.[1]

Humanistic psychology is fundamentally a psychology of personal awareness and self-management. Simply stated, a person actualizes latent abilities as s/he gains awareness and control of unconscious thoughts, feelings, and behavior. De Ropp notes that normal man lives in a state of walking sleep. He passes through his waking hours by identifying with—or reacting automatically to—whatever he happens to be doing, sensing, feeling, or thinking.

---

[1]A useful introduction to the "self" concept is the section entitled "Rogers' Self Theory" in C. S. Hall and G. Lindsey, *Theories of Personality* (New York: John Wiley & Sons, 1957). See also the revised edition, published in 1965.

Man in this state is described not as the real man but as a machine without inner unity, real will or permanent I, acted upon and manipulated by external forces as puppet activated by the puppeteer.[2]

A person who is not self-aware seems to respond continually to a stream of posthypnotic suggestions. In a similar vein, Assagioli states: "We are dominated by everything with which our self becomes identified. We can dominate and control everything from which we disidentify ourselves."[3]

Maslow and Rogers are generally regarded as leaders among the scholars who crystalized the concepts of humanism into a formal discipline. In *Toward a Psychology of Being,* Maslow saw the emerging discipline as a psychology of health, a "Third Force," a new *Weltanschauung* that was distinctly different from the first force (the behavioristic, objectivistic school) and the second force (the analytic school originated by Freud and psychoanalysis).

Maslow's basic assumptions concerning this fresh point of view were:

1. We have, each of us, an essential, biologically based inner nature, which is to some degree "natural," intrinsic, given, and in a certain limited sense, unchangeable, or at least unchanging.

2. Each person's inner nature is in part unique to himself and in part species-wide.

3. It is possible to study this inner nature scientifically and to discover what it is like (not invent—*discover*).

4. This inner nature, as much as we know of it so far, seems not to be intrinsically or primarily or necessarily evil. The basic needs (for life, for safety and security, for belongingness and affection, for respect and self-respect, and for self-actualization), the basic human emotions and the basic human capacities are on their face either neutral, premoral or positively "good." Destructiveness, sadism, cruelty, malice, etc., seem so far to be not intrinsic but rather they seem to be violent reactions against frustration of our intrinsic needs, emotions and capacities. Anger is *in itself* not evil, nor is fear, laziness, or even ignorance. Of course, these can and do lead to evil behavior, but they needn't. This result is not intrinsically necessary. Human nature is not nearly as bad as it has been thought to be. In fact, it can be said that the possibilities of human nature have customarily been sold short.

5. Since this inner nature is good or neutral rather than bad, it is best to bring it out and to encourage it rather than to suppress it. If it is permitted to guide our life, we grow healthy, fruitful and happy.

6. If this essential core of the person is denied or suppressed, he gets sick, sometimes in obvious ways, sometimes in subtle ways, sometimes immediately, sometimes later.

[2]Robert S. De Ropp, *The Master Game* (New York: Delta Books, 1968), p. 62.
[3]Roberto Assagioli, *Psychosynthesis* (New York: Hobbs, Dorman, 1965), p. 22.

7. This inner nature is not strong and overpowering and unmistakable like the instincts of animals. It is weak and delicate and subtle and easily overcome by habit, cultural pressure, and wrong attitudes toward it.

8. Even though weak, it rarely disappears in the normal person—perhaps not even in the sick person. Even though denied, it persists underground forever pressing for actualization.

9. Somehow, these conclusions must all be articulated with the necessity of discipline, deprivation, frustration, pain, and tragedy. To the extent that these experiences reveal and foster and fulfill our inner nature, to that extent they are desirable experiences. It is increasingly clear that these experiences have something to do with a sense of achievement and ego strength and therefore, with the sense of healthy self-esteem and self-confidence. The person who hasn't conquered, withstood, and overcome continues to feel doubtful that he *could.* This is true not only for external dangers; it holds also for the ability to control and to delay one's own impulses, and therefore, to be unafraid of them.[4]

Roger's self theory of personality became widely known in the 1950s, largely because of the method of psychotherapy which he originated and called "client-centered therapy." In Rogers's words, successful client-centered therapy

> would mean that the therapist has been able to enter into an intensely personal and subjective relationship with his client— relating not as a scientist to an object of study, not as a physician expecting to diagnose and cure, but as a person to a person. It would mean that the therapist feels this client to be a person of unconditional self-worth; of value no matter what his condition, his behavior or his feelings. It means that the therapist is able to let himself go in understanding this client; that no inner barriers keep him from sensing what it feels like to be the client at each moment of the relationship; and that he can convey something of his empathetic understanding to the client. It means that the therapist has been comfortable in entering this relationship fully, without knowing cognitively where it will lead, satisfied with providing a climate which will free the client to become himself.

> For the client, this optimal therapy has meant an exploration of increasingly strange and unknown and dangerous feelings in himself; the exploration proving possible only because he is gradually realizing that he is accepted unconditionally. Thus, he becomes acquainted with elements of his experience which have in the past been denied to awareness as too threatening, too damaging to the structure of the self. He finds himself experiencing these feelings fully, completely, in the relationship, so that for the moment he is his fear, or his anger, or his tenderness, or his strength. And as he lives these widely varied feelings, in all their degrees of intensity, he discovers that he has experienced *himself,* that he *is* all these feelings. He finds his behavior changing in constructive fashion in accordance with his newly experienced self. He approaches the realization that he no longer needs to fear what experience may hold, but can welcome it freely as a part of his changing and developing self.[5]

---

[4]Abraham Maslow, *Toward a Psychology of Being,* Second Edition (New York: Van Nostrand Reinhold, 1968), pp. 3–4.

[5]C. R. Rogers, "The Concept of the Fully Functioning Person," unpublished manuscript (1955) quoted in C. S. Hall and G. Lindzey, *Theories of Personality* (New York: John Wiley & Sons, 1957), pp. 475–76.

The treatment philosophy of the CSATP is indebted to the seminal teachings of Maslow and Rogers, and the above-mentioned theoreticians on the self. The CSATP is also strongly influenced by other individual persuasions under the umbrella of humanistic psychology. For example, many of the techniques used in the program are from or are modified versions of psychosynthesis: integral psychology, Gestalt therapy, psychodrama, effective communication, guided imagery, transactional analysis, conjoint family therapy, and personal journal-keeping. But these techniques are not chosen or followed according to any set formula; rather, they are used as the counselors see fit to meet the individual needs of each client. The most important contributions to the principles and methods of the CSATP come from psychosynthesis and integral psychology and they will be briefly reviewed here.

Psychosynthesis Psychosynthesis is the name given by Assagioli to his conception of the human psyche. The theory appeared in germinal form in his doctoral thesis on psychoanalysis (1910), in which he discussed some of the limitations of Freud's views. Throughout his career he expanded both the theory and the practice of his approach in numerous papers and books.

Psychosynthesis is based on the following principles: the idea of starting from within and experiencing self-identity; the concept of personal growth; the importance of the meaning a person makes of his or her life; the key notion of responsibility and ability to choose among alternatives; the emphasis on present and future, rather than on regrets or yearnings for the past; and the recognition of the uniqueness of each individual.[6]

The differences between psychosynthesis and the main body of humanistic psychology are not categorical but relative. They emanate from the emphasis Assagioli places on certain aspects: the underscoring of the will as an essential function of self; the experience of self-awareness independent of immediate I-consciousness of the various parts of the personality; a positive view of the human

[6]Assagioli, *op. cit.*, p. 4.

condition which holds that life can be exciting and joyous; the systematic use of didactic and experiential techniques that follow an individuated plan for the harmonious blending of mind, body, and spirit around the self, the unifying center of the psyche; and an assumption of the higher self, of a superconscience, manifested by drives such as creative imagination, intuition, aspiration, and genius.[7]

By practicing self-awareness and, at the same time, disidentifying ourselves from the body states, feelings, thoughts, roles, and attitudes with which we formerly identified, we learn to experience our real selves and begin to build a fuller, self-actualized personality. This is the process Assagioli calls "psychosynthesis." To begin this process, a person must formulate a plan of action. S/he must have a clear image in mind of the new personality s/he wishes to develop and the steps necessary to achieve this goal.

Assagioli distinguishes between two levels of psychosynthesis: personal and transpersonal. In personal psychosynthesis, a person learns and optimizes the ability of directing, transforming, and sublimating the fundamental psychological energies and bringing them into harmony around the awakened center of the self. These basic energies are associated with the primitive drives and with the thoughts and feelings that are stirred by the normal environment. On the other hand, transpersonal psychosynthesis suggests an upward leap towards integration of the creative aspects involving the higher aspirations of mankind. The CSATP concentrates on personal psychosynthesis and the discussion here and in Part II is limited to personal psychosynthesis.

[7]Assagioli, *op. cit.*, p. 193.

It must be noted that when a person disidentifies/desensitizes/dehypnotizes the real self from the transient body, feeling, and mind states, that person need not reject or "extinguish" these experiences. Rather, s/he assimilates and integrates them into the growth process, realizing that experiences which formerly immobilized him or her in pain or anxiety can be regarded as points of departure for growth. Moreover, an individual can assume an optimistic posture toward life and enter into situations with zest and enthusiasm instead of with anxiety and fear of dire consequences.

Assagioli underscores the importance of the will as a function of the self. He understands the will not in the usual sense of "willpower" promoted by books on positive thinking. Specifically, he does not mean a will devoted to selfish drives or compulsive upward mobility in the socioeconomic sphere by subjugation and domination of others:

> Here the first necessity is to achieve a disidentification of the personal self from those drives. This means the developing of a constructive, strong, persevering and wise will—in essence, a fusion of what we consider to be some of the fundamental energies in the human being, viz. the energy of will and the energy of love, so that we eventually have in operation a "loving will."[8]

An important tenet of psychosynthesis is that it constitutes a lifestyle that cannot be attained solely by an intellectual grasp of the concepts; to be internalized, psychosynthesis must be *experienced* through the use of specially designed exercises followed up by practice in real life situations.

Integral Psychology. Like Jung, Maslow, Rogers, and the many others whose thinking have influenced the development of humanistic psychology, Assagioli was strongly influenced by the psychologists and philosophers of the Far East. Some of the CSATP's treatment philosophy, therefore, is drawn directly from Eastern sources, in particular from the writings of Haridas Chaudhuri, founder of the California Institute of Integral Studies in San Francisco. Chaudhuri may be viewed as the Eastern counterpart of Assagioli; despite the differences in their cultural roots, the philosophies of the two men are remarkably similar. The following discussion is based largely on two books written by Chaudhuri. The first, *The Evolution of Integral Consciousness*, presents his philosophy; the second, *Integral Yoga*, develops a plan of action for implementing the philosophy. In combination, they form the discipline known as integral psychology.

Chaudhuri proposed that a life plan devoted to self-realization must include psychic integration, cosmic integration, and existential integration.[9] The treatment fundamentals of the CSATP draw primarily from psychic and cosmic integration, therefore, only these concepts will be reviewed.

[8]Assagioli, *op. cit.,* pp. 141–42.

[9]Haridas Chaudhuri, *Integral Yoga* (San Francisco: California Institute of Integral Studies, 1965), p. 83.

For psychic integration one must learn how to bring into harmony the diverse elements of personality. These are the competing impulses, drives, and urges, most of which are buried in the unconscious. Counteracting these is the rational will, which evolves as a consequence of social and cultural pressures. The demands of the elemental, natural drives must be reconciled with the demands of the social environment. Neither need be sacrificed for the other. If a person's bent is entirely hedonistic, s/he blindly follows the will-o'-the-wisp of selfish gratification and never achieves inner stability. The price paid for this course is disorientation and purposelessness.

In direct contrast to the pleasure-seeking life is one that imposes cruel standards of unbending austerity, giving no heed to the pleasurable aspects of life. Still another extremist life posture is one that adheres to religious asceticism, that denies the social and instinctual ingredients of well-being and subjects the body to unrelenting deprivation.

Self-integration means integration of all aspects of personality—the physical, mental, emotional, spiritual, and social. Chaudhuri insisted that psychic health cannot transpire if separated from society or from the unconscious psyche:

> One may criticize society and try to remould it, but one cannot ignore society or discard it. To renounce society permanently for its imperfections is like rejecting one's wife for her illness. Likewise, to suppress the unconscious for its dark impulses is like throwing away the baby with the bath water. For the light is hidden right in the heart of darkness.[10]

Chaudhuri equated nature and society with the cosmos. To achieve self-realization, one must also interact intimately with the cosmos. A person must be in harmony with nature, must respect and savor all its interdependent constituents, and must not upset the delicate balance between plant and animal life, poison the air, or disfigure the land. Chaudhuri deplored humanity's unconscionable exploitation of nature and viewed an act against nature as a double-edged sword that wounded both nature and its despoiler.[11] Repeatedly, Chaudhuri sounded a passionate plea for harmony among all people and urged that everyone should participate in social action for the betterment of all humankind.

> The more man gives himself in the spirit of love and friendship, the more he experiences the delight of self-expansion. The more he becomes concerned with the welfare of fellow beings, the more he enlarges his own being.[12]

---

[10]Chaudhuri, *op. cit.*, pp. 85–86.

[11]*Ibid.*, pp. 86–87.
[12]*Ibid.*, p. 87.

Chaudhuri understood the weaknesses and strengths of Eastern and Western philosophy. He culled and modified the best elements of both schools of thought and integrated them into a personal psychology pointed toward self-realization. Integral psychology includes the yoga or methodology for incorporating this philosophy: a psychology that implements the process of self-realization.

Two key lessons distilled by the CSATP from the teachings of Haridas Chaudhuri are: a person cannot become an effective counselor or indeed a worthwhile human being without first attending diligently to his or her own self-realization; and a person's self-realization cannot be sought successfully if s/he does not continually strive for social conditions that foster the self-realization of others.

Working Principles

The following principles were abstracted from humanistic psychology. Although they may seem oversimplified to some readers, they have been useful as teaching tools for communicating the basic approach of the CSATP to clients and particularly to members of the criminal justice system.

A person's strongest drive is to feel good. Maslow has identified a number of such needs, ranging from the fundamental needs for food, shelter, and security to a person's needs as a member of society: the needs to respect oneself and to receive respect from others; to actualize latent abilities; to belong and to feel connected; to feel that one is part of the social fabric.[13] To these must be added the need for caring: to care for oneself, to be cared for, and to care for others. Caring is a vital, genetically inherited human need. If people did not care for their progeny throughout childhood, the human species would not survive. Only when human beings feel good do they value themselves and others and develop nurturing relationships.

[13]Maslow, *op. cit.*, pp. 3–4.

Unmet needs result in hostility and aggression. It follows from the above reasoning that when a person's needs are not met, s/he feels bad. People who feel bad discharge that malaise through hostile acts either toward themselves or toward others. Those who are unable to discharge their bad feelings discover eventually that the destructive energy has been eroding their psyches, bodies, and spirits slowly and malignantly.

The self-hate/destructive-energy syndrome in an individual starts early in life. A child raised by parents who were deprived as children will seldom feel valued. Such parents feel chronically distressed and inadequate and therefore will consistently punish bad behavior by the child and rarely acknowledge good behavior. As the punitive measures become increasingly harsh, the child's self-worth and good behavior diminish. Families composed of children and parents with unmet needs form the so-called dysfunctional or troubled families. Child neglect, sexual exploitation, and battering are some of the many symptoms. Others include wife beating, divorce, adultery, psychogenic diseases, adolescent delinquency, alcoholism, drug addiction, suicide, and murder. The symptoms correlate with such variables as individual characteristics, hierarchical position, extent of the deprivations, and situational factors.

At the point when symptoms in dysfunctional families or individuals become crimes that are reported to criminal justice system officials, the response of the system can either accelerate the self-destruct cycle or stop it. If the criminal justice system personnel react as punitively as the abusive parents did, the old cycle is perpetuated. But if the officials start offenders out on a path of self-reeducation in which they learn how to meet their own needs, including the higher needs that foster social responsibility, the criminal justice system has lived up to its responsibility and creative intervention has taken place.

People are what they are. At all times, people act as they best know how to act. They do not consciously deny themselves the rewards that come from being good parents, marriage partners, workers, or friends. If they do not realize these tacitly desirable states, the obvious explanation is that they don't know how. Neither pleading nor punishment motivates people to change for the better. The father-offender in an incestuous family already knows all too well that he has betrayed himself, his daughter, wife, and family. He did not behave out of conscious choice at that point in his life; self-abusive and abusive behavior was the only response he could make to discharge the chronic state of low self-worth caused by unmet needs. The father-offender (or any offender) will stop being an offender when he is taught to become aware of all his needs for self-realization and to become personally responsible for meeting them.

The same evolutionary rule that applies to offenders holds true for the officials who handle their cases. They, too, behave the way they know best. The specific conditions and the people responsible for them are not changed through denigration, angry diatribes, and contempt. Instead, such tactics produce a defensive backlash that, for the moment at least, deters progress. Criminal justice system personnel, whose actions are vital to the success of the CSATP, will continue to use traditional methods until they are shown better ones. If the CSATP or any group claims it has a better way of treating incestuous families, that way must be proven to the satisfaction of criminal justice system personnel and other personnel intervening in the cases.

Treatment Premises Regarding the Incestuous Family

From the working principles of humanistic psychology tested by firsthand experience with incestuous families, the following major premises regarding the interpersonal dynamics of the families were developed and are fundamental to the treatment approach.

1. The family is viewed as an organic system. Family members assume behavior patterns to maintain system balance (family homeostasis).

2. A distorted family homeostasis is evidenced by psychological and/or physiological symptoms in family members.

3. Incestuous behavior is one of the many symptoms of a dysfunctional family.

4. The marital relationship is a key factor in family organic balance and development.

5. Parent–child incestuous behavior is not likely to occur when parents enjoy mutually beneficial relations.

6. High self-concepts in the mates is a prerequisite for a healthy marital relationship.

7. High self-concepts in the parents help to engender high self-concepts in the children.

8. Individuals with high self-concepts are not apt to engage others in hostile, aggressive behavior. In particular, they do not undermine the self-concept of their mates or their children through incestuous behavior.

9. Conversely, individuals with low self-concepts are usually angry, disillusioned, and feel they have little to lose. They are primed for behavior that is destructive to others and themselves.

10. When such individuals are punished in the depersonalized manner of institutions, the low self-concept/high destructive-energy syndrome is reinforced. Even when punishment serves to frustrate one type of hostile conduct, the destructive energy is diverted to another outlet or turned inward.

11. Productive case management of the molested child and her family includes therapeutic procedures that alleviate the emotional stresses of the experience and the resulting punitive action of the community and that enhance the processes of self-awareness and self-management, as well as feelings of family unity and growth.

4. The Integrated Psychosocial Approach

The fundamental aim of the CSATP is to resocialize the families that come to the program. This is done by teaching the members of the family how to develop the attitudes and skills for personal growth both within the context of the family and within society as a whole. The CSATP relies on three complementary components to achieve that objective: the professional staff of administrators and counselors plus professional people from the various official agencies; the volunteer workers; and the self-help groups, known as Parents United and Daughters and Sons United. Together the three components create the regenerative human ecology in which the process of resocialization takes place.

The CSATP described in this chapter is that of Santa Clara County, California. At this writing, 65 other CSATPs throughout the country are in various stages of development.

The client population of the CSATP is made up of the following: children molested by fathers and a smaller number of children molested by grandparents, older siblings, and extrafamilial individuals; adults molested as children; and a few carefully screened individuals who molested children not related to them; and adolescents who molest much younger children.

The Professionals

Administrators. The administrative functions of the CSATP are performed by the program administrator, who supervises the personnel and activities of the CSATP. The program administrator is responsible for selection of personnel, defining staff functions, screening volunteers, coordinating the program with the criminal justice and human service agencies, guiding the development of Parents United and Daughters and Sons United, and ensuring that the program is compatible with the requirements, laws, and mandates of the federal, state, and local agencies. S/he works closely with the program coordinator, who screens all the referrals, assigns cases to the counselors, and coordinates cases with criminal justice and human services personnel. In most counties the CSATP's administrative and coordinating functions are performed by one person.

Counselors. The counselors design treatment plans based on their evaluation of the clients' needs as individuals and as members of the family. The counselors maintain the clients' treatment records and confer regularly with the program staff concerning the clients' needs. They make appropriate referrals to supportive services both within and outside the program. All professional counselors have master's degrees in counseling or psychology, licenses in marriage, family, and child counseling or in clinical psychology, and at least three years' experience in counseling children and their families.

Interagency Cooperation. Client families are involved with a host of professional people in the criminal justice system and in human service agencies. Therefore, the professional component of the CSATP also includes all those members of the community who are responsible for the official processing of the troubled family: police, social workers, probation and rehabilitation officers, defense and prosecution attorneys, and judges.

To be effective, the CSATP must convince official interveners to agree on a consistent, humane approach typically aimed at returning the child-victim to a safe and nurturing family environment. In addition to counseling and especially during the crisis period, family members usually need help with pressing practical problems: legal requirements, financial aid, food and clothing, housing, employment, job skill training, etc. The CSATP makes sure these services are provided to clients when they need them.

The need for interagency cooperation among professionals was apparent right from the beginning of the counseling effort. In fact, it was only after some measure of cooperation existed among the probation officers, police, and the courts, and only after the self-help component started (in other words, when clients were receiving more than traditional counseling) that it was decided to name the approach the Child Sexual Abuse Treatment Program.

Volunteers

Much of the staff of the CSATP is made up of volunteers. Some of the intern volunteers are graduate and postgraduate students working for their licenses in marriage and family counseling, some are undergraduates at local colleges and universities, and some are seasoned members of Parents United. There are usually between thirty and forty intern volunteers at any one time in the CSATP.

One of the major benefits of having such a volunteer program is that it draws on the community for much of the services. Thus, the community becomes directly involved with the program not only by receiving its services but also by providing helpers. The volunteer program has also proved a valuable and effective way of educating the community about the problem of incest and of the existence of the program.

Several of the volunteers in the Child Sexual Abuse Treatment Program are seasoned members of Parents United and Daughters and Sons United whose dedication exceeds that of the average member. They are often among the most valuable and effective members of the volunteer staff, providing countless hours of intense companionship to new clients and performing many tasks for the program. Those who have demonstrated in the individual and group sessions that they have grasped the basics of good communication and have shown leadership abilities can go into training to become group co-counselors and peer counselors. These members receive additional training in group facilitation and in the techniques needed to be an effective peer counselor. If their work or school schedules allow, PU/DSU volunteers also participate in the first three days of the training program, attend intern–staff meetings, and have a representative present at the professional staff meeting.

The special classes for Parents United volunteers cover such areas as parent effectiveness, human sexuality, transactional analysis, role-playing and role reversal, communications skills, and Gestalt techniques. This introduction to humanistic psychology gives the member a better understanding of the partnership between the professional staff and the self-help component and enables him or her to serve as a volunteer counselor with greater competence.

Trained members of Parents United/ Daughters and Sons United become invaluable to the CSATP. As sponsors for new members, they make the initial telephone contacts with the new members, invite them to the Wednesday night meetings of Parents United/Daughters and Sons United, and facilitate their initiation to the organization. The trained members serve as models to the initiates who know that these veterans have undergone the same terrible experiences, yet seem not only to have survived but to be coping very well with their lives.

The Self-Help Component

To a large degree, the success of the CSATP is due to the special regenerative climate that has developed in the program over the years. Everyone connected with the CSATP contributes to this climate, which in effect provides clients the opportunity to learn the attitudes and skills needed for leading productive lives in society. Certainly the most important aspect of this resocialization process is made up by the clients themselves; the unique energy provided by the members of the organizations called Parents United and Daughters and Sons United is essential both to the healthy growth of the individual family members and to the effectiveness of the CSATP.

The group process provides clients an opportunity to compare their view of reality with that of their peers, since all the people in the group share a highly stigmatized problem. This peer situation also has the effect of emphasizing increased self-direction and personal responsibility instead of reliance on authority figures who will "cure" them. The group milieu prepares members for positive social attitudes and more confidence in their ability to cope with social problems.

Parents United. Parents United is a nonprofit and nonsectarian volunteer organization open to all who have experienced intrafamilial and child sexual molestation. Formally launched in 1972, it incorporated in June 1975. To celebrate, its three charter mother-members wrote the following creed:

To extend the hand of friendship, understanding, and compassion, *not* to judge or condemn.

To better our understanding of ourselves and our children through the aid of the other members and professional guidance.

To reconstruct and channel our anger and frustrations in other directions, *not* on or at our children.

To realize that we *are* human and do have angers and frustrations; they are normal.

To recognize that we do need help, we are all in the same boat, we have all been there many times.

To remember that there is no miracle answer or rapid change; it has taken years for us to get this way.

To have patience with ourselves, again and again and again, taking each day as it comes.

To start each day with a feeling of promise, for we take only one day at a time.

To remember that we *are* human, we will backslide at times. To remember that there is always someone willing to listen and help.

To become the *loving, constructive* and *giving parents* or *persons* that we wish to be.

The PU board of directors includes several Parents United Members, some representatives of other chapters, a member of Daughters and Sons United, two lawyers, three psychiatrists, two members of the San Jose Police Department, and two community leaders.

The Santa Clara County chapter of Parents United has grown rapidly. The chapter now has over 200 members with an average attendance of 125 members at the weekly meetings. Meetings begin with a group centering exercise, followed by a brief conference to discuss progress in growth and effectiveness. The membership then breaks up into smaller groups jointly led by a staff member and a trained member of Parents United.

The number and focus of the small groups change periodically according to the needs expressed by the membership. The groups are started at the same time and run for eight sessions, after which the members are encouraged to join other groups.

General Description of PU/DSU Groups. The facilitators usually let the group start itself after each person says his or her first name aloud. Often there's a long silence until a member chooses to speak. Any member can begin by saying anything that comes to mind— a personal or affective statement or question, perhaps. Another member usually responds to the first member. Two members can have a dialogue for awhile. Or many members can enter in and express themselves in turn. The facilitators often intervene if people are interrupting each other or if more than one person is speaking at a time.

In most groups, the facilitators will note that only a few people speak. To involve all members, it is a good idea occasionally for one of the facilitators to start the discussion by saying, "I'd like each of you to say something about what's been happening to you this past week. Jane [pointing to the co-leader] will start." Later the first facilitator also takes a turn.

The emphasis in the groups is always on personal viewpoints and personal responses. Facilitators continually but gently remind the group members to make "I statements" rather than generalizations that shift responsibility for their own perceptions to others ("we know," "you should," "the experts say," etc.).

Sometimes one member will talk at length with no other members responding: a new member relating personal experiences in detail, for example. If the facilitators decide this monologue is productive for the group and/or for the person speaking, they don't shift attention from that member. When appropriate and productive for the group, the facilitators sometimes decide to intervene with an open or closed question, a paraphrase, or a reflection of feeling. Sometimes a facilitator will initiate an exercise, such as listening dyads or role playing.

One of the members usually will interrupt a member whom s/he feels has been talking too long. Even if one member talks for a long time, however, other members may be learning from, identifying with, or reacting to what is being said. A monologue can motivate the group process, even if it has a negative tone. For example, men in the group may tire of one member's constant lament and feel themselves getting annoyed. The facilitator may help them become aware of their own feelings and it will occur to some of them that this is how they probably sound to their

families. They may think, "So this is how I've been sounding. No wonder my wife gets irritated."

Whether a session becomes volatile or emotionally charged depends on what mood the members create and what problems they bring to the group that evening. It must be remembered that groups differ and that the sessions relate to the unique "personality" and pace of the group. The group process should not be forced but encouraged to unfold at its own pace and inherent potential. Group leaders should keep an eye on each other to guard against one of them using the group as a means for displaying expertise as a group leader. The most effective CSATP group facilitators are those who participate in the group process and "facilitate" it unobtrusively and only when necessary.

The Sponsorship Program. Clients of the CSATP had a form of sponsorship right from the program's inception. The original three mothers, who eventually started Parents United, knew one another as sponsors before they met together as a group. As new mothers came into the program, the original three were able to offer their caring and support to help them through the initial days of their crises. Today's sponsors are seasoned members of Parents United, most of whom have been trained in peer counseling techniques and have learned the skills and attitudes needed to assume the role of peer counselor. Many of these veteran members are also co-facilitators of the groups which meet weekly.

The sponsor plays a key role when the new families enter the program. Often a sponsor is the first contact the new mother or father has with the program. When the police refer the family to Parents United (often the same day as the investigation), a sponsor meets and befriends the mother or father. The sponsor listens empathically and caringly to the concerns and fears of the new client, often spending hours during the first week with that person or other members of the family. Because the nature of the family problem has tended to isolate them, the new members find comfort in being able to share their feelings and perceptions with someone who has had the same problem. Because the sponsors appear to have coped successfully with their problem, they offer motivation and hope to the newcomers that they can do the same. Because the sponsors and the new members share a unique problem, the sponsors can relate sensitively to the feelings of the new members, and are able to attend to them with a depth of caring that comes from shared experiences.

If face-to-face contact with the newcomer is not possible immediately, sponsors telephone parents who have been referred and invite them to Parents United. When new members arrive for their first meeting, the sponsor makes a point of greeting them and helping them feel welcome in the group. The sponsors introduce the new members to the Parents United hostess for the evening, who gives them tags (with their first names) to pin on their upper garments like the other members do.

A workshop led by a veteran sponsor is held each month for new sponsors in the Santa Clara County chapter and other nearby chapters to teach the basic skills needed to be an effective sponsor. Some of the subjects covered in the workshop are: empathetic listening; the right things to say to new members, and what to avoid saying; the importance of avoiding direct questioning of new members (particularly that which hints of curiosity-seeking); learning how to support the new members in their moments of crisis; making no promises as to what the program will do; checking to ascertain that each family has a counselor; making sure the offender is represented by counsel and, if not, recommending one of the competent attorneys checked out by Parents United; and assisting the family with special needs such as housing, financial aid, and transportation.

Sponsors check frequently with their families during the crisis period, expressing continued interest in them and encouraging them to call their sponsors when they feel like talking. A sponsor also gives the family the number of another sponsor to call if the assigned sponsor is unavailable. Sponsors keep records of new families they contact and submit the records to the head sponsor at the end of each month. If a sponsor contacts a family that has not been referred by the head sponsor, it is the sponsor's responsibility to inform the head sponsor. Every new family is listed in the sponsorship files.

Sponsors often accompany victims and/or others when they go to the police station for the investigation. At times a sponsor will be called on to be with a mother at the juvenile probation department when she learns for the first time about the molestation. Usually, the shock is so great and the anxieties, fears, humiliation, and guilt so overwhelming that riding it out with the mother becomes a total commitment often lasting two or three days. At times, a male and female sponsor will team up to help a couple in crisis. Many an hour has been spent in the PU kitchen or at members' homes drinking coffee and lending support to the newcomers. Nowhere does the healing power of caring manifest itself so clearly as in the relationship between the new member and the sponsor.

Preorientation Group. The Preorientation Group is composed of members on their first visit to Parents United. Formerly, new members went directly to the Orientation Group, but this group grew to a size that was often overwhelming to the new members. The Preorientation Group is smaller and more relevant to their present crisis and allows them to become acclimated to the program. The group leaders, aided by other veteran members, explain the philosophy of Parents United and the services available to the new members.

The new members often think of themselves as social lepers forever banished from society. It is immensely reassuring to them to be able to witness for themselves in this group that others have survived these same feelings of despair. The new members become even more hopeful as they learn from the older members that what is likely to happen to the family is much less damaging than they had anticipated. The new members are usually ready for the Orientation Group after about three meetings.

Orientation Group. The Orientation Group, the largest of the groups, is composed of newly arrived members, members who are not ready to move on to other groups, and members who return to the group to help the newer members. The group is composed of offenders, their nonoffending spouses, adults molested as children and their mates, siblings and other relatives of molested children, visitors, and the group facilitators. New members must attend the Orientation Group for at least one eight-week cycle before moving on to the more specialized types of groups. Adults molested as children who believe that the group will continue to be helpful to them may stay longer.

The group deals primarily with problems stemming from the exposure of the incestuous situation to the authorities. The facilitators and members answer questions from the offenders regarding the criminal justice system. Many have catastrophic expectations and are relieved to hear from the members whose cases have already been settled that they are likely to receive constructive treatment from the system. Many of the wives coming to the group indicate that they intend to divorce their husbands. They have come to this decision mainly through pressure by relatives and friends. But as they see that other couples are resolving their problems, they, too, soon seem more willing to work on their marriage either in trying to renew the relationship or ending it on amicable terms.

When an eight-week cycle ends, the group facilitators will encourage members who are ready to move on to other groups to make room for incoming members. A few members are reluctant to move from their "home base" since they have found a sense of security from building relationships with other members and the facilitators. A facilitator may consult with a member's individual counselor as to whether that member is ready to move from Orientation to the more specialized growth work. Some members return to the Orientation Group after attending several of the other groups but mainly to act as models for the new members.

Spanish-Speaking Group. Led by Spanish-speaking facilitators, this group relieves the added pressure a language barrier puts on those members of Spanish descent. The group can feel comfortable expressing themselves in language most familiar to them. It can be a discouraging impediment to a person trying to express deep feelings and receive messages from others if he cannot use his native language.

The hope is that with this burden removed members can gain more insight into themselves at a faster pace. At a time when they are feeling isolated and alienated from society, they can at least identify with their heritage and be nurtured by having their ethnic background acknowledged in a positive way.

The group concentrates on constructive help and understanding and gives members a chance to get their bearings and to get centered and grounded before attending the English-speaking groups. The facilitators serve as models to the group by teaching and demonstrating the methods and results of effective communication.

With the distraction of a language barrier removed, members relax and find a secure place for themselves in the organization. They concentrate more fully on working on themselves because they are less preoccupied with "editing" and rephrasing their sentences. They are able to listen to other members better and gain a deeper understanding of the Parents United philosophy.

Open Groups. Adults who have completed the Orientation Group sessions are eligible for the Open Group. Members learn to expand their points of view as they are introduced to new ways of thinking by members whose lifestyles, occupations, value systems, ages, and roles differ from their own. The group includes single men and women and people temporarily separated from their spouses. The members also discuss subjects not directly tied to child molestation. They discover that no matter how different other members appear externally, they share many common fears, problems, hopes, solutions, strengths, and experiences. The more varied the cross-section of people in the group, the more each member benefits, since the discussions cover a broad range of roles, opinions, feelings, etc.

As in all the groups, effective communication is also stressed. Many of the members begin to see clearly that at the core of their difficulties with their former or present marital partners was their inability to communicate honestly and openly.

Women's Group. This group is composed of mothers whose children were molested, usually by their mates. The group provides a supportive amosphere in which the members can discuss their concerns as individuals, mothers, and wives. The Women's Group offers some of the members their first experience in working with other women for mutual self-betterment. By practicing effective communications, they begin to see themselves and the roles they play more clearly. They learn how they are perceived by other people by getting feedback from members who may observe, for example, that they are annoyingly submissive or domineering. By understanding what motivates them and what barriers they set up for themselves, they can begin to change their behavior and to reshape their lives. The women find that they are able to bring up and discuss problems which they would not be able to introduce if their husbands were present.

In early group sessions the women are encouraged to express their outrage at their husbands and at the criminal justice system. The prominent grievances and issues brought up by the group are:

- the betrayal of their husbands

- their inability to stop the molestation

- the uncertainty of their futures and the anger they feel from being put in the position of keeping their family from falling apart

- the tendency to blame the victims for seductive behavior or not reporting the situation to them

- feelings of jealousy toward the victims

- the inclination to blame themselves for their husband's behavior

- whether to salvage or end their relationships, and the negative and positive consequences they can expect from either course of action

- fears about seeking jobs especially if they feel they are inadequately qualified

- whether they should pursue potential careers and training plans if they stay married.

The facilitator emphasizes that the reforming of the family nucleus with their children should be their primary objective. The father cannot rejoin his family successfully if the victim, in particular, feels unsure about her relationship with her mother. The child will resist the father's efforts to reestablish his paternal position in the family unless she feels totally supported by her mother.

The group is concerned with practical considerations as well as the psychological aspects of motherhood and wifehood. By the end of the eight-week session, many members begin to understand the objectives of the CSATP in the treatment of their family and what they must do personally to achieve those objectives. The women in the group often form lasting bonds of friendship with each other.

Men's Group. The typical Men's Group member is a father-offender, but the group often includes a small number of out-of-home offenders. During their first meetings the men are inclined to spend the time complaining about their mistreatment by the criminal justice system. The facilitator allows them to express their feelings knowing that the men do so, unconsciously, to alleviate the terrible guilt they feel for betraying their roles as fathers and husbands. The facilitator also knows that they will not discuss their disgust and loathing of themselves until they learn to trust one another. The men often have been physically or sexually abused or neglected by their own parents during childhood, and the facilitator may help them trace their current anger toward authoritative figures to the reactions they had toward their parents or other people holding authoritative positions over them during childhood.

The group is likely to have at least one member whose burden of shame is so great that he cannot wait until he can trust the group. When he relieves himself of it, his despair over his actions and his vulnerability will usually elicit spontaneous support and comfort from other members. It also encourages them to disclose their own feelings of self-hatred over their abusive behavior.

Not all of the members will quickly fall in line to accomplish the primary objective of the group, which is to have each offender admit unequivocally, with no reservations at all, that they were totally responsible for their exploitive behavior, must face the consequences, and must see to it that the behavior will never be repeated. Recalcitrant members are dealt with patiently but firmly by the others. Since they share a common problem, they talk to one another with rugged honesty, yet avoiding judgmental accusations. Many offenders have been loners and the group interaction is new to them. They will do little talking out of habit, not necessarily because they wish to avoid participating in the exchanges.

Often a father will fervently declare that he would like to talk to the child he molested, to explain face-to-face how terribly sorry he is for his exploitive behavior, and to say that he intends to spend the rest of his life making up for it. The fathers usually cannot communicate with their children because they were specifically ordered not to do so by the courts.

In the latter part of the eight-week cycle, the facilitator often invites a member of Daughters and Sons United who is not related to the fathers, but who wishes to talk to them so that s/he can come to some understanding of what motivated the fathers to abuse their children. The fathers willingly try to answer this person's questions and in turn a father may be allowed to apologize to the child and to express his deep anguish over his behavior as if s/he were his own child.

Couples Groups. Since the Santa Clara County chapter of Parents United has over 250 members, several Couples Groups are required. The groups are limited to five couples so that facilitators and members can give each couple more concentrated attention. The focus is more on the relationship between the two mates and less on each person as an individual. Usually, the group members will have already received individual attention for themselves through previous participation in the men's or women's groups.

The couples are married or unmarried and may or may not be living together. Most of the couples are the parents of children who were molested by their fathers. Since a healthy, mutually-nourishing marital relationship precludes incestuous activity between parent and child, the Couples Groups are perhaps the most important of the groups conducted by Parents United.

The objectives of this group are to teach the couples to:

- relate more productively with one another and to dispense with obscure verbal messages, game-playing, or other forms of manipulation

- state their needs and wishes directly

- revise unrealistic expectations of themselves and their mates

- keep the channels of communication open and clear between each other, i.e., to listen more attentively and to respond more honestly than they have heretofore

- discuss topics in the group that have formerly been "off limits," especially those regarding their sexual relationship

- acknowledge the positive aspects of their partnership and not to dwell continually on the negative aspects

- be capable of a better balanced relationship, i.e., neither of the partners needs to take on the role of the tyrant or slave

- become more sensitive to the nuances of voice tone, phrasing, and body stances, and how these affect their relationship

- fight fair, i.e., in accordance to rules they both agree to.

When the group members begin to trust one another, they begin to explore the conditions in their individual and marital histories that led to the incestuous behavior. Listening to other couples talk to each other allows members to see that they often behave the same way. A wife may comment aloud, for example, after listening to another member speak, "I never realized it, but I sound just that shrill when I complain to my husband that he is too easy on the children."

The couples groups contribute importantly to one of the major goals of the CSATP: to teach the members to become better spouses and parents.

Human Sexuality Class. This class is offered by a local college and is led by a licensed sex therapist. It is organized specifically for members of Parents United and the professional staff. The class meets for eight weeks on an evening other than Wednesday so that members do not have to miss attending the weekly meeting of Parents United.

The leader guides intensive, in-depth discussions on sex. All aspects of human sexuality are appropriate for discussion. Both men and women attend so that more information can be exchanged than in a single-gender class. The members discuss sexuality in general and sexuality related to their own personal and marital problems. The leader uses visual aids (photos, films, crayons, and paper) and group exercises.

Members become more comfortable acknowledging that all humans are sexual and do not need to deny or be embarrassed about that part of themselves. Time is devoted to improving sexual communication between partners. The leader also assigns homework that allows them to express their sexuality without exploiting their partners.

Parenting Group. This group is open to all parents: natural, step, foster, custodial or noncustodial parents. The purpose of the group is to improve parenting attitudes and skills so that mutually satisfying relationships can be achieved with children. It is hoped that as a result of this group experience the members will be better able to:

- rechannel their anger, frustration, and dependency so that it is not directed at their children

- recognize and stop selfish, manipulative behavior

- respect their children's needs and rights

- be patient about their progress as parents as well as the developmental progress of their children.

Of importance is that group members learn that their effectiveness as parents depends on how well they satisfy their other personal needs as individuals and their relationships with spouses, co-workers, relatives, and other key people.

Adults Molested as Children Group. This group is for adults who were molested as children by a family member. Usually the offenders were their fathers, but some of the members were molested by older siblings, the spouses of siblings, or grandparents. Only an extremely small number of the offenders were females. Also, this group is usually composed entirely of female victims and the following discussion is based on this typical victim.

Commonly, a group member is in her late twenties. The incestuous situation had not been reported to the authorities and she has not been able to resolve the experience either with her mother or offending father to her satisfaction. Both parents avoid or frustrate her attempts to confront them. Ever since her adolescence, the victim has abused herself unmercifully: by promiscuity often degenerating to prostitution, by substance abuse, and/or by sabotaging or not fulfilling the potential of intimate relationships. She comes to the group angry, guilty, self-pitying, fearful of authoritative figures, and apprehensive over her sexuality and her sexual identity.

It is crucial to involve adults molested as children in a mutual support group, because it is often the only way they will learn to trust and/or to become trustworthy themselves. Many have never received any counseling or other support for this problem. Almost all have "acted out" their sadness and anger in ways they deeply regret and need to discuss. Their painful feelings have festered for years and many have carried the burden completely alone through many stages of emotional and physical and social development. Their emotional development is likely to have been arrested at the stage and age of the incidents, so they often need to go through the stages of development they have not yet experienced, almost like giving themselves a second childhood.

Most of the groups have resisted attempts to involve male facilitators in the group. Although male offenders have been used successfully in the adolescent female groups of Daughters and Sons United, this has not been the case with groups for women molested as children. The women usually must spend at least two eight-week sessions in the group before feeling ready to form the Recontact Group (described later) which includes current offending parents as well as nonoffending parents.

During the early phases of the group, the facilitator encourages the women to voice and to act out, largely through bioenergetic exercises, their suppressed anger at their offending and nonoffending parents. This is often difficult to accomplish with women who are in withdrawn states. However, most of the women gradually are able to discharge at least some of their long-suppressed rage at their parents. The facilitator is aware that the women have different ways of avoiding this necessary first step. Some use intellectual explanations, some hide behind shyness, some feign anger, and some block out all overtures by group members. Eventually, most of the members are won over as participants in the group process.

The self-help group and the unique advantages won by bringing together people with alike problems are dramatically demonstrated in this group. It must be remembered that the incestuous experience left each of the members with unattended emotional wounds. The feelings of shame, guilt, and anger resulting from an experience, which they assumed was rare and could be due only to some unique aberrations in themselves and their families, prevented them from fully facing and resolving the experience. This has been true even for those members who had been given long-term psychotherapy. The group provides them the first real opportunity to deal with the experience and its characteristic aftermath, self-sabotaging behavior.

Most of the group members leave this group feeling greatly relieved. Some go on to the Recontact Group to prepare themselves for confrontation with their real parents. Others may join the Orientation Group for less intense interactions with incoming offending and nonoffending parents, but most adults molested as children are urged to attend the Recontact Group as soon as they feel ready to do so.

Recontact Group. The Recontact Group is composed of offending and nonoffending parents, and adults molested as children. Most of the adult victims have already attended the Adults Molested as Children Group. "Recontact" refers to group members becoming aware of and resolving repressed feelings, especially those originating from sexual exploitation during childhood. Recontact is accomplished by individualized personal awareness exercises (usually of the Gestalt variety) and by role-playing exercises between the victims and the parents.

The parents in the group usually are not related to the victims in the group. In the role-playing exercises the victims confront surrogate offending parents to vent their rage at their real parents for sexually abusing them. Similarly, they discharge their anger toward their nonoffending parents for their inability to protect them.

The group does not confine itself to the catharsis of anger. Members work toward attaining congruence and inner peace of mind. They begin to develop inner resources that will enable them to satisfy their needs in socially responsible ways. They strive toward depending less on others. They complete unfinished transactions with themselves and others. Members try to provide a safe, supportive atmosphere for each other not only to give credence to the anguish they experienced, but to validate fellow members evolving persons.

Victims form bonds with parents in the group and realize in doing so that these are worthwhile people. That opens the door for victims to relearn loving and feeling close to their own parents and seeing them with new eyes. Once they experience fulfilling, trusting, nonhierarchical communication with these parent figures and receive appropriate affection and attention from them, they are on the way to reestablishing the same kind of relationship with their own parents. They learn to interact with authority and parental figures from a firm position of strength in lieu of their former helpless, dominated position.

Victims who operated formerly from an aggressive, hostile position with their parents can learn to be strong in self-esteem and assertiveness and yet be soft, vulnerable, and nondefensive. The group works on refraining from blaming others and on feeling empathy for the people they had been blaming. As the members experience catharsis from letting out their secrets and their pain, they feel more control over their lives and more distant from the former pain. Some of them at this point choose to begin working toward contacting family members with whom they have severed contact or with whom they have had mostly painful contact.

The members practice recontacting their family members by doing roles plays with other members. The role play could be a mother or father practicing what they hope to say to their own daughter or son. Or it could be a molested daughter or son practicing what he or she would like to say to parents or other family members. They say to the members what they hope to express to their own families in the future. This is their opportunity to talk to people who feel much the same as their own family members. Members of the group give them feedback about how their words might be interpreted by their own family members.

The role-playing strongly affects both the participants and the members who are watching. Since most members have never expressed themselves in this fashion before, they are very emotional and even incoherent and therefore must rehearse what they need to say several times before they can communicate clearly. Members do many role plays in succeeding sessions and modify and rephrase their messages to make them more precise and to feel more comfortable saying what they want to say.

Once members have actually confronted their own family members, they can begin to assume responsibility for the other facets of their lives. Adults molested as children often say, "If I could master this, I can master just about any difficulty that comes my way."

Members who cannot recontact relatives because they have died or the damage to their relationship is irreparable still gain much benefit from the group. They have a chance to express their anger, realize they are not alone in their suffering, and develop close relationships with surrogate family members in the group.

Parents in the Recontact Group learn to understand the victim's point of view and complaints that victims received confusing double messages from parents. An example is that the parent who punished the victim for dressing immodestly in front of family friends or peers demanded that she undress completely for him. It is often easier for parents to listen with a more objective ear to a daughter who is not their own, since there is less emotional investment.

The molested members who have felt unfinished, stuck, and unheard finally feel they have been listened to sufficiently. The parents finally have a chance to ask questions of women molested as children that they have not been able to get answered. The molested women remind the parents of how their own molested daughters will think, feel, and behave if they do not receive sufficient counseling and other support. The molested members express anger, guilt, defenselessness, shame, loneliness, and hate of their own and/or others' bodies and minds. From hearing this, the parent members usually begin understanding their own child's position more fully. Parents who have wondered how well their own daughter can come out of this experience are greatly comforted when one of the molested members successfully recontacts her own family and is able to put the pain and anger behind her.

Alcoholic Problems Group. This group is for people who do or used to drink excessively. It also includes members who do not have alcoholic problems but who have important relationships with people who do have such problems. The group carries on extensive discussions directly related to alcoholism. Their goals are to become self-managing and to overcome the need to drink uncontrollably. They strive to gain insight into the physical and emotional problems that led to the drinking and aggravated the problems.

Members discuss in personal terms how drinking affects their lives, how the dependency immobilizes them, and the individual behavioral patterns that result. They begin to recognize that they make the choice to drink even though the choice is largely unconscious, and that others are not to blame. They take responsibility for the problem and support each other in many of the same ways Alcoholics Anonymous members do. But the group deals more with the fundamental emotional problems than with the symptoms of alcoholism so that the members can learn to attend to these problems personally. Group members relate how the drinking may have facilitated the molestations, but they also acknowledge that their drunken state does not excuse the molestations.

Printed material, films, and other visual aids are employed liberally. The group is facilitated by two people who also have drinking problems. The facilitators model the behavior they hope the members in this group will emulate, and they inspire the members to realize that each of them can clean up his life and serve as a model to the next person with a similar problem who enters the program.

Making Life Happen Your Way. This group is offered to young men and women in Parents United/Daughters and Sons United and held only if at least five individuals apply. The group deals with the experiences unique to people eighteen to twenty-five years old. They discuss how to cope with stress, interact effectively with others, and sort out and resolve conflicts. They help each other identify self-realizing vocations and what each much do to qualify for and attain that vocation. Practical skills are also taught: analysis of the job market; the writing of resumes; training opportunities; how to prepare for and to present themselves in job interviews; etc.

Daughters and Sons United. This organization, an adjunct of Parents United, is composed of children five to eighteen years of age, the majority of whom are girls who were molested by fathers. DSU also includes siblings of the victims and adolescent perpetrators. The two organizations work together and share many similarities.

Giarretto formed the first groups for children in 1972, one a play therapy group for children up to the latency period and the other for adolescent girls. Both were co-led by juvenile probation officers. Because the children's groups require much more attention and professional guidance than the adult groups and because of the press of an increasing caseload on a small staff, the children's groups did not grow as rapidly as Parents United. In late 1977, a young administrative intern, Cindy DeNoyer, was assigned the task of coordinating and expanding Daughters and Sons United. Since that time, the membership has grown to over 150 members, of which about three-fourths are active while the balance attend the meetings irregularly.

The self-expressed goals of Daughters and Sons United are:

1. To alleviate trauma experienced by the victim through intensive emotional support during the initial crisis;

2. To facilitate victim and/or sibling awareness of his or her individual feelings;

3. To promote personal growth and communication skills;

4. To alleviate any guilt the child may be feeling as a result of the sexual abuse;

5. To prevent subsequent destructive behavior such as running away, heavy drug abuse, suicide, prostitution, and promiscuity;

6. To prevent repeats of the offenses by increasing victims' independence, assertiveness, and self-esteem;

7. To prevent subsequent dysfunction of emotional and sexual relationships; and

8. To break the multigenerational abusive and dysfunctional pattern which is evident in many of these families.

Daughters and Sons United's decision-making body is the Task Force Committee. The committee is presently composed of six members who meet weekly with a Parents United representative and the Daughters and Sons United coordinator. The committee establishes goals, objectives, and projects geared to enhance the development, organization, and unity of the DSU program. The DSU coordinator and interns selected for this purpose implement the Task Force Committee's decisions.

The Task Force Committee assesses all new group formats and ensures that members who act as group facilitators with the professional group leaders are carefully selected and trained. DSU helps to organize and conduct a variety of groups. Basic groups are: adolescent girls' orientation group, adolescent groups, preadolescent groups, play-therapy groups, a transitional group (to adulthood) for young people, an adolescent offenders group, and a human sexuality group.

DSU participates in the following services:

1. A **Children's Shelter Liaison** makes initial contact with a child within one or two days after admission in order to provide crisis intervention, introduce the children to DSU groups, and provide continual support and counseling throughout protective custody.

2. A *Juvenile Hall Liaison* performs the same function for children in Juvenile Hall.

3. A *Home Liaison* makes initial contact during the crisis period with those children who remain in the home.

4. In the *Sponsorship Program,* seasoned members make telephone contacts and facilitate new members' entry into the group.

5. A *Time-Out Corner* provides DSU members access to resources and reading materials that increase the children's knowledge in such areas as drug abuse, birth control, and communications skills.

6. A *support system* for police and juvenile investigations, medical exams, and court hearings means that interns accompany children through the various steps in the criminal justice system process.

7. In a *Big Sister/Big Brother unit,* interns enter into one-to-one friend relationships with children requiring sustained support.

8. A *Transportation unit* provides transportation for children to weekly groups and counseling sessions; over 115 children are transported each month.

The DSU Task Force also organizes fund-raising activities and administers the money collected. To build morale and esprit de corps, birthdays are celebrated and visits are arranged to entertainment and cultural centers.

Members of Daughters and Sons United participate in a ten-week communication workshop; they receive a certificate and high school credits upon completion. The older members also receive co-counseling training. The members are extremely supportive of one another, especially through the crisis periods.

Like Parents United, DSU is interested in social action—in making the community aware of the problems of incest and of the existence of the program. Qualified members are selected and trained to give presentations with Parents United members to schools and various organizations and to make appearances on radio and television. Assisted by a volunteer, the group has created its own pamphlet on Daughters and Sons United and arranged to have the pamphlets distributed at junior high and high schools.

Members are becoming increasingly assertive in defense of children's rights in general; and they often come to the adult groups to argue for their specific rights within the CSATP. DSU does not regard itself as the lesser half of the self-help component but as a full partner in the aims and purposes of the CSATP. It is anticipated that DSU will soon develop into a national organization based on the concept of "children helping children."

The Private Counseling Sessions

As its title clearly specifies, the Child Sexual Abuse Treatment Program was started and developed for the welfare of the victims, and all actions by the staff are done with that purpose in mind. This primary objective is restated because the attention paid by the CSATP to fathers who have sexually exploited their daughters has been misconstrued by a few critics as being "too soft" on the offenders. However, it is important to remember that the offender is regarded by his daughter more as a father than as an offender —father of the family to which the typical victim wishes to return.

To provide for the child's emotional needs as well as her overall welfare, the CSATP must ensure that she is returned to a safe and nurturing home. Therefore, both the child and her parents must be treated. Although the treatment plan concentrates on the child, her mother, and their relationship, the father also is usually seen soon after his arrest and included in the treatment plan for the family. Again, the ultimate purpose of the attention paid to the offender is to teach him to become a caring and effective father and husband.

Since it became clearly evident that the typical victim of father–daughter incest wanted to go back to her own family rather than a surrogate family, the CSATP developed a family reconstruction strategy. This strategy has been applied to the majority of the families who have been treated over the past nine years. At this writing, over 90 percent of the children have been returned to their mothers; and over 80 percent of the children have been returned to both parents.

The private counseling sessions contribute to the family reconstruction strategy. The counselor prepares a treatment plan designed around the unique requirements of each child and her family and sees to it that the clients adhere to the plan. The counselor is not a therapist in the usual sense of the word, but rather a friend and teacher who joins the other members of the CSATP in facilitating the reconstitution of the family. As part of the treatment system, the counselor and the system become more effective as the professional, self-help, and volunteer components of the CSATP become more refined and integrated.

Initial Sessions. A supportive, optimistic climate must be established by the counselor before successful counseling can take place. This climate is especially vital in the treatment of families in which father–daughter incest has occurred and been exposed to the authorities. In the initial sessions, fear is the overriding emotion in the daughter, mother, and father. They are fearful of the unknown reactions of the criminal justice system: will the child and mother be separated? will the father be sentenced to a long prison term? The counselor listens intently to their fears and allows the clients full time to express them. After giving them ample time to do so, the counselor directly addresses the principal fears and informs them that it is extremely unlikely the child will be separated from her mother, if the father remains out of the home until the court permits him to return, or that the father will be sentenced to a long prison term. In the typical case, these predictions can be made at a high level of confidence.

The clients must be given hope and reassured that their situation is not as singular or as disabling as they believe. They are told that hundreds of families with similar experiences have been helped by the CSATP. They will meet some of the family members at meetings of Parents United and Daughters and Sons United and will see for themselves that many are now managing very well. Usually the child, mother, and father are already in contact with members of the self-help groups who serve as sponsors to incoming families, and this reinforces the encouraging remarks of the counselor.

Families troubled by incest often are socially isolated and therefore distrust outsiders, especially those in positions of authority. At first the CSATP counselor may be lumped with these potentially threatening outsiders. To allay this fear, the counselor must win their confidence and firmly tell them that s/he should be regarded as their friend and can be trusted with all disclosures. No information acquired during counseling sessions will be passed on to the authorities. The client–therapist confidentiality rule will hold fast unless new incidences of molestation are reported.

The counselors are usually able to quiet the clients' fears after one or two sessions, especially if the clients are in communication with members of the self-help groups and are attending the weekly meetings. When the clients are able to listen rationally, the counselor clearly outlines the services they can expect from the CSATP. The parents are informed that families fare best if they become involved in all aspects of the CSATP: the individual, couple, and family counseling as well as the group counseling and public relations effort of PU/DSU.

The counselor advises the father and mother that the CSATP will do its part if they do theirs. For instance, the father must attend all the private and group sessions prescribed by the counselor. If not, the progress report the counselor writes for the judge during sentencing will have a negative impact on the disposition of his case.

The father is informed that if he is charged with a felony, the judge may still order him to serve a few months at the local rehabilitation center. However, the rehabilitation officer will place him on work furlough and allow him to continue with his counseling program. Whether or not he receives a jail sentence, it is certain that he will be placed on probation for two or three years.

The father is told that he must persist in his counseling program if he wishes the CSATP to influence in his favor other decisions by the court such as permission to see his daughter and eventually to return to his family, reduction of the probationary period, and expungement of his name from the criminal records when the probation ends.

Thus, the counselor not only listens to their fears sympathetically but informs the clients of the most likely developments during the period of the family's involvement with the criminal justice system and what parents, and the father in particular, must do to help themselves.

There is a tendency in some families to slip away from the counseling plan or to pursue it less diligently after the prosecution period passes. This behavior is more likely to occur in those cases where the offenses were less severe and settled at the misdemeanor level. To forestall this, the counselor has the parents sign a contract in which they agree to continue with the counseling plan until the counselor decides to terminate it. The counselor answers all questions posed by the parents regarding the contract and why the terms are necessary.

It is important for the clients to leave this session with the understanding that the services of the counselor and the CSATP are not provided solely for the purpose of tiding the family through the court process but largely for the purpose of teaching the members of the family—the parents in particular—the skills needed for forming a healthy family unit.

Family Reconstruction Strategy. The reconstitution of the family starts with the effort to cement and enhance the mother–child bond. This step is taken for the sufficient reason that the child and mother usually wish to live together. But for those who require a theoretical rationale, there are sound genetic and social evolutionary reasons for this step. The survival of the human species is dependent on the family unit and the ability of the parents to provide for their offspring until they are able to fend for themselves. Beyond enabling their children to survive, effective parents teach their children to become self-realized, socially responsible human beings. The mother is the bearer and traditionally the principal caretaker/teacher of her children. Typically, children find it extremely difficult to attain their full potential as adults without a long-term committed relationship with their mothers.

Of course, the father has an important role in the rearing of well-balanced children, but the mother remains the essential and primary parent. If the victim of father–daughter incest and her mother want their father/husband back in the home, the CSATP bends every effort to satisfy this need. But the father cannot assume his dual role as father/husband successfully if the child doesn't want him back, and she will defeat his attempts to reestablish his function in the family if she feels insecure about her relationship with her mother.

This viewpoint is confirmed repeatedly as the staff of the CSATP monitors the progress of client families. The victims (and the families) who fare best are those whose mothers give principal support to their daughters rather than their husbands. The connection between the child and mother is strengthened when the mother tells the child that she believes her story and backs this up by choosing to keep the child in the home instead of her husband.

The decision to decide between the two is often forced on the mother by the investigating officer or the court to ensure the safety of the child. In the majority of the CSATP cases, the fathers leave the home voluntarily. Some fathers hesitate in doing so, however, and rationalize this position with excuses such as that the family cannot afford separate quarters for him, that the other children need him, or that he must remain in the home so that he and his wife can work on their marital problems. Whatever his excuses, his wife will act not only in the best interests of her child but of those of the marriage and family as well if she asserts herself first as a mother who must protect her children and backs this up by insisting that he—not the child—must leave the home.

In those instances where the father denies his daughter's accusations, the mother must accept the child's word and, above all, tell her that she is not to blame for the situation. Children rarely lie when they accuse their fathers of molesting them. A few may embellish the details but fully contrived accusations are extremely rare. Of the more than three thousand children referred to the CSATP, less than one percent fabricated their stories. Even if the mother has some doubts regarding the child's statements, she must give her the benefit of the doubt. If the child indeed is lying, it is unlikely that she will continue to lie to her trusting mother, and the mother will then discover why the child was forced to lie in the first place.

When the mother assumes her primary responsibility, she begins to feel much better about herself and is able to improve not only the relationship with her daughter but the relationships with her other siblings, relatives, and friends. She will also discover, often to her surprise, that she has strengthened her marital relationship. She has won her husband's respect and helped him to clarify for himself his own role as father.

Emotional States of Clients. To begin the process of reuniting the child and her mother and from that point to reconstitute the entire family, the counselor must listen to, identify, and understand the emotions being experienced by the child, mother, and father. These emotions vary in intensity and sequence depending on variables such as the age of the child when the abuses began; the frequency and extent of the acts; duration of the incestuous period; the age of the child when the molestation stopped; the overall quality of the relationships among the child, mother, and father; and perhaps most important of all, variables such as the reactions of relatives, friends, and official interveners.

The Child. The clients are usually seen separately before being counseled as dyads. The child whose feelings are typified here is a girl about thirteen years old who is not living at home. She reported that she was being abused and, although her mother is fairly supportive, the child is uncertain as to when she will be allowed to return home or even if she wishes to return.

It must be remembered that the child took a desperate leap into an unknown world when she reported the situation. As mentioned previously, fear is her dominant emotion. She is fearful of what might happen to her family as a result of the court process and may also feel despair over the thought that she may be disowned by her mother and family. This fearful state is likely to deepen and persist if her mother rejects her or is vague about her support or if the child cannot trust her counselor and the other interveners.

The ministrations of the counselors and members of DSU are extremely important. When the child begins to accept them as friends, her fears are allayed. But the greatest calming effect is produced by her mother's solid support, and this must be strongly encouraged by members of Parents United and the staff.

As the fear begins to abate, guilt takes over as the dominating emotional state. The guilty feelings are seldom acknowledged during this transitional phase since they stem from unconscious or subconscious messages from her superego accusing her of complicity in the incestuous relationship: she seduced her father or encouraged him; she derived pleasure from the sexual acts or would have resisted him; she was jealous of her mother; she enjoyed the secret trysts and even helped to arrange them —if not, she would have disclosed the situation to her mother; she is responsible for ruining her mother's marriage and for the demise of her family. The guilty feelings are especially strong if the offender is a stepfather, and even more so if he is a younger man with whom she had related more as a lover than as a paternal figure.

The guilty feelings are manifested indirectly in various ways. If the child has some ego strength and self-esteem, she may resort to defensive devices such as declarations of anger ranging from contempt to outrage toward the authorities for their harsh and insensitive handling of the situation; toward her father for exploiting her; and toward her mother for not protecting her. The deep, uncontrollable anger may also fuel outrageous but essentially self-punishing behavior: hostile acting-out at home and at school; promiscuity; and engaging in dangerous, often law-breaking activities with rebellious groups.

A much more serious emotional problem is one that develops in a child with very low self-regard and whose chronic feelings of guilt drive her into a withdrawal state. She cannot communicate with the counselor, avoids eye contact, and may occasionally mutter a barely audible, "I don't know." The child is lost in deep anguish and remorse because she has convinced herself that she is entirely to blame for the circumstances which led to the family's hopeless condition.

In checking the backgrounds of children who retreat into this state of despair, it is often found that they had taken on many of the responsibilities of the mother/wife. In attempting to keep the family from falling apart, they had given in to their father's sexual advances to stop him from deserting the family. Such children could not depend on their parents as parents and felt forced to assume their mother's role. They blame themselves for failing in this role, and whatever anger they feel is directed inward. To sedate their painful emotional states, the children often become heavily dependent on drugs.

A counselor must be very patient with a child in a severe withdrawal state. Only by creating a reassuring, accepting climate during the sessions will the counselor be able to win the trust of the child. The trust becomes tangible when the child begins to communicate. Gradually, the counselor must convince the child that she is not to blame for the family's situation; that she was the victim of her father and not his accomplice; that she should have been protected by her mother instead of the other way around; that she has the right to be angry toward both of them.

The child's anger must be directed outward and the counselor must help the child discharge her justifiable anger toward her parents. The controlled environment of the individual and group counseling sessions provides the child the opportunity to expel her anger safely and without the repercussions that come from self-punishing acts or hostile behavior in the community.

The Mother. When the mother begins to adapt to the situation with the help of Parents United members, she too will experience guilt as the principal emotion. The mother may not always be aware of the sources of her guilty state, but in time she usually will admit to strong wrenches of guilt for not fulfilling her role as mother and wife. If she had ministered to the needs of her family instead of her own selfish wants, the incestuous events would not have occurred; had she met her husband's emotional and sexual needs, he would not have turned to her daughter for satisfying them; had she kept her ears and eyes open, she would have caught the situation and been able to protect her daughter. The guilty feelings are compounded in the mother who was aware of the sexual activities and allowed them to continue, or who suspects that she was jealous of her daughter and that this contaminated their relationship.

Reflecting their levels of self-esteem, mothers will manifest their guilty states in various ways. At one end of the continuum of possible reactions are mothers who will be in a rage against their husbands and other tormentors; at the other end are mothers who will withdraw into states of hopeless despair. Counselors facing clients in this latter category will often find that the mothers have taken on total responsibility for the survival of their families. Such mothers are parents to their husbands as well as their children. Since they assume the entire responsibility for the welfare of their families, they assume the entire blame for the present derelict states of the families. The mothers had been aware of the gradual erosion of the family's structure and were unable to stop the process. Now they have given up, feel completely defeated, and are often suicidal.

This family member, also, must be treated with extreme patience by the counselor. As the mother emerges from her mental and emotional paralysis and begins to communicate with the counselor, the latter slowly helps her to become aware of the suppressed rage she harbors against her husband in particular, and often her daughter as well, for conniving to betray her while she was absorbed in the task of keeping the family together.

The counselor must provide an opportunity for all family members to vent their anger freely in a controlled therapeutic setting. This should be a major objective especially during the early stages of counseling. It must be remembered that the mother, father, and daughter were all the unconscious victims of a dysfunctional system; they all would have preferred to be fully aware members of a healthy, well-functioning family. The counselor must help them clear their heads of the immobilizing anger, analyze rationally the parts they played in the dysfunctional family system, and then learn what each must do to contribute to a productive system.

The Father. Typically, the most difficult client for the counselor is the father. Acute dread of the reactions of the criminal justice system and of the unknown, long-term consequences of his acts to his daughter, wife, and family will persist in the father, particularly through the duration of the prosecution period but often for many months beyond. He is convinced that by breaking the incest taboo he has lost his place in society. The counselor must remember that this man is literally struggling for his survival and that his struggles are often ugly to behold. The father's fear is amplified by guilt, and this state may be revealed through declarations and behavior ranging from strong protestations of innocence or mitigating explanations for his behavior to severe disorientation and withdrawal.

The counselor will be hard put not to react with revulsion to the father who defends himself aggressively and who states that it was his wife's fault because she did not take care of him sexually; that his daughter seduced him or participated willingly; or that he did it because his daughter needed sexual education. If the counselor responds judgmentally, the client will not disclose his underlying feelings and the counseling will not be productive. The foundation for effective counseling is built as the counselor observes the client from the viewpoint that all his evasive reactions stem from fear and guilt.

The client will begin to interact with the counselor honestly when he realizes that the counselor is empathizing with him as a person in distress and fully intends to help him and his family. As the relationship strengthens, the counselor clearly explains his own position and intentions to the client:

1. Incestuous behavior cannot be condoned or rationalized.

2. The client, as father and guide, must assume the full responsibility for the incestuous situation.

3. The client must acknowledge that he had and still may have the problem of not being able to control his incestuous impulses.

4. Compulsive behavior originates from a self-punishing part of him, and client and counselor will work together to identify that part and to redirect its energy toward positive ends.

A father who sinks into a withdrawal state may pose an even more knotty problem to the counselor than a mother or daughter in a similar state. The counselor must guard against suicidal tendencies and/or substance abuse in the father. Gaining the withdrawn client's trust will usually be harder than with an aggressive father. The anger in withdrawn clients is deep-rooted and difficult to activate because it usually stems from repressed childhood experiences of parental abuse, neglect, and emotional deprivation. Nonetheless, the counselor must persevere toward the breakthrough that occurs when the father is enabled to discharge his long-held anger toward his abusive parents.

The ability to view the father as the victim of childhood abuse or deprivation is not easy to come by, despite the logical strength of the assumption that a father who abuses his child is driven by the self-hatred of the child within himself. A substantial clinical analogy exists between the behavior of an abusive parent and the behavior of an unloved child who destroys his or her most precious toys.

Methods

The methods used by the counselors are based on the humanistic principles discussed previously. Some of the techniques are adaptations of those commonly employed in Gestalt therapy, psychosynthesis, transactional analysis, and bioenergetics. Others have been invented by the staff to accommodate the special requirements of sexually abused children and their families.

Of all the CSATP counselor's techniques, however, it must be stressed that humanistic empathy is the key. More than a technique, it is an attitude that must be continually cultivated. During each session, the counselor must listen actively and be aware of not only the content but the underlying affect in the client's statements and body language; at the same time, the counselor must listen to his or her own thoughts and feelings as the counseling transactions proceed.

After the initial efforts to bring about a good working relationship, the counselor follows an iterative strategy in guiding the client through the concepts and processes of humanistic psychology. The phases are developed more in parallel than in serial fashion. A variety of techniques are used to implement the therapeutic model. None is used for its own sake or on a "let's try it and see" basis; instead, the counselor tries to respond to the client and the situation and to apply a fitting technique.

In most instances, experiential learning techniques are used to elicit affective responses; however, cognitive and spiritual needs are not neglected. To avoid professional distancing, the counselor discusses the strategy and progress of the counseling and answers questions from the client. Certain clients who begin to internalize and practice the techniques at home report profound self-enlightening experiences. These clients are given special exercises to help them to expand and integrate the breakthroughs.

Self-Assessment and Confrontation. Once a working relationship has been established and the highly charged emotional climate subsides, clients are usually ready to become aware of and begin to accept their current emotions in order to move on to the next phase of the treatment.

At this point, clients begin by taking an inventory of personal and family characteristics. Initially, during this "know thyself" exploration, the counselor underscores the positive traits. What does the victim, for example, like about herself? What does she appreciate in other family members and the family as a whole? Before she can be motivated to work actively for personal and family growth, she must believe that she and the family are worth the effort.

From this positive stance, the clients can then proceed to identify weaknesses and maladaptive habits that need to be improved or eliminated. These might include uncontrolled use of drugs, food, alcohol, and cigarettes; hostile, aggressive behavior that interferes with the progress in family, school, and work relations; inconsistent study and work habits; and, typically, the inability to communicate effectively, especially with important persons in their lives.

As the clients gain confidence in their search for self-knowledge, they begin to probe the painful areas connected with the incest. In what may be termed a confrontation–assimilation process, the counselor encourages the child, father, mother, and other family members to face and express the feelings associated with the incestuous experiences. Buried feelings such as fear, guilt, shame, and anger cannot be denied; somehow they will have their effect. If not confronted, those feelings will persist in repressed forms and will continue to harass them. With some clients, the pain-provoking memories can be dealt with fairly early in the therapy; with others the counselor finds it prudent to proceed more slowly.

In the treatment of the offender, care must be taken to avoid moralizing, no matter how subtle. From early childhood this client has had a full measure of accusations and preachments. He already feels like an outcast, and if this self-image is reinforced, the negative self-esteem that drove him to or could not control the incestuous behavior will persevere.

Moreover, a judgmental counselor may inadvertently provide an escape route to the offender if his guilt becomes intolerable. For example, he may retreat into superstition and believe he is cursed and was driven to the incestuous behavior by mysterious forces. Or the offender may convince himself that he suffers from an exotic mental disease and must rely on the doctors to cure him. The counselor's task is to guide the client to the simple fact that incest is one of the many types of dysfunctional behavior; he can learn to control this, as well as the other types, if he sets his mind to it.

It must be repeated that while listening with compassion and understanding to the father's feelings, the counselor in no manner condones the incestuous conduct or rationalization of it by the father. Sooner or later, most CSATP clients will admit to the counselor and to investigating officers that they performed the acts and were completely responsible for them. However, it must also be repeated that offenders are likely to admit to the charges only if they are convinced that the CSATP and the criminal justice system will help them and their families. If the offender and his wife anticipate destructive retribution from the court they will, of course, be inclined to deny the accusations.

Traditional counseling without a CSATP support system will seldom be effective in the treatment of incestuous families. The clients will be very guarded in revealing the details of the situation to the counselor, especially if they know that the counselor is mandated to report all child abuse cases to the police and may be subpoenaed by the court to provide incriminating evidence against them. This illustrates once again the interdependent relationship between the counselor and the criminal justice system and why it is important for the CSATP to be recognized by the system as an effective alternative to the usual devices of separation and incarceration.

The major objectives of the early stages of the counseling are to help the family through its crisis and to foster a trusting rapport with the counselor. In subsequent stages, the rapport is strengthened and the counselor facilitates awareness in the clients of personality traits and usually unconscious drives that have been negatively affecting their lives. The father, in particular, is induced to identify and control the parts in himself that have been sabotaging him and which impelled

the incestuous behavior. In a more positive vein, the clients are coached in the techniques of self-awareness so that each can develop independently the ability to observe and direct his or her own growth process. The counselor employs techniques that are best described as combined methods of Gestalt awareness and transactional analysis. Certain clients are encouraged to read and to practice the exercises provided in introductory books on self-awareness.[1]

Self-Identification. The self, conceptualized as the control center of the personality, is more than the physical, emotional, and intellectual components of an individual which are continuously in states of flux. John Lilly has an excellent metaphor for the self: "the center of the cyclone" (which he also used as the title of a book).[2] It can be demonstrated that the self as a unique entity can observe the operations of the id, ego, and superego (or the child, adult, and parent, the analagous states employed in transactional analysis.[3] A technique for self-identification used with some clients in advanced stages of counseling involves a series of Gestalt-type exercises in which the client is asked to play out conversations between the parent and child, the adult and child, and the adult and parent while visualizing the self as observing and kindly analyzing the transactions. If the client is able to identify the self, the counselor may elaborate on this line of thought by pointing out that the self as a wise observer is not ensnared by the roles he or she may play as daughter, wife, husband, student, or worker.

[1]Muriel James and Dorothy Jongeward, *Born to Win: Transactional Analysis with Gestalt Experiments* (Reading, MA: Addison-Wesley, 1971); and Dorothy Jongeward and Dru Scott, *Women as Winners* (Reading, MA: Addison-Wesley, 1976).
[2]John Lilly, *Center of the Cyclone* (New York: Julian Press, 1972).
[3]Eric Berne, *Transactional Analysis in Psychotherapy* (New York: Grove Press, 1961).

Self-Management. Once the self is identified and distinguished from the changing elements of personality, the concept of self-management is introduced. The assumption is that everyone can learn to control the way s/he behaves and, ultimately, the course his or her life will take. Each person in the family can learn the attitudes and skills for leading self-actualizing lives. The marriage and family can also be given purposeful direction. A major milestone is reached when the client realizes that all past and current experiences can be assimilated for personal growth.

It must be noted that not all the clients are interested in these advanced concepts. Most of the clients learn intuitively some of the basic ideas but are not able to verbalize them. If the extremely low recidivism rate can be used as a reliable indicator, it appears that the majority of the fathers have learned how to control potential sexual impulses toward their children. It appears also that most of the clients have improved their marital relationships as well as their effectivity as parents.

Practical Services

As a rule, the families who come to the CSATP for treatment are badly shattered and in need of practical assistance. Emergency counseling for the child, mother, and father is of prime importance. But there are also other pressing needs that require attention as well.

A CSATP staff member does not simply refer a client to one of the many community resources. If the client appears unable to make contact alone, an intern or a Parents United member will personally accompany the client to the resource.

The following is a description of principal services available to families and family members troubled by child sexual abuse. Most communities in the United States have services similar to these; the CSATP makes sure that the services are made available to the client who needs them.

Medical Aid. Valley Medical Center Hospital, the Santa Clara County hospital and medical facility, is available to the Juvenile Probation Department for any necessary physical examination, evaluation, or emergency treatment. Various police jurisdictions also use this center for examinations and treatment of victims.

Pelvic examinations for evidence of intercourse or for venereal disease are rarely given to victims of incest. The examinations are seldom necessary for the prosecution of the fathers because they admit to the accusations in 90 percent of the cases. This high confession rate is due to the skills of the police attached to the Sexual Assault Investigation Unit of the San Jose Police Department who work closely with the CSATP.

Physical examinations that include the pelvic area are usually ordered by the police for victims of "sexually depraved" homes in which the child was molested by others besides the father-figure, or by a father who was having extramarital sexual encounters during the period he was molesting his daughter, or by an older sibling with a history of delinquency.

Physical examinations are ordered routinely for children molested by strangers. They are also given routinely to children entering the children's shelter or juvenile hall before they are placed in foster homes or group homes. The doctors who examine the children do so with extreme care and delicacy and according to the needs of each child. With younger children, the pelvic area is examined as part of the general examination without arousing anxiety in the child. Older children, however, may be extremely worried about the possibility of venereal disease. After completing the examination, the doctor explains the findings clearly to the child and answers all his or her questions.

It must be cautioned that although the local CSATP has uncovered very few cases of venereal disease, this has not been true for other programs dealing with child sexual abuse, especially those serving deprived urban populations. Some of these report that venereal disease in the children they serve is rising an an alarming rate. All people working with sexually abused children should be on the lookout for venereal disease as well as other medical problems.

Legal Services. Parents United maintains a card file on the various private attorneys that clients have used. The file evaluates the quality of the service received from the attorney and specifies the average fee charged. This is a valuable resource for new clients, many of whom have never needed a lawyer before. They have access to a list of competent lawyers, and they also can get an idea of what their case might cost. For assistance in obtaining other legal information, clients are referred to the Santa Clara County Bar Association Lawyers Reference Service and receive the names of one to three attorneys. These attorneys are generally available for brief consultation at a nominal fee.

For clients who are unable to afford a private attorney, the public defender will represent them in adult court. Minor children classified as victims are represented by the district attorney in juvenile court or by the public defender if they are appearing in juvenile court on a law violation. Two full-time public defenders are assigned to the Juvenile Probation Department for consultations and for representing minors. Community Legal Services is available for consultation and representation in civil court for persons who cannot afford a private attorney. Additionally, they can represent the juvenile victim in juvenile court.

The National Organization of Women, San Jose Chapter, also maintains a reference service on female attorneys and attorneys who are well-versed in the legal rights of women, particularly relative to divorce cases and cases involving sex crimes.

Financial Aid. The Santa Clara County Department of Social Services employs eligibility workers who determine whether persons who apply are eligible to receive financial assistance through the General Assistance Plan or through Aid to Families with Dependent Children. The department also employs social workers who can provide casework services to CSATP families requiring financial aid. Although primary case management is done by a Juvenile Probation Officer and counseling by the CSATP, a social worker may contribute additional case work services in certain cases. Emergency food supplies can be obtained through the Salvation Army and St. Vincent de Paul Society; clothing can be obtained through various clothes closets, including the Volunteer Bureau at the Juvenile Probation Department.

Housing. Although used infrequently, emergency housing is available for women and children at the Brandon House, a temporary residential facility that is privately operated. Brandon House has a locked front door for the protection of the inhabitants and a full-time social worker available to help cope with any problems. The Welfare Department will help pay the rent in Brandon House for those families who meet the eligibility requirements for public assistance. New Hope Home, a Volunteers of America facility, also provides limited supervised emergency housing for women and children. The Salvation Army Hospitality House has rooms available for women or men on an emergency basis. The Red Cross will also assist in locating housing. The Santa Clara Council for Indian Affairs will locate housing for Indian families. Friends Outside, an agency that acts as a liaison between families and incarcerated offenders, will also help locate housing for families.

Emergency and protective placement of children in the Children's Shelter can be made by police and juvenile probation officers. Emergency foster home placements can be made through the Department of Social Services.

Unfortunately, the foster home system has its shortcomings as far as the daughters of incestuous families are concerned, especially those who have been rejected by their parents. The trauma experienced by the victims at times precludes a positive adjustment in foster homes. Often they deliberately sabotage the placements as a means of "getting back" at their parents. In these instances, the child, feeling rejected by her natural family, cannot readjust into a new family system or overcome the anxiety of forming new peer relationships in an unfamiliar neighborhood. The good intentions of foster parents often are not enough to ensure successful placement. The unique problems of certain sexually abused victims seem to require a special setting.

Toward this end, Parents United is attempting to obtain funds to establish a specialized group home for sexually abused children to provide a realistic, relaxed, and safe environment in which they could begin to restructure their lives. This group home would not try to replace the family, but would provide a nurturing environment to prepare the children for their return home. There the children would receive the services of counselors trained by the CSATP. The treatment goals for group home residents would be essentially the same as those for the other children in the CSATP. As members of DSU, the residents would obtain the full services of that organization, which in essence would serve as a surrogate family.

Employment. Employment is often a problem for the mother who has been a homemaker for a number of years and has been absent from the work environment. At times, a father-offender may also find it difficult to obtain work. The Information and Referral Services and Friends Outside have been very helpful in providing job leads. Parents United members are also on the lookout for employment opportunities for out-of-work members or those who wish to improve their careers. The Opportunity Industrial Center, which provides vocational retraining for industry, is a training and placement agency that has been a very important resource to the CSATP.

Hotlines and Information and Referral Services. The CSATP is listed in Information and Referral Services and with various hotlines in the Bay Area for those agencies and individuals who are not aware of the program and who are seeking information and help. The listings are cross-filed by the area served and the type of problem (housing, health, employment, legal services, child care, counseling, drug abuse, etc.). A specially trained worker gives the caller information and guidance that will assist in making an effective contact with the best available service or community organization equipped to help solve the problem.

The program is listed with every hotline in the county and Bay Area known to the staff. These hotlines are very similar to Information and Referral except that the caller is usually seeking immediate help, and the hotlines offer over-the-phone crisis counseling as well as referrals. At present, the program has official telephone coverage Monday through Friday, between 8 A.M. and 5 P.M. However, emergency calls are handled on a twenty-four-hour basis by members of Parents United who take turns providing this service.

Case Management

The Referral. The initial referral of the sexually molested child in Santa Clara County often comes to the patrolman on duty within the jurisdiction where the child lives. The child may go to a school counselor or nurse, a neighbor, a relative, or the mother, all of whom are required by California law to call the police department. The officer takes a statement from the girl and from witnesses, if any, concerning what has happened. If he feels that the child cannot receive adequate protection from her mother, he places her in protective custody in the children's shelter. That occurs much less frequently than it did before the CSATP got started. A police officer from the Sexual Assault Investigation Unit (SAIU) who has had special training in child sexual abuse cases investigates the case to decide whether there is sufficient evidence to warrant an arrest and referral to the district attorney for prosecution.

A juvenile probation officer may also receive the referral directly via a telephone call from the school, a neighbor, or another agency person and take appropriate action for the child. The juvenile probation officer is a member of two special units specifically set up to investigate cases of child neglect and abuse and also has had experience and training in the investigation of child sexual abuse cases.

Generally, the officer from the SAIU and an intake probation officer work together during the investigative stages, coordinating their efforts to minimize the trauma to the child and family during this process and to maximize services to the family. After carefully examining and evaluating the situation of the family, the juvenile probation officer makes an assessment as to how the juvenile court needs to be involved and takes the appropriate steps. The probation officer may bring the child to the attention of the juvenile court by filing a petition under section 600 of the Juvenile Court Law, which applies when the minor resides in a home "which is unfit by reason of depravity." Again, this decision occurs infrequently at this time.

The investigating officers will usually instruct the father-offender to find new living quarters for himself because he and the child will not be permitted to live together until the court so decides. But even if this step is taken, the officers should ask the child privately if she wishes to remain with her mother and siblings. Perhaps she would like to live with relatives or in the children's shelter for a few days before contending with her mother and siblings. In particular, adolescent girls who have reported the offenses without consulting their mothers should be given this choice. Commonly, they are apprehensive about the reactions of their mothers and other family members and would rather not face them at that time. The victims should be clearly informed, however, that this is a temporary measure and that they will return to their homes as soon as they are ready.

The officers' decision of whether to remove the child will be aided by the results of their interview with the mother. If the mother is obviously angry at the child and blaming her for the situation, it becomes quite evident that the child should not be placed in the mother's care until the mother fully realizes that her daughter was the victim and not the cause of the incestuous situation.

When the case is referred to the CSATP, the program coordinator assigns a counselor to the family. The counselor and the responsible juvenile probation officer confer and agree on a plan of emergency and long-range supportive action for the family. They also meet regularly thereafter; the CSATP staff takes special pains to maintain continual contact with the police and the Juvenile Probation Department. Good communication is important for proper case management and precludes the danger of having personnel from the treatment services agencies feel they are being supplanted by the CSATP.

Once the case is referred, the CSATP provides emergency counseling right away. As much as possible, crisis needs are met immediately. These crisis interventions markedly influence the way the clients anticipate their future involvement with the program.

Order of Treatment. The CSATP's first goal in each case is to provide immediate counseling to the child and her family. Incestuous families are badly fragmented as a result of the original dysfunctional family dynamics, which are further exacerbated upon disclosure to authorities. Usually, the child, mother, and father must be treated separately before family therapy becomes productive. Consequently, the treatment procedure is applied in this order:

1. Individual counseling, particularly for the child, mother, and father;

2. Mother–daughter counseling;

3. Marital counseling, which becomes a key treatment if the family wishes to be reunited;

4. Father–daughter counseling;

5. Family counseling; and

6. Group counseling.

This order of treatment is not followed invariably in each case, but all treatments are usually required for family reconstitution.

The Court Process. On average, the father's involvement in the court process lasts about three months, with the usual plea-bargaining taking place between the defense and prosecuting attorneys. Usually the charge is child molestation or statutory rape; incest laws are rarely applied. If the offender is charged with a felony, he is instructed to contact two court-appointed psychiatrists to determine if he is a mentally disturbed sex offender (MDSO). If, on the basis of their reports, the judge finds the offender to be a MDSO, the offender may be sent to a state psychiatric facility at Atascadero.

Incest offenders in Santa Clara County are now rarely diagnosed as mentally disturbed, however, owing to the growing acceptance of the CSATP by the psychiatrists as an effective alternative to Atascadero. If the offender is judged not to be a MDSO, then he can be sent to a state prison, but this has happened only once to CSATP clients.

As a rule, the heaviest sentence an incest offender gets is a year at the local rehabilitation center, which reduces to about nine months with good behavior.[4] When the offender is sentenced to the rehabilitation center, his rehabilitation officer is contacted and urged to hasten the client's work furlough and permit him to come for individual counseling and to the Parents United weekly meetings. On the increase are sentences that direct offenders to contribute several hundred hours of work to Parents United in lieu of spending that time in jail.

[4]In Kroth's evaluation of the CSATP, the court records of 127 perpetrators were checked: 52 percent were not incarcerated, 20 percent received jail sentences of which the mean length was 143.4 days, and 28 percent of the cases were still in litigation.

Criteria for Termination. Assuming that the child, mother, father, and other family members are reunited and the family is still in counseling, then the decision by the counselor and supervising agency to terminate the case is based on these criteria:

1. Is a court order for counseling still in existence? If so, must that order be modified before termination can take place?

2. Does the family feel they've made sufficient progress in their communication and interpersonal relationships?

3. Does the counselor who has been seeing the family feel they have made sufficient progress?

4. If a probation officer is involved, does s/he feel the family has progressed sufficiently to allow termination of the counseling?

The following questions are often asked to determine "sufficient progress":

1. Is molestation likely to recur? In other words, has the marital and home situation improved enough to prevent recurrence of molestation and ensure a safe home environment for the child-victim?

2. Has the offender taken responsibility for his or her behavior and learned to become aware of and to control the impulses that led to the molestation?

3. Does the child not only feel safe in the home with her father living there but wish to reestablish a father–daughter relationship?

4. Have the feelings and conflicts between all family members been dealt with openly and sufficiently so that the family has achieved a reasonable measure of harmony?

In cases where only the adult is being counseled (as an offender or as an adult woman who was molested as a child) or in cases where only the child victim is being seen, perhaps in conjunction with his or her foster family, similar questions need to be evaluated but in relation to the client's particular circumstances.

Adults Molested as Children

Although the primary function of the CSATP is to provide treatment and support to child victims of sexual abuse and their families, no description of the program would be complete without mentioning the service it offers to adults who were molested as children and who were not helped with that problem during childhood. Most of these clients have been women but recently males have been coming for treatment in increasing numbers. Adults who come to the CSATP because they were molested as children are given individual counseling and couple counseling if they are married or living with someone. If their parents are available, joint sessions sometimes include the fathers and mothers as well (this usually happens later in the counseling process). Most progress usually develops in the group sessions of Parents United, first in the group made up exclusively of adults molested as children and later in an advanced confrontation group, where they learn to understand the confusion and pain suffered by offenders and their spouses.

In role-playing exercises with these parents, the clients prepare themselves for future confrontations with their real parents. In many cases, involvement with the CSATP and Parents United has enabled people in this position to reestablish emotional ties with their parents; when this happens, a remarkable transformation takes place. Their life postures, formerly withdrawn and burdened by fear, become confident and even optimistic. This change is reflected in the improvement in their marriages, their careers, and their ability to identify sensitively with the feelings of others and to articulate these feelings.[5]

Often when this breakthrough occurs, the clients want to help others. Several of these clients continue their involvement with the program, helping young victims individually or serving as facilitators in the group sessions of Daughters and Sons United and Parents United. In this sense, they find what so many of the staff and clients of the CSATP have found: helping others is an important phase in their own therapeutic process. In fact, the main theme of the integrated psychosocial approach of the CSATP can be summed up thus: *people helping people.*

[5]See appendix 1.

Writing to Women Molested as Children

This is an example of one form letter the CSATP has used to respond to the thousands of inquiries received from women molested as children.

Dear   ,

I can't tell you how bad I feel for being unable to answer your letter sooner. I, too, was sexually molested by my father as a child and understand the pain and confusion you felt and are still feeling. I also appreciate how important it must be to you to confide your feelings to someone who will listen and understand them. In my case, I found even more relief when I shared my pain with other women who had gone through the same experience.

That's why I'm writing to you and why Hank and Anna Giarretto are asking me and other women in Parents United who were molested as children to answer each letter in the caring manner it deserves. Hank feels that even if he could answer all the letters personally—an impossible task—a letter from someone like myself would be far more meaningful. He does want you to know that he has read your letter, however, and sends his love and also that all of us here are more determined than ever to carry on our work in this terribly neglected area and invite you to join us.

If there is any comfort in numbers—and I never quite understood this idea—you and I should derive a great deal of it from knowing that we have received hundreds of letters from women like ourselves (not to mention the hundreds of children and their families who are coming in for treatment as a result of the nationwide publicity our program is receiving). I think the real comfort lies not in realizing there are millions of us in the same boat but in that some of us are able to talk about our problem and help each other.

What I really want to accomplish with this letter is not to cry on each other's shoulder—both of us have done enough of that—but to pass on to you some of the steps I've taken to help myself grow out of the pit of pain and to come to a better understanding of myself, my father, and my mother, and the situation in which we were all entangled.

Hank and the other counselors have developed these exercises and not only use them in counseling sessions but encourage the women to do them at home. If you have a therapist, discuss these exercises with him or her and ask if s/he feels comfortable with them and if you should or could do the exercises under his or her supervision. If you don't have a therapist, try to get together with a friend you can trust. If your friend herself was molested as a child, agree to help each other by taking turns in doing the exercises. Plan to meet once or twice weekly, go through two or three of the exercises, and discuss the results. Don't rush through them or do those you can't seem to handle; respect your limits. I was very hesitant in doing some of them, but after trying one or two, I discovered not only that I survived but actually felt a great deal of relief after I finished. Gradually, I was able to do them all and even was able to invent some of my own.

There are two sets of exercises: the first set is for *venting* the pain and anger; the second set is for coming to terms with or *assimilating* the experience. Even though I've placed the exercises for each set in serial order, you don't have to follow them in order, do them all, or stop doing them after you have completed the list. Whenever you feel pain or anger welling up inside, turn to the list and do the exercise you feel is the appropriate one.

Ventilation Exercise

1. Write a letter to your father, a letter you know you cannot send but wish you could. Pour into it all the terror, guilt, feelings of betrayal ("Why did you deny me the fathering and protection I needed from you?"), etc. Don't edit or try to be reasonable. Curse him, call him all the dirty names you can think of, tell him how his exploitation of you for his own pleasure has affected your life. If you have a tape recorder, you may prefer to use it instead of, or in addition to, the letter. Don't hesitate to yell out your feelings. Playing back the tape will be very helpful in teaching you the importance of self-awareness and the danger of repressing your feelings like a smouldering fire within you.

2. If you have angry feelings toward your mother, repeat the first exercise with her as the subject.

3. With your friend looking on, place two chairs so that they face each other. Sit down on one of them. Imagine that your father is sitting in the chair opposite you. Again, go into your rage with no holds barred. Cry out your confused feelings until you're exhausted. Your friend can be helpful by standing in back of you and adding what she thinks you are forgetting to say or are holding back.

4. Repeat this exercise with your mother as the subject. (Remember that if your friend was molested as a child, she's to do the exercise also.)

5. Sit down with your friend and tell her all the torture you would like to put your father through. Let your imagination go; do not be ashamed at some of the cruel things you are thinking. It's better to let them out. Remember that this is the purging stage: you are surfacing and letting go of the feelings of helplessness, which came from being forced to do things you didn't want to do. The vengeful reactions are natural. (One of our women almost gleefully imagined chopping her father up and running the pieces through the garbage disposal—and felt a great relief after she was done.) After I did this exercise a few times, I noticed that I felt much less hate and hostility toward my father.

   Your friend should help you with this exercise by contributing her own devices of torture. After you have finished, she should conjure up her own torture ritual for her father, and this time you will be helping her. Remember that you should *not* force each other to do this or any of the exercises if you don't have the stomach for it.

6. Throw a tantrum. Lie on your back on a bed, preferably king-sized. Thrash about wildly, working yourself up to a pitch, kicking and punching out. At the same time, yell out all your frustrations over what your father did to you. But this time you are fighting back and yelling, "NO! NO! NO! I won't let you do it. Leave me alone!" etc. Turn on your stomach and pound the bed with your fists and forearms. For better leverage, get on your knees beside the bed and continue with your pounding and yelling.

7. Get an old tennis racquet. Place a pillow on your bed. Raise the racquet over your head and hit the pillow with the flat side of the racquet, slowly at first but with increasing force. Put all your body into it, but do it rhythmically without straining your back. (If you have a back problem, avoid this exercise.) As you beat the pillow, your friend will be saying tauntingly, "You will! Yes, you will!" and you will be responding by yelling out with more and more conviction, "No, I won't! No, I won't!" etc., continuing until you're exhausted.

After each of these exercises, you and your friend should discuss them, telling each other the feelings that were aroused and if you experienced a sense of relief afterward.

Assimilation Exercises

1. Get the letter you wrote to your father. Close your eyes for a few moments and try to imagine what your father would be feeling as he opens up the letter and starts reading it. Read the letter slowly and try to experience the emotions and thoughts he is experiencing as he reads your letter. Now get a sheet of paper and answer your letter in the way you think your father would, again trying to "be him" as much as you can. Continue this "correspondence" with your father by writing a series of letters and responses.

2. Repeat this exercise with your mother as correspondent.

    (I've got a stock of such letters. As I read them over and over again, I continually learn more about myself and about my father and mother. I found that this was a necessary preparation for the letter I finally sent my father to get the response I needed from him. I know now that if I had actually sent him the letter I had first written, his answer would have been evasive and defensive and we would have remained in the same "stuck place." Some of our members have done these exercises and have come to a more peaceful place, despite the fact that their fathers were dead or otherwise impossible to contact.)

3. Repeat Ventilation Exercise 3, but this time play both roles. In one chair, you are yourself, saying to your father what you need to say, expressing whatever emotion you are feeling. Now and then, sit in the opposite chair and "become" your father, trying to imagine what he is feeling, what he is thinking, and how he would respond to your accusations and questions.

    Your friend can help by suggesting when you should exchange chairs. A good time to change is after you've asked an important question or series of questions. ("How could you have done those awful things to me? What in the hell was going on in you?" etc.) After doing this for a while, start becoming *aware* of what you are feeling inside—the knot in your stomach, the lump in your throat. Again, your friend can help by asking, at appropriate pauses in the "conversation," what you are feeling at that moment. You'll both get the hang of this exercise after a little practice.

4. Repeat Assimilation Exercise 3, but this time the conversation will be with your mother.

5. Sit down with your friend in the opposite chair. Close your eyes and "become" your father as he is now. Do it as a character actress would in getting ready to play a role. Try to make contact with whatever may be going on in him as he evaluates his life. ("Most of my life has passed me by and I've made a mess of it. . . . My wife and I live in the same house together and yet we are strangers. . . . I've made no real contact with her for years. . . . The kids come to visit as little as they can but they come mostly for her. . . . When did my life start to go wrong?" etc.) Your friend can join in this exercise, adding her comments as she too tries to identify with your father. After you've finished, then it's her turn to do the exercise.

6. Repeat the exercise with your mother as the subject.

I have repeatedly done these exercises and similar ones that I've picked up in books I've been reading. Incidentally, there are two books I recommend highly. The first is *Born to Win* by Muriel James and Dorothy Jongeward; the second is *Women as Winners* by Dorothy Jongeward and Dru Scott. I strongly urge you to carefully look over the exercises in these books and to do those that apply to you.

I'd like to tell you about some of the main insights that have come to me since I've been with the program:

(a) I can do a lot to help myself—I don't have to depend on someone else to "cure" me.

(b) The more I learn the habit of self-awareness, the more I can contend with life and where I'm headed. I've found that when I deliberately try to be aware of my pain, pinpoint it in my body and feelings, that most of it goes away.

(c) I've learned that my life is a process of ups and downs; that it would be boring if it did not vary; and that the events in my life which I once considered as problems are really opportunities for growth. Most of all, I've discovered that the stresses produced by my abnormal relationship with my father are now becoming a source of strength for me. Hank once told me something I'm slowly beginning to understand: "Have you ever considered the possibility that your present strengths—the abilities to listen, to be sensitive to others, to be able to nurture others and yourself—may, for the large part, stem from the fact that you were molested as a child and that this event in your life forced you to look inward, to experience the whole YOU more fully and therefore has made you more appreciative, more caring of yourself and the kids and adults who come to you for help?"

(d) There is one more idea that Hank has tried to pass on to me, while I'm having more difficulty with but which is slowly beginning to make sense. He told me that my father would really have preferred to have been a good father. The greatest personal rewards come from being effective (loving and lovable) fathers, mothers, wives, husbands, workers, friends, etc. He said that my father didn't add up to a good father simply because he didn't know how to become one. Hank added that it is foolish to think of anyone deliberately holding out on himself, of deliberately punishing himself, or of deliberately denying himself the inner peace and self-fulfillment that comes from living the good life.

I guess the most important thing we're learning here at Parents United is how to live good lives. And we've discovered the best way of accomplishing this is by working together to help one another assimilate old pains and turn them into positive energy that we can use for our growth and for helping the children and their families who are presently experiencing the traumas of incest. The best self-help is to help others.

I strongly believe that you can start to do what we're doing here—by contacting your local Child Protective Services Agency and offering your services for helping the sexually abused children who are coming to their agency for help. Once you get involved, then you can urge them and assist them to set up a program similar to the one we have here. If you get to this stage, write to me and I will send you additional information regarding the start-up and development of such a program.

I sincerely hope that this letter has been helpful, but even if you are unable to use some or all of the suggestions, please know that the heart of this message is LOVE from me, Hank and Anna, and all of us here at Parents United.

Peace and Love,

5. CSATP Growth and Results

The Child Sexual Abuse Treatment Program has provided services to over three thousand families since it began in 1971. During the first three years, the program received about thirty referrals a year. In 1974, the referral rate rose sharply to 135 cases mainly because of the growing reputation of the program as a source for help to sexually abusive families and because of funds from public revenue-sharing and from the Rosenberg Foundation. This money was used to increase the staff and begin a public education effort that soon bore fruit. There were over 700 referrals in 1980, and the CSATP expects the referral rate to continue increasing, despite the fact that many cases which would have been referred to the Santa Clara CSATP are now being referred to the new CSATPs in nearby counties.

Since it is reasonable to suppose that the actual rate of incest itself has not changed significantly in Santa Clara County during the past few years, this growing referral rate means that many child-victims and their families are now receiving help who would not have received such help were it not for the CSATP, its ability to gain the cooperation of the criminal justice system, and its positive reception by the press and public.

Another significant measure of the effectiveness of the CSATP is the immediate and long-lasting help given to the children and their families. The marked improvement in the treatment of families troubled by incest compared to the way they were treated formerly largely accounts for the program's growth and the markedly increased referral rates.

An Independent Evaluation

Previous to this year, the effects on the clients due to the services of the CSATP were measured by the staff, and the findings were considered by some to be questionable because of potential bias. Early in 1978, however, the review committee selected by the California State Director of Health appointed an independent investigator to collect and analyze data on the performance of the CSATP. In their final report of June 1978, this evaluation team discussed the results of a survey of comparable groups of clients at three stages in the treatment program: at intake, at midterm, and near termination. The following sections discuss the principal findings of the evaluation.

The Daughter. Child victims of incest in Santa Clara County who were removed from their mothers by the authorities are being returned to their mothers much sooner than they were before the CSATP was formed and sooner than in other communities throughout the country. Giarretto estimated in 1976 that around 90 percent of the children were returning home within the first month and that 95 percent were returned eventually. Based on a sample of 127 active cases, the findings of the independent evaluator substantially concur with this estimate: the median time out of the home for these girls was 90 days, and 92 percent could be expected to return home eventually.[1]

[1]Jerome A. Kroth, *Child Sexual Abuse: Analysis of a Family Therapy Approach* (Springfield, IL: Charles C. Thomas, 1979).

Although not objectively measured, it was clearly apparent to the staff that there was a decline, both in intensity and in duration, in the typical self-abusive behavior of child victims. It appeared that the coordinated approach of the CSATP prevents truancy, decline in school performance, promiscuity, and heavy drug use, primarily by helping the girls overcome their strong feelings of betrayal and guilt. The evaluation team measured this self-abusive factor as a "failure to deteriorate" and found, from a sample of seventy incest victims, that during the prior two months only four percent had gotten drunk or high on drugs, only three percent had shown signs of sexual promiscuity, only one percent had stayed out overnight without permission or run away from home, and only six percent had become involved with the authorities. These figures are extremely low compared with any other figures in the literature on child sexual abuse.

Put, perhaps, in strong terms, if one supposes that children who experienced incest have an increasing tendency toward social maladjustment and are, as a consequence of the molestation, more prone toward delinquency, sexual acting-out, substance abuse, etc., receiving family therapy intervention entirely contradicts such a prognosis.[2]

Undoubtedly related are the evaluator's findings on the psychological health of the victims during the course of treatment. The evaluation found, for example, that the percentage of girls with such symptoms as bedwetting, nail-biting, fainting, etc., declined from 47 percent at intake to 6 percent by termination. Important, too, are the findings that show a marked improvement of the girls' relationships with their peers and the other members of their families, particularly their fathers.

Although it is too early to say with documented confidence, it can be expected that the CSATP will have contributed to the mental health of these girls as they become women and mothers.

The Father. The father-offender also seems to benefit from involvement with the CSATP. As noted before, men who formerly would have received long jail or prison sentences are now being given short jail terms or suspended sentences as a result of increasing recognition of the CSATP by the judiciary as an effective alternative to incarceration. Of 127 cases analyzed, 52 percent were not incarcerated, 20 percent spent some time in jail, while 28 percent were still in litigation, or no information was available.

For successful treatment to take place, it is vital that the father accept full responsibility for the molestation. In the evaluator's sample, 89 percent were ready to accept most or all of the responsibility for the molestation at termination of the study period. Significant, too, is the finding that feelings of extreme general guilt were reduced at the same time: the number of parents feeling "strong guilt" declined from 65 percent of the sample at intake to 24 percent near termination. This ability to distinguish responsibility and guilt is one of the important goals of the treatment: the former is a necessary step toward self-management; the latter is self-defeating.

The CSATP has markedly speeded up the process of rehabilitation for the offender. Before the program started, individual or marriage counseling did not occur, if at all, until after the offender was released from long periods of incarceration. Now, counseling and involvement with Parents United is started soon after his arrest and continues during and after incarceration to carefully considered termination. This protracted counseling and participation in Parents United strongly influences those who decide whether the offender is rehabilitated. In this regard, the CSATP was effective in helping to restore the licenses of two commercial pilots and two real estate men, to regain the secret clearances of two engineers in the aerospace industry, to have two postal service employees keep their civil service positions, to prevent the loss of careers to five men in the military services, and to save the jobs of numerous men in private industry.

The CSATP has been very helpful in the delicate matter of rebuilding a normal relationship between men and the daughters they have abused. This goal, once considered by many to be undesirable and/or impossible, has proven crucial to the future mental health of both the child and her parent, as well as to the family as a unit. In the evaluator's sample, worsening relationships between father and daughter decreased from 17 percent to 4

[2]Kroth, *op. cit.*, p. 100.

percent, while improving relationships increased from 22 percent to 50 percent.

The Mother. In the typical incestuous family treated by the CSATP, the mother is often the first to receive tangible help in the form of immediate counseling and emergency practical assistance. Before the program existed, mothers usually found themselves alone in a hopeless situation. The bureaucracy involved was badly fragmented and the mother had no guidance in securing the various kinds of help needed for her family. The CSATP has made great strides in mobilizing typically disjointed and often competitive services into a cooperative effort.

It is interesting to note that while the mother's strong sense of guilt declines during the course of treatment (as does the father's), she, too, learns to accept her share of responsibility for the poor marriage and her inability to protect her daughter. By termination, 50 percent of the evaluation's sample admit that they were "very much responsible" as opposed to none at all at intake. This change of attitude comes from learning that a failing marriage is, invariably, one of the precursors to incest.

The Marriage and the Family. The positive influence of the CSATP on both parents is revealed in the evaluator's measure of "attitudinal changes." Near termination, 82 percent of the mothers and fathers surveyed agreed with the statement: "I feel more open, honest, and in control of myself," and all affirmed that "things are a lot better than they used to be." The percentage of those who disagreed with the statement: "Right now I feel devastated emotionally" rose from zero percent at intake to 76 percent near termination. Similarly, the percentage of those who felt "not close at all" to a nervous breakdown rose from 12 percent to 88 percent.

As a result of the CSATP's policy of initiating counseling as soon as possible after referral and continuing it to successful termination, far more marriages have been saved than formerly was the case. Giarretto had estimated in 1976 that about 90 percent of the marriages were saved. The evaluation determined that 76 percent of the couples were still married at the end of the study period and 14 percent were separated. Many of the separated couples were still in the early stages of counseling. From past experience, it can be expected that many of these will eventually reunite. Therefore, it is reasonable to predict that the gap between the two findings will close. Kroth notes that in any case, even the 76 percent figure is a success rate unmatched by any other known study.

In many cases, the husbands and wives confide that their relationships are better now than they were before the crisis, or, for that matter, better than they have been for years. As one couple confided, "This is the first time in our marriage that we have ever been able to communicate."

The evaluator found tangible measures of improved marriages during the course of treatment. Near termination, 59 percent of the sample reported that their relationships had improved, whereas only 6 percent reported that their relationships had deteriorated. Their sexual activity increased both in frequency and quality. There is a corresponding improvement in the husband's sense of his own sexual health. Those marriage partners who argued "quite a lot" at the beginning of the study argued much less at the end; the decrease in arguments ranged from 38 percent at intake to zero percent near termination.

Recidivism rates are an indication of the CSATP's success in preventing remolestation. Despite the fact that four out of five fathers return to live with their families and their daughters, only three repeats have been reported among the more than 1,500 families who have received treatment to formal termination. The recidivism rate to date for all client families is less than one percent. The recidivism rates found by the evaluator in the literature ranged from two to twenty percent. In an unpublished report obtained by the CSATP on a study at Atascadero State Hospital, the report noted that "91 subjects representing 15 percent of all 617 subjects released into society qualified as sexual recidivists." Of the 91 subjects, 11 percent were incest recidivists.[3]

[3]Kroth, *op. cit.*, p. 124.

However, Kroth feels that the recidivism rate is not as significant as the number of the referrals to the CSATP:

> In effect the single most important statistic which reflects on the efficacy of treatment is not recidivism or anxiety level, or the grade point averages of victims in treatment, but the rate at which victims, offenders and families come forward! In this regard the CSATP referral record is superb . . . since 1974, for example, *there has been an average increase of about 40 percent in the number of clients coming forward each year, and it is likely 98 percent of these new clients will not repeat the offense merely on the basis of the fact that the molest has been reported and the family secret broken!*[4]

The Failures. Of course, the Child Sexual Abuse Treatment Program is not equally effective with all clients and fails utterly with some. About ten percent of the referrals elude the efforts of the CSATP. They will not come in for the initial interview, or they will drop out soon after treatment has begun. In the first two years of the program, four couples were dismissed by Giarretto because the father and/or his wife would not admit to the offender's culpability but continued to place the blame entirely on the child-victim and her "seductive" behavior. In these instances, extraordinary effort was required in the treatment of the deserted child. After many attempts, the four girls adjusted to foster homes. Three are now married and seem to be doing well. But the wounds of alienation between children and parents seldom heal.

The decisions to deny the services of the program to the four couples was made with the hope that a firm no-nonsense stand would shock the couples into facing their responsibility as parents. In retrospect, however, the counselor regrets these decisions since the victims were not reunited with their families. Perhaps more patience on the part of the counselor and the staff might have gradually won the parents over. It is now the policy of the CSATP to provide treatment to clients as long as they wish it, no matter the reasons or how recalcitrant they appear to be.

As mentioned above, only three cases of recidivism have been reported among any of the families that received full treatment and were formally terminated. There have been about fifteen known cases of recidivism in families whose treatment was not completed. One, for example, involved a family in another county. Not eligible for individualized treatment, this family regularly attended the group counseling sessions provided by Parents United and Daughters and Sons United. The offender, fifty-two, was on probation but was not permitted to reside in the family home. He broke this order while his wife was hospitalized and persuaded his fifteen-year-old stepdaughter to submit to thigh intercourse. As soon as he left, the girl called her mother, who immediately contacted the CSATP.

Another case also concerned a stepfather, thirty-two, who had served a nine-month jail sentence for sexual intercourse with his fifteen-year-old stepdaughter. A year after leaving jail, at a party while in a drunken state, he openly attempted to fondle the breasts of the girl, then seventeen. This man had refused to come in for counseling after his release from jail despite the strong urgings of the CSATP personnel and his probation officer. He had a serious drinking problem and could not bring himself to find steady treatment.

The CSATP works for most families because the approach is based on multifaceted treatment to the point where the staff and the client agree that no further help is required. When this formula is not followed, the results often confirm that, used separately, traditional therapies such as the self-help aspect, incarceration, and social work are not sufficient. The comprehensive, integrated strategy of the CSATP must be applied until the client becomes self-managing and the parents are able to lead their families effectively.

---

[4]*Ibid.*, p. 125. Italics in original.

Not all families are equally motivated toward involvement in the CSATP. They come for different reasons, some simply with the hope that doing so will soften the blow of the law. Others require more intensive treatment than the CSATP can provide currently. The position of the CSATP, however, is that it is the staff's responsibility to motivate the clients and that the variety and depth of services must be continually improved.

It is true that the CSATP receives many more referrals than it can handle efficiently. The problem of keeping facilities and personnel adequate will probably never be solved. But the fact that the staff may be overextended because of a sharply accelerating referral rate is no solace to the family that is asking for help and does not receive it.

In spite of these lapses, however, the cases and personal statements of clients in this manual attest to the general effectiveness of the CSATP. Clients develop close ties with the CSATP staff and co-members of the self-help groups, and these links very likely help to prevent or reduce the severity of new offenses. In most cases of known recidivism, the CSATP was informed of the molestations within a short time after they happened. The girls told their mothers as soon as they could, and the mothers, in turn, reported the recurrence immediately, although they knew that doing so might lead to the incarceration of their husbands.

Previously, these girls had been sexually exploited for several years before they could muster the courage to confide in their mothers or in anyone who could help them. Some of the mothers had failed to report the earlier crimes, fearful of the reaction of their husbands, and of the criminal justice system. All of the mothers had attended the women's group of Parents United. One of the themes explored by this group is the need for some of them to develop self-sufficiency—that excessive economic and emotional dependence on their husbands diminished them as persons, unbalanced their marriages, and weakened their abilities to protect and parent their children. Apparently, then, these mothers (as well as the girls) had profited from the CSATP treatment at least to the extent that they were able to stop their husbands (and fathers) from continuing the abusive behavior.

Still another example supports the view that the CSATP helps prevent new offenses. This example is typical of several similar ones in which the clients demonstrated that they had internalized the ability to monitor residual and potentially dangerous impulses. In this case, a father who had been terminated from individual therapy a year before called the counselor and asked for an appointment. He confided that he was beginning to have sexual feelings toward one of his older daughters. On the following day, the daughter he had originally molested also called the counselor and said, "I wish you would talk to Dad. I think he's beginning to act funny with Betty." A few days later, it was discovered that, in a conversation with one of the mothers she had befriended at Parents United, the mother had voiced some misgivings about her husband's increasing attention to Betty. This type of multiple "early warning" or monitoring system makes the CSATP staff fairly confident that it learns of most of the recidivism that occurs.

Winning the Support of the Community

The Criminal Justice System. When justice is distorted in incest cases by retribution in the form of long-term incarceration for the offender and separation of the child from her family, the effects are destructive and expensive both to the family and the community. Perhaps even more disturbing is the fact that, in those communities wherein the criminal justice system has a reputation for being cruelly punitive, families troubled by incest will not report the situation and the victims continue to be victimized.

The CSATP is based on the assumption that incest occurs within the context of an unstable or failing marriage which in turn creates dysfunctional family relations, and that the best treatment of the problem is to reeducate the father/husband and the mother/wife so that they become more effective as individuals, spouses, and parents. The CSATP has continually promoted these views to the criminal justice system and the public at large.

The CSATP has been in a good position to influence the criminal justice system since the program developed within the Juvenile Probation Department, which is part of that system. Earning the confidence and cooperation of the juvenile and adult probation officers, the police, the prosecuting attorneys, and the courts has been a gradual and persistent effort, and one accomplished more by demonstration than by polemics. Without the cooperation of the system, a program for coping with child sexual abuse would be severely limited and in fact would not be a CSATP at all.

Family Service Center
Naval Submarine Base New London
P.O. Box 93
Groton, Connecticut 06349

At first only a few probation officers referred their clients to the counselor, as if on an experimental basis. The results with these cases were apparently worthwhile, and more probation officers began to think of the counseling effort as the appropriate resource for incest cases. They found it convenient to direct the clients to the on-site resources for therapy rather than to agencies scattered all over town and found that their case management problems improved. The probation officers were also very helpful in winning the cooperation of the police and eventually the other members of the criminal justice system. And it was only after this cooperation began to take shape that the counseling effort began to be regarded as a "program."

The task of getting all the interveners in incest cases to cooperate is, of course, never completed; and the CSATP staff continues with this effort primarily by employing its principal persuader: the meetings of Parents United and Daughters and Sons United. Police, prosecuting and defense attorneys, probation officers and judges are invited to the weekly meetings to witness first-hand the effects of the program on the clients. In addition, presentations on the program are conducted at meetings of these various jurisdictions.

Members of the staff also appear in court on behalf of the clients, in particular the children, and are able to convey the objectives of the program directly to the judges and the attorneys. Letters to probation officers by the counselors regarding the progress of the offenders in their counseling plans have been instrumental in reducing the severity of sentences in most cases. The program is now regarded by most of the judges as an alternative to long-term incarceration. Most sentences, whether suspended or requiring jail terms, include strong orders for continued therapy with the CSATP. Increasingly, recent sentences also order certain offenders to contribute several hundred hours of work to Parents United in lieu of spending that time in jail (see appendix 4A).

Another example can be given of the effort to influence positively the way incest and other forms of child sexual abuse are handled, especially in minimizing trauma to the children. An indication of progress in this area was the request by the Crime Prevention Unit of the San Jose Police Department for suggestions and endorsement of their proposal for funds to create a special sex offense resource team that would act to reduce the damaging effects of the investigation of a sex crime on the victims. With the help of the CSATP, the police department eventually was granted the funds that support the very successful Sexual Assault Investigation Unit previously mentioned in this publication.

The foregoing discussion noted that the CSATP grew within the Juvenile Probation Department by taking advantage of this position for gaining the cooperation of the criminal justice system. It must be emphasized that other agencies holding jurisdiction over child sexual abuse cases, such as child protective services and similar agencies, can establish CSATPs and be equally productive in developing cooperation among the responsible workers. Indeed, most of the sixty-five new CSATPs that resulted from the training project were started and are currently being coordinated by members of child protective services agencies who were trained by the project.

The Community Awareness Unit. Just as it is necessary to demonstrate to the criminal justice system that a humanistic method of handling incest cases is more effective than a punitive one, it is necessary to educate the community at large that families troubled by incest are deserving of compassion rather than social vilification. By combatting the pervasive dread of incest, the CSATP encourages troubled families to seek help voluntarily at the earliest possible time.

The community awareness unit of the CSATP is supervised by a member of the administrative staff and of Parents United. They train speakers, book their engagements, promote coverage by the media, and disburse written material upon request. Although the primary focus of this effort has been on local communities, the community awareness unit also meets the increasing demand from people throughout the nation for information about the program and about the problem of child sexual abuse.

Members of the CSATP professional staff have spoken to a variety of groups, such as child protective service workers, mental health personnel, college classes, the Santa Clara County Task Force on Child Abuse, therapists, and numerous other agencies and concerned community people. Members of the staff have conducted seminars and workshops for human service groups all across the country. Presentations have been made at major national and international conferences on child abuse.

Many members of Parents United and Daughters and Sons United also have been active in the field of public education through the Parents United Speakers' Bureau. The Speakers' Bureau meets every two weeks to train new speakers who wish to relate their stories and who know that this is one of the best ways to educate the public. The members are taught facts about the CSATP and about child sexual abuse in general and are trained to develop the skills necessary to address an audience.

Presentations are usually given by a team consisting of a CSATP staff member and one or more members of PU/DSU. The staff member describes the treatment approach of the program, and the PU/DSU members relate their own experiences and describe the structure and functions of Parents United/Daughters and Sons United. Speakers are sent to groups as diverse as the Kiwanis, the Optimists, the National Organization of Women, as well as to radio and television shows. In 1980, presentations were given to 180 groups.

Stimulating public awareness on the subject of incest has a strong beneficial effect on the parents and children who participate in the Speakers' Bureau. They learn they can modify the attitudes and policies of the agencies whose decisions may affect their families adversely. Therefore, they learn that they can have more control over their lives if they become socially responsible.

The Media. As mentioned above, the CSATP staff and members of Parents United and Daughters and Sons United have appeared on numerous radio broadcasts, a majority of which were audience-participation shows. Newspaper coverage of the CSATP has ranged from the local papers to *The New York Times* and the *Washington Post*. Support has come from columnists whose audience vary widely: in *Playboy* Howard Smith and Brian Van der Horst described the program and expressed a hope that readers could "look for these enlightened techniques to spread across the county"; Ann Landers also praised the program in her advice column, saying, "We need dozens more. Here's a project for PTAs all over the nation," and included an article by Giarretto in her *Ann Landers Encylopedia*.[5]

Articles about the CSATP have appeared in journals that range from the highly specialized (*Children Today* and *Family Practice News*) to the mass-market magazines (*Readers Digest, People, Family Circle,* and *Ms.*).

A video tape has been produced by *Newsweek* and distributed to fifty television stations across the country. The CSATP was featured on "The Today Show," "The Tomorrow Show," and "The Phil Donahue Show." The National Broadcasting Company developed a documentary on the CSATP and Parents United, which they aired nationwide on their ninety-minute program *"Weekend"* on May 7, 1977. This documentary reached an audience of several million people and has been used subsequently as an educational aid to enlighten various communities throughout the United States on the problem.

Exposure through the media was not easy to achieve at first. Incest is a delicate subject, and most editors and producers in the early 1970s were fearful of a negative audience reaction. At the national level, the *Washington Post* and NBC were the first to stir widespread attention to incest. The response of the public indicated that open discussion of the problem was long overdue. After the NBC special, for example, the CSATP received hundreds of letters from women all over the country who had been abused as children by their fathers or stepfathers. In many cases, these letters were the first time the women had ever told anyone about the secret that was still haunting them. More important to current victims of child sexual abuse were the large number of letters from agencies and professionals wanting to know more about the approach of the CSATP.

Information Disbursal. Thousands of information packets have been sent all over the country to people who have requested them. (The CSATP responded to approximately 960 such requests between October 1977 and March 1978.) The packet contains an overview of the CSATP and Parents United, as well as information on child sexual abuse. Toward the same purpose, a brochure has been developed for mass mailing or for distribution through doctors, law enforcement agencies, public service agencies, high schools, etc. There is also a flyer appropriate for posting in the community.

The importance of the public information effort cannot be overstressed. As a result of alerting the public about the widespread problem of incest, thousands of children here and elsewhere are receiving the treatment they would otherwise have been denied.

The problem of child sexual abuse may never be eliminated from our society, but it can be reduced by removing from it the shroud of mystery and shame. For too long, incest has been a topic that few are willing to discuss. The public should be made aware of the problem and of the resources for help. Laws must be enacted that are effective and consistent, neither permissive nor cruelly punitive. Finally, comprehensive procedures must be established in each community to treat sexually abused children and their families to prevent future violations and to enhance these families' chances for reconstitution into healthy, growth-promoting units.

[5]Howard Smith and Brian Van der Horst, "Innovations on Incest," *Playboy* Magazine (September 1976), p. 213; Ann Landers, "More Incest Treatment Centers Needed," *Daily News* (New York; August 26, 1977), p. B-2; and Ann Landers, *The Ann Landers Encyclopedia* (Garden City, NY: Doubleday, 1978).

II

The CSATP's Two-Week Training Course

Unit I. Orientation

Unit Description

This unit is divided into five modules, each consisting of various learning activities designed to introduce trainees to the history and philosophy of the Child Sexual Abuse Treatment Program (CSATP) in Santa Clara County and to give them their first exposure to the program's professional and self-help components. In addition, Unit I gives the trainees an overview of the content of the training program; on this first day, trainees are given examples of what they will be learning and experiencing in greater depth during the next two weeks.

Presentations are given by the director of training and by representatives of the adult and child self-help groups, with emphasis on the philosophy and development of these components. The principles and methods of the program are introduced. The speakers narrate their personal experiences, telling how their own development kept pace with that of the program.

A film produced for television by NBC serves as an introduction to the problem of incest in America and the way it is dealt with by the CSATP. Trainees are then given a preliminary introduction to the program's administrative and interagency coordination functions. Finally, the community training organizer describes the course work of the training program itself and explains the schedule of events for the two-week period.

Unit Goals

To provide trainees the opportunity to:

1. Learn about the history of the Child Sexual Abuse Treatment Program;

2. Learn about the humanistic philosophy of the program, how it affects the treatment approach, and how it enhances interagency cooperation;

3. Meet members of the counseling staff and of Parents United and Daughters and Sons United who will relate personal experiences;

4. Learn about the roles and functions of the administrative personnel; and

5. Begin to get a sense of purpose and commitment to increasing their effectiveness in dealing with sexually abusive families.

Unit Content, Module Design, and Activities Requirements

Module	Time	Activity	Time	Materials
1. General Introduction to the CSATP	2½ hrs.	1. Registration 2. Introductions 3. Historical background of CSATP 4. Historical Background of Parents United 5. Historical Background of Daughters and Sons United 6. Question-and-Answer Session	30 min. 5 min. 1 hr. 20 min. 20 min. 15 min.	Felt pens, name tags, sign-in roster, handouts and training kits, supplies for coffee and other refreshments. Space requirements: A room large enough to seat trainees and trainers in a circle. Ambiance should be comfortable—the room should be carpeted, if possible—and pleasant.
2. Lunch with Staff	1½ hrs.			
3. NBC Film Presentation	2 hrs.	1. Film showing 2. Discussion	1½ hrs. 30 min.	16mm sound projector, wall screen or portable screen, NBC film. Additional staff: a projectionist
4. Introduction to Administration and Interagency Cooperation	1 hr.	1. CSATP Administration 2. CSATP Interagency Coordination	30 min. 30 min.	Organizational charts Flow charts
5. Schedule and Training Locations	1 hr.			Schedule and maps (if necessary)

Unit Rationale

The trainees are a special group of workers with a unique mission: they will be expected to introduce into their communities an innovative approach to the treatment of child sexual abuse. Unit I is designed to make them aware of the scope of this mission and the realities of the problems they must face when they return to their agencies, as well as the personal satisfaction they can expect to receive as CSATP workers. It is the task of the trainers to motivate the trainees to accomplish the job, and to assure them that upon completion of the training they will have the skills and tools to start their own programs. Toward this end, Unit I gives the trainees:

1. An understanding of the problem of child sexual abuse, particularly when it involves father–daughter incest;

2. A description of how the typical community ignores the problem or magnifies it by using punitive tactics;

3. An introduction to the CSATP approach to the problem; and

4. personal accounts of the obstacles as well as the rewards experienced by the principal developers of the CSATP.

Unit Objectives

At the end of this unit, trainees should be able to:

1. Begin to understand how CSATP programs are started and developed;

2. Be cognizant of the overall goals and objectives of a CSATP patterned after the Santa Clara County model;

3. Anticipate some of the practical problems and issues they will be dealing with in their own communities;

4. Begin to reevaluate the hopes and expectations they brought to the training program;

5. Begin to clarify their present and future roles as child sexual abuse workers; and

6. Have an idea of what their personal investment will be in dealing with the problems of child sexual abuse and in developing a CSATP in their own communities.

Module 1: General Introduction to the CSATP

Description

This module presents an overview of the historical and philosophical development of the CSATP and its self-help components, Parents United (PU) and Daughters and Sons United (DSU). The director/trainer describes how he started the program in Santa Clara County, including a personal account of how his own evolution as a humanistic psychologist influenced the development of the CSATP.* Representatives of the self-help components share their personal treatment histories and discuss their involvement as leaders of PU/DSU. Throughout the morning, the trainees are urged to ask questions; these are answered in a way that will encourage effective communication between participants and staff members.

*Here and throughout this manual, activities are described as they occur in the Santa Clara County program. The personal pronoun "he" is used here, for example, only because the director/trainer in Santa Clara County happens to be male. It in no way suggests a gender preference or recommendation.

Goals

To provide trainees the opportunity to:

1. Begin to get a philosophical grounding in the humanistic approach of the CSATP;

2. Be motivated to start programs in their communities, knowing that this can be accomplished by one or two dedicated persons;

3. Begin to learn the skills and format for starting CSATPs utilizing both private and official resources within their communities;

4. Learn about a model of treatment in which the clients can learn to lead self-managing and socially responsible lives;

5. Understand that an accepting, educative, and cooperative stance in CSATP developers—rather than an adversary attitude—is effective not only with clients but also in winning the support and cooperation of personnel in the criminal justice system and other agencies that have an impact on clients; and

6. Understand that trainees and trainers alike are there to learn from one another and to help each other now and after the training is over.

Rationale

The trainees will be required to absorb a great deal of information about all aspects of the CSATP. This module gives them an overall understanding of how the CSATP works as well as how various elements within the program function. One of the basic concepts of the CSATP is the importance of working together. Therefore, the activities in this module are designed to introduce the trainees to one another and to some of the trainers so that all people involved will make the most of the training course.

Objectives

At the end of this module, trainees should be able to:

1. Have an overall picture of the CSATP from both a philosophical and a historical perspective;

2. Begin to visualize and anticipate the tasks they will face when they return to their communities;

3. Have a good idea of the problems involved in changing entrenched institutions;

4. Begin to ask critical questions about the CSATP approach and to challenge it;

5. Begin to understand the importance of self-knowledge and working on their own basic attitudes and feelings about child sexual abuse before attempting to persuade others to change their belief systems; and

6. Begin to experience within the group the concepts basic to the program: caring, empathy, cooperation, trust, and cohesion.

Activity 1. Registration

The trainees are greeted by trainers and other staff persons. They sign in and receive name tags. Hosts introduce trainees to each other and to other persons present and encourage them to help themselves to refreshments. Trainees socialize until all participants have arrived and signed in. During this activity, trainers make every effort to make trainees feel welcome and cared for, help them relax and feel at home, and encourage them to become acquainted with each other.

Activity 2. Introductions

Seated in a circle, the trainees and trainers take turns introducing themselves briefly (where they are from, the agency they work for, and their job title), stating why they chose to come for training, and explaining what their hopes and expectations are relative to the special needs of their community agencies.

This activity gives the trainees a chance to know one another more intimately and to begin to get a sense of cohesion and common purpose. It also provides the trainers with an opportunity to become familiar with the group personality, as well as the individual personalities of the trainees, so they can tailor the training around individual or group needs.

Training Kit Table of Contents

Note: The handouts and training kit will include whatever materials the trainers deem necessary or appropriate to their particular training program. This is an example of what might be included.

Activity 3. Historical Background of the CSATP

Santa Clara County's director/trainer gives a brief historical and philosophical overview of the CSATP.

Director's Opening Talk

Hello and welcome. I'm going to give you a brief history of the Child Sexual Abuse Treatment Program: how it got started, the basic ideas behind it, and some of the growing pains as well as the rewards. I'm going to make it a personal story because many of you will be having similar experiences.

The CSATP is made up of three components: the professional component, the self-help component, and the volunteer component. All three are necessary for a true CSATP. I'll begin by telling you how the professional component took form. In 1971, the Juvenile Probation Department here was getting about thirty referrals a year of cases involving child sexual abuse. Most of them concerned fathers who were molesting their own daughters. Some of the probation officers were getting very upset over the way cases were being handled. It seemed that the law enforcement people either ignored the victim's complaints or came down very harshly on a family if the father admitted the crime. In most instances, the reaction of the system resulted in jail for the father and a break-up of the family.

When a case came to them, the probation officers could do very little with it. Usually it was necessary to find a new home for the child because her own home was not considered safe, and no counseling was available for the parents that merited their confidence. There was no case management to speak of.

Eunice Peterson, who supervised the intake and placement section of JPD, talked to Bob Spitzer, the consulting psychiatrist to the department at that time. Bob thought that families troubled by incest needed conjoint family counseling. He had seen Anna (my wife) work with a family and liked the way she did it. He called our office and asked Anna to come to his office to talk about his family therapy plan. I went along out of curiosity.

I don't quite remember how we came to that conclusion, but it was decided that I would try my hand at counseling the families. Eunice, Bob, and I agreed that I would do the counseling at the Juvenile Center so that the service would be immediately available to incoming families—at the time they needed the most support. This was a good decision, one that we follow as much as possible to this day.

We decided on a pilot effort of eighty counseling hours spread over a ten-week period, and Bob said he would contribute eight hundred dollars to the effort. So our start-up budget was a huge eight hundred dollars. After the ten-week period was over, there was no question as to whether I would continue seeing the families. I was so involved with the clients that I just kept coming to JPD. In fact, before long I found myself spending most of my working week with the families. Luckily, I had a fair practice with other paying clients, and Anna was working.

After the pilot phase ended, over two years went by before we received some revenue-sharing funds for my salary and a small grant from the Rosenberg Foundation that paid for the part-time salaries of Dorothy Ross and Vicki Imabori. So for over five years, the three of us made up the paid staff of a program that, by 1976, was handling several hundred referrals per year. We finally were able to augment the staff in the spring of 1977 when we got the funds for the California Training Project.

I'm giving you these financial details to impress upon you the fact that very little or no extra community funds are required to operate a CSATP. Over sixty CSATPs throughout the country, modeled after the local CSATP, are being operated by child protective service agencies with trained members of their staffs. Many of these CSATPs include counselors from public mental health agencies. Again, any community that wishes to establish a CSATP can do so with personnel from existing public agencies trained for this purpose.

Of course, the increasing referral rates will in time require more personnel. But these added costs to the community will easily be counterbalanced by decreased costs in foster home placement, welfare payments, and incarceration, not to mention the other economic losses to the community when a father loses his job. Clearly, a CSATP copes with a sexually abused child and her family not only more humanely but more economically.

I believe, also, that the lack of funds had much to do with the way the CSATP took shape. I'd like to say that I had a master plan or a completely worked out strategy for a child sexual abuse treatment program, but during the first months it never occurred to me to dignify what we were doing with the word "program." A program did eventually develop, not by design but out of necessity, and even out of desperation. I quickly discovered that I could not cope with the enormous needs of the families by myself. So I turned to the juvenile probation officers for help.

When a JPO sent me a family, he or she and I would work on the case together. We essentially became co-counselors; the JPO would see the mother and daughter at home, or see the daughter at the children's shelter, while I would counsel the family members at the Juvenile Center. And I'm sure that in this expanded role the JPOs gave the families more than the usual attention, especially in helping the mother deal with the many problems that came with the exposure of the situation. Along these lines, the first girls' groups—one for adolescents, another a play-therapy group for young children—were organized and led by a JPO and myself.

I learned an important lesson while working with the JPOs, one we still follow and will stress during the next two weeks: it makes good sense to *involve* the other official interveners in the CSATP instead of trying to shut them out. By participating in the treatment process, they become allies; by being cut off, or by having their efforts disparaged, they become enemies. Nobody likes being displaced or having his turf invaded.

We began to use this participation tactic with the police, pretrial officers, adult probation officers, defense and prosecuting attorneys, and eventually the judges. This is how the professional component of the CSATP began to take shape, how we began to coordinate the services of the official interveners in a case. It was a slow process and one that we continue to develop and refine. We try to prove the merits of the CSATP approach by demonstration and proven results rather than by argument and exhortation. We try to keep the CSATP an open system that anyone in an official capacity can examine and question. But our main effort is to get the police, the probation officers, and the rest to join us in implementing and improving services to the family.

I don't want to give you the impression that all members of the criminal justice system and associated agencies have jumped on the CSATP bandwagon. Some still look at us with doubt, if not deep suspicion, especially some of the deputies from the district attorney's office. On the whole, however, we are working together and pointed toward the general objective of reunifying the family if it's in the best interests of the child-victims. And in at least nine out of ten instances, the child does want to return and is returned to her family.

Even while the professional component was developing satisfactorily, I felt the professional counseling and the other services did not meet all the needs of the families. I hit upon the self-help idea by having one of the more advanced clients talk to a new client over the telephone. That this was a good idea quickly became apparent when I saw the enormous emotional relief expressed by a new mother-client after talking over her situation with another mother who had already gone through most of the early trauma stemming from the discovery of the incestuous activity and of its exposure to the authorities. Soon three of the mothers wanted to meet in person. Other mothers began to meet with them, and after a while some fathers joined the group. That's how Parents United—the second component of the CSATP—got started. And, incidentally, that is how most new Parents United groups get started.

The children's groups were and can be started the same way: girls who contact each other by telephone soon want to meet personally. As the girls saw Parents United develop into an organization, they felt that they too could form a group of their own—a Daughters United. Some time later, when a few boys started coming to the group meetings, the title of the organization was expanded to Daughters & Sons United.

As the families kept coming in, Dorothy Ross, who was coordinating the services to the families, and I, the only counselor, still felt that the families were not being provided all the services they required. More administrative and counseling help was needed. So Dorothy and I began to gather volunteers. The first was Vicki Imabori, who very quickly was engulfed by the paperwork and other administrative tasks and who remains in that state.

A bit later, we began to attract local college students who were working on their master's degrees in family counseling and who hoped to get their state licenses in that field. To qualify for the license they needed supervised counseling experience. Since I was able to offer this supervision to the students, they began to trickle in. We called these students counselor interns to distinguish them from the volunteers who transport kids to counseling sessions and who do administrative and office work (the administrative interns). We now have about thirty administrative and counselor interns; this cadre of "Support and Services" volunteers makes up the third component of the CSATP.

To sum up, a CSATP is made up of three interdependent components: professional, self-help, and volunteer. All three are necessary, all three are complementary, and together they create the environment—called a "regenerative environment" by a recent visitor—that resocializes families troubled by incest, changing them from dysfunctional to productive families.

This afternoon and again during the training program, Bob Carroll, our program administrator, and Dorothy Ross, our program coordinator, will describe in detail the structure of the CSATP and the tasks of administration, coordination, and case management. For the time being, I want to emphasize that the CSATP is organized primarily for the child-victims. We've discovered, however, that we serve the child best if we can return her to her own family under the condition that the parents replace the former exploitive climate with one that provides care and nourishment. And we've found that most of our parents can be taught to become good parents.

We start to reconstitute the family by concentrating on what we call the mother–child core. The family can be rebuilt into a productive one for the child only if the child feels secure in her mother's love. Most children wish to return to their mothers and families, and most mothers want them back. The desire to be with one another may not be apparent at first, especially if the girl is in her teens. She is usually filled with fear, anger, and guilt. Guilt is the dominating emotion in the adolescent child, for she feels (usually unconsciously) she has betrayed her mother and siblings, first by allowing the incestuous situation to continue without confiding in her mother, and secondly by reporting it to the police and thereby placing her family in jeopardy.

Before the child can return to her mother and thrive in the relationship, her mother must be able to convince her unequivocally that she was not to blame for the sexual activity and that her father has assumed full responsibility for the incidents and the troubles now facing the family. The child must also be told that both her father and mother are receiving treatment. Usually, the mother must be given individual counseling before she can be thoroughly convinced that her daughter was the victim of the bad marriage and not the cause of it. We usually find that after the child has been returned to her mother and a sound mother–daughter relationship has been established, the child then will begin to be concerned about her father's welfare and what must be done to have him rejoin the family.

The average family is provided the following types of counseling, roughly in this order: individual counseling for the child, mother, father, and, if necessary, for certain siblings; mother–child, marital, and father–child counseling; and family counseling including the child, mother, and father, and eventually the entire family.

The type, intensity, and duration of the treatment plan must be designed to meet the specific needs of each family. In terms of treatment, the emotional consequences of the incestuous acts are more significant than the actual acts and their legal definitions. Each child (and other family members) will react differently to the specific incestuous act or series of acts, depending, in most part, on how she generally feels about herself (her self-esteem); the overall quality of her relationships with her mother, father, and siblings; and the reactions of the persons, especially those in an authoritative position, to whom she has reported the situation.

The effective counselor listens to the feelings of the child and responds accordingly rather than projecting alarmist expectations of what the child should be feeling. The responses and attitudes of the people in contact with the family during the crisis period following exposure of the incestuous situation will markedly affect the family's recovery from the crisis.

Certainly the most profound influence on the emotional state of the family comes from its involvement with Parents United and Daughters and Sons United. Contacts by PU/DSU sponsors have an immediate calming, stabilizing effect. Family members no longer feel they are pariahs facing banishment from human society. Beyond the crisis period, the family that makes the most progress toward productive reunion is the family that continues its counseling program, attends the weekly meeting of PU/DSU, and becomes actively engaged in promoting the development of the organization.

An active PU/DSU member becomes involved in some or all of the following functions: providing support to new members; public speaking, through the speaker's bureau; co-leading group counseling sessions; and or participating in various committees and task forces.

During the next two weeks, you will be spending a good deal of your time with PU/DSU members. You will be working with them in the personal and group counseling sessions and in the task forces. Let me sum up the aims of the treatment program, which we would like each family to pursue: the individual counseling sessions foster personal awareness and self-management; the marital and family counseling sessions are designed to develop a healthy, productive family unit; and participation in the functions of PU/DSU leads to improvement in interpersonal relationships and social responsibility. One would expect that the families who take advantage of all aspects of the CSATP fare best. Indeed, such was the finding of a recent study of the CSATP by an independent researcher.

Before I end this talk, I'd like to say a few words about the humanistic treatment philosophy of the CSATP. It is fairly well covered in your kit of materials. It's a philosophy that is easy to explain but difficult to internalize and live by. But the best way to understand it is to experience it, as you will with us during the next two weeks. You'll find some inconsistencies in our own behavior because we are still in the process of learning it. As I said, it's easy to say but hard to do.

Let me review two basic assumptions of the humanistic viewpoint. The first assumption is that man's strongest drive is to feel good, to seek well-being. This is a state of being that even the newborn recognize and that we strive for continually throughout our lifetimes. To feel good, our needs must be met. Abraham Maslow, one of the founders of humanistic psychology, tells us that we have a hierarchy of needs. The basic needs are the needs for survival, security, belongingness, and self-esteem—which must be satisfied before we can satisfy such higher needs as truth, caring, justice, and social service.

There is a negative side to this picture. If our needs are not met, we feel bad and may discharge that state through hostile acts. Although they usually involve others important to us, such acts are essentially self-abusive. When we're in this despairing state, we act much like unloved children who destroy their most precious toys.

This concept applies with force when we check the histories of abusive parents. Typically they were raised by punitive and generally uncaring parents. As children and later as adults, they seem to trigger rejecting and even hostile responses from siblings, relatives, acquaintances, teachers, and others. They continue with this general lifestyle when they form their own families. Abusive parents are not able to lead rewarding lives. Therefore, they stew in a state of chronic resentment which can be relieved only through hostile behavior toward persons important to them.

Let me repeat, this behavior is primarily, although largely unconsciously, intended to be self-punishing. The sexually abusive father does not use his child (typically the one he loves the most) primarily for sexual gratification but principally for reconfirming and discharging his self-hatred. He also expects to be severely punished for this behavior, so when the authorities follow suit, the self-hatred cycle is reinforced once more. A major purpose of the CSATP is to break this cycle.

The second key assumption of the humanistic viewpoint directly influences our ability to have a positive effect on our clients. It is the premise that people are what they are and not what we want them to be. At all times in our lives, we behave in accordance with both our genetic background and our social conditioning. We would all prefer to behave according to the standards of good social behavior. In the long run, the most rewarding social status is to be a respected spouse, parent, worker, and citizen. When we act in ways that prevent us from achieving this status, we do so only because we don't know how to stop. This statement is hard to believe when we see what appears to be deliberate abusive behavior by apparently intelligent people. Again, let me repeat that all hostile behavior is motivated by an essentially unconscious state of abiding self-hatred. One cannot control the behavior until one controls self-loathing.

If you don't believe this, talk to a reformed convict or drug addict. Or ask one of our former offenders with Parents United why he molested his daughter, the daughter he said he felt closest to. You'll find him to be an articulate, intelligent person who says something like this: "I don't know why I did it. All I know is that I couldn't stop it." On closer questioning, you'll usually find that he, too, was abused and neglected as a child.

Fortunately, people who are inadvertently conditioned to abuse themselves by abusing others can be taught not to do so. Beyond that, they can be taught to lead productive lives. But before they will allow themselves to be taught, they must trust the teachers. If we send them the accusing judgmental messages they have heard all their lives, they will add us to the long list of people who have hurt them in the past. To gain the trust of our clients, we must fully accept them as they are: as worthwhile, evolving human beings.

Okay, I think that most of you will agree that the words "empathy" and "acceptance" represent the key concepts for successful counseling. Now let's put the accepting counseling attitude to the test. Imagine that you're sitting in your office and Hitler walks in and wants to be counseled. No, let's make it Nixon—he's more familiar and still alive. He looks at you with that famous scowl and says, "Counsel me." How accepting do you feel, especially if you're a Democrat?

Let's make the test nonpartisan and closer to our immediate area of concern. Imagine that you are reading the police report on your next client. You read that he has admitted to having his five-year-old daughter orally copulate him. You have this image in mind when he walks in. What are your immediate, unedited feelings about this man right now? I know what mine were. This man was one of my first clients and as I read the report, I was not accepting of him at all. I felt murderous hatred.

All right, these are some of the problems we'll be dealing with over the next two weeks. They are not all so grim. As you join us in working through them, I think you'll find that we're all part of a big caring self-help group.

Note: It is likely that the person(s) charged with training and or starting a CSATP may not have the prior experience with the historical development of a CSATP and its self-help components, Parents United and Daughters and Sons United. It is suggested that the trainers address themselves, in such cases, to the need in their communities for an alternative approach to child sexual abuse cases, citing the historical development of the Santa Clara County program and being prepared to give examples of the results of that program. Part I of this book is a valuable reference for such an introductory talk.

Trainers representing existing treatment programs might discuss how child sexual abuse cases were handled in their counties before their own programs were developed, illustrating what happened to families—and particularly to child victims—as they were processed through the criminal justice system. Trainers are encouraged to speak of their own evolution as workers or therapists, their interest in child sexual abuse, and their conviction that enlightened case intervention must replace the typical punitive methods.

Materials in this book provide a sample of the issues and areas a speaker might wish to cover, but any talk should be tailored to fit the speaker's own experiences and the needs of the given audience.

Activity 4. Historical Background of Parents United

Male and/or female representatives of Parents United, preferably those who have been with the chapter since it was first organized, take turns relating their personal experiences with the organization from the special vantage point of being both members and people who have assumed leadership roles.

Parents United Representative's Opening Talk

I was the first offender to join what was the beginning, the birth of Parents United. Three mothers, one of whom was my wife, met with Hank Giarretto weekly in a group to discuss their trauma. This was the original core group of what later became Parents United. The weekly session served the two functions that are still being served: socializing and therapy.

My request to join them arose from my need to share my feelings with others who had experienced child sexual abuse in their family. I was serving time in jail, was very depressed, confused, and lonely. I desperately needed that contact. My weekly individual counseling session with Hank couldn't fulfill all my needs. Meeting with the three mothers gave all of us a forum to express ourselves, to make appropriate connections with others. We all began "opening up" to ourselves and each other. This was when I could stop being so self-engrossed and begin to change and grow. I also used to telephone Hank at all hours to vent anger and frustration, because I needed even more contact than the individual and group sessions afforded.

It became apparent to Hank how beneficial it was to the four of us to be able to meet together in a safe, accepting environment to get what he couldn't give us: contact with each other. He realized how much the mothers benefited from listening to and talking to a male offender and how much I benefited from being with the mothers. Hank observed that therapy occurred spontaneously: the group opened up to each other, nurtured each other with comfort and support. We were helping ourselves and each other faster than he could help us and faster than we could help ourselves without the group.

Hank asked a juvenile probation officer to join our small original core group (Hank, the three mothers, Anna and me). The probation officer helped Hank and Anna lead our weekly group sessions and became convinced that our group was a valuable community resource. Then my rehabilitation officer from the county jail joined us at Hank's and my request. That officer acknowledged that we were members of his community trying to take responsibility for ourselves, and he became convinced of the value of these meetings. He realized then that what we were doing was constructive. It was a safeguard that benefited the entire community. So he gave permission to some of the other offenders serving time for child sexual abuse to attend our meetings. He also persuaded other rehabilitation officers to allow their prisoners to attend the meetings because the group sessions were a crucial part of the rehabilitation process.

That was the real beginning of our growth. As the group increased in number, instead of having just that one group, we began dividing into three smaller groups. A staff member and/or intern led each group. More groups and more types of groups evolved as there was a need or request for them. In June, 1975, when there were between sixty and eighty members, we incorporated and attained nonprofit, tax-exempt status. Because we were growing at such a fast pace, we needed and obtained independent monies through private foundations to carry out our functions. All those families who had become members were depending on us and needed us to give them what no other organization in the community had to offer.

Later, we obtained state funds through AB2288 for training purposes. That allowed us to have a paid, full-time representative who would establish other Parents United chapters in California. I was hired to fill that position. I had the responsibility of helping to start the Orange County chapter (in Southern California). I was really frightened and apprehensive about breaking all of that new ground and taking on all that responsibility. There were no previous guidelines or precedents for me to follow. I also felt privileged to be able to carry on this very important development of our program in other parts of the state.

Since I'm both a member of PU and a paid coordinator, I have a special vantage point from which to view Parents United. And I have a double role to fill. In my role as member, I try to be a model for other members. I model leadership skills when I co-facilitate the weekly orientation session. When I carry out a speaking engagement in the community, I model effective, open communication and interaction as well as self-confidence. I take responsibility for myself and am a productive member of the community, contributing to society. I work toward being "un-stoic" and leaning on and reaching out to this extended family we call Parents United. I continue my quest for self-knowledge, following the PU philosophy that I can't know or help the next member unless I continually know and help myself. These are my internal functions.

In my external function as paid staff, I organize chapters throughout California and other states. I'm the contact person for the other chapters. I visit them to get them started and then visit them again after they're established. I send them material to use as their guidelines. I document the spread of our chapters and support them during their "growing pains."

Parents United operates on five basic concepts:

1. **Self-help**. We're a self-help group, and that means we must understand and help ourselves so we can understand and help other members. In the beginning, Hank pointed out what he observed about us (members) as we talked to each other in the sessions. Then we used his observations to grow and to help the next member grow. And that's what we are still doing.

2. **Sponsorship.** There is no need for any member to suffer alone and handle the problem without support and comfort from other members. We urge members to exchange phone numbers and to call each other between weekly sessions. An established member can sponsor an incoming member by giving him or her extra attention through face-to-face and phone contact. Contact only once a week at the meeting and group sessions just isn't enough, as I found when I was in crisis. New members can survive their crisis and grow beyond it, but they are likely to believe me or any other member before they'll believe a professional. When I knew what a comfort it was not to suffer alone, I wanted to spare others from the isolation I had felt. Being able to call someone who listened, who didn't judge me, and who supported me really eased the pain.

3. **Teamwork and equality.** Hank didn't set himself up as an expert. We all learned together, and we're all still working on ourselves. That includes the staff. Group leaders don't separate themselves or hold themselves up as a distinct entity. And members can become group leaders. We all pull together in this work, and we share our personal lives and vulnerable feelings with each other.

4. **Informing the community.** Hank began community outreach by taking members with him to speaking engagements. That started our Speakers' Bureau, and we encourage new members to get involved in this effort as soon as they feel comfortable giving talks. The people who have experienced child sexual abuse are the "experts," and it's important that the community hear from us. When the public hears us speak first-hand, they understand what we're confronting and overcoming. They learn who we are and realize we're members of their community, too. They can see that we want to grow, help ourselves, and reconstitute our families.

We're learning effective communications as part of our growing process. By speaking candidly to the community about our problems, we're modeling open communication and reaching out to our fellow man. When I had reached a certain point of development in my own growth, I asked myself, "Why shouldn't I be able to share my experiences with the community as well as with members of PU?" These speaking engagements also fulfill our social responsibilities. Our philosophy is to give back in service what we've gotten from the program and the community. Members can give back only when they can look beyond their own crisis. Accepting speaking engagements indicates they've helped themselves and are ready to give to others.

5. **Helping victims.** The prime concern of Parents United is the welfare of children who have been sexually abused, the Daughters and Sons United. As you'll hear several times during training, we offer many types of self-help groups to the adult members. That's mainly because we want our help to result in a better, safer future for the children in our families. We offer several types of groups to the adult members, but the Daughters and Sons United Groups and the Play Therapy Group for Children are a main focus of our organization.

Parents United began with only one weekly group (there were just four members to consider). As our membership grew, so did our need for more groups with a staff counselor or intern leading each group with a PU co-facilitator. We've now developed to the point that we can offer an orientation group for all new members, a mothers' group, a men's group, a group for women molested as children, several couples' communication groups (for married couples or paired couples to work on in-depth communication problems), a parenting skills group, a women's group, an open group (for members who are separated or single and wish to work on problems with members of the opposite sex), a leadership training group (to develop co-facilitators for groups), and a recontact group (where women who were molested as children can work with mothers and fathers as surrogate parents, or parents can use role-playing to work on situations that give them difficulty). We also have established groups where single people can work on learning social skills, where any member having an alcoholic problem can receive help, and where women can learn how to be more independent and handle the practical matters they have always left to their husbands' care.

As you go through your training, I am sure you will have many questions about Parents United. Please jot them down: I will be available during your stay to answer them for you, and I will be happy to help whenever I can.

Activity 5. Historical Background of Daughters and Sons United

The Daughters and Sons United (DSU) Coordinator (or another DSU representative) introduces herself, relates her background, and explains how she became involved with DSU, and recounts the historical background of DSU.

Daughters and Sons United Representative's Opening Talk

Daughters and Sons United is primarily an organization for child victims of sexual molestation, but it also includes some siblings of victims and some minor perpetrators. The organization complements Parents United, and the two organizations work together and share many responsibilities. However, DSU manifests its own unique personality. The DSU groups have evolved to meet the specific needs of their members who are all striving to rebuild their lives and overcome the trauma of the molestation and its exposure to the community.

The original self-help groups for children involved in the CSATP—an adolescent group and a play therapy group for the younger children—were started by Hank Giarretto in 1972. However, children's groups require much more attention and guidance than adult groups, and the early years were marked by problems, mainly in support services such as providing transportation for the children to and from the meetings, finding an adequate place to meet, and getting co-facilitators for the groups. The first groups were co-led by Giarretto and juvenile probation officers. The groups met haphazardly until late 1973 when interns began to join the program and were pressed into service providing transportation and assistance as group co-leaders. The groups began to meet on a more regular basis. With a growing referral rate, attendance at the groups swelled.

Late in 1977, two administrative interns, one of whom eventually became the present DSU Coordinator, recognized that members devoted tremendous energy toward providing support and caring for one another. The interns surmised that this energy could be used to build a stronger self-help entity with a structure and personality of its own, and with which youngsters could identify. It would be run for and by members and would provide the corrective emotional experiences needed to overcome the initial crisis and to learn the attitudes and skills necessary for self-fulfilling lives. These interns prompted the formation of Daughters United.

In 1978 an important decision was made to help preadolescent and adolescent boys feel a stronger affiliation with the CSATP, and Daughters United officially became Daughters and Sons United.

Today there are ten groups: a play therapy group for both sexes ages six to ten, a preadolescent group for girls ages ten to thirteen, an orientation group for adolescent girls who are new to the program, four adolescent groups for girls ages thirteen to eighteen who have been in the program for at least eight weeks and are ready to move into more advanced groups that focus on self-awareness and life control issues, a transition group for girls eighteen to twenty-two who are striving to become independent and require practical skills for living and self-support, a preadolescent boys' group, and an adolescent boys' group. If there are a sufficient number of members, a group is formed for adolescent offenders.

DSU brings together children who have been sexually molested. DSU also includes a few children who have molested other much younger children. Newcomers are introduced to one another so that they may share similar problems and feelings that accompany the exposure of the molestation. More seasoned members also have their own groups. Both kinds of groups bring youngsters together with well-established members who have been with the program for a year or longer, who have demonstrated leadership skills, and who are assisting staff members and interns as co-facilitators. It is from interactions with these established members that newer members can take hope: they too can move through the crisis and learn to lead satisfying and productive lives. Most of all, the ongoing support and reinforcement among members is a tribute to the power of, and the need for, caring. It is hoped and can be expected that newer members will reciprocate at some time in the process and reach out to others in the DSU organization and elsewhere.

The principal service provided by DSU is support for its members. When a new youngster first enters the program, she is surrounded by a support system that lets her know people really care about her. Support comes from many quarters, including the counselors, interns, and other staff persons; but most especially it comes from the DSU sponsor and other DSU members who surround the new member with care.

The sponsor, who is an experienced and seasoned member of DSU, may accompany the new girl to the police investigation, other steps of the law enforcement process, or the clinic (if a medical examination is required). She offers comfort and support through the initial days following exposure. The sponsor invites the girl to the self-help group, meets her there, and may sit with her to help ease her way into the unfamiliar situation. The sponsor will continue to maintain contact in person or by phone until the new girl feels welcome and at ease.

Often the sponsor is the first person to whom the new member confides her feelings. The sponsor acts as a bridge between the group and the newcomer. She provides an important social connection that helps the newcomer feel a sense of belonging. The support system is by no means confined to the early days of a girl's entry into the program but continues to meet her needs for warmth, friendship, and sharing for as long as she is a member.

Another support service provided by DSU is a Children's Shelter liaison, a counselor-intern who contacts the child within a day or two of her arrival and provides immediate crisis counseling. She continues to meet with the girl biweekly for the length of her stay in the shelter. Another intern is the liaison to girls in Juvenile Hall. Youngsters who remain at home are contacted and invited to join the group by the DSU coordinator and/or a DSU member.

DSU coordinates and organizes transportation to weekly groups for children in hardship cases only. This service remains a problem for DSU, as it was in the early days of the organization. Interns are required as a part of their internship to provide two hours of transportation weekly. Several of the administrative staff also fill in. Transportation is provided for 115 to 130 children each month. Except for hardship cases, parents (usually mothers) are expected to transport their own children as a part of their counseling contract.

The decision-making body of DSU is the Task Force Committee. It is made up of carefully screened youngsters who meet once weekly with a Parents United representative and the DSU coordinator. The coordinator's task is to facilitate the group's awareness of what they want and to help implement its decisions. Counselors and interns wishing to start new groups must submit their plan to the Task Force, which decides if the groups are appropriate. If the committee approves, the plan goes to the program administrator and the director of treatment and training for final approval. The Task Force later ensures that DSU group facilitators chosen to work with the professional leaders of any new groups are carefully selected and trained.

Again, the Task Force is made up of youngsters who have been highly screened by the committee. Applicants must write up why they want to serve, are required to sit in on a Task Force meeting, are interviewed by Task Force members, and finally are voted on. Applicants must have records of responsible behavior and make a commitment to attend meetings on a regular basis.

A major premise of DSU is that the self-help group reduces the sense of alienation that comes from feeling unique and alone with a molestation problem. Since all members share a problem that is highly stigmatized, they find comfort in sharing their feelings with peers and counselors. Another premise is that the self-help group experience will increase feelings of personal worth and power to control one's life. In the groups and in the organization as a whole, children learn how to feel good about themselves, to value themselves and others, and to develop meaningful and nurturing relationships with family and peers. In the group, they learn to deal with self-abusive behaviors stemming from guilt, shame, repressed anger, and self-deprecation. The children learn to enhance self-esteem through self-understanding, social action, altruism, and cooperation with members, which fosters social responsibility. In believing that one must have a connection with society that is mutually beneficial, DSU is philosophically bound to Parents United.

DSU members actively publicize the problems of incest and the existence of the program. Many members have volunteered to share their experiences before community groups and on radio and television. These children learn they can be productive and responsible members of society, and they return to society some of what they have received.

Activity 6. Question and Answer Session

Although the trainees are encouraged to ask questions throughout the morning, time is set aside here specifically for that purpose. Trainees are encouraged to ask any questions that may have come up during the morning's activities, particularly on specific issues and concepts that they find confusing or controversial. Their questions are answered in a way that will encourage productive communication between participants and staff members.

Module 2: Lunch with Staff

Description

This module consists of one activity. The trainees and staff go to a local restaurant, eat together, and become better acquainted.

Goals

To provide trainees the opportunity to:

1. Continue the process of sharing and discussing common problems and goals;

2. Enjoy friendly interaction between trainees and staff; and

3. Continue the morning's discussion in an informal setting.

Rationale

This module illustrates the value of informal get-togethers for workers with a common purpose. To build the closeness required for effective collaboration, trainees are encouraged to socialize with one another and with trainers whenever possible.

Objectives

At the end of this module, trainees should be able to:

1. Begin to see that personal learning and team effectiveness are enhanced when co-workers socialize; and

2. Note that friendly get-togethers, though sometimes spontaneous, often must be well organized and must give consideration to individual needs and obligations.

Module 3: NBC Film Presentation and Discussion

Description

The trainees are shown a shorter version of the NBC documentary film that was broadcast nationally on the "Weekend Show," May 7, 1977. Made in cooperation with the professional staff and PU/DSU members of the Santa Clara County CSATP, this fifty-minute film examines the problem of incest in this country and the traditional ways in which the criminal justice system handles the problem. The director of the Santa Clara County program is interviewed, as are other staff persons and members of PU/DSU. Special focus is put upon the experiences and feelings of offenders, their spouses, and the child victims before and after their exposure to the community. The film ends on the hopeful note that the problems of incestuous families can be resolved through the creative approach taken by the Santa Clara County treatment model.

Listening to the personal stories of the families involved in the incest crisis generally evokes many feelings in the viewers. The film is followed by discussion, and trainees are encouraged to disclose their feelings and reactions. (Unfortunately this film is not available from NBC; the training project currently is negotiating with NBC in an attempt to make the film available as a training tool to others.)

Goals

To provide trainees the opportunity to:

1. See a dramatization of the problem of incest in America today and to hear and see from clients in treatment that society's typical reaction often magnifies the problems of the incestuous family;

2. Be familiar with the CSATP's humanistic model of treatment as a viable alternative to the traditional approaches of the criminal justice system and associated agencies;

3. Be motivated to take action toward starting CSATPs in their own communities;

4. Begin to become aware of their own feelings surrounding issues of child sexual abuse and inept case management;

5. Continue to be oriented to the overall Santa Clara County program; and

6. Further develop an understanding of both the client family and the system with which it must interface.

Rationale

It is essential that trainees understand the seriousness and scope of incest and child sexual abuse in our society. Understanding the shortcomings of traditional methods in dealing with these problems is also important. The NBC documentary is an excellent introduction to these issues. And since self-exploration is stressed throughout the course, the discussion after the film encourages the trainees to explore and express their usually repressed feelings on the subject of incest and child sexual abuse.

Objectives

At the end of this module, trainees should be able to:

1. Begin responding on an affective level to the trauma of the victim and family in the incest crisis and the web of retribution that further exacerbates the problem;

2. Begin to develop determination and motivation to introduce some new approaches to case management of sexually abusive families in their community agencies; and

3. More fully understand that the CSATP's humanistic approach to sexually abusive families can rebuild lives rather than destroy them and, most importantly, can create a nurturing family climate for victims and their siblings.

Activity 1. NBC Film Showing

Before viewing the documentary, trainees are advised to pay particular attention to a comparison between the traditional criminal justice system methods for dealing with intrafamilial molest and a humanistic model of enlightened and creative intervention in these cases. Trainees are also asked to be keenly sensitive to the feelings the film evokes in them as they listen to the personal accounts of persons who have experienced incest.

Activity 2. Discussion of NBC Film

A question-and-answer period allows the trainers and trainees to discuss the film they have just seen. The content of the film often evokes feelings of anger, revulsion, and/or compassion, and determination in the trainees to change the manner in which child molestation cases are handled in their own communities.

Module 4: Introduction to Administration and Interagency Cooperation

Description

In this module, the program administrator and the program coordinator introduce trainees to the administration and coordination aspects of the CSATP. The intent of the module is to provide an overview of administrative and coordination principles and methods as developed by the CSATP, with emphasis on the guiding principle of teamwork in the resocialization of the sexually abusive family.

Goals

To give the trainees the opportunity to:

1. Become familiar with the administrative and coordination services of the CSATP and learn how the program interfaces with the criminal justice system and other human services agencies;

2. Learn about the attitudes and personal skills needed to win the support of the above agencies;

3. Continue to absorb the cardinal principles of understanding and accepting the way other people interpret their jobs, and understand that a relaxed, educative stance is more productive in effecting change than a self-righteous one;

4. Absorb the core principles of cooperation, common purpose, and the team concept as the most effective ways known to resocialize abusive families;

5. Begin to learn the methods and procedures of congruent and consistent case management from referral through termination;

6. Understand, through examples and statistics, the effect the humanistic, team-concept approach has on the reporting, referral, and confession rates;

7. Understand in some detail the referral and intake process, and the role of the professional staff and PU/DSU members in providing immediate supportive and crisis intervention services to the victim and the family; and

8. Witness self-disclosure as the speakers describe their experiences, feelings, and how their personal growth has kept pace with that of the program.

NOTE: During the two-week training session, trainees will have ample exposure to local criminal justice and associated agency personnel, as well as to the process of mobilizing and coordinating their energies toward creative case management.

Toward the end of the training program, participants will once again meet with the program administrator and program coordinator to pull together what they have learned and to begin developing action plans for marshaling agency support in their home communities.

It should be noted that while coordination procedures are similar from county to county, some of the problems facing the program administrator of the Santa Clara County CSATP may be unique because of the advanced state and responsibilities of this particular program. In typical county programs, the functions of coordination and administration are assumed by one person.

Rationale

Human energy is most productive when knowledge is pooled and directed towards finding better ways of satisfying human needs. Ineffective treatment of abusive families is usually caused by competitiveness and a lack of trust among agencies associated with the criminal justice system. A territorial, contentious environment arises when there is little understanding, especially among civil servants, of what makes human beings behave as they do. The CSATP leadership strives to create a cooperative, constructive environment where all public servants involved with troubled families work together to create a mutually beneficial working atmosphere for their clients and for themselves.

Enlightened case management—management that does not deal a lethal blow to the family struggling to maintain itself—is needed. If families know they will be treated with respect and kindness and that the goal of the official agencies is to help them reconstruct their lives and families, they will be less inclined to stiffen their resistance to official interveners out of fear that they will be harshly punished. As the CSATP gains reputation as a helpful treatment resource, families who are experiencing the trauma of incest will be more inclined to step forward to report their problem voluntarily, and the professionals from private and official agencies will be encouraged to refer clients to the CSATP.

Objectives

At the end of this module, trainees should be able to:

1. Be familiar with the multiple agencies whose cooperation they will want to enlist and have some ideas for approaching these agencies and persuading them to use the CSATP approach;

2. Have a fuller understanding of the importance and significance of the team concept of cooperation in the resocialization of abusive families and begin to understand the skills and attitudes required to sell the team approach to others; and

3. Have a more thorough knowledge of productive case management, the various referral processes, and of how both the staff and veteran clients cooperate to involve a new family in the counseling program and in Parents United and Daughters and Sons United.

Activity 1. CSATP Administration

The program administrator briefly describes his functions:

1. Hire or select personnel and oversee their duties.

2. Define administrative staff functions.

3. Plan and assist in the training of the administrative staff.

4. Avoid and/or resolve conflicts with the criminal justice system.

5. Act as inter- and intra-departmental liaison responsible for all administrative duties related to the effective functioning of the program.

6. Ensure that the program satisfies the objectives of projects funded by federal, state, county, and private agencies.

7. Ensure that program operations meet the requirements, laws, and mandates of applicable federal, state, and local regulations.

8. Supervise and help prepare all administrative reports required by funding sources.

9. Seek new funding sources and assist in the preparation of grant applications.

10. Assist in the development of other CSATP community projects including community development, out-of-county program organization, and the training of out-of-county personnel.

11. Assist in the recruitment and screening of interns and volunteers.

12. Coordinate the program with the criminal justice system and human services agencies.

13. Supervise and assist in the public education effort.

14. Monitor the budgets of the CSATP and of Parents United.

The administrator also discusses the skills needed to establish a CSATP. Among them are an aptitude for diplomacy, a capability to mediate between factions, a firm belief in the humanistic principles and methods of the program, and an ability to educate others in these principles and methods.

Referral rates (specifically, those for Santa Clara County) are reviewed. The rapid rise in referrals is attributed to the community awareness program, which the program administrator describes. Approximately 39 percent of the cases are self-referrals; 36 percent come from police and juvenile probation departments; 25 percent from other agencies; and the remainder come from outside the county.

Referral Statistics

The rate of referrals has risen dramatically since the inception of the program in 1971. In its first three years, the program received about thirty referrals a year. In 1974 the referral rate rose dramatically, mostly because of the program's growing reputation, partly because of the new child abuse reporting laws, and partly because of revenue sharing and other funds given to the program by the Rosenberg Foundation. This money was used to increase the staff and to begin a public education effort.

The annual referral rate jumped to 135 families in 1974 and has risen steadily every year. There were over five hundred referrals in 1977 and over seven hundred in 1980. There are an average of 140 consultations and anonymous telephone referrals per year. The total active caseload is approximately 400 victims and families at any one time. Currently, each counselor handles about 80 cases at any one time; most cases require individual, couple, and group counseling. (Obviously, this would be an impossible task were it not for the assistance of volunteer interns and members of PU and DSU.)

Since it is reasonable to suppose that the rate of incest itself has not changed appreciably in Santa Clara County during the past few years, this growing referral rate is all the more significant. It means that many children and families are now receiving help solely because of the CSATP and its ability to gain the cooperation of the criminal justice system and a positive reception by the press and the public.

The majority of referrals come from the criminal justice system agencies such as the juvenile and adult probation departments and the police. Minor victims of child molestation are also referred by delinquency probation officers who handle minor offenders sexually involved with younger children, usually siblings or children they have been babysitting; from juvenile hall and from the children's shelter; and from schools, church groups, mental health agencies, public health agencies, hospitals, departments of social services, daycare centers, and other community agencies.

An increasing number of self-referrals come from mothers who suspect or have discovered that one or more of their children are being molested by their husbands. Occasionally, a father will report himself to the CSATP or to the police. Relatives (such as grandparents, aunts, or older sisters) and nonrelatives (such as a neighbor or the mother of a victim's girlfriend) in whom the victim has confided often call in. Additionally, the CSATP receives calls from women who were molested as children and who have not had the opportunity to resolve their feelings about the situation. Rarely, calls are received from men molested as children.

The program administrator discusses the direct services offered to sexually abusive families through close communication and cooperation with other agencies and support systems. Among the most important of these services is crisis intervention at the time of exposure of the incest.

The growth and development of the volunteer work force is then traced. This component has proved invaluable in augmenting services to clients and in relieving the workload of the professional staff.

The Child Sexual Abuse Treatment Program has relied heavily on the volunteer services of administrative and counseling interns since 1973, when the first volunteers began to provide ongoing support and counseling services to victims and their families. The earliest volunteers helped in the office, provided children with transportation to Daughters and Sons United group sessions, and assumed big-sister and group leadership roles in DSU. As the program grew and the referrals and caseloads increased, more and more interns joined the program. Eventually the majority of the volunteers were the counseling interns who assisted the staff counselors with their caseloads.

In recent years, the program has had as many as forty administrative and counseling interns and as few as twenty, with a ratio of about five counseling interns to one administrative intern.

One of the major benefits of a volunteer intern program is that it draws its personnel from the community and thus involves the community directly with the program. Intern applicants generally hear of the program through the offices of the universities they attend. The community-awareness program has helped to inform graduate students also: Speakers' Bureau people are frequently asked make presentations to classes in human sexuality, family therapy, and child growth and development.

Most degrees in counseling and psychology have practicum requirements that can be met through an internship with the CSATP. Adequate supervision by licensed personnel is usually an important consideration, so students seeking supervised internships will be influenced by the quality of the supervision program.

One of the principal criticisms that has been directed at the Santa Clara County CSATP internship program is the inadequacy of the supervision. Initially, the program did not have sufficient personnel who were qualified to supervise, and the program was growing so rapidly that the staff counselors who could supervise were hard pressed to find time. With the addition of licensed personnel and with four of the staff counselors providing at least two hours of supervision weekly, this problem has been largely alleviated.

In addition to supervision, the CSATP has at times been able to pay its interns a small weekly stipend. Interns who have shown the most dedication and have been with the program the longest are the first to be considered when money is available, but recent budgetary restrictions do not permit compensation to interns for the present.

The final incentive is that new openings in the professional counseling staff are filled by licensed counselors who formerly served as interns in the CSATP.

Administrative interns are generally undergraduate students at local universities. Others are nonstudents interested in volunteer services with the program. These interns work in the capacity of big brothers or sisters with minors referred to the program, assist with the clerical duties in the office, provide transportation for youngsters to and from group therapy sessions, co-lead groups (if properly trained) for adolescents, accompany youngsters to the hospital for evidence-gathering examinations when this is necessary for the police investigation, and contribute speaking time for public awareness and community education. The administrative interns are under the supervision of the coordinator.

Most counseling interns are enrolled in the last third of a masters' degree program in marriage and family counseling (or related disciplines) at local universities. A few doctoral candidates have applied for internship as well, although these applicants usually find employment before the year's commitment to the program has been served. Because the CSATP wishes to minimize intern turnover, it gives preference to masters' degree candidates working toward the state licensing examination in marriage, family, and child counseling.

Counseling interns applying to the program initially contact the program coordinator. An appointment is made for them to come in and fill out the initial application form. The applicant is then given a packet of information about the program and is asked to read it prior to the initial interview.

Because it takes time to train a counseling intern in the program operation, its philosophy, and its integrated psychosocial approach to the abusive family, and because the intern needs time to acquire the basic attitudes and skills used in counseling these families, applicants are asked to give the following: a one-year commitment to the program; twenty hours per week of client contact, which may include group leadership functions; two hours of transportation of children to and from group therapy sessions each week; attendance at the weekly interns–staff meetings; attendance at one hour of group supervision weekly; and participation in the first three days of training.

Questionnaire for CSATP Interns and Volunteers

NAME: _____ PHONE: WORK: _____

                                                                   HOME: _____

ADDRESS: _____

_____ DATE: _____

Are you presently working? Yes_____ No_____

If yes, what do you do? _____

Are you a student? Graduate (what degree)_____ Undergrad. (major) _____

Yes _____ School you are attending _____

No _____ Graduate or degree when_____

Are you applying for internship or practicum work _____ Other volunteer work (Specify)

_____

Do you need hours per week and if so how many _____ How long will you be with CSATP if accepted?_____ Specify in qtrs. or semesters.

For counseling trainees and interns please check below the areas of counseling you are most interested in:

1. Whole Family
2. Marital Pair only
3. Men only
4. Women only
5. Daughters (victims)
6. Children (other sibs as well as victims)
7. Small group leadership
8. Other

Do you have any particular skills you could teach or that we could utilize in the counseling process such as art, dance, music, Tai Chi, meditation and relaxation, etc. _____

_____

What has been your past experience in counseling if any? _____

_____

Please write a brief statement about why you would like to be an intern in the CSATP and what you would hope to gain from the experience. _____

_____

_____

The prospective intern is informed of these requirements at the initial interview. The interviewers—the program administrator and/or program coordinator—are also concerned with the applicant's needs and requirements, his or her expectations, and his or her reasons for wanting to be a part of the CSATP. If the initial interview goes well and the applicant feels he or she can meet the requirements, and if the interviewers think the prospective intern will contribute to the program and enhance its services to clients, the applicant is interviewed by a staff counselor. The counselor assesses the applicant's counseling skills and experience as well as his or her attitudes and feelings about sexually abusive families and estimates how much training and supervision the applicant will need to become an effective agent for change in the families assigned to him or her.

Prospective interns must also effectively demonstrate to the principal interviewers that they are self-motivated and can withstand the demands that would be placed on them through involvement in the CSATP. Frequent turnover is detrimental to the clients and to the program. Each time an intern becomes competent enough to assume some of the caseload and then leaves the program for personal reasons, the supervising staff counselor must take over the intern's families and/or transfer the family to another intern. The change imposes hardship on both the clients and staff counselors. While they understand that many interns must support themselves and their families and that many have school requirements, the CSATP staff tries to ensure that applicants will stay for at least a year. In return, the CSATP offers the prospective intern a wide variety of experiences in counseling children of all ages, couples, families, and groups, and opportunities for client contacts seldom equaled elsewhere.

Following the applicant's interview, the staff counselor sends an evaluation to the program administrator and/or coordinator. If the interviews have gone well up to this point, the applicant is asked to attend a meeting of Parents United and is also put in contact with an established CSATP intern, who also meets with and evaluates the prospective intern.

When all the evaluations are in and if the interviews have progressed well, the person is asked to fill out all the forms required by the juvenile probation department's volunteer bureau, including an application for the county driver's permit needed to assist in transportation of minors to and from counseling sessions. The volunteer bureau has been very cooperative in screening intern applicants, although they usually do not interview them directly. However, they do run a California investigation and identification check on the applicant to ascertain if the applicant has a crime history. They also run a reference check. Once this process is completed and cleared, the intern becomes an official volunteer of the Santa Clara County Juvenile Probation Department and has completed the requirements for entering the CSATP as an intern.

For the first month, the new intern is required to come into the office on a regular basis to assist in such areas as answering telephones and doing clerical work. This experience provides an overview of the operations of the program and affords ongoing contacts with staff members of Parents United, Daughters and Sons United, and probation officers. The new intern also begins to attend meetings of Parents United, Daughters and Sons United, and of interns and staff.

Supervision from a staff counselor is also provided, though the intern may not yet have families to work with. When the intern and the supervising counselor agree that the intern is ready to start counseling clients, the counselor determines which cases to assign to the intern. The counselor will continue to supervise the treatment, although interns are generally allowed considerable latitude with their clients.

The program coordinator assists interns in working cooperatively with the criminal and juvenile justice systems. Additionally, the coordinator helps the interns write letters of evaluation regarding the clients to the juvenile and criminal justice agencies. All interns are required to keep client-progress notes, which are read and initialed by the coordinator and which are filed in the client file. If the coordinator sees something that should be called to the supervising counselor's attention, he or she sends the notes to the counselor.

Whether they see clients directly or serve as consultants to counselor-interns, the supervising counselors are responsible for all active families. The supervising counselor determines when to release a family to an intern and makes sure the transition is smooth and not disturbing to the clients. Then the counselor monitors the family's progress: the assigned intern is responsible for regular check-ins with the counselor, who will also make the final decision regarding termination of treatment.

Every counselor-intern must receive at least one hour per week of group supervision from a staff counselor, who may or may not be the counselor who assigned the particular case. Interns may also seek individual supervision sessions with any counselor on the staff.

About 350 families are currently being treated by the Santa Clara CSATP. The caseload is distributed among five staff counselors, ten fully active interns, and several partially active interns. An intern is considered fully active if he or she has at least five client families and is counseling a minimum of ten hours per week. A partially active intern either has fewer than five families and counsels less than ten hours weekly, or does group counseling only and leads a Parents United or Daughters and Sons United group. These interns generally are those whose job and school requirements limit the time they can give to the program.

Recently the interns as a group decided they wanted more of a say in the tasks assigned them. They asked that they be consulted on administrative policies that directly affect them. For many valid reasons, some of the interns cannot participate as fully as others in some of the ancillary activities required of them by the CSATP, so the group felt it should determine who would be excused from certain services. The intern experiencing difficulty meeting a requirement would present the problem during an interns–staff meeting, where interns could decide each case on its own merit. Although final decisions still rest with the program administrator, interns now have the opportunity to contribute their viewpoints regarding the tasks assigned to them.

The staff and interns work in the following areas: new case contacts, counseling sessions, consultation and evaluation, cultural enrichment of clients, crisis intervention by telephone, progress reports, community information, public relations, training of personnel in and out of county, program development, transportation, conferences, and seminars. During five months in 1977, a total of 2,830 hours of direct counseling services to CSATP clients were logged by staff and the twenty-two counseling interns.

Activity 2. CSATP Interagency Coordination

The program coordinator describes her job and duties. Together with the program administrator, the coordinator is responsible for mobilizing and coordinating all official, public, and private agencies that deal with the sexually abused child and family.

The intent is to minimize the family's trauma and confusion and to promote the resocialization of that family. This objective is attainable only if services are not contaminated by duplication, overlap, or territorialism, so coordination has been essential to the success of the CSATP.

The coordinator is also directly responsible for the following tasks and functions:

1. Screening all referrals and assigning cases to counselors.

2. Coordinating CSATP services with those of personnel from the juvenile and adult probation departments, the police department, rehabilitation units at the county jail facility, the pretrial release program, the children's shelter, juvenile hall, county juvenile rehabilitation facilities, and any agency attached to the juvenile and criminal justice systems officially involved with a minor and her family.

3. Winning the cooperation of professionals who are involved with the family by adequate communication. When other agencies are not fully cognizant of the handling of a case by the CSATP, they may have doubts about whether the requirements of law enforcement are being met. These doubts are allayed by ongoing face-to-face contacts and telephone calls.

4. Increasing confidence in the CSATP by attending unit meetings in the Juvenile Probation Department and monthly meetings with police officers who investigate child molestation cases, thus acting as a bridge between law enforcement and the CSATP.

5. Attending to immediately or trying to forestall any difficulties in communication or case management that arise between CSATP personnel and juvenile and criminal justice personnel.

One such area of misunderstanding might arise if these workers suspect that the CSATP counseling staff is overstepping its boundaries as a treatment resource by interfering with the prosecution of cases. To preclude such occurrences, the counseling staff is frequently reminded that its responsibility is to provide treatment to the clients and to write evaluations of client progress to adult and juvenile probation officers that they can incorporate in their recommendations to the court.

The counselors are not permitted to send their evaluations directly to the court or to defense attorneys. Nor may they suggest the type of sentence that should be passed by the judge. Letters of evaluation prepared by staff counselors, counselors, or counseling interns are reviewed and countersigned by either the coordinator or the administrator.

These letters, despite their circuitous routing, are now welcomed by the court. The judges want as much information as they can get to make sound decisions. They want to know how severely the child was traumatized and how she and her family are responding to counseling. For example, if the juvenile probation officer and the counselor jointly agree that a family is ready to provide a safe environment for the child, the judge wants to know specifically how they came to this conclusion. Judges with adequate information make good decisions.

The criminal justice system wants to do its best by troubled families and is willing to cooperate when the CSATP has demonstrated its worth as an alternative to harsh punishment and separation. Judges serving in adult courts are likely to decide in favor of low or probationary sentences for the offender if they have sufficient information regarding his progress in counseling. The CSATP has spent much effort in educating the judges and people associated with the court process.

At one point CSATP staff members were becoming too visible in adult court. Now they will appear in court only by subpoena. On the other hand, the CSATP staff tries to make as many appearances as are necessary in juvenile court, even if a counselor is there only to hold the child's hand. It is important for the CSATP to demonstrate continually that its focus is on the treatment and protection of the child.

The educative goal of the coordination effort is to promote a humanistic stance throughout the entire spectrum of agencies that encounter the family. The program coordinator stresses the importance of developing an open communication system with agency personnel. This will ensure child protection and legal controls over the offender and the family, and it will hasten the reconstitution of the family when in the best interests of the child.

Case Management: Referrals

The program coordinator defines the different kinds of referrals and explains how they are processed.

Referrals from the police

1. The police refer the case to the CSATP. A staff person fills out a Referral and Intake Form at the time of the contact by the officer.

2. A counselor is usually assigned at this point.

3. The case is entered into the log book by name (or alias) of victim. Case numbers are assigned in sequence and include year and month. For example, case 79-02-112 was referral number 112, and it was received in February 1979.

4. If the referral concerns a family that requires emergency treatment, the referring officer will call CSATP as soon as he has finished his investigation. On occasion, the police officer requests a PU member and/or staff person or counselor to assist in interviewing the child and/or the offender and his spouse. More often, a probation officer from the dependent intake unit will assist the officer in the interview to save the child from having to face another interview later on.

A CSATP staff person, counselor, or Parents United sponsor will meet the mother and child at the police station and accompany them to the CSATP office unless the officer brings them over personally. At the CSATP, someone from the staff and/or a PU volunteer will talk with the mother as quickly as possible and make every effort to alleviate her anxiety. The CSATP always gives top priority to the victim, and a counselor and DSU member will talk to the child as soon as she is available.

5. The assigned counselor will try to see the mother and/or child the same day or soon thereafter.

6. Telephone or personal contact will be continued by the PU sponsor who will invite and/or accompany the mother to the next PU meeting. Similar attention is given to the child by the DSU sponsor.

7. If the case is not an emergency, or the mother cannot go to the CSATP for whatever reason, the officer will refer the case to the CSATP office where it is logged as usual and a counselor is assigned who will contact the mother for an appointment.

8. If he is free on bail or on his own recognizance, the father is passed on to a counselor and a PU sponsor after the police investigation.

9. Usually by the first PU meeting, both the mother and father have made connections with PU sponsors who may spend many hours giving them critically needed comfort and support in the days following exposure of the case.

10. Depending on her age, the victim will be talking to a DSU sponsor and will have been invited to the DSU group meeting. If the child is in protective custody either at juvenile hall or at children's shelter, the CSATP liaison person at the center is notified and instructed to see the child as soon as possible. The liaison tries to contact the victim within forty-eight hours and continues to give her support during her stay in these institutions, even though the victim is also being seen by the assigned counselor. The children seem to need this extra contact, and the liaison is an important link between the child and the counselor.

11. The staff person taking the referral from the police must inform the clients that the juvenile probation department has also been contacted regarding the situation. The police occasionally forget to notify the dependent intake unit of JPD.

12. The assigned counselor or counselor-intern will contact the probation officer as soon as possible to coordinate services to the family. The counselor or intern also informs the investigating officer who will be treating the family.

Referrals from Juvenile Probation Department

1. If an intake juvenile probation officer gets the case before the CSATP, the officer may fill out the CSATP Referral and Intake Form while conducting her/his own evaluation of the case. Otherwise, the CSATP staff person taking the referral will complete the form.

2. The staff person, usually the program coordinator, takes the initial information, particularly the victim's name and whereabouts, the parents' names, addresses, telephone numbers, the name and relationship of the perpetrator to the victim, and the name of the family member who will contact the CSATP or the CSATP or PU member who will contact the family.

From this point, the case management proceeds as it would with a police referral.

Referrals of minor offenders

1. Referrals of minor offenders normally may come from the police or delinquency probation officers. The offenses generally involve the sexual exploitation of younger children: siblings, a child cared for in the home, a neighbor's child, or a child the offender was babysitting. A few minors have been referred for exhibitionism or voyeurism.

2. The procedures are essentially the same as in referrals from juvenile probation or the police, and the case is assigned to a counselor.

3. A PU or DSU referral is made to get the offender and parents into group counseling as soon as possible.

4. If the offenses were intrafamilial, it is usually advisable to treat the victim and the offender separately at first and together later.

5. If the molestation did not involve a family member, a separate case folder is set up for the victim and her/his family and the offender and his/her family.

Referrals from public and private community agencies

If the situation has already been reported to the juvenile probation department and to the police, referrals from schools, church groups, mental health agencies, public health agencies, hospitals, departments of social services, daycare centers, etc., are processed essentially the same way as referrals from the police. If the offenses have not been reported, the agency contacting the CSATP is informed of its responsibility to report the matter and is instructed on how to do so. A follow-up check is made to be certain that the agency did report the case.

If the reporting party is unable to contact the mandated agencies, the person receiving calls will take down the information and make the necessary contacts. The agencies are encouraged to do the reporting themselves, however, because they have the most information regarding the case.

Self-referrals and anonymous phone calls

Self-referrals usually come from victims, mothers who suspect or discover that one of their children is being or was recently molested, or, in rare occasions, the fathers refer themselves. Sometimes referrals come from relatives, friends of the family, or neighbors.

If the person contacting the CSATP is determined to report the situation, they are informed about the CSATP services and are immediately directed to the dependent intake unit of JPD, the Sexual Assault Investigation Unit (SAIU) of the San Jose Police Department, or other appropriate police or sheriff's department. They are given the names and telephone numbers of the persons to contact. Follow-up is made to ensure that the reporting has taken place.

Most self-referrals and nonagency referrals are seeking information. They want to know the alternatives open to the family. When a referral of this nature comes to the CSATP, the first question usually asked by the person answering the telephone is, "Is this a matter that has to be reported?" If the caller responds "Yes," or "I think so," the next question will be, "Has it already been reported?" If the caller says it has not, then s/he is told that no identifying information is going to be taken until the caller has discussed this with a CSATP staff person.

The staff person, who in most instances will be the program coordinator, will listen to the caller's concerns, offer support and assistance, and answer questions as accurately and honestly as possible. She informs them of the help the family can expect from the CSATP if the offenses are reported. But if the matter goes unreported, the molestation is likely to go on, the victim will continue to suffer, and the family cannot receive the comprehensive help it requires.

The caller must at no time feel that the staff person is attempting entrapment. The decision to report must remain with the caller. If the caller is concerned about the way the case will be handled by the probation and police departments, the staff person explains that s/he can make no guarantees as to how these agencies might react. S/he advises the caller to talk directly to the official personnel and explains that can be done anonymously. The staff person then asks the caller to hold while s/he finds out who is available at the

appropriate agency in the caller's jurisdiction. The staff person then gives the caller the name and phone number of the police officer (or juvenile probation officer) on duty and encourages the caller to voice his/her fears directly to the officer. Usually the caller will take this suggestion.

If the anonymous call is from a mother or father offender, the staff person will ask the caller to speak with a PU member for first-hand information about the alternatives available to the family.

All persons talking to the anonymous caller must listen empathically to the concerns of the caller and convey the message that there is caring help available for the family. If the calling party does reveal the identity of the family and reports the situation, all CSATP support systems including PU and DSU are applied as quickly as possible. The actions may include having a PU person accompany the parents to the police and/or probation departments; having the child accompanied by a DSU member either prior to, during, or after being interviewed by the police or probation department; having a counselor contact the child immediately after admission to the children's shelter; and having counseling services available to the family soon after the reporting phase. All actions are coordinated with the investigating personnel to preclude interference with the investigative process.

Referrals from adults molested as children

Phone calls are received frequently from women who are experiencing difficulties as a result of having been molested as children. If the molestation occurred more than three years previous or if the caller was not a minor while being molested within the last three years, the situation does not have to be reported to the authorities in the state of California.

An example of a situation that would have to be reported would be a nineteen-year-old caller who says she was being molested while she was seventeen years old. Again, the consequences of reporting would be made clear prior to taking any identifying information from the caller.

Adults molested as children who come into the CSATP are usually women. They are assigned to a staff counselor who connects them with the PU group for women molested as children and arranges for individual counseling if necessary. If a sufficient number of males molested as children are available, a PU group is formed for them.

Consultation calls

The CSATP receives a large number of consultation calls from local people and from people in various parts of the nation. Consultation calls include a worker from a social agency inquiring anonymously about potential services for a particular client; a private therapist working with a family in which incest is occurring and wants to know what has to be done; a therapist seeking clinical consultation with a CSATP counselor; or an attorney who wishes to connect his client with the CSATP.

Most of the calls are taken by the program coordinator. Those she cannot handle personally are relayed to the appropriate CSATP staff members.

Module 5: Schedule and Training Location

The training coordinator is in charge of the training recruitment and organization. He briefs the trainees on the training schedule, describes the activities they will be participating in over the next two weeks, and answers questions. If the trainees are to meet at other locations, maps are passed out and explained. The coordinator recommends places the trainees can go to for entertainment and meals. The trainees are encouraged to enjoy their stay, to do things together, and to get to know one another.

Goals

To give trainees the opportunity to:

1. Hear about the training schedule and ask questions about it;

2. Become familiar with the local area, things to do, places to see, restaurants, etc; and

3. Develop goodwill and friendship among themselves to encourage collaboration in the future.

Rationale

To set an example of the caring attitude necessary for working in the field of child sexual abuse, the trainers must make every effort to make the trainees feel welcome and to inform them clearly of the training that will be provided.

Objectives

At the end of this module, trainees should be able to:

1. Have a clearer understanding of the coursework that will be provided;

2. Estimate whether the coursework fits their expectations and requirements; and

3. Request minor modifications to suit their individual requirements.

Note: Some adaptation of the schedule is usually possible for the three-day trainees as well.

Unit II. Experiential and Didactic Workshop

Unit Description

This unit is divided into four modules, each consisting of a variety of discussions, group communication techniques, and special exercises designed to increase knowledge about sexually abused children and their families and the trainees' current attitudes toward these clients. The trainees learn the value of honest communication and of self-awareness exercises for their personal and professional development. The unit gives special attention to unconscious attitudes about child sexual abuse, particularly incest. The importance of the art of self-management both for trainees and for their clients is stressed. Trainees are given the opportunity to examine and evaluate their personal philosophy and to compare it with that of the CSATP. Primarily by means of experiential exercises, they assess their general behavior and world view.

An inductive approach is favored in which exercises are followed by discussion and didactic analysis. If possible, trainers for the experiential and didactic workshop should include members of Parents United and/or Daughters and Sons United, whose personal inputs lend validity to the training messages.

Unit Goals

To provide the trainees the opportunity to:

1. Assess their reactions to Unit I;

2. Gain knowledge and skills in counseling and program coordination;

3. Practice effective communication and cooperative action;

4. Engage in self-exploration at an affective level;

5. Increase their respect for the group process; and

6. Discuss the history of the incest taboo and its current personal impact.

Unit Rationale

A judgmental attitude in the counselor evokes defensive reactions by the clients—a good indication that they don't trust the counselor and fear that if they reveal their faults this information will be used to hurt them or make them feel even more guilty. On the other hand, a counselor with an attitude of calm but sincerely concerned acceptance of the client as a person engenders a trustful client–counselor relationship. (Acceptance of the client as a person does not mean that the counselor condones the dysfunctional behavior.)

Trainees cannot be accepting of their clients if they are not accepting of themselves. To gain self-acceptance, the trainees must delve into their pasts, recall both pleasant and unpleasant experiences, and acknowledge them as natural phenomena in their histories. Much more difficult is the probing and surfacing of repressed feelings from painful events stored in the unconscious. The general state of anxiety and irritability that affects many human beings is in major part due to an abiding suspicion, arising from repressed feelings, that we have been and are being manipulated by parents, spouses, or other close people in our lives. In fact, we *are* being manipulated, but not so much by others as by the repressed memories in our unconscious minds.

The unconscious (a concept used loosely here) can be likened to a repository of undigested memories or disorganized brain imprints. To bring these under rational control, we must first identify and label them. We must take an inventory. Counselors who don't do so remain under the control of unarticulated feelings and project their own fears and doubts onto their clients. They cannot be accepting of their clients if they are not accepting of themselves.

In this unit and throughout the training course, trainees are engaged in group exercises designed for developing self-awareness of repressed painful feelings. Trainees doing these exercises discover that when they open the Pandora's box of their minds and confront the ghosts therein, they experience a deep sense of relief—the relief that comes from assimilation or reclamation of undigested "mental garbage."

The relief often turns into exhilaration when they discuss their new insights with other group members and realize that the contents of the unconscious can be reclaimed and turned into energy for positive action. They learn the art of self-management as they become aware of and control repressed feelings that formerly controlled them.

Unit Objectives

At the end of this unit, the trainees should be able to:

1. Practice self-exploration as an on-going daily habit and realize that awareness and identification of conscious and unconscious feelings and thoughts are prerequisites for self-management;

2. Listen actively, reveal their own thoughts and feelings during conversations, and note that these abilities are vital for effective communication;

3. Begin to have confidence in their ability to cope with clients during individual and group sessions;

4. Appreciate the value of perseverance and patience and understand that the advantages of CSATP methods over traditional methods must be demonstrated rather than argued about in order to gain the support of co-workers and personnel from other responsbile agencies; and

5. Have a better understanding of the incest taboo, its origin, its continuing impact on society, and its effect on their own sexual attitudes and behavior.

Unit Content, Module Design, and Activities Requirements

Module	Time	Activity	Time	Materials
1. Review of Experiences of the Previous Day	1 hr. 20 min.	1. Discussion of Previous Day's Experiences	20 min.	Space requirements: large (20′ × 30′) room, chairs and/or pillows for all participants. Room should be pleasant and floor should be carpeted, if possible.
		2. Expression of Leftover Feelings from Previous Day's Experiences	30 min.	
		3. Trainer Elaboration of Humanistic Philosohy and Didactic Material on the Incest Taboo	10 min.	
		4. Questions and Answers	20 min.	
2. Self-Awareness and Communication Techniques	1 hr.	1. Relaxation Exercise and Guided Use of the Imagination	15 min.	
		2. Effective Communication and Trust-Building Exercise	45 min.	

Module	Time	Activity	Time	Materials
3. Lunch	1 hr. 30 min.			
4. Developing a Humanistic Attitude	3 hrs.	1. Trainer Describes Case and Gives Instructions	5 min.	
		2. The Judgmental Counselor	20 min.	
		3. The Coldly Clinical Counselor	20 min.	
		4. The Over-Protective Counselor	20 min.	
		5. Discussion of the Role-Playing Exercises	30 min.	
		6. Break		
		7. Client Empathy	30 min.	
		8. Expressing Reactions to the Client Empathy Exercise	20 min.	
		9. Question and Answer Session and Farewell Circle	20 min.	

Module 1: Review of Experiences of Previous Day

Description

Trainees are encouraged to reveal both negative and positive reactions to the previous day of training. They express their feelings about what was said by the staff and PU/DSU representatives and the residual effects of the documentary film. Using group process techniques, the trainer urges participants to make personal rather than general statements, to take responsibility for their own feelings and perceptions, and to respect such feelings and perceptions as normal phenomena both in themselves and in others. The trainer helps them tie current feelings to past events in their lives.

The trainees are given initial practice in communication theory—how to listen actively and respond honestly. The philosophy of the CSATP is tested and discussed in depth at appropriate times.

The activities listed for this module are not necessarily conducted sequentially. A flexible approach is used because group interaction is a dynamic process and the group leaders must be sensitive to the needs of the participants. However, lengthy intellectual discourses are discouraged so that most of the time can be spent in experiential learning.

Goals

To provide the trainees the opportunity to:

1. Discuss impressions about the training up to that point;

2. Challenge and test the humanistic philosophy of the program;

3. Examine the incest taboo and its personal impact;

4. Evaluate personal philosophy and attitudes in relationship to the program's philosophy; and

5. Practice techniques in effective communication.

Rationale

During the first day of training, trainees were exposed to a great deal of thought-provoking information, and they saw an emotionally stirring film. They have now had a night to reflect on their experiences and are usually anxious for an opportunity to air both their positive and their negative feelings and thoughts. The trainers respond to the reactions and augment them with their own.

Trainees are encouraged to question critically the philosophy and methods of the CSATP. The discussion inevitably turns to the incest taboo, and as the trainees learn about its origin and history they are often surprised to discover that the taboo has markedly influenced their own lives.

Objectives

At the end of this module, trainees should be able to:

1. Have a better understanding of the humanistic approach to treating sexually abusive families and to gaining interagency cooperation, and see how this approach is congruent with what they have experienced in their training experiences thus far;

2. Appreciate the importance of effective communication and start using the methods during training and during off-hours with the other trainees; and

3. Assess the continuing impact of the incest taboo on society and on themselves, especially the effect on their sexual attitudes.

Activity 1. Discussion of Previous Day's Experiences

The trainer leads a discussion about the previous day of training. The focus is on trainees' experiences, negative and positive thoughts, questions, and opinions. They discuss, for example, statements made by members of the staff and of PU/DSU, the NBC film, the criminal justice system, and the philosophy of the CSATP.

The aim is to clarify the information thus far obtained by the trainees and to assure them that the trainers are more than willing to discuss with them whatever reservations or disturbing thoughts they may have.

Activity 2. Expression of Leftover Feelings from Previous Day's Experiences

The trainer encourages the trainees to focus on their emotional reactions. The trainers help them to probe these reactions and to trace them to events in their lives that may have aroused feelings yet to be resolved. The probing is gentle and accepting of current feelings. It is not designed to expose and embarrass. Trainees thus learn to trust the trainers and other trainees, and they eventually realize that clients will not reveal themselves if the counselors are not trustworthy.

Activity 3. Trainer Elaboration of Humanistic Philosophy and Didactic Material on the Incest Taboo

Interspersed at appropriate turns in the discussion, this activity traces the history of the incest taboo. The trainer reviews the cultural and biological theories about the origin of the taboo, myths surrounding it, and how the taboo influences our sexual conditioning to this day. S/he explains that, normally, our early sexual conditioning takes place in the nuclear family and that, therefore, most of us have experienced incestuous feelings; but the incest taboo forces us to repress them, particularly when the sexual feelings involve our parents. The trainer reviews human psychosocial, physical, and spiritual needs, why human societies often fail to meet these needs, and how the humanistic philosophy of the CSATP and its emphasis on caring as a life-long pursuit counteracts the failings of society. The trainer underscores the optimistic viewpoint of the CSATP and its confidence in the human potential for growth. Each individual is important and deserves acceptance and nurturing. Each individual can be taught to be responsible for his or her own perceptions and to control his or her behavior. The rewards of a self-directed humanistic life style are described and elaborated.

Activity 4. Questions and Answers

Again comingled when appropriate with the other activities, this activity invites critical assessment of the philosophy and methods of the CSATP and the positions taken by the trainers. The special focus is on answering the trainees' questions to their satisfaction. The questions may be intellectually abstract or specific (example: "What should my goals be when I work with a family?" or "Do all societies have an incest taboo?"). The trainees are encouraged to express feelings, too (example: a trainee may relate sexual problems stemming from negative sexual influences by her or his parents).

Module 2: Self-Awareness and Communication Techniques

Description

Self-awareness and communication exercises are conducted for the trainees' personal and professional use. The exercises complement one another. Trainees interact to build rapport, trust, and group cohesion.

Goals

To provide the trainees the opportunity to:

1. Practice exercises for inducing and self-inducing relaxation and for guiding the imagination to evoke positive images;

2. Practice communication techniques: listen actively; accept—not judge—what they hear; and respond honestly and personally, rather than advising or lecturing their partners; and

3. Become better acquainted and to encourage frequent and positive interactions during the balance of the course.

Rationale

Since many of the trainees attending the CSATP training course will lead similar programs in their own areas, it is important for them to develop the habit of self-understanding and guidance and to learn the skills of effective communication not only for dealing with clients, but also for building sound, harmonious working relationships.

Objectives

At the end of this module, trainees should be able to:

1. Appreciate the effects of self-induced relaxation and see that this ability would be useful as a daily habit and/or during stressful periods;

2. See the value of relaxation exercises as a preparatory step for the group process—to see that it helps group members center down, to "stop spinning their wheels," and to attend more quickly to group dynamics;

3. Understand that the imagination can be guided to recall positive images and past events to counteract those negative ones brought up by the uncontrolled imagination;

4. Bring to the surface repressed feelings and thoughts and note that this is the only way such feelings and thoughts can be assimilated;

5. Discover that self-acceptance precedes acceptance of others;

6. Learn that active listening and honest self-disclosure are the necessary components of effective communication and productive transactions with clients (whereas a hostile attitude in the intervener, whether communicated aggressively or through passive contempt, leads to alienation and to a breakdown in communication with the client); and

7. Know each other better and feel a sense of common purpose and unity.

Activity 1. Relaxation Exercise and Guided Use of the Imagination

Trainees are instructed to clear their hands of objects, assume a reclining position that is comfortable for them, and close their eyes. The trainees are guided through any typical exercise that will help them learn to consciously relax their bodies and minds. The exercise should include instructions for being aware of one's breathing; becoming aware of one's body and relaxing it; and acknowledging (not editing) the flow of thoughts, noting that the relaxed observation of the thinking process often releases repressed thoughts and feelings which are natural reactions to the way trainees view life now.

When the trainer feels the relaxation exercise is completed (it should not extend beyond five minutes), s/he moves into the second part of Activity 1, the guided use of the imagination, without a break in speaking rhythm.

The guided imagination exercise is intended to teach the trainees that the imagination can be employed creatively. The trainer begins by asking the trainees to imagine sitting in a theater and viewing a motion picture of their lives.

Sample Relaxation Exercise

The trainer instructs the trainees to clear their hands of objects, choose a position that is comfortable for them, and close their eyes. The trainer speaks in a calm, clear voice to help relax the trainees, using an exercise like the following.

"Be aware of your breathing but don't try to change it. Be aware of your emotions, what you are feeling. Whatever you're experiencing now is fine. Whatever your experiences will be as we proceed with this exercise are okay. Give yourself permission to simply notice what those experiences are. Become aware of what you are feeling at this very moment."

(Pause for a few minutes of silence.)

"Keep your eyes closed and keep in your comfortable position. Begin to be aware of the different parts of your body, starting with your toes."

(Pace each sentence so the pause between thoughts is long enough for the trainees to experience how each part of the body feels as it is mentioned.)

"How do the spaces between your toes feel?"

"Move up to your ankles."

"Then to your lower leg."

"How do your knees feel? Notice that, but don't try to change how they feel."

"Notice how your thighs feel."

"And your buttocks on the pillow or the floor. Is there any tension in any part of your body? Follow the line up from your buttocks to your lower back and see how it feels. Then move around to the front and up to your chest."

"Keep noticing your breathing, whether you are taking long, slow relaxed breaths or shorter, more intense breaths. Move up from your chest to your shoulders."

"Then move down your arms. Go down to the tips of your fingers."

"Now shift to your neck and see how tense it is."

"And how does the inside of your throat feel? Is it tight or relaxed?"

"Whatever is there, just experience it. Move up from inside your throat to your mouth. Then notice your eyes."

"And the space between your eyes."

"Notice the muscles near your forehead. Then end up at the top of your head."

"Get a sense of your whole body being a field of energy, from the bottom of your feet to the top of your head."

(Proceed to the guided imagination exercise without a break.)

Sample Guided Imagination Exercise

This exercise is to be used after the group has been led through a body-awareness/relaxation exercise. Without changing the level or tone of the voice used to help relax the trainees, the trainer leads the group into a guided fantasy as follows:

"Keep sitting comfortably. Without opening your eyes, come with me on a trip. Enter a movie theater with me and get ready to view a film. The film is about you and your life: your past life and your present life. Remember the highlights of your life, including your earliest sexual experiences. What took place, and how did you feel about those experiences? Put what you learned from those experiences into your film. Take about ten minutes to make your film of your life.

"If you remember something that's uncomfortable for you, place it in your film, noting what you learned from it, how it might have contributed to your present ability to deal with life. Remember you are the writer, producer, and director of your film, and its theme can be positive. Everything that has happened to you, no matter how painful, can be viewed as a learning experience, one that has added to your present capacity to identify with another person's feelings and to think creatively. It is a fact that on the whole you are coping with life quite well."

(Pause for ten minutes of silence.)

"Now start ending your film without giving it a definite ending. You can come back to your film later and add other parts of your life. When you are ready to come back to the group, open your eyes."

Activity 2. Effective Communication and Trust-Building Exercise

This activity demonstrates the importance of concerned listening and honest self-disclosure in promoting effective communication. The trainer instructs the trainees to be aware of their feelings (shyness, irritation, etc.) as they choose a partner.

After partners have been selected, the trainer says, "Decide who will listen and who will speak. Each speaker will be given fifteen minutes to relate his or her imagined movie and the feelings it evoked."

After the fifteen minutes are up, the trainer says, "I'll ask you to reverse your roles. As a listener, try to experience your partner fully. Really be with that partner. Appreciate who he or she is. Say nothing about yourself while listening, although you may ask questions for clarifying your partner's story. As a speaker, be aware of what thoughts you don't feel safe enough to disclose, what you are censoring or editing."

After the partners exchange roles and the exercise is completed, the trainer asks the trainees to reconvene as a group with the partners of each dyad sitting together. Partners then take turns relating to each other what they experienced as listener and then as speaker. They are to communicate with their partners directly, as if they were in private conversation, even though the group is "eavesdropping."

To complete this exercise, the trainer says, "I would like you each to end this conversation by saying to your partner what you perceive to be his or her strengths and virtues." Almost invariably, trainees will remark with wonder about the closeness they achieved with each other through this simple exercise. In the half-hour allotted to the exercise, they were able to divulge experiences in their past lives which they have been unable to relate even to close friends.

Trainees may also confide that they seldom receive or give genuine personal "strokes" and were surprised to discover that they found the exchange of positive comments about themselves pleasureable. Trainers may point out that, despite repeated research pointing to the advantages of positive reinforcement, we are still more inclined to notice and condemn bad behavior than to notice and compliment good behavior.

Trainees are also reminded that the conditions for good communication must often be set up deliberately and preferably agreed on by the communicants.

Module 3: Lunch

The trainees are told in advance that they have the option of bringing a brown bag lunch or going to a restaurant (if there is one on or near the premises). Either way, the trainees spend their lunch time with one another. Trainers may join the trainees during all or part of the break.

Module 4: Developing a Humanistic Attitude

Description

This module examines a case of father–daughter sexual abuse, the roles of the family members in the case, and the ways case-workers react to them. Trainees play the roles of three family members and three counselors with predetermined attitudes, as described by the trainers.

Goals

To provide the trainees the opportunity to:

1. Discharge typical initial emotions vis-a-vis a child victim, the father offender, and the child's mother through role playing;

2. Understand clearly the nonproductive results of angry, judgmental attitudes by experiencing them, and to compare the outcomes with those they experienced in the effective communication exercises in Module 2; and

3. Realize that parents will deny the existence of an incestuous situation if they are convinced that admission of the problem will lead to the destruction of the family.

Rationale

In Module 2, trainees learned a technique for effective communication. In Module 3, they learn (again by experiential exercises) what happens when workers approach their clients with a judgmental attitude, openly hostile or camouflaged by a cold, professional stance. Thus, they are able to compare the rapport they felt toward each other during the effective communication exercise with the anger and frustration they feel as the client condemned and rejected by the counselor.

Objectives

At the end of this module, trainees should be able to:

1. Become conscious of normally angry and judgmental feelings toward father-offenders and their wives and over-protective feelings toward the child-victims;

2. Observe how such feelings subvert the rapport that must be established between client and counselor before effective counseling can ensue; and

3. Use techniques for discharging these feelings before meeting with the clients.

Activity 1. Trainer Describes Case and Gives Role-Playing Instructions

The trainer describes three typical reactions counselors try to hide from clients but which nonetheless contaminate the counseling sessions if we don't become aware of them. Trainees are advised that these attitudes are deliberately exaggerated in the exercises so that they can be clearly identified and contrasted with the friendly, accepting attitude practiced in the previous exercise.

A case familiar to all workers in child sexual abuse is described—that of a mother who supports her husband's denial of the victim's accusations. Due to lack of evidence the district attorney refuses to prosecute the perpetrator, who returns to his family after the victim is placed in a foster home.

The trainees are asked to choose partners and to take turns playing the following roles and scenarios: an angry, judgmental counselor berating a denying mother; a coldly clinical counselor "psyching out" a molesting father; and a cloying, over-protective counselor talking to a molested child about eleven years old.

Activity 2. The Judgmental Counselor

The trainees examine how it feels to vent their anger and frustrations regarding denial of the charges by the mother* and the rejection of the daughter by both parents. The trainees are asked to let go—not to try to control their anger as professionals.

Sample Dialogue

Counselor: How can you refuse to believe your little girl about the molestation? You know very well she's telling the truth.

Mother: She's lying this time. If anything had happened, I'd be the first to know. Can you imagine my husband choosing her for sex instead of me?

Counselor: All I hear is that you are refusing to support your child, even though you are her mother. That you are sticking by your husband because you're a coward—you're afraid of being left alone, of making your own way. Imagine how your daughter, an eleven-year-old child, feels when she's deserted by both her mother and her father. You're a disgrace both as a mother and as a spouse. . . .

Activity 3. The Coldly Clinical Counselor

The trainees are asked to simulate a counseling session in which the counselor assumes a coldly clinical, objective stance with the perpetrator. The trainees take turns playing these two roles with the same partners they had for Activity 2.

Sample Dialogue

Counselor: Mr. Nevelson, I am a licensed counselor and I will be meeting with you biweekly at a mutually convenient appointed time. Shall we begin?

I understand you are denying the charges made by your daughter. I don't intend to argue with you. Just simply answer the questions I put to you.

(From this point on, he gives the client no feedback except an occasional grunt as he fills out his questionnaire.)

*If time permits, this exercise can be expanded to include the perpetrator in a similar exercise with the judgmental counselor.

Activity 4. The Over-Protective Counselor

One of the partners in each dyad plays the over-protective counselor while the other enacts the role of the molested daughter. When they have done this, the partners switch roles and repeat the exercise.

Sample Dialogue

Counselor: (Sitting too near the child, holding both her hands and speaking in a pollyannish tone.) Julie, honey, I'm your counselor, Mrs. Sunman. You can call me by my first name, Katie. You and I are going to be great chums and tell each other all our secrets.

Child: (Trying to pull away from the counselor's grasp and feeling smothered.) Oh.

Counselor: Julie, honey, I know all about the horrible, scary things your father did to you. You tell Katie all about it, sweetie. And don't be afraid because I'm going to take good, good care of you. If your mother can't take care of you, we'll find another nice lady who will.

Child: I want Mommy to take care of me. . . . (She breaks away from the counselor's hands.)

Activity 5. Discussion of the Role-Playing Exercises

The trainees discuss their reactions at the end of each role playing exercise: how it felt while playing the counselor and how it felt while playing the client. Do they feel that the communications were productive? Are they really free of judgmental/moralistic attitudes?

Ten minutes are provided for discussion at the completion of each activity. The trainer advises them not to feel guilty about judgmental feelings but to be aware of them and to find ways of airing them, such as with a co-worker or in role-playing exercises during staff meetings. The trainer suggests that staff meetings should be held regularly for this purpose.

Activity 6. Break

Activity 7. Client Empathy

The trainer instructs the trainees to do a three-part role-playing exercise in the following manner. Trainees are divided into groups of five, and each group sits in a circle on the floor. Group members are asked to identify with the perpetrator in Activity 3 and to guess what is going on inside the man.

One person in each group volunteers one sentence that comes to mind (example: "I've always been a loser. Now I've lost everything."). Another person in the group adds a sentence that may or may not relate directly to the first sentence ("How could I have destroyed the people I love the most?").

All group members add sentences as thoughts occur to them. By the end of the ten minutes allotted to this part of the activity, the trainees have completed a composite study of the inner emotional state of the perpetrator.

The second part of the exercise, done the same way, concentrates on the denying mother in Activity 2 (examples: "Why did he do this to me?" "How will ever be able to trust anyone again?" "What will happen to me and my family?").

The third part of the exercise, again done the same way, attends to the victim's feelings ("I can't even look my mother in the eye. She'll never take me back." "We're in a terrible mess. . . . What will we do if Dad goes to prison?"). The trainees adopt the facial expressions, postures, voice intonations, and attitudes that correlate with the feelings expressed.

Activity 8. Expressing Reactions to the Client Empathy Exercise

The trainer leads a discussion in which the trainees analyze and comment on Activity 7. They express what they experienced within themselves and what they observed about other trainees. They often note that the exercises involved the same mother and yet there was a radical difference in the way they perceived the mother during the judgmental exchange and the way they perceived her during the client empathy exercise.

Activity 9. Question-and-Answer Session and Farewell Circle

The trainers answer questions concerning the day's activities. Afterwards, everyone stands and the group forms a circle. Each person puts his or her arms around the waists of the people on either side. The trainees are instructed to close their eyes and experience the energy they give and receive from each other.

As they depart, many of the group members may embrace, thank each other with warm comments, and make arrangements for the evening's activities.

Unit III. The Criminal Justice System, Co-Counseling Sessions, and Parents United

Unit Description

This is a long day. Starting at 10 A.M., the trainees meet with a member of the Sexual Assault Investigation Unit of the San Jose Police Department, a deputy of the District Attorney, and the legal consultant to Parents United. The focus of these discussions is on the coordination of interventions by law enforcement personnel and personnel of the CSATP. Issues of the law pertaining to confidentiality are also discussed.

In the afternoon, the trainees attend a general staff meeting, after which they are assigned to counselors and/or interns and participate in counseling sessions with CSATP clients. In the evening, the trainees spend time with members of Parents United and Daughters and Sons United during dinner, attend the weekly PU meeting, and may join members of PU after the meeting for coffee and more discussion.

Unit Goals

To provide trainees the opportunity to:

1. Be introduced to the law enforcement aspect of the CSATP and learn how the CSATP and the criminal justice system interact;

2. Become familiar with issues of confidentiality;

3. Observe how the administrative and counseling staff deal with the problems that arise;

4. Get first-hand experience in the counseling of incest cases; and

5. Be a part of the PU and DSU group meetings as an introduction to a self-help concept that includes social responsibility in the personal growth process.

Unit Rationale

The trainees will be observing and participating in many aspects of the CSATP in action. The greatest value of this day for the trainees comes, of course, from the fact that they will be learning by doing. Experience with group after group of trainees has shown that "total immersion" training to be the most profitable.

Unit Objectives

At the end of this unit, trainees should be able to:

1. Have an idea of what they must do to enlist the cooperation of the criminal justice system in modifying its approach to child sexual abuse cases;

2. Understand the implications of confidentiality and understand that they must familiarize themselves with the confidentiality laws of their own states and communities;

3. Appreciate the importance of regular staff meetings to keep all members of the staff informed, and to provide an opportunity for staff members to express their frustrations;

4. Have a better idea of the development of counselor–client rapport;

5. Have a basic sense of the workings of self-help groups, and understand their mechanics as well as their therapeutic value; and

6. Have an understanding of the role of self-help groups in the resocialization of the family.

Module 1: Law Enforcement and the Criminal Justice System

Description

Trainees learn how the police investigate cases of child sexual abuse and how they use the CSATP as a resource. They learn what happens in the criminal justice system as the offender moves through it from his initial contact with the authorities to his sentencing. The role of the District Attorney's office in both the juvenile and the adult justice system is described. The legal issues of client confidentiality and the laws pertaining thereto are covered.

Goals

To provide the trainees the opportunity to:

1. Gain information concerning the process and procedures of the criminal justice system from the initial report stage to the sentencing of the offender;

2. Learn about the special investigative procedures of the Sexual Assault Investigation Unit (SAIU);

3. Learn how the police use the CSATP as a resource to help obtain confessions and to convince the family to enter treatment to reduce the chances of lengthy incarceration for the offender and separation of the child from her mother;

4. Appreciate the importance of a close working relationship between the criminal justice system and the CSATP (one that has in Santa Clara

Unit Content, Module Design, and Activities Requirements

Module	Time	Activity	Time	Materials
1. Law Enforcement and the Criminal Justice System	2 hrs.	1. Police Investigation Methods and Procedures	1 hr.	Blackboard, chalk, and handout on "Special Techniques of Child Witnesses."
		2. Role of the District Attorney	30 min.	
		3. Confidentiality and Reporting Requirements	30 min.	Handouts: "PU Guidelines to Confidentiality," and "Authorization for Release of Confidential Information."
				Additional staff needed: officer from the Sexual Assault Investigation Unit; district attorney or attorney familiar with the DA's functions; and legal consultant for Parents United.
Lunch	1 hr.			Preordered lunches, hot and cold beverages, paper plates and utensils.
2. Staff Meeting	1 hr. 30 min.	1. Introduction to the Staff	5 min.	
		2. Business	30 min.	
		3. Guests	30 min.	
		4. Explanation of Co-Counseling Training Schedule and of PU/DSU Groups	25 min.	Training schedules

Module	Time	Activity	Time	Materials
3. Practicum I, Co-Counseling Sessions	3 hrs.*	1. Briefing, Feedback, and Discussion	1 hr.	*NOTE: The three hours allotted for these two activities are spent at the discretion of the counselor, according to need. Usually there are two co-counseling sessions of one hour each; Activity 1 comprises the other hour.
		2. Co-Counseling	1 hr.	
4. Dinner and PU Meetings	1 hr. 30 min.	1. Dinner with PU Members	1 hr.	Seating and tables to accommodate the group, dining and coffee equipment, food (brought by members and interns).
		2. DSU Group Meeting	30 min.	Name tags, felt-tip pens, coffee equipment.
		3. PU General Business Meeting	30 min.	Name tags, felt-tip pens, coffee equipment.
		4. Self-Help Groups	2 hrs.	Enough chairs and/or cushions to seat everyone comfortably. Space required: Enough separate rooms or partitioned areas to accommodate each group comfortably and privately.
		5. Optional After-Group Get-Together	1 hr. 30 min.	

County resulted in important changes in the investigative process, the law enforcement process, and the methods of prosecution); and

5. Recognize how these changes have vastly increased the rate of referral and of admissions, while minimizing the trauma to the victim and her family.

Rationale

When the sexual abuse of children by parents warrants the intervention of the authorities, the family is already severely weakened by internal stresses. The first officially responsible members of the community to contact the family are law enforcement personnel. If a mother knows she and her family can get help, she will be encouraged to report; and if the father understands that he can get help for himself and that his family will not have to suffer unduly, he will be motivated to admit his crime.

It is important for trainees to understand the mechanics of the criminal justice system (CJS) to develop a cooperative working relationship with CJS personnel in their communities—this relationship being one in which all agree in substance on a course of action that minimizes trauma to the child and initiates a healing process for the family. More than any other factor, the cooperative relationship between the CJS and CSATP accounts for the dramatic increase in referrals and the high rates of admissions from offenders in Santa Clara County. It enables hundreds of families and, most importantly, victims to receive help they would not otherwise receive.

Objectives

At the end of this module, trainees should be able to:

1. Be generally familiar with the local criminal justice system process, both adult and juvenile, from the time of the initial report of the molestation through the sentencing of the offender;

2. Understand the special techniques used by officers in the SAIU to investigate cases of child molestation and obtain a confession from the offender, and understand how these methods differ materially from the harshly punitive procedures employed in the past;

3. Understand how law enforcement agencies cooperate with the CSATP in a way that maximizes the flow of help toward the victim and her family during and beyond the initial crisis of exposure of the molestation;

4. Begin to realize what the key factors are in the high rates of admission and the ever-increasing referral rate; and

5. Begin to think about how to enlist the cooperation of the criminal justice system in their own communities.

Activity 1. Police Investigation Methods and Procedures

An officer from the San Jose Police Department's Sexual Assault Investigation Unit (SAIU) goes through the law enforcement process step by step, from the initial report of a child sexual abuse case to sentencing. (See also Appendix 4C, "The Gathering of Physical Evidence.")

Note: The following speech paraphrases or quotes talks by Sgt. Gene Brown and other officers in the SAIU. Each officer has a somewhat different way of gathering evidence while using the techniques developed by the SAIU. By combining elements from each of several officers' presentations, we hope to present a more comprehensive view of the investigative tactics of the SAIU.

The Sexual Assault Investigation Unit Officer's Talk To Trainees

Incest is a crime, and the investigation of incest is a law enforcement function. However, the San Jose Police Department has broken from the traditional police thought, image, and action in dealing with sex crimes, and particularly sex crimes that involve in-house molestation (where the child identifies the offender as being a member of her household).

Our traditional task used to be to make an arrest, write a report, and testify in court. But now we have taken on the additional responsibility of investigating in-house molestation because there is no one else to do it. We assumed the additional function of becoming the initial contact person between the family and the courts, which required special investigative techniques that respected the sensitivities of the family, and particularly of the victim, but made it easier and more likely for us to make a case against the offender at the same time.

The whole case is shaped by how the police handle the family because they have the initial contact. And how well the police handle the family is one of the elements that makes the CSATP the successful program it is.

One step we have taken is to move away from the direct interview with the child. The adult witness's testimony is as valid as the child's and is taken as if it were said by the child. The beat officer who responds to the reporting party's initial call can take information from the reporting party as if it were coming from the child. What this means is that if a child has told her mother, a teacher, a relative, a counselor, or a neighbor that she is being molested, the officer who responds initially talks to that person. This prevents the child from having to be exposed to a uniformed officer who may frighten and intimidate her if he lacks the expertise in investigative techniques and who could adversely effect the case at the outset.

The patrolman does the initial report but does not conduct an in-depth investigation. He talks with the reporting party, asks what he or she knows—dates, times, how long has it been going on, and when the victim confided about the molest, etc.

Timeliness of the victim's report to the adult has evidentiary value in prosecuting the case. If the molest occurred over thirty days prior and the child is just now reporting, it reduces the child's credibility. In the prosecution procedure a timely report means the reporting party can testify as an exception to the hearsay rule. If the report is not timely, it may be regarded as hearsay evidence.

If the victim is present, the patrolman sometimes gets a general statement from her as to what happened. He will want to know dates, time of day, and as much as she is able to tell him; but he does not go into details about the molestation, as that is the responsibility of the investigators.

The patrolman then writes a report for the Sexual Assault Investigation Unit (SAIU); as soon as possible, an officer from the SAIU becomes the contact person for the entire family. However, if it is an emergency and the child appears to be in immediate danger, the responding officer will call the SAIU and the on-call investigator will respond to the scene or will bring the mother and the victim to the bureau. The patrolman may decide that the child is in jeopardy and will place her in protective custody.

He may be at the school where the child has told the school nurse, and the child is afraid to go home because she's tried to tell her mother before and the mother has not believed her, or has blamed her, or told her there wasn't anything she could do, or the father has threatened to do bodily harm to her if she told. Or, maybe her father is home and the mother is at work.

The officer must decide whether the child's immediate safety and psychological well-being are at stake. If the child is home and the mother or reporting party seems concerned and cooperative and is willing to come down to the SAIU and talk to someone, or if it's established that the father will not live in the family home while the victim is there, then the officer will leave the child with her mother.

For several reasons, we prefer to conduct our investigation downtown. It helps us maintain control. At home the siblings are running around and asking questions, the TV is on, the young children need attending to, the phone rings, the neighbors call. We also want the mother and victim to come in as inconspicuously as possible, so we don't take the child out of school. We are in plain clothes when they meet us, and we try to make it as easy and free from embarrassment as possible for the victim.

We also want the witnesses here so we can tape-record their statements. We tape everything. We don't have to tell them we are taping and we tape any investigative interview surreptitiously. We aren't trying to trick them, but if they know they are being taped they will be conscious of what they say or ham it up for the microphone.

Taped interviews can be used as evidence in court. The tapes give us a ready reference. Then if the offender denies, we play the child's tape to him, and usually he will fall apart and admit. We do what we have to do to get the father to admit and to protect the child. If the mother is nonsupportive of the child and two weeks later decides to change her story, we can play the tape and bring her back in line. If the child goes on the stand at the preliminary and says she was having nightmares and what she told the officer was not true, her tape will contradict that.

The process of getting facts is informal and conversational. When the mother and child come in, we talk to the mother first and occupy the child elsewhere with games and toys. We talk about the family situation, the dynamics. For example, the father may have been out of a job, and the mother may have gone to work; or she may have been ill for a long time. We try to get an in-depth understanding of the whole family: what its problems are, and what its fears are about the molest and its exposure. We develop rapport with them, build their trust, generate confidence in the system's desire to help, and explain that there is help for the family from Parents United.

We tell them what the judicial alternatives are and also disclose the price of noncooperation. This is not done so much as a threat as a revelation of the truth. Everything we say is calculated to encourage the mother's confidence in us, to give her hope that the situation is not hopeless and can be dealt with, and to encourage her to support and protect her daughter.

While the officer is talking to the mother, he is assessing how supportive she is. He recognizes how threatened her security is by the exposure and by the possible consequences to her husband: the possible loss of his job and the family income, and the loss of her companion and the children's father. The mother will usually stand by the daughter at this point and want to proceed with whatever must be done.

We want the child to be able to remain at home with her mother, but the mother must be supportive and agree to keep the father away. She must believe that what the police are doing is in the best interest of the family. If she feels that the police action will destroy the family, she will not cooperate.

We must convince her that cooperation offers considerably more hope for the future than noncooperation. Consequences of noncooperation may be: husband in jail, the daughter removed from the home, damage to the children who must appear in court to testify against their father, and adverse consequences to the child if the case is not prosecuted. We also spell out the advantages of cooperation: help for all the family, the probable reconstitution of the family, and the emotional health of the victim now and when she's an adult.

When the investigation of the mother is completed, the officer interrogates the victim. We ask her whether she would rather her mother be present or see the officer by herself. The younger child usually feels more secure with her mother present while the older victim feels embarrassed and that she is betraying her mother by discussing the details of the molestation in front of her. We respect the child's wishes either way.

Often we ask an investigative juvenile probation officer to work with us during the investigation of the child. Probation officers are also peace officers. In some counties Child Protective Service workers have the responsibilities that our probation officers are charged with in this county.

Having the probation officers present at the investigations and interrogations precludes the child's having to tell her story twice, once to the police officer and again to the probation officer. Probation officers, particularly if women, can often elicit answers to questions when the police officer cannot. The police officer can leave the room while the probation officer talks to the child.

How the investigation is handled also depends on the age of the child. With the very young child we have to go very carefully. We may spend the better part of an hour just playing with her and building rapport before we begin the questioning. Even before we go into the interview, we talk to them and say, "Now I understand something may have happened, and I want to talk to you about it." We say "may have happened" because we haven't heard from her yet, and we want it in her own words.

We tell them we want them to know that they are victims and haven't done anything wrong. We really want them to understand that they are *victims,* and we take whatever time we need to make sure they understand and can explain to us in their own words what a victim is. We tell them, "A victim is somebody who gets hurt by somebody else, so if I reach over and hit you, then I've hurt you and I've done something wrong. You're the victim and I'm the one who did wrong." We associate pain and emotion, which they have experienced in the molestation.

We talk to them for a while in this manner and then ask, "Now do you think you've done anything wrong?" And they may still answer that they think they have, so we explore their feelings, give them support, continue to support the idea that a victim is one who has been hurt or wronged. Finally, we say, "Do you realize that you are a victim, that you haven't done anything wrong, and that you did the right thing by telling?" Then when they agree, we ask them to tell us in their own words what a victim is and how they are a victim.

Then we say, "I've been told that Daddy may or may not have done something to you that you don't think is right," We talk about that, and this leads into the interview. Sometimes they can tell what happened with ease and sometimes they can't. Sometimes they don't know words like "vagina," "penis," or whatever. They use their own words and we tell them to use their own words, but we make sure their words and our understanding are the same. So when the child uses the word "pee-pee," we say, "Well, what is a pee-pee?" or "What does Daddy do with his pee-pee?" If the child answers, "It's a thing he uses to go to the bathroom," we know we have the same usage for the word. We make sure we have a clear understanding of all their special words, and then we use those words in the interrogation.

The child can usually tell us when the incident happened. For example, when mommy went to the hospital to have Jeremy. We ask her when that was, and she may say she doesn't remember, but maybe she knows how old Jeremy is. Or, we can bring the mother back in and ask her when she was in the hospital having Jeremy, and she gives us a date. We may have to take the victim backward from the most recent incident, which is the freshest, to the earlier ones. We get her to relate incidents to memorable events such as the end of school, a birthday, a holiday, or a vacation.

When someone else reports the molestation, the children may deny it to us at first. Then we approach them with, "Daddy may have a sickness. Now if Daddy had a broken leg, we would want him to go to the orthopedic doctor and get his leg fixed. An orthopedic doctor is one who fixes broken bones. You'd want him to go to the doctor for his broken leg, wouldn't you?" She can't deny that. "And if Daddy had appendicitis, we would take him to a surgeon who specializes in people with sick stomachs, and you'd want him to get to that doctor as soon as possible, wouldn't you?" They can't deny this either. "And if Daddy has something wrong with his head, with how he thinks, we would take him to a psychiatrist to get him help. You would want him to get help for any of these things that are wrong, wouldn't you?"

The victim usually will concur by now. So we say, "Okay, I've been told that maybe Daddy has a little sickness in his head and we're here to try to help Daddy get better." We have to be honest with them so when they ask, "What's going to happen to Daddy?" we say, "I can't say for sure. Maybe he'll have to go to jail for a little while, or maybe he won't have to go at all. But it won't be permanent. If he does go to jail, he'll be gone for a little while, only a few months."

So we finish the interview with the child, getting information about how the perpetrator approached her, things he said to her, where he touched her and she him, when he asked her to, and whether he bribed her or told her it was a secret to be kept between them, etc.

Before the mother and the child leave the bureau, we do two things. Even if a crisis situation does not exist, we want to get the family hooked into the CSATP as soon as possible. Once the officer has gotten statements from both the mother and the victim, he goes to the telephone and calls the CSATP office. He tells a responsible person there—usually the program coordinator but sometimes a staff person or Parents United volunteer—what the situation is and that he would like someone to talk to the mother and her child.

Some of the mothers are in severe crisis, fearing the end of their families. Such a mother isn't just given a number and asked to get in touch with the CSATP, because she probably would not do so. She feels helpless but her tendency is to withdraw, to distrust having more people know what has happened. The program coordinator will talk to the mother at length and often enlist the help of the PU mother volunteer in the conversation. An intern and/or a PU volunteer will pick up the mother and victim and drive them back to the CSATP, or the officer takes them over personally. He wants to bond them immediately to a source of help and support and get them crisis counseling.

If they can't see someone at the CSATP for whatever reason, a PU sponsor will contact the mother at home and maintain this contact until the next PU meeting, where she will be met by the sponsor and helped to feel at home with the other PU members. We must remember that the mothers are fearful of exposure, rejection, and the fantasized wrath of others. A sponsor who has been in the mother's shoes at an earlier time is immensely helpful in tiding the new client over the crisis.

If the family is not in immediate crisis they may go home, and we contact the CSATP so a PU sponsor can begin to call them and urge them to come to Parents United, and the DSU sponsor can encourage the girl to attend a group also. When the father gets over to the CSATP there will be a father member of PU to support him, too. If the family returns home we tell them they will be contacted by someone from PU and a counselor with whom they will make an appointment. There never is any question that they will make a connection one way or another with the CSATP. We let them know that this is part of the way they will cooperate with us.

The second thing that usually happens before the mother leaves the police bureau is that, providing she is cooperative, she is encouraged to bring the father in. She calls him and tells him where she is and that the police know everything, and that if he comes down voluntarily and cooperates with the police he will be treated respectfully and will probably be able to go on with his job and daily life much as before.

We do have to be careful that we don't make the mother an agent of the police. If we do then everything is lost. Any admission he would make would be lost, so some officers prefer to call the father themselves. We call him at home and say, "Hey, I'm Sergeant So-and-so, and come down here because I want to talk to you." They usually come right away because they are carrying this enormous weight on their shoulders and they're ready to unload it. Or, we'll call them at their job and tell them to come down after work. We rarely go to their place of employment and take them off the job. But sometimes a man won't come in. Then the department must use whatever means it has available to bring him in and get a confession.

There are generally two kinds of fathers, the ones who are so relieved to have the molestation exposed that they confess everything to the officer at once, and the others who deny or partially deny because they're too afraid to admit. When the father comes in, he is read his Miranda rights, and the officer asks him if he wants to talk now that he knows his rights. The man may request an attorney, but this occurs infrequently. Although there are some who will try to bluff their way through and say they'll talk because they have nothing to hide, most of the men now want to admit the charges.

If he comes in voluntarily and is willing to talk, we use the same respectful tactics as we use with the mother and the child. We have to break through his resistances and fears of harsh treatment and the humiliation of exposure to the community. It is just as important for him to feel confidence in the system as his wife.

If the offender has been cooperative, we allow him to self-surrender and he has to leave his job for only a few hours. The attorney calls the police to let them know their client will cooperate, so by the time the police get the complaint from the district attorney, we don't have to put him in jail. The offender comes in, is processed, and is released on his own recognizance (OR) on the promise to appear at the arraignment. By this time the molester is usually convinced he isn't going to be crucified, and he and the family will get the help they need. He is convinced he must stay out of the home as the police and his attorney have told him to do. He has also been told to begin counseling and to attend Parents United as a condition of his OR release.

Sometimes the man is too afraid to admit and we have to use different interview techniques. We have the basic information from the child, the mother, or other witnesses, and it isn't necessary to get a full confession. Denials or partial denials are all right because we are already well armed with evidence. Those who deny, however, may only persist in the denial for a short time. We start out with, "Well, this is what Barbie said happened," and then describe the latest incident. He'll often say, "Yeah, it happened." We'll say, "And she also said it happened a week before that on Sunday," and he may admit to that but qualify it and say, "But it wasn't intercourse." The officer may respond with, "But she said it was. Suppose you tell me what happened."

The father may then describe how he had her play with him, then put his penis between her legs and had her move back and forth. So the officer clarifies that is called thigh intercourse or thigh masturbation, and determines whether he ejaculated between her legs. And he'll confess that he did. The officer clears up what Barbie at age eleven thought was intercourse—that she thought he was inside her.

But it is not always so easy to get the confession. Some fathers might say, "I don't know where she got those ideas." Then we can use the tape of his daughter, the daughter he cares so much about, and let him listen to her sobbing and telling her emotionally packed story. Or we just describe Barbie and what a beautiful girl she is, and relate to the father what this child had said to the officer and how badly she felt, and that she was choked with tears and saying that she loved her father and didn't want to hurt him. "And you're going to sit there and tell me she was lying with those tears coming down and not wanting to hurt you, when it was hurting her so badly?"

Another tack is to say his daughter described the sexual acts in explicit detail; how can someone describe something she has not experienced? Sometimes this works.

Sometimes we have to use traditional tactics and team up on him. One of us will play the good guy, and the other the bad-guy routine. Sometimes we have to turn around the collar and be the father-confessor. One officer can become the empathic listener saying, "Your whole world is falling apart, you're confused and don't know what to do. You're afraid you'll lose your job, your family, rot in jail." And the man will say, "Yeah." Then the officer tells him how his kid and wife are hurting; he wants them to get help, doesn't he? Doesn't he want his daughter to grow up to be okay and undamaged? and he'll say, "Yeah." Then the officer says, "So suppose you start telling me what happened, so we can start getting you people some help." The officer appeals to the father's sense of duty and responsibility towards his family, the people he loves.

If the father still won't admit, the officer tells him to make a call—only the officer dials the number and hands him the receiver. He has him talk to a Parents United father. The two talk and then make arrangements to talk in person. Later the father is met by the sponsor at Parents United. Parents United members can get him to start talking often when the police have failed.

His confession may come out in bits and pieces, half admissions, and even large denials of guilt, but that's all right because we have the victim's testimony on tape. By the time of the preliminary he is usually ready to make a full confession because it is harder and harder to continue to disappoint the family. Parents United has been talking to him, and he doesn't want to hurt the family any more.

It is the officer's duty to do what is best for the total family. After the confession, whether partial or complete, we have two ways to go. We can arrest him or let him go on his own recognizance. We don't want to arrest him. We want to keep him on the street, going to his job, maintaining as normal a routine as possible. If the family has been cooperative and has said they will go along with the CSATP, and if the father agrees to move out immediately, then there will be no arrest at that time. He is released on his own recognizance, ordered to have no contact of any kind with the victim, and told to begin attending the CSATP. Before he leaves we advise him to get an attorney, either one of his own choosing or one recommended by Parents United. Attorneys suggested by Parents United are familiar with the program's work and the necessity for bringing the case to trial quickly.

One compelling reason not to arrest the man and send him to jail is that he would be easily recognizable and vulnerable to being sexually assaulted and humiliated by others there. Molesters are designated for protective custody, given distinctively colored uniforms, and are at the bottom of the jail hierarchy. "Baby Rapers" are not safe in the city jail.

It is so much easier when we get a cooperative offender. If we have to act punitively toward him or threaten him and his family, his sense of survival stiffens his resistance to us, and we are placing the whole family in a difficult bind. We have to come from the stance that we will help him if he goes along with us. The process of investigation and connecting the family to the CSATP is compressed into a few hours. We get a confession from the father, he is persuaded to stay out of the home and not have contact with his child, the connection to CSATP and the PU sponsors is made, the police go right to the district attorney with the evidence, and a complaint is filed.

The family doesn't have time to disappear. While the complaint is being sought, the family is being surrounded by the people in the program and receiving help and support from so many quarters they don't have time to change their minds. Even if the mother has a change of heart in the ensuing week, if all her old fears come back and the police again become the enemy, there are the PU people and the counselor, all of them caring, all of them sharing their experiences and encouraging the family to stay around and be helped. It is estimated that in the first week following exposure, the family receives twenty-two hours of contact with persons in the program beginning with the initial contact with the police.

Finally, offenders usually express a need to be punished. Their confessions are the first step. When the offender confesses, he begins to take responsibility for his act and therapy has begun. As he gets further along in the program, that acceptance and responsibility grow. The police play only the first part. But again the whole case is shaped by how the police handle this initial contact with the family. In gathering evidence we may indeed play the "mind game" to fulfill not only the police mission but the family mission as well. And if we can do this by remaining helpful and caring, we can start this family on a path that will eventually restore it to health and productivity.

Activity 2. Role of the District Attorney

A deputy district attorney or an attorney familiar with the DA's functions describes the role of that agency in prosecuting child sexual abuse cases. When the investigating officer reports a case to the DA, the DA listens to the officer's opinion regarding the case, particularly as to whether the alleged offender will cooperate with the system, decides what charges are appropriate, and whether there is sufficient evidence to warrant filing a complaint. The complaint is taken to the courts and is reviewed by a judge who decides whether the charges the DA has asked for are sound. If the judge decides the charges can hold up, he issues a warrant for the arrest of the offender. The officer will then contact the man and inform him of the charges, tell him what bail has been set, and make arrangements for him to contact an OR (own recognizance) or pre-release specialist. The officer tells the father that he can be released on his own recognizance so he won't be going to jail or have to lose his job.

On the other hand, an officer might fight OR for a number of reasons: if he felt the father would not observe the no-contact order, if the father were obnoxious and needed to cool down in jail for awhile, or if he were violent and might do harm to his family.

The father will have hired an attorney or public defender who calls the investigating officer to ask if he feels all right about releasing his client on his own recognizance. If the officer has determined that the man will be cooperative and meet the OR requirements, that the OR is supervised and conditional on no contact with the victim and immediate participation in the CSATP, then he okays it.

The father is warned again not to contact the victim or there will be no hope for OR, and that because there is probable cause to arrest, the officer could just walk over and book him on the spot if he wanted to. The officer may underscore his warnings by saying that if there is any contact whatever with the victim, she may be removed from the home and placed in protective custody, and that the law will act strongly and decisively against the father for his disobedience.

The attorney then contacts the OR people, and OR contacts the police to verify that they approve the OR. At this point the father is interviewed by the OR specialist.

If the victim is under fourteen years of age—or sixteen years depending on the charges—the DA files along with the complaint a request to the judge that this matter be brought before the courts for a preliminary hearing within thirty days. This time element is important because the victim will tend to forget details and her testimony can be impeached by a defense attorney, who, hoping that the victim will impeach herself, is interested in extending the time of the preliminary as much as possible. In Santa Clara County the preliminary is usually scheduled for around twenty days from the date of filing. The father will usually plead out at this time and waive the preliminary so the victim does not have to testify in court against him. Parents United has been telling him not to put the child through this ordeal, and he doesn't want to hurt her any more.

At the preliminary, the DA must demonstrate to a judge in the Municipal Court that there is probable cause to believe that the defendant committed the offenses with which he has been charged. Both the DA and the judge will question the witnesses. This can be emotionally devastating to both the defendant and the witnesses, and particularly to the child who must testify in court against her father while he is sitting there. However, the father usually has had contact with other Parents United people by this time, as well as a counselor, who have admonished him that putting the child on the stand can be emotionally damaging to the child who is already experiencing strong feelings of guilt, shame, and betrayal. Most fathers will plead out to a felony at this time, waiving the preliminary hearing. The case is remanded to Superior Court.

The defendant will be arraigned in Superior Court, and the judge will usually allow the offender to remain OR. A date for the pretrial conference is set. At the pretrial conference, the DA and the defense attorney will attempt to settle the case by having the defendant plead out to the charges or by entering into a "plea bargain." If the defendant pleads guilty at the preliminary, the case goes to an adult probation officer who will investigate and provide the judge with a presentence report. At that time the judge will set a date for sentencing.

Several months usually elapse between the preliminary and sentencing, giving the offender and his family time to participate in counseling and Parents United. All this will be taken into consideration by the probation officer when writing his presentence report. He will also have had frequent contact with the CSATP counselor, who has kept him apprised of the client's progress and who will submit a client evaluation report to the probation officer, which will be considered in the probation officer's recommendation of sentence to the court.

The probation department usually recommends that the court first determine whether or not the defendant is MDSO (Mentally Disordered Sex Offender). The judge orders the defendant to be examined by two court-appointed psychiatrists who make a determination. The psychiatrists must both find the man to be MDSO beyond a reasonable doubt before he can be so labeled. In Santa Clara County, the CSATP offers a viable alternative to state prison for in-family sex offenders, and most of the examining psychiatrists are aware that men who go through the CSATP do not remolest.

After the psychiatric evaluations are in, the offender returns to Superior Court for sentencing, usually within two weeks of the findings. The offender being sentenced for a felony will usually be sentenced to a few months in the county jail, and/or placed on probation for a few years, ordered to pay a fine, and ordered to attend and participate in the CSATP. Sentences to prison are extremely rare.

Most intrafamilial offenders who are in the CSATP are not found MDSO. The psychiatrists and the judges are convinced that such offenders are not chronic child molesters and that enrollment in the CSATP will be more productive than imprisonment. Local judges usually consider the CSATP rehabilitative of the entire family, whereas a prison term precludes therapy for the entire family and may lead to its disintegration.

Nevertheless, some deputies may press for a state prison sentence. For this reason, educating the district attorney's office as to the superiority of the CSATP approach over imprisonment is as critical as educating the police in this regard. Another reason for convincing the deputy DA to retreat from his adversary position is to protect the child from repeated questioning.

Pressure by the deputy counteracts any tendency by the CSATP to reduce its own pressures on offenders to complete their treatment programs. If the offender is uncooperative with the program or with the court orders regulating his activity, the program must report this noncompliance to his probation officer, and the deputy DA will use this information in the prosecution process.

A deputy assigned to the Juvenile Court represents the victim if the court determines it has jurisdiction and can issue orders on behalf of the child. The deputy may ask that a victim be removed from a home that is unfit by "reason of depravity." But often what the deputy wants for the child is in conflict with what the child wants, which is to go home.

In Santa Clara County, the district attorney's office is beginning to declare conflict of interest in such cases and often requests the court to appoint an outside attorney for the child. One outcome of the CSATP approach is that about 67 percent of the children are not removed from their mothers at all, with the fathers moving out instead. In all, about 92 percent of the children return home within the first two months.

Activity 3. Confidentiality and Reporting Requirements

The attorney who serves as legal consultant to Parents United makes a presentation to the trainees in which she tries to clarify the nebulous issues of when to report clients' confidences and when and what to keep confidential. (See also appendix 4D, "Parents United Guidelines to Confidentiality.)

Sample Presentation

The client–counselor privilege is the right of clients to depend on counselors not to reveal confidences. Although clients are assured of this right, there are exceptions; counselors will not be able to keep everything clients say confidential. What information counselors have to divulge is controversial and confusing; and some aspects still are not settled.

Everyone agrees that it is important for clients to be able to speak freely to counselors in both individual and group sessions. Law enforcement agents who visit Parents United (PU) agree not to divulge to any third party what they hear during group sessions.

If members did not have some assurance of confidentiality, their inhibitions and resistance would hinder their progress. Confidentiality is essential, since they are expected to bare their souls and reveal their dreams, shame, and entire selves to their counselor. It facilitates successful treatment when clients do not have to worry that their confidences will be revealed on the witness stand by their counselors or anyone else. That was the Supreme Court's rationale for giving the privilege. They strengthened the privilege by declaring it part of the Ninth Amendment.

PU volunteers, interns, counselors and other staff members appreciate and abide by the confidentiality rule. They realize it is crucial for developing a trusting environment. They are in a dilemma, though, because they also appreciate the need to abide by the reporting requirements set by law. Our staff warns first-time callers who are prospective PU members that if they state their name we must report them as an incoming case. That way they can choose to remain anonymous until they are ready to report themselves. That privilege establishes trust, and about 40 percent of the callers report themselves after phoning us anonymously only two or three times. Once their case is reported, these incoming PU members are assigned a counselor. That counselor does not need to divulge any more information about that particular offense than was taken during the investigation phases.

PU has adopted three policies so that clients, staff, and volunteers can have guidelines to follow and know what to expect. That facilitates developing trust. First, we must inform law enforcement if we learn any new information indicating that any PU member has repeated sexual abuse on the victim. Second, we must tell law enforcement if any client molests or had molested a child other than the one(s) reported before entering our program. Third, law enforcement needs to know if any client violates a court order.

We adopted these policies because the staff must abide by the legal constraints placed on them. We want to follow these policies because we need to align ourselves closely with the criminal justice system. We need the resulting leverage, which gives the families the place and time they need to get help with their resocialization process. Since these are exceptions to the client's privilege of confidentiality, the counselors or other staff members must inform members of these policies.

The member must agree to abide by these limitations before being considered to have a formal relationship with our program. An agreement between the counselor and client is crucial so that the counselor cannot be sued later. A verbal agreement is not enough. It is best to have the client sign a statement also signed by the counselor, signifying that the client understands the exceptions to his privilege of confidentiality. This should be done before a client is formally admitted to the program.

The counselor should also get a signed release from the client authorizing him or her to talk to any third party about that client. The release should specify whom the counselor will be consulting and what he or she intends to say about that client. If the counselor finds it necessary to talk to that third party again in the future, an oral waiver from the client is enough authorization after the first time. Even a mention in the counselor's notes saying the client agreed to the times after the first time is sufficient. But do not rely on an oral waiver to be an adequate release to write letters or reports about the client. Get a written waiver for that.

Authorization for Release of Confidential Information

NAME OF MINOR/CLIENT: BIRTH DATE:

ADDRESS:

FATHER:

ADDRESS:

MOTHER:

ADDRESS:

I,_____ , hereby authorize_____

_____

to give specific information concerning _____

_____

in my program records to _____

Referred by:

Date:

Signed _____ Date _____

Relationship (if principal is a minor) _____

Witnessed by _____ Date _____

It would be fatal to our program for us to be forced to reveal confidences unnecessarily. The burden of proof is on staff counselors—not on clients—to prove they have acted appropriately and that they have taken measures to maintain confidentiality. We must also prove we informed the clients fully of the restrictions on their privilege. We must prove the client agreed it is okay to divulge information to others about them when necessary and appropriate. The client–counselor relationship should not begin until these matters are taken care of by the counselor.

PU formulates its policies of confidentiality according to the underlying principles of our program, case law precedents, and three codes that are sources of California law: the Evidence Code, the Penal Code, and the Welfare and Institutions Code. Each of these codes perceives the counselor–client confidentiality privilege differently. (In these codes, the term counselor includes marriage, family, and child counselors; licensed clinical social workers; clinical psychologists; and psychiatrists.) All three codes agree that a counselor can consult other counselors without breaching the client's privilege of confidentiality.

A counselor must explain to the client that he will have the confidentiality privilege as a client as long as he intends to have it. The counselor must abide by the privilege unless and until the client changes his intention and states verbally or in writing that he has changed it. That is waiving the privilege voluntarily.

An exception to the client's privilege occurs when his mental condition is in question and the client waives his privilege involuntarily. Another exception is when a person claims he has a neurosis that is the result of an accident and brings suit to win damages. In that situation, the court appoints a therapist to talk to the person bringing suit at the defense attorney's request. The attorney uses the information gotten from the therapist to build the defense. So naturally, the therapist can not keep confidential what information the person divulged.

In situations where the client has not waived his privilege, the counselor must remain silent even if he or she is sent to jail for contempt of court. But there are other situations that supersede the privilege. When a client threatens potential danger to a third party, the counselor must not keep that information confidential. The "dangerous patient" exception states that clients who might harm someone must be reported and cannot maintain their privilege. This exception applies to all counselors, whether or not they are covered by the Welfare and Institutions Code definition of being a state-employed worker.

Victims could sue a counselor who kept silent and did not warn them of the possibility of danger. Any counselor, including a community mental health worker, invites a lawsuit and will lose that lawsuit if s/he fails to report potentially dangerous clients. According to the Evidence Code, this is the only situation that warrants the counselor's divulging any client confidences.

The Tarasoff case set a precedent about this situation. It held a counselor responsible for harm to a victim even though the counselor had made efforts to avert danger—efforts that were sabotaged by his supervisor and by the police. The court held that counselor liable, not the supervisor and not the police. If we apply the Tarasoff decision, then we must report *all* active cases. And we must report not only to the mother or guardian but the police also. To report just to a child's caretaker is not sufficient protection for the child. The caretaker is emotionally involved and cannot be relied on to take the necessary legal action. Still the caretaker should be informed, because she is responsible for the child's welfare.

A mere counseling session is not sufficient protection from possible danger. This interpretation fits with both the Penal Code's and the Evidence Code's legislative intent. If a client is being held in an institution involuntarily when he threatens danger, the counselor does not need to report threats, because the potential victim is safe from harm. It is a breach of confidentiality for the counselor to report the threats unless the client agrees to it.

When a PU/CSATP client has mandatory attendance requirements, it limits his privilege because dates of sessions and attendance records are not privileged information. Content of what clients say in sessions is usually confidential except for the exceptions I am discussing with you. Counselors must report what a client divulges only if it fits the exceptions.

If a counselor or other staff member violates a client's privilege without one of the exceptions as the reason, the client can sue her or him. The client can also sue the entire program. The state could choose to revoke counselors' licenses so we must always act as if any information is confidential unless we know otherwise. Do not discuss cases with third parties. Do not leave case files or notes open to view. Avoid negative legal ramifications and keep the trust intact in the relationship you have worked so hard to build with that client. According to the Evidence Code, your primary duty is to your client and to society, whether your salary is paid by private or public monies.

According to the Penal Code's mandatory reporting requirements, everyone in the helping profession must report any suspected case of molestation. This includes doctors, teachers, counselors, social workers, psychologists, psychiatrists, law enforcement agents, and others. If we suspect molestation, we must report even if there are no physical or tangible trauma signs. We should report when we hear evidence from the victim, not a third party. We must report both to local law enforcement and to a second resource. In this county the second resource is the Juvenile Probation Department. In other counties it may be the dependency unit of Children's Protective Services, for example.

Laws concerning sexual abuse of children were afterthoughts to the other types of child abuse, namely physical abuse and neglect. So words about sexual abuse were tacked on later. As a result they are phrased clumsily and ambiguously. The laws as they stand now confuse people and are interpreted several different ways. The various codes add to this confusion. The Penal Code *requires* counselors to breach the client's privilege of confidentiality if they suspect sexual abuse. The Evidence Code does not require reporting; it just permits reporting. But the Penal Code carries more weight and overrides the Welfare and Institutions Code also.

The Welfare and Institutions Code forbids state-employed workers to breach confidences. In reality, though, if you fail to breach a client's confidences when you should, you are liable to be sued. A 1976 case in this county held a physician liable for child abuse injuries. Public policy is so strongly in favor of a child being protected that protection is the primary concern. So any private citizen can report suspected molestation. And if the report is made in good faith, the citizen does not need to fear any reprisals for reporting. Any worker in the helping professions—a probation officer, for example—must report any harm to a child s/he suspects was inflicted purposely and not by accident. S/he does not need to fear liability unless the report is malicious or unless s/he did know or should have known it was a false report.

The Welfare and Institutions Code's definition of the client's privilege of confidentiality differs from the other two codes. It states that under the Lanterman–Petris–Short Act all state workers should keep confidences. It also states that if a worker breaches confidences, the client deserves restitution from that worker. Remember though that the courts interpret that the Penal and Evidence codes take precedence over this third code. The legislative intent is to value the child's protection more than the client's right to the privilege of confidentiality. The legislative intent is the determining factor that makes the difference and carries the weight. The distinction also applies to what a child says concerning herself. If a child client confides she was molested, the counselor must report that immediately. This includes state-employed workers.

The courts are the ones asked to resolve conflicts and determine what statutes take precedence over other statutes. They try to resolve the conflicts harmoniously when they can. The Tarasoff case decision and one section of the Evidence Code conflict with the Welfare and Institutions Code, which demands that workers adhere strictly to keeping client's confidences. The Supreme Court evaded this conflict when the Tarasoff case came to light. The court said that owing to "grounds of immateriality" they could not resolve the issue, because the counselor was not a state-employed worker. The court will continue to be asked to make decisions to settle these conflicts. And the court must maintain that exceptions apply to all counselors, no matter who employs them. Whether their salaries are paid by public or private funds, whether they are private counselors or community mental health workers, counselors cannot be held to different standards. That denies them the equal protection that the Fourteenth Amendment guarantees.

Finally, a few comments about children's rights as clients. After a case is reported, a child can depend on his or her counselor to keep the confidences from that time forward except for the exceptions we have discussed. The exceptions to the privilege of confidentiality is just as strong, sound, and necessary for child clients as for adult clients. Even a three-year-old has the privileged relationship with her counselor. A 1978 Santa Clara County case decided that. The court ruled against a father who tried to uncover information his child had confided to her counselor. A child's interest may differ from her parents' interests. The court has ruled that a child is entitled to have her own legal counsel to represent her interests. The law lags behind the times on this matter in many counties. There is confusion about children's rights, too. The term "help" regarding how workers should help children is defined several different ways. It is not helping a child to divulge her confidences outside of the exceptions I have specified. Even if your rationale in divulging her confidences is that you are trying to help her, remember that what she needs most from you is someone she can confide in and trust.

The importance of upholding a child's right of confidentiality was recently addressed in a Santa Clara County Superior Court hearing. Recognizing that our program and others like it would be seriously crippled if children under sixteen were held to have no right of confidentiality under Evidence Code section 1027, or if the custodial parent were automatically deemed to have the right in all cases to exercise or waive the child's right of confidentiality, the court held that the child who was three years old or older did have the privilege of confidentiality with her counselor. The court also held that the child's interests may diverge from those of the custodial parent, and that therefore the child was entitled to have independent counsel represent her interests in her right of confidentiality. The court also ruled that just because the child's custody and her father's rights of visitation were in issue did not mean that the child was a party to the action. In other words, parents could not make a child a party to the action simply by declaring that such was the case.

The significance of this decision is threefold. First, by upholding the child's right of confidentiality, the court recognizes that it must act to protect the rights of children even when the legislature has failed to do so; second, that it is against the interests of child victims to allow third parties to interfere with their counseling; third, that children are not merely the property of their parents; they have rights separate from and sometimes in conflict with those of their parents. These rights include that of the counselor–client privilege.

The issues raised in this talk are also the subject of the handouts "PU Guidelines to Confidentiality" and "Authorization for Release of Confidential Information." We will probably see many changes in the next few years regarding confidentiality and the reporting requirements, and it is important for all workers in the field of child sexual abuse to stay current on what the laws expect and require.

Note: The trainees will break for lunch before joining the staff meeting. They are encouraged to eat and spend time together, to get to know each other, and to exchange thoughts, feelings, and ideas about the training just completed.

Module 2: Staff Meeting

Description

The CSATP staff meets once weekly for one and a half to two hours. The staff meeting is closed to trainees and visitors for the first half hour. This gives the staff time to gather together for an intimate few moments of sharing personal feelings, reestablishing contact with one another, and reaffirming the group's sense of community. The trainees join the staff meeting for the last hour and a half of business.

Meetings are attended by all members of the counseling and administrative staffs as well as assigned representatives of Parents United and Daughters and Sons United, and a counseling-intern liaison.

The staff meeting provides a forum for sharing and exchanging information and for facilitating operations and relations between agency personnel and the CSATP. For this reason, the meetings are also often attended by selected guests from the criminal justice system and from official and private human services agencies. Keeping the CSATP open to the community is a matter of continuing effort.

The principle function of the staff meeting is the exchange of information to promote maximum cooperation and effectiveness among the various agencies and personnel responsible for the abusing families. In addition to airing problems within the CSATP, any issue concerning the promotion of understanding and cooperation between the CSATP and elements of the criminal justice system are heard and discussed, often with CJS personnel present and contributing to the exchange of information and joining in the problem-solving process. Parents United and Daughters and Sons United representatives share their concerns to integrate their interests and efforts with those of staff members.

Toward the end of the regular staff meeting, the co-counseling schedule is given to each trainee and explained by the training coordinator so each trainee knows which counselor he or she will be training with for the next week and a half and what hours are set aside for this training. The DSU and PU groups that will meet that evening are described so that trainees may be thinking about which groups they will wish to attend.

Goals

To provide the trainees the opportunity to:

1. Participate in a CSATP staff meeting and observe how the staff tackles the problems that arise;

2. Be exposed to the immediate problems as well as to the preparation of the long-range plans of the CSATP;

3. Note how the staff meeting functions as part of a total support system that embraces not only CSATP personnel but also the agency personnel with whom the program collaborates; and

4. Witness the educative aspect of the CSATP as its personnel interact with other agency personnel in the exchange of mutually beneficial information, in the solving of problems, and in effecting sound case management and treatment of abusive families.

Rationale

The three major components of the CSATP—the professionals, the self-help groups, and the volunteers—can best be understood as a dynamic system. The components as well as the individuals comprising them are interdependent. To make the system viable, the relationships among all elements and components of the system must be functional, congruent, and beneficial to all participants.

The staff members as well as the clients of the CSATP believe that a well-functioning organization can best meet the needs of its members by continually improving the channels of communication. Effective communication is essential for productive transactions with families, and all intervening personnel.

Conflicts in attitudes and methods arise constantly in a developing program such as CSATP, which relies heavily for its success on the official and private resources of the community. The CSATP continually strives to improve communications at every level of interaction.

The weekly staff meeting, the counselor-intern meeting, and the counselor–staff meeting all attempt to meet the psychological and practical needs of the participants by sharing information, dealing with negative feelings, negotiating differences, solving problems, learning new skills, providing support and comfort, and fostering cooperation and goodwill. Repeatedly, the trainees are urged not only to observe but to participate in all the operations of the CSATP.

Objectives

At the end of this module, trainees should be able to:

1. Have a sense of the numerous problems and issues that the CSATP, in an advanced state, contends with and some understanding of the ways the organization deals with these problems;

2. Augment their appreciation of effective communication as they observe the CSATP and other agency personnel working together to share information and solve ongoing operational problems; and

3. Begin to experience how staff meetings attempt to meet the needs of the participants, and understand that the concept of mutual support or self-help embraces everyone and not just the families for whom they are responsible.

Activity 1. Introduction to the Staff

The trainees join the CSATP staff meeting after the first half hour. Trainees will have met many of the staff during the first two days of the training; however, this is their first opportunity to meet the other staff members. Introductions around the room are made with each person stating his or her job title.

Activity 2. Business

There is usually considerable information to share and discuss at the staff meetings. Problems in administration and coordination, the budget and funding, training, interns' concerns, and issues concerning Parents United and Daughters and Sons United are some of the numerous topics that come up weekly. It is important to keep the entire staff informed on a regular basis so that everyone can contribute intelligently to group decisions concerning immediate problems or long-term policies of the CSATP.

Questions arise frequently over case management and coordination of services, often focusing on the specific management of a difficult case. Interagency relationships among law enforcement, human services, and community groups are reviewed continually, as effective case management and delivery of services depends on their cooperation and goodwill.

Parents United and Daughters and Sons United chapter development around the country and at home is reported on and discussed. Also discussed are questions of policy regarding interns: their supervision, their ancillary duties (such as providing transportation to clients), their recruitment, and qualification requirements for new interns.

Activity 3. Guests

The staff often invites personnel from other agencies such as law enforcement officers, defense attorneys, judges, prerelease officers, probation officers, or other community-based resource personnel.

Sometimes the guests will come just to share information. For example, a prerelease officer may talk about the criteria for determining whether an offender should be released on his own recognizance or on bail. A district attorney may speak of his office's suspicions that the CSATP is "soft" on offenders and reunites families too quickly. A police officer may wish to clearly delineate what his department defines as police responsibility and what is the CSATP's responsibility and when the CSATP is interfering in law enforcement matters.

The presence of such guests affords the CSATP and other agency personnel the opportunity to work through problems of interagency coordination, improve the communication feedback process, and ensure a cooperative working relationship.

Activity 4. Explanation of the Individual Training Schedule and of PU/DSU Groups

The community training coordinator distributes and explains the training schedule. The coordinator mentions that the schedule is flexible and allows trainees a number of options. For example, a trainee who is particularly interested in the play therapy group may wish to trade with a trainee scheduled to sit in on that group but who would prefer a different kind of training session.

Training Schedules

INSTITUTE FOR THE COMMUNITY AS EXTENDED FAMILY

P.O. Box 952, San Jose, California 95108

TWO WEEK TRAINING COURSE

PRACTICUM I

Thursday, 2:00 PM–5:00 PM, _____

Session IA: Individual Counseling Sessions

Location: Parents United House
467 S. Third St., San Jose

TRAINEES	COUNSELORS
_____	_____
_____	_____
_____	_____
_____	_____
_____	_____
_____	_____

Session IB: Play Therapy and Pre-Adolescent Groups

Location: Parents United House   )
467 S. Third St., San Jose) Play Therapy Group

Parents United House   )
467 S. Third St., San Jose) Pre-Adolescent Group
)

TRAINEES	COUNSELORS
_____	Options indicated below*
_____	'' '' ''
_____	'' '' ''
_____	'' '' ''
_____	'' '' ''
_____	'' '' ''

*Bee Brown and Anne Myers for Pre-Adolescent Group,

Ellie Breslin and Laura Costello for Play Therapy Group.

I/P-41 (6/80)

INSTITUTE FOR THE COMMUNITY AS EXTENDED FAMILY

P.O. Box 952, San Jose, California 95108

TWO WEEK TRAINING COURSE

PRACTICUM II

Monday, 10:00 AM–1:00 PM, _____

Session IIA: Administrative Issues

Location: Juvenile Probation Center, Room 307
              840 Guadalupe Parkway, San Jose

TRAINEES

_____

_____

_____

_____

_____

_____

INSTRUCTORS

Bob Carroll and Dorothy Ross

,,   ,,   ,,   ,,   ,,

,,   ,,   ,,   ,,   ,,

,,   ,,   ,,   ,,   ,,

,,   ,,   ,,   ,,   ,,

,,   ,,   ,,   ,,   ,,

Session IIB: Individual Counseling Sessions

Location: Parents United House
              467 S. Third St., San Jose

TRAINEES

_____

_____

_____

_____

_____

COUNSELORS

_____

_____

_____

_____

_____

INSTITUTE FOR THE COMMUNITY AS EXTENDED FAMILY

P.O. Box 952, San Jose, California 95108

TWO WEEK TRAINING COURSE
PRACTICUM III

Monday, 2:00 PM–5:00 PM, ———————

Session IIIA: Legal Issues

Location: Parents United House
467 S. Third St., San Jose

<table>
<tr><td align="center"><u>TRAINEES</u></td><td align="center"><u>INSTRUCTOR</u></td></tr>
<tr><td></td><td align="center">Elizabeth Cobey</td></tr>
<tr><td></td><td align="center">,,   ,,</td></tr>
<tr><td></td><td align="center">,,   ,,</td></tr>
<tr><td></td><td align="center">,,   ,,</td></tr>
<tr><td></td><td align="center">,,   ,,</td></tr>
<tr><td></td><td align="center">,,   ,,</td></tr>
</table>

Session IIIB: Individual Counseling Sessions

Location: Parents United House
467 S. Third St., San Jose

<table>
<tr><td align="center"><u>TRAINEES</u></td><td align="center"><u>COUNSELORS</u></td></tr>
</table>

INSTITUTE FOR THE COMMUNITY AS EXTENDED FAMILY

P.O. Box 952, San Jose, California 95108

TWO WEEK TRAINING COURSE
PRACTICUM IV

Thursday, 2:00 PM–5:00 PM, _____

Session IVA: Individual Counseling Sessions

Location: Parents United House
             467 S. Third St., San Jose

TRAINEES   ### COUNSELORS

_____   _____

_____   _____

_____   _____

_____   _____

_____   _____

Session IVB: Play Therapy and Pre-Adolescent Groups

Location: Parents United House   )
             467 S. Third St., San Jose)   Play Therapy Group

             Parents United House   )
             467 S. Third St., San Jose)   Pre-Adolescent Group
)

TRAINEES   ### COUNSELORS

_____   Options indicated below*

_____   ”   ”   ”

_____   ”   ”   ”

_____   ”   ”   ”

_____   ”   ”   ”

                                                ”   ”   ”

*Bee Brown and Anne Myers for Pre-Adolescent Group,
 Ellie Breslin and Laura Costello for Play Therapy Group.

I/P-44 (6/80)

Trainees are told they will be going with the counselors wherever their counselors may go, whether to the Children's Shelter, Juvenile Hall, on a home visit, or to court on behalf of a client. The trainees are informed that they will begin to sit in with the counselors and their clients at their next regularly scheduled appointment, which should begin shortly after the end of the staff meeting.

Finally, the weekly PU and DSU counseling groups are described, so that trainees can decide which ones they will wish to observe that evening.

Module 3: Practicum I: Co-Counseling Sessions

Description

This three-hour module includes two activities: the two one-hour counseling sessions and the third hour used at the counselor's discretion for discussing cases before and after the sessions. (The trainee will have received a schedule at the staff meeting indicating with whom he or she will be working, and at what times, for the remainder of the training period.)

Over the two-week period, each trainee will co-counsel with a staff counselor and participate in up to ten hours of counseling sessions. Trainees who are more concerned about administrative problems are permitted to spend part of the ten hours with the administrators.

The counselor endeavors to schedule appointments that include a variety of counseling situations such as individual sessions with offenders, mothers, and victims of all ages (including women molested as children); dyadic sessions with mother and daughter, father and daughter, and the marital pair; and family counseling sessions. (With two exceptions, all group counseling takes place in Unit III, Module 4, Activities 2 and 3. The exceptions are a play therapy group for children ages six to ten and a group for preadolescents eleven to thirteen which meets after school one day a week for approximately one and a half hours.)

The trainees accompany the counselor in whatever activities s/he engages in during the module period. In addition to the counseling session in the counselor's office, the counselor may have a session with a child at the Children's Shelter or Juvenile Hall. The counselor may visit the family home and conduct a session there. The counselor and trainee may go to Juvenile Court on behalf of a child, or to adult court if the counselor is subpoenaed by the offender's lawyer. Face-to-face consultations with the probation officers or other agency personnel are a usual part of a counselor's day, and the trainee will participate in many or all of these activities.

Goals

To provide the trainees the opportunity to:

1. Make intimate contact with clients and counselors and take part in an intense and varied experience that goes beyond mere intellectual understanding of treatment concepts;

2. Become familiar with the different kinds of crisis counseling as well as the methods and techniques used to further the goals of self-knowledge, beneficial interpersonal relationships, self-managed growth, and social responsibility;

3. Observe CSATP counselors using the skills that will enable them to implement the methods and principles of humanistic counseling with their own clients;

4. Become more self-aware as they attend to the client's process and feelings;

5. Become acquainted with the multifaceted work of the counselor and its contribution to client growth and productivity; and

6. Ask questions and challenge CSATP counseling methods and their effectiveness, and to begin to assess how CSATP methods and counseling styles compare with their own.

Rationale

The fundamental aim of the CSATP is to resocialize families referred to the program. This resocialization is achieved by teaching the parents to be better parents and better spouses and the children to meet their own obligations within the family—essentially, teaching family members that harmony within the family usually engenders harmonious relationships outside the family.

The counseling sessions will expose the trainee to counseling methods and techniques that teach personal awareness and self-managed growth, promote satisfying interpersonal relations, and foster social responsibility. Of course, with new families the counseling sessions concentrate on the immediate crisis. Effecting social awareness and responsibility is one of the treatment objectives for the more advanced clients. Trainee participation in the counseling sessions is regarded as one of the ways in which this objective is furthered. Most clients wish to share their experiences and progress when they know that trainees will use this knowledge to assist other families with the same problem. Trainee participation in the individual sessions is, therefore, viewed as a part of the client's counseling process. The emphasis on teaching clients social responsibility by practicing it in the community is one of the characteristics of the CSATP approach that distinguishes it from other approaches, particularly those that try to "rehabilitate" offenders within an institutional setting.

Objectives

At the end of this module, trainees should be able to:

1. Have gained some practical experience in counseling many kinds of clients and have learned some preliminary skills that will enable them to achieve the goals of humanistic counseling with their own clients;

2. Begin to internalize a positive and humanistic stance in the treatment of sexually abused children and those who abuse them;

3. Cope with their own negative feelings toward abusive parents and know that these negative feelings will not permit productive intervention based on understanding of the psychological dynamics that led to the abusive acts; and

4. Understand how the counselor's commitment to an integrated psychosocial counseling approach means building a treatment structure that meets the multiple needs of the family and provides a regenerative environment that will further the process of resocialization.

In addition, the trainees should be asking and answering for themselves the following kinds of questions:

1. Does the counselor demonstrate rather than preach the virtues of respect, caring, warmth, and empathy?

2. Is there a feeling of trust and congruence between client and counselor?

3. Does the counselor teach attitudes and skills that raise the client's self-esteem?

4. Does the counselor systematically aid the client in removing blocks to self-awareness?

5. Does the counselor manifest him/herself as a person primarily, instead of as a therapist, and is the counselor also learning from the encounter?

6. Does the counselor get involved in obtaining practical assistance and emotional support for the new client?

7. How well does the counselor exploit the client's interactional patterns and make apparent facets of the client's personality not previously seen?

8. Does the counselor experience the client's feelings with comfort, allowing for and encouraging their full expression?

9. How completely does the counselor personify the humanistic principles and methods of treatment?

Activity 1. Briefing, Feedback, and Discussion

In this loosely-structured activity, counselors meet the specific requirements of the counseling session and the needs of the trainee. A counselor may choose to use ten minutes prior to each of the two counseling sessions to brief the trainee on the client's history and current progress and the counselor's goals for the client.

The time between and after sessions is also important for the trainee's questions regarding the process and methods used by the counselor. Often a session triggers powerful, hidden emotions in the trainee that the counselor must attend to before the trainee leaves. An important aspect of the training is to provide the trainee an opportunity to become aware of parts of his or her personality that need further exploration and work.

In fact, the feedback portion is important for both the counselor and the trainee, giving each a chance to comment on the work of the other, compare counseling styles, and give suggestions for resolving certain problems encountered during the session. The spirit between trainee and counselor is one of mutuality, cooperation, and learning that flows in both directions.

Activity 2. The Co-Counseling Session

Prior to the counseling session, the counselor decides whether the trainee will enhance or inhibit the counseling process with the scheduled client. The counselor has made an effort to schedule clients who are willing to have trainees participate, but this is not always possible. Particularly when a client is at a critical phase, such as the trust-building stage with the counselor, the presence of a stranger can endanger the process.

Generally, the counselor receives the client's permission for the trainee to participate in the session before the day of the appointment. Nevertheless, it is important to get the client's permission again on the day of the training session, and not in the presence of the trainee. Although they rarely object to the participation of a trainee, allowing clients to express their feelings about it is important for several reasons. The most obvious is to show the counselor's respect for the client's feelings. Anxiety about the trainee's presence may interfere with the work of the session, but the client will be encouraged to share time with trainees on future occasions if the experience is positive.

With clients who have worked with trainees previously, the counselor can use precautionary words such as, "I'm working with Bill from———County today. I know you didn't mind having a trainee sit in last time—how about today?" The client who has been prepared for the trainee's presence usually agrees.

The client and trainee are then introduced to each other, and the trainee helps put the client at ease by describing his or her job and desire to help others in the client's same difficulty.

It is advisable to set the tone for the work by allowing all persons in the session to express their fears and reservations about the change in the counselor–client relationship caused by the presence of the trainee. If anxiety seems to be high, it is sometimes beneficial to do a relaxation exercise to reduce anxiety and to focus awareness.

As the session proceeds, the client usually becomes absorbed in the work and is not deterred by the trainee's presence, particularly if the trainee is acting as a co-counselor rather than an aloof observer. Before the end of the session, the counselor asks the client for feedback about working with the trainee. Any client resentments and appreciations are encouraged at this time, and in this way, all feelings are dealt with in the present and closure of the session can be effected.

Generally, clients express positive feelings about the experience and the added dimension brought to the session by the trainee. The trainee then thanks the client for allowing him or her to participate, and the session ends.

Module 4: Parents United and Daughters and Sons United Meetings

Description

In this module, trainees have an opportunity to meet with members of Parents United at dinner or to attend the Daughters and Sons United self-help group. Then they attend the general Wednesday evening business meeting of Parents United. In the Santa Clara County Chapter, about 150 PU members are usually present at this meeting. The focus of the evening is on the self-help group sessions following the general business meeting.

The fifth activity in this module—a get-together with PU members after the group sessions for socializing at a local restaurant—is optional.

Goals

To provide the trainees the opportunity to:

1. Interact with Parents United members personally and in group sessions;

2. Become involved at an experiential level with PU and DSU members;

3. Observe the members' feelings, attitudes, levels of awareness and growth, expectations, traumas, etc., at various stages of treatment; and

4. Understand the value of the group process.

Rationale

The intention of this module is to make trainees fully and directly aware of what transpires when PU members convene weekly as a group. Personal interaction with group members enables the trainees to experience directly the emotional reactions and positive changes taking place in the family members. Trainees will have met a few PU and DSU members on an individual basis during the first three days of training, but this is their first opportunity to meet the family members in a group, to listen to them express their feelings to each other, to feel the impact of group interaction.

Generally, trainees will discover that the results of the humanistic approach of the CSATP are vividly evident in the atmosphere created by the members when they come together on Wednesday evenings. This so impresses the trainees that most of them will join the forty or fifty members who gather at a local coffee shop at the end of the formal meeting, despite the late hour (about 10:30 P.M.). (The caring climate created by a PU/DSU group is not unique to the Santa Clara County chapter. It can be found at any of the more advanced chapters now flourishing in various parts of the country.)

Objectives

At the end of this module, trainees should be able to:

1. Visualize how PU and DSU groups in their own community will interact when they convene weekly;

2. Be familiar with the main issues and growing pains they will encounter after they establish a PU chapter;

3. Anticipate what may evolve during self-help group sessions and meetings; and

4. Begin to clarify for themselves their future roles as PU group organizers, coordinators, facilitators, etc.

Activity 1. Dinner with PU Members

In this optional activity, the trainees share a potluck dinner prepared by members and interns in the training building or at the nearby home of a member (unless members have chosen to go to a restaurant instead). Some of the staff, interns, and members attend. The conversation is usually convivial and informal. Trainees may ask members questions about their personal experiences and about the program. This is one of the activities that satisfies the socialization needs of both the members and the trainees.

Some trainees may choose to attend a DSU self-help group session instead of the dinner, or may take a break until the start of the PU meeting.

Activity 2. Daughters and Sons United Group Meeting

Of the ten Daughters and Sons United groups, seven meet from 6:00 to 7:30 P.M. on Wednesday evening. (The Transition Group for girls eighteen to twenty-two meets from 8 to 10 P.M.; the Preadolescent Girls' Group meets one afternoon each week from 4:00 to 5:15; and the Play Therapy Group for latency-age children meets from 3:30 to 5:00 on another afternoon.)

All the DSU members present for the evening groups come together in a large meeting room at 6 P.M. for socializing and business. Announcements are made regarding fund-raising activities, trips, and parties being planned. The Task Force informs the members what it is working on. Occasionally, the adult leaders of the CSATP address the DSU members to inform them of the overall progress of the CSATP and how DSU has contributed to it.

At 6:30 the children go to their small groups. There is an Orientation Group for adolescent girls who are new to the program. Some of these youngsters are in protective custody and come from the Children's Shelter. There are several groups for girls who have been in the program for eight weeks or longer and for whom the initial crisis of exposure is past. There are also groups for molested preadolescent boys and for older boys, and a group for young male offenders. Occasionally, the older boys will meet with one of the girls' groups for a mixed group session.

The children have been told during their counseling periods that there are trainees present who will want to join them in some of the small group sessions. The trainees have been advised that permission to participate in the small groups must be granted by the group members, who will decide by vote when they convene. The members have never voted to exclude a trainee, although some have voiced their reservations. Most recognize the importance of sharing their experiences with people who will be assisting other children with the same problems.

Each trainee chooses and joins a group. Before the sessions begin, the trainees introduce themselves to the members of the groups and explain their interest in DSU and what they hope to learn from them. The group sessions then commence and usually last about one hour.

Many of the dynamics that develop in the DSU group sessions are similar to those that develop in the PU group sessions. The differences lie in the ages of the members of the two groups and in the concerns unique to victims who are also children in various stages of growth and development. The sexually abused child must deal with feelings of guilt, shame, and betrayal that are often overwhelming for one with such limited life experiences and coping skills. The usual growing pains characteristic of various age groups are intensified by the molestation, often exacerbating problems of adjustment to family, school, and peers.

There is often a volatile undercurrent in DSU groups. Children who are resolving difficulties with their parents help stabilize the group's emotional climate, whereas the children who have been rejected by their parents are apt to disturb it—or to shun participation in the interactions. In her confusion and despair, and to indicate that she is beyond help, the abused child may act as if she were beyond control.

The group experience is intended to support her through the trauma left by the molestation and its subsequent exposure, to decrease the negative effects of the juvenile and criminal justice systems, and to help her retain her self-esteem by reinforcing positive behavioral and attitudinal changes.

Leaders of the DSU groups must have special skills and must be carefully selected. They must have extraordinary patience, not be overly directive, not be fearful of the potentially explosive group environment, and must allow the group's process to unfold without undue interference.

Activity 3. Parents United General Business Meeting

Before the thirty-minute general business meeting, members, staff, interns, visitors, and trainees interact for about fifteen minutes. During this time, people arrive randomly, make name tags for themselves, drink coffee, and socialize. Name tags should display first names in large print readily seen from a distance of fifteen to twenty feet. Calling a person by the first name is especially desirable during group sessions. Trainees' name tags should also include their functions and the agencies they represent.

At 7:30 P.M., everyone present gathers in the meeting room. Trainees and visitors introduce themselves and tell what organizations they represent and their purpose in visiting. One member takes a turn leading that week's five-minute relaxation exercise. The relaxation exercise usually includes a simple breathing exercise, a body tension awareness exercise (see sample relaxation exercise in Unit II, Module 2), and at times an inspirational reading or a guided fantasy. Members are encouraged to be creative in getting the group relaxed and getting its attention centered on the immediate goings-on rather than on the world outside.

After the exercise, the PU president presides over the twenty-five minutes devoted to business matters. A typical agenda might include:

1. An announcement by the Speakers Bureau of organizations they have addressed during the week and of new requests for speakers.

2. Progress reports on projects of special committees (e.g., fund-raising activities toward establishing a group foster home for daughters).

3. Requests for volunteers (e.g., to coordinate a picnic, to organize a flea market, or to contribute to the monthly newsletter).

4. Reports on media coverage of PU: articles in the newspaper, radio and TV appearances by members, etc.

5. Personal announcements (e.g., fathers tell the progress of their court cases and relate any sentencing or probation conditions they have received).

6. Requests, questions, etc., from members, staff, and interns.

Visitors include psychiatrists, psychologists, educators, mental health workers, police, social workers, attorneys, judges, physicians, nurses, politicians, etc. Many come from outside the county. Members are encouraged to welcome visitors. The PU chapter depends on the goodwill of the community for its success as an alternative to traditional methods of dealing with child sexual abuse. At the end of the general business meeting, everyone is given a ten-minute break to get a cup of coffee if they wish before going to the rooms where the smaller groups meet.

Activity 4. Self-Help Groups

Each trainee chooses the group that most interests him or her. Once in the group, the members and the trainees introduce themselves by their first names. The trainees observe and eventually participate as members in the group's drama.

A staff counselor and a PU member who has had leadership training usually co-lead the group. If a trained PU member is not available, co-leadership is provided by another staff member or intern. At the end of the two hours, the facilitators call attention to the time and terminate the session; the group usually ends with a farewell circle.

Activity 5. Optional After-Group Get-Together

After the sessions, trainees are given a few minutes to make personal contact with anyone who has especially touched them during the group sessions. Afterward, most trainees join various PU members, staff, and interns at a nearby coffee shop for an informal get-together.

Unit IV. The Intern-Staff Meeting and Co-Counseling Sessions

Unit Description

The fourth day of training introduces the trainees to the volunteer intern component of the CSATP. As described in Module 4 of Unit 1, volunteer interns are either administrative interns who assist in the CSATP office, or counseling interns who counsel clients under the supervision of staff counselors. The interns and staff hold meetings every Thursday morning, and these meetings are particularly vital to the interns' training: they provide the interns with a supportive group setting in which to learn the skills and attitudes necessary for productive counseling of sexually abused children and their families. The meetings also give the interns a chance to discuss the CSATP and its dealings with the criminal justice system and the official community in general. But the principal purpose of the weekly meetings is to provide an opportunity for interns to know each other more intimately so that they can air and exchange anxieties and frustrations as well as the satisfactions they experience in their work with clients. The

interns and staff must be able to work together harmoniously in the treatment of clients.

The meetings commence at 10 A.M. with a half-hour business meeting. The group encounter portion occupies the balance of the morning (from 10:30 until 12:30 P.M.). Following the lunch break, trainees join assigned counselors for the second module of this unit, in which they continue to learn counseling skills by participating in a variety of individual, couple, and family counseling sessions.

Unit Content, Module Design, and Activities Requirements

Module	Time	Activity	Time	Materials
1. Intern-Staff Meeting	2.5 hrs.	1. Introductions and Welcome	15 min.	Coffee and tea
		2. Business	30 min.	
		3. Group Encounter	1 hr. 40 min.	Training props, if any
		4. Closing	5 min.	Space requirements: a room large enough to accommodate 25 people. The most satisfactory meeting places have been in homes, where the atmosphere is more conducive to intimacy than typical institutional settings.
2. Practicum II, Co-Counseling Sessions	3 hrs.	1. Briefing, Feedback and Discussion	1 hr.	
		2. Co-Counseling Sessions	2 hrs.	

Unit Goals

To provide trainees the opportunity to:

1. Learn about the volunteer intern component of the CSATP;

2. Experience an intern–staff meeting and learn its functions;

3. Continue to learn about counseling clients by participating in actual counseling sessions; and

4. See how interns participate directly in the counseling of sexually abusive families.

Unit Rationale

The strong volunteer intern program has been absolutely essential to the success of the Santa Clara County CSATP. For one thing, it provides a work force without which the program's efforts would be severely hampered. Moreover, it draws on the community directly for its workers, thus involving and educating the community by making citizens aware of the program's existence and the way it deals with incest and child sexual abuse in general.

Again, rather than simply learning about the interns by hearing a lecture, the trainees meet with the interns, join them in their work, and have an opportunity to listen and respond as interns voice both their positive and negative feelings. In the meeting, they learn the practical problems as well as the emotional problems of child sexual abuse, with which the interns must cope. And in the practicum, which occurs in the afternoon, they participate with the counselors in sessions with sexually abusive families.

Unit Objectives

At the end of this unit, trainees should be able to:

1. Understand the importance of a volunteer intern program to the success of any CSATP;

2. Know what to expect of volunteer interns in a CSATP: what interns should be able to contribute and how they can best aid the counseling staff in its work;

3. Understand the value of weekly meetings that put into practice the humanistic philosophy and methods of the program; and

4. Begin to have an idea of how to establish a volunteer intern program for the CSATP in their own community.

Module 1: Intern–Staff Meeting

Description

The interns and staff meet each week, usually at someone's home. A typical meeting has many functions, including the sharing of information, the voicing of conflicts of interest between the criminal justice system and the CSATP, and the discussion of issues of confidentiality and client privilege. Meetings also provide a forum for interns to voice complaints and to suggest improvements in the program. In a learn-by-doing process that enables participants to internalize the experience rather than just adding it to their intellectual larder, the sessions also provide training in specific counseling techniques such as gestalt, transactional analysis, and bioenergetics. And the meetings furnish an opportunity for interns to staff difficult cases and to get feedback and input on possible interventions.

The principal purpose of the meetings, however, is to provide a group format where both staff and interns can vent feelings of frustration, revulsion, inadequacy, and fear. These emotions inevitably arise when working intensively with sexually abusive families, and the interns and staff must explore, resolve, and assimilate these feelings for their personal and professional growth.

The weekly intern–staff meetings are open to as many counseling and administrative interns and staff as can attend. Representatives of Parents United also may attend. Probation officers, officers from the Sexual Assault Investigation Unit, and other cognizant professionals from official and nonofficial agencies frequently are visitors.

Group leadership rotates among interns every two months. Another intern is responsible for taking notes on the business part of the meeting. The first thirty minutes are for introductions and business, and the remaining time is devoted to personal interaction, sharing professional and personal frustrations and satisfactions, and learning new skills and techniques.

To finish getting important information from visiting professionals, the business portion of the meeting is occasionally extended. On the other hand, if one of the group members has a pressing need to discuss a sensitive personal issue and does not wish to reveal it before visitors or believes that visitors will interfere with the group's ability to cope with the issue, then s/he may request that visitors not be included in that part of the meeting. Such requests occur rarely because staff members fully recognize and endorse the importance of the meeting to the trainees. However, staff members participating in a group process must be given the same consideration as clients, who have the right not to discuss their problems before visitors.

In sum, the meetings provide a warm and mutually supportive atmosphere that helps avoid burn-out and feelings of isolation. It is a time of intimate sharing and contact that fosters trust and cooperation between members of the team.

Goals

To provide trainees the opportunity to:

1. Participate directly in the intern–staff meeting;

2. Become familiar with the meeting's multiple purposes: to deal with CSATP administrative tasks; to share information about the criminal justice system and its relationship with the CSATP; to coordinate counseling services to the family; to exchange mutual help and support between members of the staff and volunteers; and to provide specific group skills training;

3. Experience the group process as a way of internalizing core CSATP concepts such as the value of teamwork and the importance of reciprocal caring and support in human relationships;

4. Observe that a staff meeting not restricted to business matters alone can engender an atmosphere of trust, effective communication, and due recognition to the unique contributions of interns; and

5. Note that the intern–staff meeting is in fact a self-help group where intimate interpersonal encounters can help to dissolve the feelings of alienation that lead to burn-out.

Rationale

A sensitive observer visiting a typical agency will often note that the relationships among workers are often taut, distrustful, and defensive. Some of the workers may try to neutralize the atmosphere of uneasiness and anxiety by light, teasing conversations or displays of rough camaraderie. However, these devices can readily be seen as attempts to cover up the underlying competitive tension. Such agencies usually are inefficient, have contentious relationships with other agencies, and have high rates of employee turnover, sick leave, and other evidences of burn-out.

A proven initial step toward changing this poor work climate is to hold weekly meetings which not only allow time to settle the normal business problems but which include sufficient time (at least one and a half hours) for a structured group process led by two people, preferably one female and the other male. The leaders should have skills in encounter group techniques, such as those for effective communication, transactional analysis, gestalt awareness, and bioenergetics.*

However, an agency that would like to set up a weekly encounter group session should not be dissuaded if the leaders are not knowledgeable of all the techniques mentioned. If they know the methods of effective communication, they can get the group started; the more sophisticated techniques can be learned later. It is not difficult to teach people how to listen actively to a speaker without judging the content or the feelings in the statement, and it is not hard for them to learn to assume responsibility for the messages they send back to the speaker. Most group members soon learn the techniques of effective communication because the rewards come quickly.

*For examples of group techniques, see H. R. Lewis and H. S. Streifield, *Growth Games* (New York: Harcourt Brace Jovanovich, 1970).

Objectives

At the end of this module, trainees should be able to:

1. Appreciate the value of regularly scheduled intern–staff meetings;

2. Recognize that the meetings must include a structured group process that allows personal and job-related frustrations and anxieties to be vented in an atmosphere of acceptance and trust, and that such a process fosters the warm, cooperative work relationships that prevent burn-out; and

3. Begin to learn how to conduct effective staff meetings.

Activity 1. Introductions and Welcome

When the group has gathered, the group leader asks for introductions around the room. Trainees tell which agencies they work for, their job titles, and the counties they are from; CSATP people tell what their job functions and titles are. Other visitors also introduce themselves. The trainees are welcomed by the leader and encouraged to participate fully in the meeting.

Activity 2. Business

The business meeting deals with new and old business. It might include such topics as tightening screening procedures for new interns to reduce turnover, setting criteria for selection of interns, coordinating transportation for DSU children, what constitutes a maximally active intern in terms of families being seen, CSATP requirements for supervision of interns, procedures for hearing intern complaints, problems of recruitment of interns, training needs of interns, and other intern-related business. In general, unless the topic under discussion is very pressing, the business part ends promptly on time so that the experiential portion of the morning can begin.

Activity 3. Group Encounter

The group encounter develops in various ways. The following examples are taken from the experiences of the Santa Clara County CSATP. Although they are only illustrations (and certainly not a program of scheduled events), they show what sorts of things might happen in an intern–staff meeting.

Example 1. A counselor presents a troubled drawing by an eight-year-old girl who was raped by her grandfather. The counselor offers an interpretation of the drawing based on her experience with the client and her understanding of such drawings. She and the others present express their feelings of revulsion and anger as they analyze the drawing and the ugly visions it elicits.

The group leader asks the members of the group to form dyads with one person play-acting the grandfather and the other the counselor. The grandfather role may be improvised as the actor perceives him: as being resistant, blaming, unremorseful, defensive, nonchalant, or denying. The counselors respond with their own feelings, giving words to their anger, disgust, frustration, and helplessness.

The "counselors" and "clients" then switch roles so that each has a chance to identify with the grandfather. In reflecting the grandfather's feelings, the counselor (or intern, trainee, etc.) may become aware that s/he often experiences similar feelings. By arriving at some understanding of these less pleasant aspects of oneself, s/he can better accept such feelings in a client.

Example 2. An intern says he often feels uninvolved and bored leading a Parents United group. The group leader asks the intern to contact his feeling of uninvolvement by giving it a voice. (See sample dialogue on next page.)

Example 3. An intern shares her feelings about the end of her marriage and impending divorce. She feels sad, hurt, and afraid. The others listen with sympathy and give her time to unburden herself. They then share their own experiences of relationships ending. They offer understanding, compassion, and support. The intern cries and is comforted by the group.

Sample Dialogue

Intern:	I feel out of it, like I'm really bored with you people and your endless conflicts and hassles. I don't really like you, or being here with you, but I have to pretend to because I'm supposed to be helping you. I'd rather be home.
Group leader:	(After a pause.) What are you experiencing now?
Intern:	I feel like they're all watching me and judging me. I don't think they like me at all.
Group leader:	Be "them" for a moment and express what you're imagining they are thinking and feeling.
Intern:	He's such a bore and I don't like being here with him, but I'm stuck because I have to be here by court order. This guy doesn't know what he's doing, but I still have to pretend I like being here.
Group leader:	Repeat this statement as if it were your own.
Intern:	I'm a real bore, really a drag. I don't know what I'm doing and I'm afraid to let on. I don't believe they like me or want to learn anything from me, and I can't give them anything worthwhile. I feel very unsure of myself right now and doubt if I'll ever make it as a counselor.
Group leader:	(With a sigh of recognition.) Yes, that's how I often feel. (Most of the group members and their heads in firm agreement.)

Activity 4. Closing

Arms around each other, the group forms a circle and stands silently for a few moments, absorbing the group energy. A few may wish to express their appreciation of the group and the meaning that the experience of being together has had for them.

Module 2: Practicum II: Co-Counseling Sessions

Description

This module is a continuation and elaboration of the practicum of the previous day, the co-counseling sessions. This time the trainees will each be attending client counseling sessions with a different counselor. This holds true for the remainder of the co-counseling sessions, with trainees rotating through the counselors, so that at the end of the sixth session each trainee will have had the opportunity to work with different counselors.

When counselors are not available for one reason or another, the more advanced counselor-interns share their time with the trainees. Since the staff counselor's time for a particular family may be limited by a demanding case load, complementary counseling responsibilities are delegated to the counseling interns to ensure sufficient counseling services to the family. For example, the staff counselor might concentrate on the marital pair, while the intern counsels the victim and her mother, individually and/or together, under the staff counselor's supervision. The intern might arrange to see the daughter at school during her noon hour, or at the family home, if she cannot come to the office.

Interns usually can devote more time to a family than a staff counselor. Trainees who spend time with interns will see other facets of the treatment, such as those taking place in the home, at the children's shelter, or at Juvenile Hall. The counselors describe and discuss the dynamics of each case with the trainee before and after the counseling session.

Goals

To provide trainees the opportunity to:

1. Gain exposure to a variety of counseling styles, have counseling experiences with a broad spectrum of clients, and become familiar with the different transactions that take place during a counseling program for a family (for example, at the initial interview, at midpoint counseling, and at termination of counseling);

2. Increase their participation in counseling sessions and augment their counseling skills by practice and feedback from the counselor;

3. Observe how counselors elicit emotions and explore deeper feelings, fantasies, and memories as a means for enhancing the client's self-understanding;

4. Observe how the counselor validates the client's subjective reality and respects the client's personal boundaries;

5. Note that counseling techniques are not used for their own sake but are tailored to the client's needs;

6. Evaluate the nature of the relationship between the counselor and the client and determine whether it is one in which the client has confidence in the counselor's competence and feels that the counselor genuinely cares about his or her welfare; and

7. Witness how each counselor in his or her own way adheres to the humanistic approach.

Rationale

Trainees should be exposed to the styles of a variety of counselors. They should also be shown the advantages to the family of cooperative counseling between a staff counselor and an intern. By working with interns, trainees will appreciate their value and realize that eventually the professional staff of their own CSATP must be complemented with trained volunteer interns so that vital, cost-effective, and community-based services can be provided to families.

Objectives

At the end of this module, trainees should be able to:

1. Be more confident about their ability to deal with a variety of clients and counseling problems;

2. Internalize some of the humanistic counseling methods employed by the counselors;

3. Become increasingly aware of feelings evoked in them by the clients and be able to disclose and discuss these feelings with the counselor at the end of the session;

4. Be more at ease in challenging the interventions of the counselor and requesting feedback on their own work; and

5. Understand some of the ways the counselor disrupts the family's dysfunctional patterns and teaches its members to replace them with productive patterns that abet the family's evolution to a healthy system.

Unit V. Experiential and Didactic Workshop and Review of the Week

Unit Description

This is the last day of the first week of training. The day's three modules are devoted to discussions and experiential learning exercises. In Module 1, trainees recall, discuss, and question the instructional materials presented in the previous four days of training. They continue to explore early experiences in their family of origin, including their early sexual development and key experiences and insights during adolescence, young adulthood, and recent life phases. The trainees break for lunch (Module 2) before beginning Module 3, in which they discuss case management and how to build effective teamwork. Toward the end of Module 3 they are asked to start thinking of their personal requirements in preparing themselves for the task of establishing CSATPs in their own communities

and to request assistance from the trainers in this regard before the training course ends.

Unit Goals

To provide trainees the opportunity to:

1. Gain confidence and competence in the group process;

2. Become increasingly aware of their own attitudes and feelings, in particular those that have been repressed;

3. Learn additional methods for self-management;

4. Learn more about CSATP administration and case management; and

5. Assess the training in terms of the requirements and constraints of their own communities to make sure they have the information they need before they leave.

Unit Content, Module Design, and Activities Requirements

Module	Time	Activity	Time	Materials
1. Review and Personal Interaction	2.5 hrs.	1. Recalling the Week's Training Experiences	10 min.	Space requirements: large (20' × 30') room, chairs and/or pillows for all participants. Room should be pleasant and the floor should be carpeted, if possible.
		2. Sharing of Experiences	1.5 hrs.	
		3. Analysis of Experiences	50 min.	
2. Lunch with Staff	1.5 hrs.			
3. Administration and Coordination	3 hrs.	1. Administration and Case Management	1 hr.	Interagency Relationship chart, case management forms.
		2. Interagency Coordination	1 hr.	
		3. Typical Action Plan for Starting a CSATP	1 hr.	

Unit Rationale

The two experiential and didactic workshops of the first week and the two given in the second week are designed for intense practice and discussion of the principles and methods of the CSATP. The concepts are fundamental and are not difficult to describe. How well they are practiced with conviction, however, depends upon how well they have been absorbed. For example, most people will agree that a judgmental attitude in a counselor will not simply nullify his or her effectiveness but will be harmful to clients. But we live in a judgmental society, and all of us, including counselors, are continually conditioned accordingly.

The converse of a judgmental attitude is an accepting attitude. Again, most professionals will agree that human beings, as natural phenomena, are as they are and not as we want them to be; and counseling for positive changes in a client's behavior starts with acceptance of the client as s/he comes to you. In this unit the discussion on an accepting versus a judgmental attitude in the counselor is usually thorough and intense and ends with the participants nodding their heads in unanimous agreement. But when the principles are put to the test in the experiential transactions that occur in the group sessions and in the dyadic role-playing exercises, the trainees and the trainers alike are surprised to discover that their judgmental conditioning has had a more powerful influence than they thought.

This unit and Units VII and X of the second week of training are therefore intended to impress on the trainees the importance of continually practicing the methods they are being introduced to if they wish to become humanistic counselors. And they are informed repeatedly that this same humanistic attitude must be exercised in their dealings with co-workers if they wish to convert them to the CSATP approach.

In addition to understanding and implementing the rule that the leader of a CSATP will be successful to the degree that s/he has adopted a humanistic attitude, trainees must also learn certain basic skills. Therefore, in the third module of the unit, the trainees thoroughly review the problems of administration and coordination and how these apply to case management.

Finally, the trainees should ensure that the training course provides all the information it can for their unique needs. To this end, they are asked to reflect on the specific requirements of their communities.

Unit Objectives

At the end of this unit, trainees should be able to:

1. Be more confident about their future performance as counselors and leaders of CSATPs in their regions;

2. Know how to continue to work on their personal and professional development;

3. Realize that respect for their clients' processes depends on their respect for their own processes;

4. Apply some of the group exercises in their future work as group leaders;

5. Have a better understanding of CSATP administration and case management;

6. Begin to integrate the training and to anticipate how the knowledge will be helpful in starting up their own CSATPs; and

7. Begin to ask for information specific to their own needs and those of the communities they represent.

Module 1: Review and Personal Interaction

Description

This module takes up the entire morning. Assembled as a group, the trainees share their reactions to co-counseling experiences and feelings about the first four days of training. The trainer guides the discussion and concentrates on affective communication. As cases are brought up, the trainer encourages the trainees to discuss the dynamics in terms of their own experiences in their families of origin, in particular their sexual development and values and how these were influenced by parents, siblings, relatives, and other significant people.

Goals

To provide trainees the opportunity to:

1. Recall thoughts and feelings from the co-counseling sessions and try to trace them to early experiences in their nuclear families, especially those relating to their sexual development, and share them with group members;

2. Describe some of their own cases of sexually abusive families and form ideas of how the training will affect future contacts; and

3. Discuss positive and negative reactions about the training in counseling.

Rationale

By this point it should be clear to the trainees that counseling sexually abusive families requires a great deal of self-examination on the part of the counselor. This module gives the trainees practice in this art, particularly in exploring those aspects of the self that may have been long repressed. This morning's work may open up avenues of thought and feeling that trainees have never been aware of before. The trainees must learn to recognize the significance of personal exploration for their own growth and for their effectiveness in helping their clients.

Objectives

At the end of this module, trainees should be able to:

1. Start to integrate their counseling experiences and skills from the first week of training;

2. Understand better how sexual attitudes derived from their family of origin affect their interactions with clients; and

3. Anticipate problems they will encounter in their work.

Activity 1. Recalling the Week's Training Experiences

The trainees are asked to relax themselves, using the exercise they learned in Unit II or their own techniques. (The trainer may ask for a volunteer to conduct a group relaxation exercise.) They are given five minutes for the relaxation exercise and then are instructed to reflect on the week's experiences, especially those in the co-counseling sessions and in the PU/DSU groups.

Activity 2. Sharing of Experiences

The trainees are encouraged to express their thoughts and feelings about the training to date. Here is a typical discussion:

Trainee A: *I'm aware now that we must confront our own feelings each time we work with an incestuous family . . . our feelings about our own sexuality. Our emotions are involved whether we want them to be or not.*

Trainee B: *You're right. Incest is a common denominator that affects all of us, because it affects our sexuality, our most basic biological drive.*

Trainer: *(To Trainee B.) Jane, could you tie that statement to a personal experience—one perhaps that happened in your own family?*

Jane: *(Pausing and reflecting.) Well, I remember an incident that kind of set the tone for changes in my relationships with my mother and father. I was about twelve years old and beginning to develop. Before going to bed it was my habit to kiss my mother and father. This time I was in my nightgown. Mom was standing and I gave her a hug and a kiss. Dad was sitting down watching TV. I sat on his lap and gave him a strong hug and a kiss. It felt good and I lingered a bit.*

When I got up, I noticed a strange look on my mother's face and she said something like, "Janie, you're growing up now and I think you should wear a robe over your nightgown."

What she said was innocent enough, but it was the look on her face that was strange. I suddenly felt embarrassed and guilty . . . and the relationship between my father and me became less close.

The conversation continues along these personal lines. When it deviates, the trainer intercedes and gently guides it so that it becomes personal again. Occasionally the trainer also contributes with a personal story or feeling. At a later point the discussion turns to experiences as parents:

Trainee C: *Yeah, I know what you mean. We kiss on the mouth in our family. My daughter's fifteen and when we kiss I realize now that I feel differently than when I kissed her as a child. It's a mixed-up feeling of exhilaration, pride, uneasiness, and even stubbornness. I'm gonna continue to kiss her on the mouth as long as she feels okay about it.*

Trainee D: *Are you sure she feels okay about it? I hate it when my husband kisses my daughter that way.*

Somewhat later, Trainee D says: "We try not to be sticky about nudity in our house. Last week my son, who's sixteen, had just finished taking a shower. The bathroom door was open and as I passed it I saw him standing naked in front of the mirror getting ready to shave. He was lithe, tanned, beautiful. I felt a gush of excitement—maybe he reminded me of my husband when his body was that way. Anyway, the excitement wasn't motherly entirely. I can now remember and tell you without shame, but with some wonder, that the female part of me wanted to embrace him."

Activity 3. Analysis of Experiences

The trainer leads the group in an analysis of the experiences exchanged in Activity 2: the feelings they had in the co-counseling and PU/DSU sessions and how these were related to feelings stemming from events in their own families. The analysis helps the trainees to understand how the principles and methods of the CSATP were derived. The trainer sums up the discussion at appropriate points. Here are some points a trainer might make in this activity: "I think you see now why we keep stressing concepts like 'acceptance' and 'self-awareness.' Several of us remembered sexual feelings towards members of both our original and current families. We repressed these feelings because we were told that they were bad, unnatural. Of course, we still haven't brought to self-awareness all these feelings.

"I'm sure I haven't—there must be many 'close calls' in my past of sexual stimulation involving my sisters, mother, and daughters that I must have repressed. Maybe I'm rationalizing these and the ones I've become aware of when I say they are natural.

"But it makes good sense to say they are natural, because we all have sexual drives and they start from birth. In fact, erections have been detected in X rays of male infants even before birth, and the penises of boy infants will often pop up when they are placed on their mothers' stomachs after delivery. Several mothers have confided to me—often with some shame or chagrin—that they remember coming to orgasm while breast-feeding. . . .

"Now, if I can accept as natural my sexual feelings towards my daughter and learn to become aware of them when they arise, I can learn to control them. I can see clearly that if I allow myself to act out these feelings I would be exploiting my daughter, that I would be denying her the fatherly love and guidance she most needs from me. And I would be denying myself the great, deep-seated pleasure that comes from being a good father.

"If, on the other hand, I unconsciously repress my sexual feelings towards my daughter through guilt, they will come out somehow in ugly ways beyond my control.

"Some common examples of uncontrolled behavior dictated by repressed sexual feelings in the father are: he avoids her when she tries to recapture the closeness between them during childhood; he makes sarcastic comments about her clothes; he rejects her boyfriends to the point of forbidding her to see them; he harasses his wife about her supposed inability to control the daughter's comings and goings; and so on.

"In extreme cases, the father's dissatisfactions with his life come to the boiling point. He feels alienated from his wife; his job isn't going right; he feels continually resentful, bored, fretful, and anxious. Now and then we come to the even more extreme case of a father who has been abused and rejected by his parents as a child and is in the down period I just described. This father finds himself irresistibly drawn to his daughter, he finds or makes opportunities to be with her alone, and eventually he loses all control and compulsively begins and continues to molest her.

"Before we can treat this father we must be able to accept him as an evolving human being. Before we can accept him we must learn to be accepting of ourselves. Again, I must emphasize that accepting him as a person does not mean that we must also condone the specific dysfunctional behavior. Before we can teach him the self-awareness than enables self-management, we must learn these arts for ourselves."

Module 2: Lunch with Staff

The trainees and staff eat lunch together. They can bring a brown bag lunch to eat at the training building, or they can eat at a nearby restaurant.

Module 3. Administration and Coordination

Description

This module focuses on the problems of starting and coordinating a CSATP. The trainees review the information they have received from the administrative staff of the Santa Clara County CSATP and ask for clarification of any points that they don't understand. The case management of a typical family is discussed in detail. The trainees are reassured that the administration problems they will face in the early stages of their CSATPs will not necessarily be the same or as complex as those faced by the Santa Clara County CSATP, which has been in operation for over ten years.

The trainees are requested to start thinking of the initial actions they will take during the start-up stages of their own CSATPs. For example, they should think about the following questions: Which people would they like on their CSATP staff? Which supervisors must they convince for releasing these people for roles in the CSATP? What are the functions of the start-up staff, and to whom will they be assigned? What are the important initial tasks and who will be responsible for doing them?

The trainees are advised that only a general, preliminary discussion of the questions will be undertaken in this module. The purpose of the discussion is to motivate them to start thinking about the unique requirements and constraints of their own regions. They should see to it that the questions that come to mind will be answered by the trainers during the second week of training.

The trainees are also informed that on the last day of training the trainers and the group will collectively help each of them to devise a specific plan of action for starting a CSATP in their own communities.

Goals

To provide trainees the opportunity to:

1. Discuss and clarify the administrative functions of the Santa Clara County CSATP;

2. Study in detail the case management of a typical client family; and

3. Start thinking of their own unique situation so as to make sure that in the following week they will receive information that will help them satisfy their own specific requirements.

Rationale

It is important for the trainees to observe the operations of a CSATP in advanced stages of development to appreciate the benefits the clients (and the staff) derive from a mature program. But the trainees should be exposed also to the daily problems the staff must deal with to keep the program on course. For example, the trainees will see that although the program has won the general support of co-workers and personnel from other official agencies, this support is hardly unanimous. Many will question, at times harshly, the humanistic stance of the program, and the trainees should observe how staff members contend with difficult policemen, deputy district attorneys, defense attorneys, and other official interveners.

Some trainees will feel overwhelmed by and inadequate to the task of getting a CSATP under way. They are reminded repeatedly that the local program has been several years in the making and that their start-up effort will not be difficult once they decide to go ahead with it. In this last module of the first week of training the trainees begin to focus on immediate objectives and to gather the specific tools for their initial tasks when they return home. Usually, these tasks will be to get their supervisors to agree to let them specialize in child sexual abuse cases; to build a small core team—at the beginning, one or two CPS workers and one or two mental health workers are sufficient; to start seeing clients; and to start Parents United and Daughters and Sons United groups as soon as they have two or three client families.

Objectives

At the end of this module, trainees should be able to:

1. Have a better grasp of the administrative operations of a CSATP in its advanced stages, especially regarding the processing of clients; the coordination of official interventions such as police, social services, defense and prosecuting attorneys, and probation departments; the development of the self-help component (Parents United and Daughters and Sons United); the selection and administration of counselors; the development of a cadre of volunteers for administrative and counseling functions; and client data gathering and management;

2. Realize that a CSATP such as the one in Santa Clara County requires years to develop;

3. Begin to identify some of the initial tasks facing them when they return to their communities;

4. Start a list of questions regarding these anticipated tasks to get all the help they can from the trainers before the course ends; and

5. Understand that the trainers will be available to them by telephone even after they return home and that they can expect at least one visit from the training staff to help them start a CSATP.

Activity 1. Administration and Case Management

This activity concentrates on CSATP administration, particularly case management of client families. A typical family is described by the trainer and taken through the system step by step, from the point of entry (or referral) to release from the program. The decisions that must be made by the staff at various junctions in the process are described, and differences in the handling of child-victims, mothers, siblings, and offenders are pointed out.

The trainer uses the Interagency Relationship Chart, auxiliary flow charts and case management forms as aids in describing the process.

Child Sexual Abuse
Treatment Program
Initial Evaluation and
Treatment Plan

Victim's Name _____

Family Name _____

Persons Seen _____

Date(s) _____

Staff Counselor doing evaluation _____

    I.   Initial Evaluation

   II.   Treatment Plan

       A.   Victim

          1. Individual counseling by staff counselor . . . .   Yes____ No____
          2. Participation in Daughters & Sons United . . . .   Yes____ No____
          3. Other _____   Yes____ No____

       B.   Offender

          1. Individual counseling by staff counselor . . . .   Yes____ No____
          2. Marital counseling. . . . .   Yes____ No____
          3. Family counseling. . . . .   Yes____ No____
          4. Participation in Parents United . . . .   Yes____ No____
          5. Other _____   Yes____ No____

       C.   Spouse

          1. Individual counseling by staff counselor . . . .   Yes____ No____
          2. Marital counseling. . . . .   Yes____ No____
          3. Family counseling. . . . .   Yes____ No____
          4. Participation in Parents United . . . .   Yes____ No____
          5. Other _____   Yes____ No____

   III.   Comments relating to above treatment plan:

   IV.   Treatment plan for other members of the family or persons significant to the situation:

Santa Clara County Juvenile Probation Department Child Sexual Abuse Treatment Program Case Progress Report

_____ 1st Report
_____ Quarterly Report

DATE DUE ___/___/___

COUNSELOR _____

INTERN _____

FOLDER NAME _____ AKA _____ FILE # _____

MO./Sub. _____ FA./Sub. _____ OTHER _____

VICTIM 1 (V-1) _____ VICTIM 2 (V-2) _____ SIBS. _____

Indicate # of hours in counseling or type of contact and with whom

Date	Mo.	Fa.	Oth.	V-1	V-2	Sibs.	Mar.	Family-code participants	No Show	Follow-up

CHANGES IN RESIDENCE (if foster/group home placement, include name of placement)

NAME	REL.	NEW ADDRESS & TELEPHONE

COURT STATUS

JUVENILES—Disposition of JPD case (SAI, IS, W&I 300/601/602) or changes in status

NAME	Vic/Sib/Perp.	DISPOSITION	PROBATION OFFICER	COUNSELING ORDER?

ADULT PERPETRATORS Stage in criminal justice process, i.e. complaint pending, settled w/o complaint, arrested, O.R., convicted, sentence (specify)

NAME _____ DISP. _____ COUNSELING ORDER? _____

LIST OF INDIVIDUALS SEEN DURING REPORT PERIOD, RELATIONSHIP, INTERN ASSIGNED IF ANY

NAME	RELATIONSHIP	INTERN	NAME	RELATIONSHIP	INTERN

WHAT INDIVIDUAL ARE YOU NO LONGER SEEING AND SHOULD BE TERMINATED AND REASON

SHOULD THIS CASE BE TERMINATED?_____ COMPLETED BY _____ DATE _____

Santa Clara County Juvenile Probation Department Child Sexual Abuse Treatment Program Termination

Case Name(s)_____ AKA_____

File #_____ County of Residence_____

Reason for Referral_____

_____

Individual(s) being terminated (LIST)_____

_____

Did client(s) complete the program?   ☐ YES   ☐ NO   If NO, explain_____

_____

Are you terminating the *complete* case?   ☐ YES   ☐ NO

PARENTS UNITED/DAUGHTERS & SONS UNITED

D&SU Participation (who, length of time, frequency)_____

_____

    Will the child(ren) continue in DSU?   ☐ YES   ☐ NO

PU Participation (who, length of time, frequency)_____

_____

    Will the adult(s) continue in PU?   ☐ YES   ☐ NO

AGENCIES INVOLVED

☐ Police Agency (specify department)_____

☐ Juvenile Probation Department_____

☐ Juvenile Court_____

☐ Adult Probation Department_____

☐ Adult Court_____

☐ O.R. Release Program_____

☐ Other (specify)_____

Was the Juvenile Probation Officer notified of termination? ☐ YES ☐ NO

    If NO, explain_____

Was the Adult Probation Officer notified of termination? ☐ YES ☐ NO

    If NO, explain_____

REASON FOR TERMINATION_____

_____

_____

_____

_____

_____

COUNSELOR: DATE:

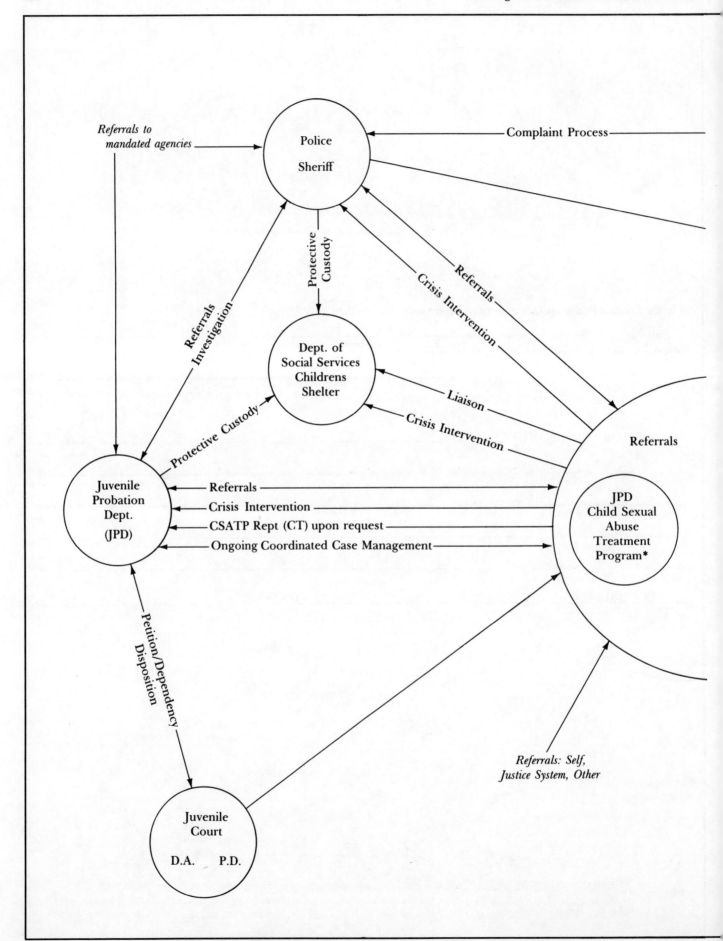

*CSATP and PU are separate but linked programs. Services are closely coordinated for maximum case management. The type of linkage with other impacting justice system agencies usually involve both CSATP and PU. Thus, to facilitate the creation of this chart, both programs are shown within the dotted enclosure.

Activity 2. Interagency Coordination

This activity focuses on the methods employed by the staff in winning the approval of the CSATP approach from police, defense and prosecuting attorneys, social service workers, probation officers, judges, and rehabilitation officers. It is emphasized, again, that approval and cooperation are achieved by patience and demonstration rather than through argument and exhortation. The trainers recount early experiences and tell how police and probation officers were gradually won over.

The importance of the self-help groups is underscored not only for the benefits they provide to clients but also for convincing key personnel in the official system of the effectiveness of the new approach. This is accomplished by inviting such people first to Parents United meetings and later to the children's meetings. (Usually a Parents United group is ready to accept one or two visitors after a few meetings.)

Activity 3. Typical Action Plan for Starting a CSATP

A Child Sexual Abuse Treatment Program based on the Santa Clara County model is usually started by two workers attached to Child Protective Services (CPS) or an equivalent agency who have been authorized to take on this responsibility. One of the workers does all the investigations while the other takes on the task of case management and the key responsibility of leading the development of the CSATP.

In sparsely populated regions, however, CPS may be forced to assign all functions to one worker. The worker in this case will be faced not only with the leadership role, but also with the delicate (but not impossible) task of conducting an investigation while convincing the client-family that s/he will perform this service and future case management services with the best interests of the family in mind.

It must be emphasized that a CSATP cannot be started if child molestation cases are dispersed randomly among agency workers. To cope effectively with such cases, a CPS agency must focus its energy by funneling all cases to a small, strongly led team of workers who will develop a comprehensive network of service to sexually abused children and their families, i.e., a CSATP. The same rule applies to mental health agencies who wish to take part in setting up a CSATP. At first, all incoming cases should be referred to one counselor who thus will be given the opportunity to develop the special counseling skills required for incest cases and other forms of child molestation. In addition to the counseling function, this worker will collaborate with other CPS workers in organizing a CSATP.

Assuming that a typical team has been formed, the cases flow from the investigator to the coordinator, who does the initial crisis work and takes the next step in the treatment process by involving the client-family with the mental health worker for long-term counseling.

Once a small case load is accumulated, the team begins to form the self-help component. The first step is to arrange telephone contacts between members of a new family and corresponding members of a family in a more advanced stage of treatment. The telephone conversations between the mothers, victims, and perpetrators of the two families usually will motivate them to meet personally. The first group meeting of the adults forms the nucleus of a future Parents United chapter wherein group sessions are led by two members of the CSATP organizing team. Similarly, the nucleus of a Daughters and Sons United chapter is formed as soon as the children get together for their first group meeting.

The PU/DSU component becomes the core source of energy for the growth of a CSATP. After a few meetings to allow the group to gain confidence and a sense of unity, the group leaders remind the members that one of the principal functions of a Parents United group is to educate the community, particularly the people acting in official capacities in child sexual abuse cases. These officials must learn to understand families troubled by incest by interacting with them personally and observing first-hand how the families begin to cope with their problems by helping one another. Only by educating the official interveners such as the police, lawyers, probation officers, and judges can the members of Parents United hope for enlightened handling of their cases and those of members to come.

The trainees are advised to spend little time in holding meetings to "sell" the merits of a CSATP to personnel from other agencies, though. It is recommended instead that they concentrate on the following course of action (in which it is assumed that a CPS worker and a mental health worker from the same community have come together for training):

1. Convince their supervisors to route all child sexual abuse cases to them. This is a key first step because it is the only way in which expertise can be developed in an agency. Most CPS and mental health agencies distribute new cases to workers on a case load and/or geographical basis. Usually, in communities which do not have a CSATP, only a relatively few cases of child sexual abuse cases are reported.

   To start a CSATP, all these cases must be sent to one CPS worker and to one mental health worker. A CSATP begins to form and to develop in effectiveness and size as the case workers become more expert and as the new resource is made known to the community, particularly if the new resource includes a PU/DSU component.

   The number of workers to be assigned the responsibility of developing a CSATP will, of course, depend on the size of the community and the referral rate of child sexual abuse cases. However, the referral rate of the average community of half a million inhabitants without a CSATP rarely rises above fifty cases annually, and a CSATP will get started only when the cases are assigned exclusively to one or two case workers in each agency.

2. Start working with clients. The CPS worker will be responsible for the coordination of services to the family and for helping the mental health worker in the crisis counseling. The mental health worker will be responsible for the in-depth, long-term counseling.

   (In discussing this step and the following associated steps, the trainers review in detail the case management and family counseling procedures described in Part I.)

3. As the case load begins to build, ask the clients in more advanced stages of treatment to contact the new clients.

4. Arrange weekly group counseling for the adult clients and the children, in which the CPS worker and the mental health worker act as co-leaders.

5. Aid the clients in forming Parents United and Daughters and Sons United chapters.

6. Get permission from the groups to invite key official personnel to the meetings.

Once these steps have been described, the trainees discuss the potential exceptions to this general action plan. They are asked to begin to consider carefully and anticipate the special requirements and pitfalls of the communities they represent and to ask for assistance in meeting them from the administrative staff and other cognizant trainers during the last week of training.

The trainees are also informed that on the last day of the course the trainees and the group co-trainers, aided by the legal consultant and representatives of PU, will collaborate in devising a start-up plan of action for each of them. To prepare themselves for a critical assessment of their personal training requirements, the trainees are instructed to read carefully the sections in Part I on case management, on family counseling procedures, and on the development of the self-help component.

Family Service Center
Naval Submarine Base New London
P.O. Box 93
Groton ,Connecticut 06349

Unit VI. Co-Counseling Sessions 3 and 4 (Practicum III)

Unit Description

This day is divided into two modules, each being a co-counseling session of three hours. The morning session begins at 10 A.M. The trainees break for lunch at 1 P.M. and return for the start of the afternoon session at 2 P.M. As indicated in the schedule handed to them, trainees sit with a different counselor in each of the two sessions.

As in Unit III, Module 3, two clients are scheduled for each three-hour session. Each counseling interview lasts about one hour, leaving the third hour for discussion of the cases before and after the interviews.

If an emergency requires the counselor to visit a youngster at the Children's Shelter, talk with a probation officer, attend the juvenile or adult court, or arrange a home counseling session, the trainee will accompany the counselor unless the client's interests would be jeopardized.

Unit Goals

To provide trainees the opportunity to:

1. Continue to work with different counselors and to observe their modes of counseling with a variety of clients in a variety of situations; and

2. Sharpen their awareness of their personal feelings and reactions as they participate in these sessions, which will assist them in understanding and assimilating these feelings with the help of the counselors.

Unit Content, Module Design, and Activities Requirements

Module	Time	Activity	Time	Materials
1. Co-Counseling Sessions	3 hrs.*	1. Briefing, Feedback, and Discussion	1 hr.	* There are three hours for these two activities, and time is spent at the discretion of the counselor according to need. Usually there are two co-counseling sessions of one hour each, and the other hour comprises Activity 1.
		2. Two Co-Counseling Sessions	2 hrs.	
2. Co-Counseling Sessions	3 hrs.*	1. Briefing, Feedback, and Discussion	1 hr.	
		2. Two Co-Counseling Sessions	2 hrs.	

Unit Rationale

Exposing trainees to all kinds of counseling is important because it increases their experience and enhances their confidence. It also allows the counselors to observe the trainees' style and evaluate their skill level. Although it is difficult to expose trainees to all the kinds of counseling done with a variety of clients, every effort should be made to do so. The counselors' backlog of clients should include father-offenders, mothers, child victims of all ages, and adults molested as children. It is desirable for the trainees to gain experience in individual sessions, dyadic sessions (with the marital pair, the mother and daughter, and, if possible, with the father and daughter), and family group sessions.

The counselors and the trainees can discuss the trainees' contributions following the sessions. Trainees are encouraged to ask questions and comment on the counselors'

work as well. This feedback is important to both counselor and trainee; it involves them in a mutual learning process, which confirms the advantages of collaborative counseling.

At the end of the session the counselor can illuminate and expand on his or her interventions and at the same time encourage the trainee to share how s/he would have handled the same situation.

Unit Objectives

At the end of this unit, trainees should be able to:

1. Demonstrate increased ability in the counseling methods used in individual, dyadic, and family counseling of incestuous families;

2. Have a better understanding of the basic humanistic counseling attitude that helps the clients cope with their current trauma and which, with more advanced clients, foster self-awareness and self-management; and

3. Begin to practice the self-directed process of assimilation—of turning the negative energy generated by repressed feelings into positive, growth-promoting energy—and to pass on this ability to their clients.

Module 1: Co-Counseling Sessions

Description

This module is the first of two co-counseling sessions scheduled for the day. It begins at 10 A.M. and lasts until 1 P.M. The intent of the module is again to further the experience of trainees with different counseling styles and a variety of clients. An extremely valuable experience for the trainees, if it can be arranged, is to observe the counselors working with a new family in crisis, at which time the counselor develops a therapeutic structure designed to provide maximum support for the family, instill hope in the family members that they will receive the help they need, and pave the way for future growth and positive changes in the family system.

In the initial session, the counselor attends primarily to the feelings of the client (usually the victim or her mother), listening with empathy and compassion to her often overwhelming feelings of shame, anger, guilt, fear and despair. The counselor recognizes these feelings as manifestations of current inner states and does not question them, but rather chooses to listen and reflect, permitting the client to appreciate the counselor's acceptance of these feelings.

The counselor's intent for the initial session is to build trust and rapport with the client by generating a warm, supportive atmosphere. Highly charged emotional states due to exposure of the incestuous situation must be dealt with before the clients can move on to recall and confront the feelings associated with the incestuous experiences.

In the early sessions, therefore, the counselor does not doggedly go about the task of filling out an interview form. Although the data is necessary, it is obtained gradually during opportune openings. The clinical history of the client is also obtained as an integral part of the counseling objectives and not to satisfy the curiosity of the counselor or to fill historical gaps while overlooking the emotions aroused in the client while s/he tells his or her story.

Occasionally an appointment will be cancelled. When this happens, the counselor and the trainee should spend the time discussing that case or others and in answering the trainee's questions about the program. When this is impossible—if, for example, the counselor has been subpoenaed to appear in a closed court session that excludes the trainee— the trainee may double up with another trainee, sitting in with another counselor.

Of course, this must never be done at the expense of the client, whose feelings must be respected in these matters. A client who feels mildly uncomfortable with one trainee may feel overwhelmed by the presence of two. The counselor must carefully check out the change in conditions with the client, and then weigh the benefits to the client versus the benefits to the trainee. This is especially important with a new client in crisis.

As important as it is for trainees to understand how the counselor generates the climate for future work, the counselor must show total respect and regard for the needs of the client at any particular moment, and this may mean excluding the trainee from the session. Despite these precautions, CSATP counselors have rarely found it necessary to exclude trainees from the counseling sessions. Indeed, when the trainees participate as co-counselors, the clients are usually grateful for the added support. The more advanced clients often welcome the trainees during the introductions. Such clients are motivated to "spread the word" to other counties, a milestone in their counseling progress which reflects the CSATP's emphasis on social responsibility.

Goals

To provide trainees the opportunity to:

1. Make intimate contact with clients and counselors and to take part in an intense and varied experience that goes beyond mere intellectual understanding of treatment concepts;

2. Become familiar with the different kinds of crisis counseling as well as the methods and techniques used to further the goals of self-knowledge, beneficial interpersonal relationships, self-managed growth, and social responsibility;

3. Observe CSATP counselors using the skills that will enable them to implement the methods and principles of humanistic counseling with their own clients;

4. Become more self-aware as they attend to the client's process and feelings;

5. Become acquainted with the multifaceted work of the counselor and its contribution to client growth and productivity; and

6. Ask questions and challenge CSATP counseling methods and their effectiveness, and to begin to assess how CSATP methods and counseling styles compare with their own.

Rationale

The fundamental aim of the CSATP is to resocialize families referred to the program. The counseling sessions expose the trainee to counseling methods and techniques, and most clients are proud to share their experiences and progress when they know the trainee will use this knowledge to help others. Thus, trainee participation in the counseling sessions also helps foster the client's sense of social responsibility.

Module 2: Co-Counseling Sessions

Description:

The second of two co-counseling sessions scheduled for this day, this module begins at 2 P.M., following the lunch break. The training procedure is the same as the one described for Module 1. However, it is hoped that by this time trainees will risk active participation in the sessions as co-counselors rather than remain detached observers. Participation will strengthen the trainee's confidence in his or her ability to work with clients in the sensitive area of child sexual abuse, and will help to put clients at ease as they experience the co-counselor's interest and involvement.

The counselor has a double duty in these co-counseling sessions. In addition to being sensitive to the verbal and nonverbal cues from the client and being conscious of his or her own feelings, thoughts, and fantasies, the counselor also must be aware of the trainee's process as the counseling transactions take place.

The goals, rationale, and objectives for this module are the same as for the preceding module.

Objectives

At the end of this module, trainees should be able to:

1. Have gained some practical experience in counseling and have learned some preliminary skills;

2. Begin to internalize a positive and humanistic treatment stance;

3. Cope with their own negative feelings toward abusive parents and know that these negative feelings will not permit productive intervention; and

4. Understand how the counselor's commitment to an integrated psychosocial counseling approach helps to meet the multiple needs of the family and to provide a regenerative environment that will further the process of resocialization.

In addition, the trainees should be asking and answering for themselves the following kinds of questions:

1. Does the counselor demonstrate rather than preach the virtues of respect, caring, warmth, and empathy?

2. Is there a feeling of trust and congruence between client and counselor?

3. Does the counselor teach attitudes and skills that raise the client's self-esteem?

4. Does the counselor systematically aid the client in removing blocks to self-awareness?

5. Does the counselor manifest him/herself as a person primarily, instead of as a therapist, and is the counselor also learning from the encounter?

6. Does the counselor get involved in obtaining practical assistance and emotional support for the new client?

7. How well does the counselor exploit the client's interactional patterns and make apparent previously unseen facets of the client's personality?

8. Does the counselor experience the client's feelings with comfort, allowing for and encouraging their full expression?

9. How completely does the counselor personify the humanistic principles and methods of treatment?

Unit VII. Experiential and Didactic Workshop

Unit Description

This unit, divided into three modules, continues in the vein of the workshops of the previous week. In the experiential portion of the unit, additional group process techniques are employed for more in-depth exploration of feelings stirred in the co-counseling sessions and in personal and group contacts with adult and minor members of the self-help groups. In the analytic portion of the unit, it is expected that the trainees will now have a more sophisticated understanding of the principles and methods of the CSATP and be more perceptive in challenging them and in evaluating them in terms of the requirements of their home counties. Members of Parents United and/or Daughters and Sons United are included as facilitators to add validity to the workshop.

Unit Goals

To provide trainees the opportunity to:

1. Examine with greater acumen their new feelings and attitudes about responses to clients;

2. Practice self-exploration and group process techniques for their personal and professional use;

3. Assess the philosophy and methods of the CSATP more concretely and in terms of personal practicality; and

4. Receive more individualized attention from the trainers.

Unit Content, Module Design, and Activities Requirements

Module	Time	Activity	Time	Materials
1. Exploring Reactions to Co-Counseling Sessions	2.5 hrs.	1. Discussion of Reactions to Co-Counseling Sessions	1 hr.	Coffee, other beverages, and supplies.
		2. Role-Playing: Connecting Current Feelings to Past Events	45 min.	Space requirements: A room large enough for trainers and trainees to sit comfortably in a circle and for two or more people to have ample space for role-playing.
		3. Role-Playing: Returning to Client Transactions	45 min.	
2. Lunch	1.5 hrs.			
3. Bioenergetics	3 hrs.	1. Bioenergetics	2 hrs. 55 min.	Three large cushions, one or more tennis rackets, one extra empty chair, enough room for two people to walk around near the cushions during the exercises.
		2. Farewell Circle	5 min.	

Unit Rationale

The training course uses an iterative approach, aimed at enabling trainees to gain an initial but firm grasp of the key concepts and methods of the CSATP, to motivate them to start their own programs, and to increase their skills (especially in counseling), not only by on-the-job opportunities but also by additional schooling.

This unit and the ones that follow give repeated emphasis and instruction on the value of self-exploration for awareness, in particular of negative feelings usually linked to painful childhood experiences, to reduce potential projection of such feelings onto clients; acquiring a positive, empathic attitude for dealing productively with clients as well as with colleagues for building a cooperative treatment system; self-help groups and how to start them and help them develop; and efficient record-keeping, administration, and coordination.

It is impressed on the trainees that the effectiveness of a CSATP depends on the degree to which the staff has internalized the principles and methods of the humanistic approach. Cognitive understanding and verbal facility in discussing the concepts are often self-deceiving. The trainers acknowledge that they are continually on guard against complacency and realize they must practice humanism as an ongoing discipline.

By using themselves as models, the trainers demonstrate humanism and avoid a tutorial, know-it-all demeanor. As mentioned previously, the trainers for the experiential and didactic workshop include, if possible, members of Parents United and/or Daughters and Sons United. Their personal inputs help to keep the training messages "honest."

Unit Objectives

At the end of this unit, trainees should be able to:

1. Be more competent in many of the self-exploration and group process techniques employed by the CSATP staff;

2. Visualize more clearly the early stages of their own CSATPs and the obstacles they may face in getting them started; and

3. Be more assertive in asking for attention and information from the trainers for their personal needs and in preparing themselves for the preliminary steps they intend to take for getting their CSATPs started.

Module 1: Exploring Reactions to Training and Continued Practice in CSATP Methodology

Description

In this module, Gestalt techniques in particular are used to explore the reaction of trainees to the co-counseling and group sessions. The trainers start the group process by asking the trainees to discuss their reactions to the counseling and group sessions and their contacts with the staff. Disturbing reactions are listened to and may be traced, if it is in the interest of the trainee, to past distressful experiences.

The cases of clients brought up by the trainees are analyzed to identify similarities and differences in the psychological dynamics during the incestuous period and following exposure. The treatment plans for different families are discussed and analyzed.

The trainees are cautioned about reliance on psychological theories and generalizations in the treatment of incestuous families and about the dangers of a presumptive counseling stance. They are reminded that humanistic treatment implies individualized treatment.

Goals

To provide trainees the opportunity to:

1. Continue their practice of humanistic principles and methods;

2. Circle ever closer towards satisfying their personal and community requirements for starting a CSATP, especially in winning the support of their supervisors; and

3. Start relating to members of the self-help groups attending the workshop more as persons in their own right and less as clients.

Rationale

Trainees can become effective change agents with clients only after working on themselves first. They will be able to attend to their clients' needs only if they are not hampered by negative feelings toward themselves and hence toward their clients. If a client disturbs them, it may be because that client has touched some unresolved issue in their personal life.

This module is designed to help trainees learn to become aware of and to assimilate distressful experiences so that residual painful memories and feelings will not taint the counseling session. The trainees will learn and practice techniques that they will find useful continually throughout their work in the field of child sexual abuse.

Objectives

At the end of this module, trainees should be able to:

1. Realize that the group process is beneficial to staff members as well as to clients;

2. Resolve to arrange similar meetings with their own co-workers;

3. See clearly that the inhibitory effects of projection in their dealings with clients and with colleagues may in large part be avoided if they become conscious of disturbing feelings as they arise, try to pinpoint their origin, and discuss the feelings with some one they trust; and

4. Appreciate the self-help group members in the workshop as full, evolving personalities (rather than as victims, mothers of victims, or child molestors) with whom they can share many life-coping experiences.

Activity 1. Discussion of Reactions to Co-Counseling Sessions

The trainer starts the morning's meeting with a relaxation exercise. After the trainees settle down, s/he asks the trainees to discuss their reactions to the counseling sessions of the previous day. The trainees bring up feelings of empathy toward the victim or animosity towards the victim's mother and/or the perpetrator, express doubts or approval about the counselor's methods in the transactions with clients, and express their confidence or concern about their own abilities.

The trainer employs basic effective communication methods for clarifying and personalizing the statements and then begins to focus on specific problems brought up by the trainees by setting up role-playing dyads: typically, trainee–mother, trainee–offender, and trainee–counselor.

The Gestalt empty-chair technique (see Appendix 1), in which the trainee addresses an imaginary person in an empty chair, may be used; or the trainer may ask a group member to play the other protagonist. If a father-offender is participating in the workshop, he may volunteer to play the role of the imaginary offender. Similarly, if a victim's mother is attending she, too, may volunteer to play the part of an imaginary mother.

Activity 2. Role-Playing and Gestalt Techniques: Connecting Current Feelings to Past Events

Here is an example of how role-playing follow-up by a Gestalt method is used in this activity.

Trainee: *I was very frustrated yesterday because I wanted the counselor to be much more directive than he was being. The mother was showering hostility all over him and the counselor was just taking it.*

The trainer then asks the trainee to demonstate what she would have liked to say by enacting her fantasy with another person in the group. The trainee asks another trainee to play the role of the hostile mother. At appropriate times—usually when a question is asked—the trainer asks the players to exchange roles. When the role-playing is over, the trainer asks the trainee to recall the feeling associated with a particular accusation by the other during the exercise.

Trainer: *What was going on in you when, as the counselor, the mother said to you, "You're supposed to be helping me and my family but the probation officer tells me that you won't okay that my daughter be returned to me?"*

Trainee: *Well, I felt very angry at the client. I knew that the counselor couldn't give the child back to her mother, because the child didn't trust her mother. She suspected that her mother would sneak her father into the house despite the no-contact order of the court and that the mother was still blaming her for the incestuous situation.*

Trainer: *Yes, I can see that you're still angry as you were when you called the mother selfish and angrily accused her of still being a marshmallow as far as her husband was concerned.*

Trainee: *Yes, I'm still very angry.*

Trainer: *Please close your eyes and attend to your body. Try to locate the anger. Where is it in your body?*

Trainee: *A lot of it is in my stomach—like a fiery ball . . . the size of a grapefruit.*

Trainer: *Can you remember an event or events in your childhood that made you feel somewhat like you do now?*

Trainee: *(After a pause.) Oh, yes. It happened when my parents boxed me in. My mother used to do that a lot, especially when I was in my late teens. Like hassling me about why I couldn't get a boyfriend. When rarely I did manage to get close to someone, enough to invite him to my house, she'd talk to him with disgusting coyness—even flirtatiously—if she liked him. Or she'd make cutting remarks if she didn't approve of him.*

Trainer: *Get back to that ball in your stomach. Really feel it.*

Trainee: *(Concentrating.) Well, it's still there, but it seems somewhat smaller.*

The trainer continues in this vein or may set up a role-playing exercise involving the trainee's mother. Occasionally the trainer cuts in and brings the trainee's attention back to the angry ball in her stomach. Usually the trainee discovers that it gradually diminishes in size and may even disappear.

In this particular example, which includes only portions of the actual training episode, the trainee did a role-playing scenario based on the mother's anxiety about the trainee's lack of boyfriends. The insightful highlight of the dialogue came when the mother, played by the trainee in a role reversal, tearfully confided to her daughter that she and her husband were having terrible marital problems at that time.

Activity 3. Role-Playing: Returning to Client Transactions

The role-playing goes back to dialogues with clients. For instance, the trainee who did the role-playing with her mother in activity 2 was asked to engage the client-mother who aroused her anger in another dialogue. At this point, the trainees are usually better able to empathize with the clients.

The trainers and other trainees give feedback to the trainees who have explored feelings from their family backgrounds. Some admit to similar feelings from similar experiences, and the group members' relationships become closer. This activity prepares the trainee for the upcoming afternoon bioenergetic exercises.

Module 2: Lunch

This module permits relaxed interaction among trainees during lunch.

Module 3: Bioenergetics

Description

Up to this point the trainees have been introduced to the basic concepts and some of the methods of psychosynthesis, Gestalt counseling, and a combined form of transactional analysis and Gestalt as interpreted and modified by the CSATP counseling staff. It is hoped that despite the limited exposure the trainees will appreciate the effectiveness of the methods and resolve to obtain more schooling in them when they return to their home counties.

This module emphasizes bioenergetics, a method that concentrates on the body and the way it manifests the repressed reactions to painful events, of which the most significant are sexual traumas experienced during early childhood.

The childhood memories that were revived in the morning session provide a natural introduction to bioenergetics. Following each trainee's completion of the basic bioenergetics exercise in Activity 1, the other group members communicate to him or her the feelings stirred in them while observing the trainee's responses during the exercise.

The bioenergetics exercises are very effective in the surfacing of repressed distressful experiences and in relieving the muscular tensions that the body unconsciously develops in suppressing the feelings associated with the repressed experiences. The group seems to enter a new, more animated phase after the exercises and group members interact with greater warmth and intimacy for the balance of the course. The module ends with a farewell circle.

Goals

To provide trainees the opportunity to:

1. Relieve muscular tension resulting from repressed childhood experiences;

2. Discuss and assimilate the newly conscious childhood experiences and associated feelings; and

3. Learn a new technique for promoting self-awareness for their personal and professional growth.

Rationale

The way the mind processes the sensory influx from ongoing experiences is clearly evident through facial expressions such as smiling, frowning or crying and in muscular tension seen and felt in the jaw, shoulders, diaphragm, and other parts of the body, as well as in the general posture of the body. When humanistic psychologists speak of self-awareness, they mean to include awareness of both emotional feelings and how certain loci in the body manifest the feelings. Chronic body pain or muscular tension is due to the mind's efforts to repress the feelings associated with past traumatic experiences.

Traditionally-trained therapists or ego therapists attempt to resolve repressed feelings on a verbal or mental level; behavior therapists use conditioned-response methods to desensitize feelings causing maladaptive behavior; Gestalt therapists help the client to assimilate verbally described painful feelings by having the client become aware of the bodily expression of those feelings; and practitioners of bioenergetics employ physical exercises designed to discharge muscular tension in order to help the client to identify and resolve the repressed feelings that lead to the tension.*

A cardinal rule of the CSATP is that all counselors on the staff must experience a technique personally before they are allowed to employ it in counseling. Therefore, the trainees will be introduced to bioenergetics largely by having each of them perform one of the principal exercises of this discipline. Further, they are cautioned to seek additional training in bioenergetics and to feel competent in the discipline before attempting to use it with clients.

This module is very important since the trainees will eventually be working with clients whose pent-up anger will require physical release to prevent its often subtle but always negative effects on their lives. Bioenergetics provides a channel, safely controlled by the counselor, for helping clients discharge anger contained in the body and to trace that anger to its sources: repressed feelings stemming from the incestuous situations and/or other traumatic experiences. Bioenergetics is particularly valuable in the treatment of adults molested as children.

Objectives

At the end of this module, trainees should be able to:

1. Appreciate the interdependency of body and mind;

2. Understand the rudiments of bioenergetics and resolve to get more training in this discipline; and

3. Relate with group members more openly and honestly.

*This description and comparison of therapeutic approaches is, of course, highly simplified. A more thorough discussion of Gestalt techniques and bioenergetics and of how they can be used in a complementary way is provided in activity 1 and in Appendix 1.

Activity 1. Bioenergetics

The trainer discusses briefly the rationale of and the way to do a bioenergetics exercise. S/he explains that this exercise will help them acknowledge pent-up anger from repressed feelings and permit them to express it physically without fear of repercussions. The exercise might be thought of as a vehicle for regaining power formerly given away to someone they perceived as more powerful than they (e.g., an authoritarian parent).

The trainer gives the trainees time to air their apprehensions. If no one volunteers, s/he will ask one of them to participate; this person usually acquiesces. The trainees are asked to identify with the trainee doing the exercise and to be aware of their own reactions.

The participant is given a tennis racket and positioned before a stack of three or four large cushions, about three feet high. The position is similar to the one taken for log-splitting: the feet are planted firmly on the ground, knees are slightly bent, toes point slightly inward, and the body leans slightly backward, bending from the hips.

The participant begins by lifting the racket overhead and smashing the flat part of it against the top pillow. The participant develops a natural pace and rhythm while repeating this motion over and over. S/he is coached to achieve a powerful but fluid motion, with eyes open and focused on the target, the center of the pillow.

The trainer stands to the side of the participant and now and then interjects comments designed to stimulate and release suppressed anger. As the smashes against the pillow become more powerful, the participant will usually indicate the source of the anger and frustration, and the trainer tunes in with appropriate comments.

For example, if the participant says, "I'm moving out," the trainer will say with authority, "Oh no you won't." If the participant says, "I won't live here anymore," the trainer will brook no nonsense and say, "Oh yes you will."

The trainer's commands are intended to goad the participant to a level of physically aggressive behavior which s/he normally would not permit. The trainee reacts by hitting the pillows progressively harder. The trainer reminds the trainee to look directly at the pillow while hitting to keep herself grounded in reality, to stay in the present rather than get lost in the childhood years and her sense of powerlessness. The trainee will feel better able to cope with life if she can keep in mind that she is now a mature person and will not permit others to control her.

At some point the trainer may ask, "Who am I?" The answer from the trainee helps the trainer to formulate fitting remarks. For example, if the participant says, "You're my mother," the trainer will say something like, "I was a fine mother and you'd better appreciate me." This remark usually elicits a new and more powerful series of blows.

After the participant is exhausted and hands back the tennis racket, the trainer continues to work with him or her, attempting to help the trainee integrate the experience. For example, while maintaining eye contact with the participant, the trainer may ask in a kindly tone, "What would you like for yourself at this moment?" The trainee may respond, "I'd like to hide my face from all of you." Using a Gestalt technique, the trainer will ask the participant to step in front of each group member in turn and say clearly and strongly, "I feel like hiding my face from you."

As the participant goes from person to person, s/he is able to make this statement more firmly. If the tone wavers, the trainer will remind the participant of this and ask that the statement be repeated again and with more conviction.

Soon the participant realizes that his or her fears were unwarranted and that, in fact, group members are responding with greater warmth and friendliness. This revelation usually prompts remarks such as "I'm not afraid any more," or "I feel so safe with all of you, now that it's over."

The trainer continues to attend to the participant until the participant's needs are satisfied. The trainees, who have been watching the process, express empathy for and closeness to the trainee who has just finished the exercise. The remarks usually come to admissions of similar suppressed feelings of frustration and anger, and expressions of admiration to the participant for having the courage to do the exercise and to let go: "Wow, you looked beautiful as you got into the rhythm of it. I didn't realize you were that strong," or "I envy you. I don't think I have the guts for letting go," or "I was with you all the way. I helped you in every smash. I want to get my hands on that racket." Invariably one of the trainees will embrace the participant.

After all the trainees take turns doing the exercise, the remaining minutes of the afternoon are spent in discussion. The trainer points out that the pillow-pounding exercise is useful for venting current frustrations concerning spouses, co-workers, clients, etc. The trainees are informed that training in bioenergetics is available in most cities. The book *Bioenergetics* by Alexander Loven, M.D., is recommended, as well as others (listed in the bibliography). See also the articles on Gestalt and Bioenergetics in Appendix 1.

Activity 2. Farewell Circle

The trainers and trainees form the usual circle to provide closure to an especially intense day. The trainees are reminded that they have only three more days to spend with each other and to take advantage of the brief time remaining.

Unit VIII. CSATP Administration and Coordination, Practicum IV:

Unit Description

The eighth day of training is another long day, beginning with a three-hour module that elaborates on the administrative functions of the CSATP. The trainees spend the morning with the program administrator and the coordinator, continuing their discussion of case management and methods for enhancing interagency cooperation.

After a one-hour break, the trainees again join their assigned counselors for co-counseling sessions. Trainees may then take a breathing spell until the start of the Parents United meeting, or they may sit in on one of the adolescent boys' and girls' groups that meet from 6:00 to 7:30 P.M. As in Unit III, trainees may join Parents United members in an informal social gathering during and following the evening meal.

Unit Goals

To provide trainees the opportunity to:

1. Delve more deeply into the structure of the CSATP and its administration within the Juvenile Probation Department, mainly to foresee how a CSATP may be developed in their own agencies;

2. Learn more about interagency coordination and how this is achieved;

3. Follow the flow of clients through the CSATP from initial referral to termination;

4. Learn about the screening and selection of interns and the preparation of letters of evaluation to the court;

5. Add to their knowledge of counseling methods;

6. Join as observers and participants in the Parents United/Daughters and Sons United group meetings to further their understanding of the self-help component of the CSATP; and

7. Note how the professional staff and the self-help component join hands in the family resocialization process.

Unit Rationale

The success of a CSATP depends on a great many factors. The program's primary function —to resocialize and teach self-management to people whose lives have been affected by child sexual abuse—is seen most directly in the counseling sessions. But equally important are the self-help component and the cooperation of all the agencies responsible for these people's welfare. This day exposes the trainees to all these aspects of the CSATP's operation. Again, the trainees learn by direct experience.

Unit Objectives

At the end of this unit, trainees should be able to:

1. Understand the organization of the Santa Clara County CSATP more completely and start conceptualizing a CSATP for their own communities and how it might fit into the local official structure;

2. Appreciate fully the importance of interagency cooperation in building an efficient CSATP, since lack of cooperation among the responsible agencies will seriously hamper the ability of the CSATP to be fully effective in the treatment of clients;

3. Feel more competent in working with clients;

4. Identify the areas in which they feel deficient and would like more training; and

5. Be more at ease in their interactions with members of the self-help component as a result of getting to know them as persons (not as patients) and getting a fuller understanding of the characteristics of self-help groups.

Unit Content, Module Design, and Activities Requirements

Module	Time	Activity	Time	Materials
1. CSATP Administration, Coordination, and Record-Keeping	3 hrs.	1. CSATP Administration	45 min.	Handouts: "PU Organization Diagram," "Santa Clara County Chapter of PU/DSU," and "CSATP and PU/DSU Flow Chart."
		2. CSATP Coordination	1 hr.	
		3. Record-Keeping Forms Used by the CSATP	15 min.	"CSATP Referral and Intake Form," "PU/DSU Sponsorship Referral," "CSATP Referral to Dependent Intake and Police Department," "Case Contact Record," "Case Management Forms," and "Case Management: Referrals"
		4. Lunch	1 hr.	
2. Co-Counseling Sessions	3 hrs.*	1. Briefing, Feedback, and Discussion	1 hr.	* There are three hours for these two activities, and time is spent at the discretion of the counselor, according to need. Usually there are two co-counseling sessions of one hour each, and the other hour comprises Activity 1.
		2. Two Co-Counseling Sessions	2 hrs.	
3. Evening with DSU and PU	3.5 hrs.	1. Participation in DSU groups or interaction with PU members before the meeting (optional)	1.5 hrs.	
		2. PU group meeting or DSU group meetings for adolescents	2.5 hrs.	
		3. Informal get-together with PU members (optional)	1.5 hrs.	

Module 1: CSATP Administration and Interagency Coordination

Description

The program administrator and program coordinator meet with the trainees for a three-hour session that includes having lunch together. The module is designed to elaborate on the administrative and interagency coordination operations of the CSATP. The discussion covers the topic of case management, outlines the unified approach to child sexual abuse cases, and describes the mobilization of services into a cooperative effort that channels maximum help toward the family.

The trainees are informed that some of the administrative tasks of the CSATP which in Santa Clara County are divided between the administrator and the coordinator will probably be performed by one person as they get their own CSATP started. The trainees are assured, however, that much of the material presented in this module is for historical information only, to show them some of the administration problems faced by a CSATP in a mature stage and which also has training responsibility. It is suggested that they filter the material for information of immediate use to them in their initial plan for starting a CSATP—to concentrate, for example, on the ways clients are handled at intake and the cases managed thereafter, on the importance of the self-help component in this process, and on the methods used by the CSATP to win over the cooperation of personnel from other agencies, particularly law enforcement personnel.

Goals

To provide trainees the opportunity to:

1. Observe the intake procedure and case management and the critical role of PU/DSU members in this process;

2. Study the division of responsibility of child sexual abuse case workers within the Juvenile Probation Department of Santa Clara County and how this compares with their own agencies;

3. Note that the coordinated approach has made the intervention of law enforcement and human services agencies more humane and efficient;

4. Compare the advantages and disadvantages of having treatment and investigation under the jurisdiction of a single agency;

5. Realize the importance of becoming familiar with the operations and characteristics of the agencies in their own counties as a necessary first step in the coordination task;

6. Observe the coordination methods of the CSATP, especially the way the lines of communication are kept open among agency personnel through a planned feedback system;

7. Study the various flow and organizational charts and the forms used for record-keeping from intake to termination;

8. Recognize the importance of the counselors' letters of evaluation to the probation officers regarding their clients' progress in the program and note how these letters are screened for correct and useful information to the courts as well as to make certain that the counselor is not interfering in the judicial process;

9. See that the counselor–client relationship is improved when the counselor appears on behalf of the client in the juvenile and/or adult court;

10. Appreciate the importance of the community awareness program in attracting clients to the program and in winning support from private and public agencies, county supervisors, citizen groups, etc.; and

11. Note that the cost effectiveness of a CSATP in their own communities should be similar to that of Santa Clara County.

Rationale

By now the trainees should be aware that effective and efficient case management in the CSATP depends on the cooperation and coordination of many individuals. This module gives them more specific information on what happens to a family in the course of its association with the program, on the people and agencies directly involved in the family's welfare, and on how the CSATP has managed to win the support of these people and agencies. This information will be of great value to the trainees when they return to their communities and begin the task of building an effective, community-based resource for families troubled by child sexual abuse.

Objectives

At the end of this module, the trainees should be able to:

1. Understand CSATP case-management and how the self-help component contributes to this process;

2. Have a more complete grasp of the administrative operations of a CSATP in its advanced stages;

3. Start making distinctions between the local CSATP and the forms their own programs will take;

4. Begin to visualize their own roles and the other roles that must be filled to get their CSATPs off the ground;

5. Start asking precise questions regarding information they need to cope with the problems they anticipate while starting their own CSATP;

6. Have a clearer picture of the relationships of the professional, self-help, and volunteer components of the CSATP;

7. Recognize the pivotal position of the self-help component in launching a CSATP and keeping it operational; and

8. Start making plans for the key initial steps in forming Parents United and Daughters and Sons United groups. (For trainees who are already seeing sexually abused children and their families, the first step would be to arrange telephone contact between members of a family in more advanced stages of treatment with equivalent members of a family in the initial stages of crisis.)

Activity 1. CSATP Administration

The program administrator reviews and expands on the information given to the trainees in Unit I concerning the administrative functions of the CSATP. The following points are stressed:

1. Because of the advanced state of the Santa Clara program, these functions are divided between two workers: the program administrator and the program coordinator.

2. The success of a CSATP depends on the ability of the administrative staff to integrate and render more humane and efficient the interventions of the criminal justice system, the human services agencies, the cadre of volunteers, the counselors, and the members of the self-help component.

3. To be productive, the case management of a family must reflect a consistent humanistic philosophy and must ensure that services to the family are sufficient and organized efficiently.

4. The Juvenile Probation Department (JPD) of Santa Clara County is one of four JPDs in California that handle child abuse cases; in other counties, these cases come under the jurisdiction of the Department of Social Services.

5. Divisions of responsibility within the JPD fall between intake (which investigates the case), dependent supervision, and placement if the child becomes a ward of the court.

6. The JPD is administratively responsible for the overall operation of the CSATP. The principal advantage is that CSATP services are available to the clients as soon as the intake interview is completed by the JPD worker.

   One disadvantage in the JPD process is that the functions are handled by different workers. For example, at a time when it is important that s/he be given a sense of stability, the child sees one worker at intake and another for supervision and placement.

   A solution might be to have services performed by the same worker; another, less preferable, is to have intake and placement workers in the same unit so that the transfer of the child to another worker could be done more smoothly and less disturbingly to the child. But the CSATP has not been able to convince the top management of the JPD to implement either one of these solutions.

7. It is recommended that trainees starting their own CSATPs have investigation and placement done by a worker who is not also responsible for the counseling. Where a shortage of workers requires the performance of official and counseling services by one person, s/he must convince the child and her family that s/he is primarily concerned for the overall welfare of the family despite his or her role as investigator.

8. The relationship of the administrative and counseling staff to Parents United is explained with the help of organization charts.

Santa Clara County Chapter of Parents United Inc. Organization Chart

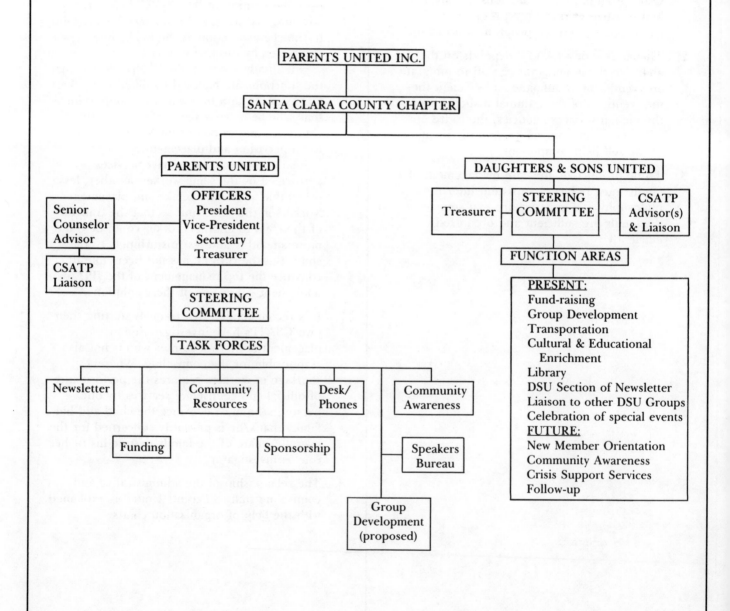

Parents United, Inc. Organizational Diagram

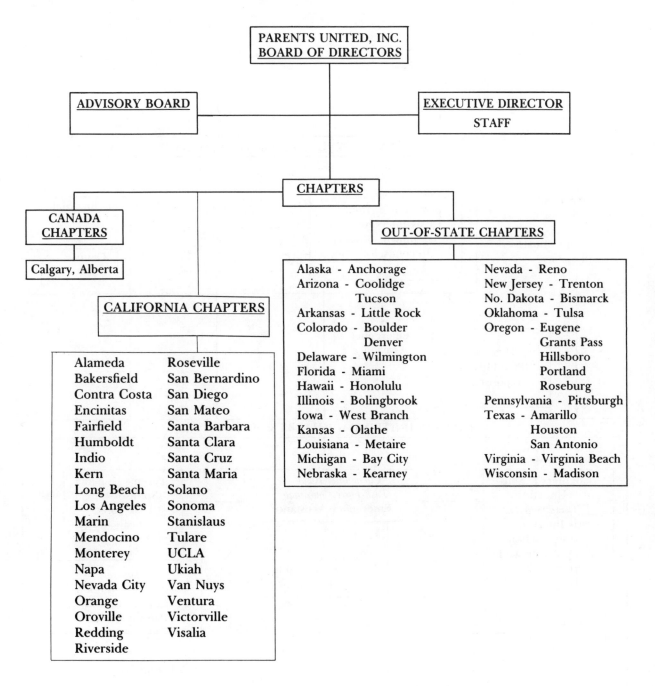

CSATP and PU/DSU
Flow Chart

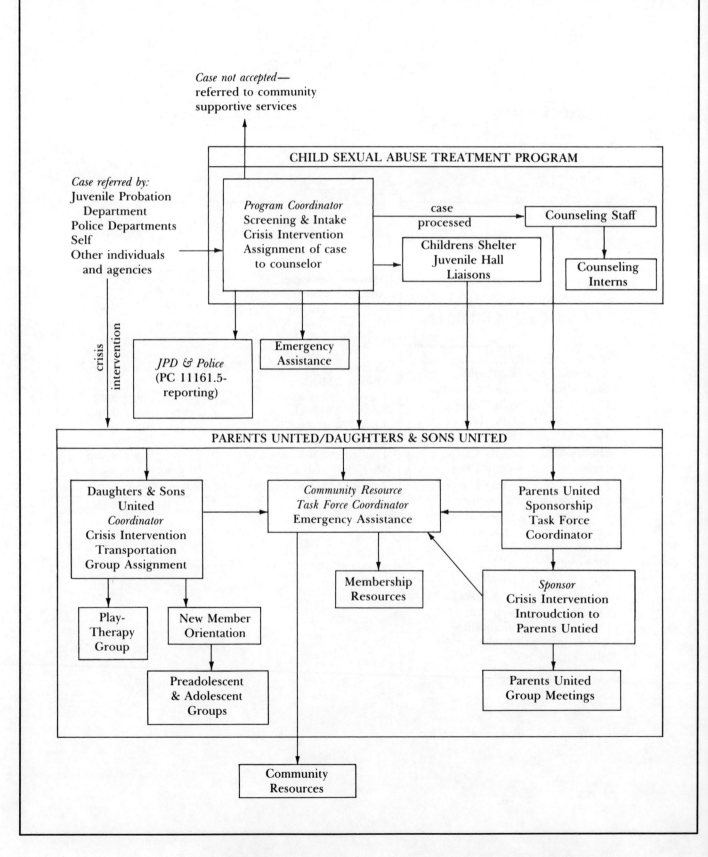

Case not accepted—
referred to community
supportive services

CHILD SEXUAL ABUSE TREATMENT PROGRAM

Case referred by:
Juvenile Probation
    Department
Police Departments
Self
Other individuals
    and agencies

Program Coordinator
Screening & Intake
Crisis Intervention
Assignment of case
to counselor

case
processed

Counseling Staff

Counseling
Interns

Childrens Shelter
Juvenile Hall
Liaisons

crisis
intervention

JPD & Police
(PC 11161.5-
reporting)

Emergency
Assistance

PARENTS UNITED/DAUGHTERS & SONS UNITED

Daughters & Sons
United
Coordinator
Crisis Intervention
Transportation
Group Assignment

*Community Resource
Task Force Coordinator*
Emergency Assistance

Parents United
Sponsorship
Task Force
Coordinator

Play-
Therapy
Group

New Member
Orientation

Membership
Resources

Sponsor
Crisis Intervention
Introudction to
Parents Untied

Preadolescent
& Adolescent
Groups

Parents United
Group Meetings

Community
Resources

CSATP Referral to Independent Intake and Police Department

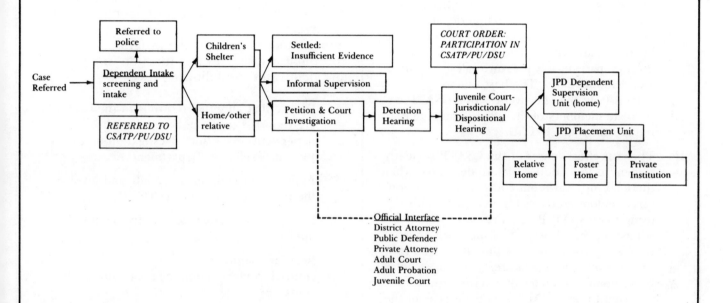

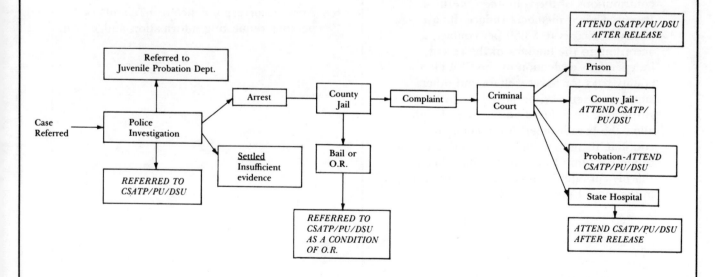

See Parents United's brochure, "General Guide to the Criminal Justice System" for details.

9. An outreach team made up of the professional staff and members of the Santa Clara County chapter of Parents United will visit the trainees at their communities to help them start their CSATPs. Telephone contact is maintained as the CSATP develops, and additional visits are arranged if necessary.

10. A new chapter can be formed (or receive help in addition to that provided by the Santa Clara County chapter) with the assistance of an established chapter in a nearby county.

11. An important function of the CSATP administrator is to win the support of the official community: the police, the DA's office, the judiciary, and the probation department, as well as the county executive offices and the board of supervisors. This support comes through patient, low-pressure salesmanship and demonstration. The best way to demonstrate the effectiveness of a CSATP is to invite members of the official community to the meetings of PU/DSU.

12. The cost effectiveness of the CSATP is clearly evident in that court costs are decreased when there are no drawn-out court procedures and cases seldom go to trial; investigative police using the CSATP/PU as a resource obtain admissions in 90 percent of the cases, thus decreasing the amount of time they need to spend investigating; children are kept at home or go home soon after they have been removed to protective custody, because of the emphasis on mother–child counseling; the contributions of the volunteer interns and Parents United members reduce the average counseling costs to $3.80 per contact, according to the findings of the recent independent evaluation of the CSATP; the county pays for fewer welfare and other supportive services, because jail sentences are suspended or reduced and work furloughs allow the breadwinner in the family to continue to support the family; and the costs of incarceration to the county have been sharply curtailed with corresponding reduction in the loss of tax revenues.

Activity 2. CSATP Coordination

Many of the functions of the program administrator and the program coordinator overlap and are mutually dependent. They both share the responsibility of mobilizing and coordinating the many official interventions in a child sexual abuse case into a cooperative effort that will provide a consistent treatment approach to the sexually abused child and her family.

However, the coordinator also has the specific responsibility of coordinating the case management of each family from intake to termination. As trainer, the program coordinator discusses this function in detail and delineates the following tasks.

1. Ensure that all initial referrals to the CSATP are reported to the police and to the dependent intake and investigation unit of the Juvenile Probation Department.

2. Assign counselors to the family and involve the family members in PU/DSU.

3. Interview and screen prospective counseling interns.

4. Read and approve counselor and counselor-intern letters of evaluation to the court.

5. Review case terminations.

6. Answer correspondence from clients or persons requesting information and/or route

these letters to appropriate members of the staff.

7. Act as a group leader in Daughters and Sons United groups.

8. Assist the counseling interns who are liaisons for minors in Juvenile Hall and in the Children's Shelter and ensure that these children get on-site counseling and other supportive services.

9. Assist in the public information effort by presentations on the CSATP to criminal justice and community agencies.

10. Provide training to departments of social services, foster parents, police officers, head-start programs, etc.

Again, the program coordinator reassures the trainees that they will not be faced with most of these tasks either in kind or in degree during early stages of their CSATPs. Some of the tasks are unique to the Santa Clara County CSATP and its special responsibilities.

Activity 3. Record-Keeping Forms Used by the CSATP

The administrator and the coordinator go over the various forms used by the CSATP for record-keeping from intake to termination.

1. "CSATP Referral and Intake Form." Filled out by either dependent intake or a staff person in the CSATP office.

2. "Parents United/Daughters and Sons United Sponsorship Referral." Completed by an administrative staff person and those persons responsible for assigning PU and DSU sponsors, such as the DSU Coordinator and a PU member who has been cleared to work in the office as a volunteer.

3. "CSATP Referral to Dependent Intake." Used when referrals come in to the CSATP that must be reported to dependent intake and the police. A copy is made out for intake, one for the police, a third for the CSATP files.

4. "Case Contact Record." Used to record CSATP or probation officer communications with various agency personnel regarding a client. This could be an office visit, phone call, or home visit contact.

5. "The Child Sexual Abuse Treatment Program Close Out." Used for case termination.

CSATP Referral and Intake Form

Referred to CJS by _____   Date   _____
CJS agency receiving   County   _____
    initial report _____   JPD #   _____
Referred to CSATP by _____   JPD Officer   _____
Agency & tele. _____   Police Agency _____
                                               Police Officer _____

		SEX	D.O.B.	AGE AT MOLEST'S			INTRAFAMILIAL	
1.	VICTIM'S NAME	SEX	D.O.B.	BEGIN.	END	REPORT		
(a)	_____						YES	NO
(b)	_____						YES	NO
(c)	_____						YES	NO
(d)	_____						YES	NO

2. PERPETRATOR'S NAME_____ SEX_____ AGE____D.O.B. _____

RELATIONSHIP TO VICTIM(S) (a)_____ (b)_____ (c)_____ (d)_____

3. MOTHER'S/SUB. NAME_____ AGE____ D.O.B. _____

4. FATHER'S/SUB. NAME_____ AGE____ D.O.B. _____

5. MARITAL STATUS OF PARENTS/SUB(S):(Circle)
   Legal Marriage: A. Intact   B. Separated   C. Divorced   D. Death
   Consensual Union: A. Intact   B. Separated   C. Terminated D. Death

6. FAMILY ADDRESS_____ TELEPHONE #_____

7. WHEREABOUTS OF VICTIM(S) _____

8. WHEREABOUTS OF PERPETRATOR _____

9. TYPES OF REPORTED MOLEST: (Use code numbers shown below)

	ACTS COMMITTED BY PERPETRATOR ON VICTIM	ACTS COMMITTED BY VICTIM ON PERPETRATOR	TOTAL # OF INCIDENTS	DURATION	MEDICAL EXAM	
VICTIM (a)					YES	NO
VICTIM (b)					YES	NO
VICTIM (c)					YES	NO
VICTIM (d)					YES	NO

TYPES OF MOLEST (Use appropriate codes for question #9)

1. Propositioning for sexual acts
2. Shown pornographic or other material intended for adult sexual stimulation
3. Voyerism
4. Exhibitionism
5. Forced to watch sexual acts others
6. Fondling—waist up (including kissing in an overt sexual manner)
7. Fondling—waist down (including hand–genital contact/manipulation)
8. Fellatio
9. Cunnilingus
10. Simulated intercourse
11. Attempted vaginal penetration
12. Intercourse
13. Attempted anal penetration
14. Anal intercourse (sodomy)
15. Other (PLEASE SPECIFY)
16. Unknown

10. CIRCUMSTANCES OF INITIAL REPORT _____

_____

11. WAS MOTHER AWARE OF MOLEST?   (Circle)   YES   NO   NOT/APPL.   UNKNOWN
    If yes, how and for how long? _____

    WAS PERPETRATOR ARRESTED?   (Circle and fill in appropriate spaces)
       A.   Pending
       B.   Yes (charges and outcome _____
       C.   No (why

13. ATTITUDE OF MOTHER TOWARD VICTIM _____

14. ATTITUDE OF MOTHER TOWARD PERPETRATOR _____

15. IS THERE A COURT COUNSELING ORDER?   (Circle)   YES   NO   PENDING

16. IMMEDIATE TREATMENT NEEDS:

    Victim _____
    Mother _____
    Father _____
    Siblings _____

****** C S A T P   U S E   O N L Y ******

TYPE: ____ V/F (____I-F ____EX-F ____BOTH)   CSATP # _____

      ____ ADULT MOLESTED AS CHILD   FILED UNDER: ____Anon. ____Con. ____Reg.

      ____ PERPETRATOR (____Minor ____Adult)   APPT. WITH: _____

      ____ OTHER _____   DATE _____
                                                      TIME _____

Parents United/ Daughters & Sons United Sponsorship Referral

THIS SECTION TO BE COMPLETED BY CSATP

Date of Referral to PU/DSU _____ Counselor _____

NEED TO CONTACT

Name _____ Role _____

Telephone _____ Available _____

Name _____ Role _____

Telephone _____ Available _____

Name _____ Role _____

Telephone _____ Available _____

CIRCUMSTANCES

Type of Case _____

Reported: _____JPD _____POLICE _____NOT NECESSARY

Child's Whereabouts _____

COMMENTS:

_____

_____

_____

*   *   *   *   *   *   *

THIS SECTION TO BE COMPLETED BY PU/DSU

SPONSOR ASSIGNED

PARENTS UNITED:

1. _____ Date of Initial Contact_____

2. a. _____ Date Assigned_____

    b. _____ Date Assigned_____

DAUGHTERS & SONS UNITED:

1. _____ Date of Initial Contact_____

Comments_____

_____

_____

_____

FOLLOW-UP COMMENTS   (Use reverse side)

Original: PU/D&SU Records
Copy: CSATP Case Folder

CSATP Referral to Dependant Intake and Police Departments

Date _____

VICTIM'S Name _____

Birthdate _____

Legal Address _____

Telephone _____

_____

Present Address (if differs) _____

Telephone _____

_____

PARENTS: Mother _____   Father _____

                     Address _____   Address _____

                     _____   _____

                     Telephone _____   Telephone _____

SUSPECT'S Name _____   Relationship to victim _____

Address _____   Telephone _____

_____

REFERRING PARTY'S NAME _____

Address _____   Telephone _____

_____

Circumstances for referral _____

_____

_____

_____

POLICE AGENCY _____ Officer reported to / handling _____
                                                        (circle)

Date referred to / received from policy agency_____
          (circle)

CSATP counselor assigned _____ Completed by _____

Case Contact Record

Minor/s	Address	B.D.	File#	P.O.	DSS# & Worker

	Name	Address	Phone	Work Phone
Father				
Mother				
(Stepparent)				
Other (Custodian)				
(Guardian)				

OV   PC   HV   With_____ Relationship _____

Address_____ Phone _____

Topic _____

Summary of Conversation _____

_____

_____

_____

_____

_____

_____

_____

_____

_____

_____

_____

_____

_____

_____

Was the Adult Probation Officer notified of termination? ☐ YES ☐ NO

If NO, explain_____

REASON FOR TERMINATION_____

_____

_____

_____

_____

_____

_____

_____

_____

_____

_____

_____

_____

_____

Date_____ Probation Officer _____

Santa Clara County Juvenile Probation Department Child Sexual Abuse Treatment Program Termination

Case Name(s)_____ AKA_____

File #_____ County of Residence_____

Reason for Referral_____
_____
_____

Individual(s) being terminated (LIST)_____
_____

Did client(s) complete the program?   ☐ YES   ☐ NO   If NO, explain_____
_____

Are you terminating the *complete* case?   ☐ YES   ☐ NO

PARENTS UNITED / DAUGHTERS & SONS UNITED

D&SU Participation (who, length of time, frequency)_____
_____

   Will the child(ren) continue in D&SU?   ☐ YES   ☐ NO

PU Participation (who, length of time, frequency)_____
_____

   Will the adult(s) continue in PU?   ☐ YES   ☐ NO

AGENCIES INVOLVED

   ☐ Police Agency (specify department)_____
   ☐ Juvenile Probation Department_____
   ☐ Juvenile Court_____
   ☐ Adult Probation Department_____
   ☐ Adult Court_____
   ☐ O.R. Release Program_____
   ☐ Other (specify)_____

Was the Juvenile Probation Officer notified of termination?   ☐ YES   ☐ NO

   If NO, explain_____

(see pp. 162-163)

Module 2: Co-Counseling Sessions

Description

As the trainees engage in another three-hour co-counseling session, they should be feeling more comfortable collaborating in the counseling process. However, some trainees are more advanced in counseling skills than others, and the counselor needs to be sensitive to this. More advanced trainees may desire training in the use of psychosynthesis, bioenergetics, or Gestalt techniques, but a counselor must never sacrifice the client's interests in order to display techniques that are not consistent with the client's needs at that stage in the treatment process.

The less skilled trainee may need some help with the more basic counseling skills such as empathetic listening and reflection. Again it must be stressed that the counselor's capacity for empathy is essential to productive counseling in general—and perhaps even more essential for clients who have experienced the trauma of incest.

The chances for successful treatment are augmented when the counselor is aware of his or her core feelings of rage, helplessness, dependency, fear, and the like that may be associated with typically repressed incestuous feelings. The counselor must be willing to disclose these feelings when in the client's interests; inasmuch as the counselor identifies and accepts these feelings, the client dares to push his or her own limits in accepting and disclosing similar feelings.

The counselor should continually be on guard, of course, against assuming that his or her feelings are also being felt by the client. Trainees who tend to question the client's feelings and thus interfere with the counseling process must gently be sidetracked and later reminded that this tendency must be controlled.

Trainees often need help in listening for feeling as well as content in the client's communications. When the direction of dialogue is allowed to flow from the client with the counselor reflecting, summarizing, and responding empathically, the counselor is respecting the client's way of feeling, thinking, and responding and is in step with the client's process.

Questions that place the client in a vulnerable position may be interpreted by the client as intrusive. The questioner keeps a safe emotional distance from the client and risks very little of him/herself. Trainees who feel uneasy or frightened of the counseling situation may try to relieve their anxieties by questioning tactics. The counselor needs to be sensitive to the trainee's discomfort and be willing to work with this aspect after the session ends.

Goals

To provide trainees the opportunity to:

1. Make intimate contact with clients and counselors and take part in an intense and varied experience that goes beyond mere cognition of treatment concepts;

2. Become familiar with the different kinds of crisis counseling, methods, and techniques used to develop self-knowledge, beneficial interpersonal relationships, self-managed growth, and social responsibility;

3. Observe CSATP counselors using the skills that will enable trainees to implement the methods and principles of humanistic counseling with their own clients;

4. Become more self-aware as they attend to the client's process and feelings;

5. Become better acquainted with the counselor's multifaceted work and its contribution to client growth and productivity; and

6. Ask questions about, challenge, and compare CSATP counseling methods and their effectiveness to their own.

Rationale

As the trainees become more involved in the counseling sessions, they begin to understand how the counselor contributes to the principal objective of the CSATP, i.e., teaching the clients to improve their life-coping abilities. Effective counseling relieves the client's emotional trauma, provides opportunities for experiential learning in self-management, teaches problem-solving methods that lead to increased mastery over formerly disabling situations, helps overcome the client's abiding state of social isolation and alienation, and furthers the client's ability to make lasting, mutually beneficial relationships.

It is not claimed that the training provided to students in the two-week course will produce counselors fully competent in humanistic counseling. It is hoped, however, that even relatively unschooled trainees will leave the course with at least some preliminary skills in counseling and an appreciation of the CSATP approach that will motivate them to learn additional counseling skills when they return to their jobs.

Objectives

At the end of this module, trainees should be able to:

1. Demonstrate rather than preach the virtues of respect, caring, warmth, and empathy;

2. Feel that they have established a feeling of trust and congruence with their co-counseled clients;

3. Begin to feel confident in their ability to teach attitudes and skills that raise the client's self-esteem;

4. Understand how a counselor can systematically aid the client in removing blocks to self-awareness;

5. Manifest him/herself as a person primarily, rather than a counselor, and be able to learn from his or her encounter with the client;

6. Get involved in obtaining practical assistance and emotional support for the new client;

7. Help the client become aware of his/her interactional patterns and previously unseen personality traits;

8. Experience the client's feelings with comfort, allowing for and encouraging their full expression; and

9. Personify the humanistic principles and methods of treatment.

Sample Client–Counselor Dialogue Exploring Deeper Feelings

Dramatization I:

Counselor: Can you tell me what you've been experiencing since I saw you last?

Client: Very bad feelings, very scared, like I've lost my bearings and can't find my way. The familiar landmarks have disappeared, and I feel as if something terrible will happen.

(Counselor listens carefully and nods head at appropriate times.)

Client: It's like being caught in a runaway system and there's nothing I can do. It's the worst thing I've ever experienced.

Counselor: Sounds terrifying, like your very existence is at stake.

Client: Yes. I've had scary things happen before, in the war and all, but not like this.

Counselor: Tell me some of those scary things.

Client: Well, I can remember when my mother shipped me out to my aunt's in Kentucky. I was eight, and I asked her when I could come home again and she said she'd come for me soon, when things got better. But she didn't come for three years, and I thought I would die before I saw her again. Or, she would die and I'd never see her again. I'd ask my aunt and she'd say she was okay, but I thought she must be dead because she didn't come, or write, or anything.

Counselor: You felt abandoned by her.

Client: Yes. All alone. My aunt didn't like me that much. She had her own kids.

Counselor: The anxiety you're having now, that you talked about a few minutes ago . . . I'm wondering . . . does it have any of the same quality to it as you experienced as the abandoned little boy?

Client: Hmm . . . [thoughtful and silent for a while, then tears begin to well up]. Yes, they're similar. I'm afraid my family will abandon me, and I'll be alone. [He begins to sob freely.] Yes, now that I think about it, I feel just like I did when I was a kid, in the dark and alone.

Dramatization II:

Counselor: I see you're back in Juvenile Hall, what happened?

Client: Oh, I got into a hassle at my group home so they took me back to the hall Sunday night and dumped me off. I got all upset when I called my mom. I just wanted to tell her that I loved her and all that shit. You know? But she wouldn't talk to me.

God, it's all so unfair. Like all I wanted was to say hello to my little brother. He's five, you know. I mean, I raised that kid. I took care of him right since birth like I was the *mother* and then . . . you know . . . god, I love that kid. He's so cute and I haven't seen him in over a year. . . . [At this point, sobbing begins quite heavily.]

Counselor: It's been that long?

Client: Yes, and it's all because of my stepdad. He'd been molesting me ever since I could remember. Finally I told my mom about it, but she wouldn't believe me. She said I had to be lying, that he wouldn't do a thing like that.

Counselor: It must have been terrible not to have your mother believe you, and that you had to leave instead of him.

Client: That's right. It's just not fair. He's free to go anywhere and he doesn't come to the program, or nothing. They put me in the shelter. And now my mom's sick and the boys give her a hard time.

Counselor: Sounds like you're worried about your Mom.

Client: Yes, I am. I really am. She has a drinking problem, you know. My stepdad doesn't do nothing to help her, and I worry about my little brother a whole lot.

Counselor: It sounds to me that you feel bad that you told your Mom about the molest.

Client: That's right, I do. If I hadn't told, I would be home now helping my mom and my little brother. We wouldn't be in such a mess.

Counselor: How do you feel about your mom still not believing you?

Client: Oh god, I just *hate* her for it. It makes me so MAD. They're all at home having Christmas and things, and I'm stuck in that lousy rotten group home. It just isn't fair.

Counselor: So there is a part of you that's mad at your mom for not believing you and another part that worries about her and feels guilty for having told her about the molest.

Client: That's about it. I feel all twisted up inside, like it's all my fault. My stepdad hates me now, my mom won't talk to me and won't have anything to do with me, and I'm out in the cold.

NOTE: The above dramatization is a fairly verbatim dialogue between a counselor and a sixteen-year-old client. During the year preceding this interview, she got heavily into PCP and was raped twice. The father was not charged. The young girl had never been in any trouble before the molest came out. Following this interview, she disappeared and has not been heard of since.

Module 3: Evening with Daughters and Sons United and Parents United

Description

The trainees participate once again in the Wednesday night meetings of Daughters and Sons United and Parents United. Several options are open to the trainees: (1) to participate in the DSU meeting from 6:00 to 7:30 P.M., or take a break before the PU meeting, or hobnob with PU members before they meet; (2) to participate in one of the adolescent DSU groups from 7:30 to 10:00 P.M.; (3) to participate in one of the several groups conducted by PU from 7:30 to 10:00 P.M.; (4) to socialize with PU members informally after the meeting. (Descriptions of these activities are given in Unit III, Module 4.)

Goals

Module 3 is designed to provide trainees the opportunity to interact once again with members of PU/DSU, both by personal contacts and by participation in the group sessions.

Rationale

It is expected that, between the first and second meetings of the self-help groups, the trainees will have made personal contact with the members in the counseling sessions and in other interactions and therefore will be better able to participate intimately in the group sessions. The best way to underscore the importance of the self-help component in the resocialization process is to have the trainees experience this effect in the group meetings.

Objectives

At the end of this module, trainees should be able to:

1. Be more at ease in contacts with victims, mothers, and father-offenders and appreciate fully the recuperative influence of the expanded self-help format of PU/DSU; and

2. Decide that they, too, must start a PU/DSU organization and start making plans for getting one under way in their own communities.

Unit IX. Staff Counselors' Meeting and Practicum V: Co-Counseling Sessions

Unit Description

This unit contains two modules. Module 1 is the CSATP biweekly meeting of the staff counselors for the purpose of discussing unusual cases, sharing the problems of difficult ones, and deciding whether different counselors and/or additional interns should be assigned to certain cases. Module 2 is the sixth and final co-counseling session.

Unit Goals

To provide trainees the opportunity to:

1. Participate in the staff counselors' meeting to observe how difficult cases are analyzed and why new counselors and/or more interns may be assigned to a case;

2. Observe the counselors' use of the group process for resolving negative feelings and blocks that hinder effective work with clients or may add to the hazards of burn-out;

3. Present problem cases that they are treating in their own agencies and receive pertinent feedback from the group;

Unit Content, Module Design, and Activities Requirements

Module	Time	Activity	Time	Materials
1. The Staff Counselors' Meeting	1.5 hrs.	1. Case presentation by staff 2. Dealing with supervisors' feelings 3. Reassignment of counselors or interns 4. Case presentations by trainees	20 min.* 30 min.* 10 min.* 30 min.*	Space requirements: the space for module 1 should be as comfortable and relaxing as possible. It should provide sufficient privacy to allow for open discussion of specific cases and for the counselors to do some venting or self-work if they desire. *Flexible
2. Co-Counseling Sessions	3 hrs.**	1. Briefing, Feedback, and Discussion 2. Two co-counseling sessions	1 hr. 2 hrs.	Recommended books and reading material **The three hours are spent at the discretion of the counselor according to need.

4. Be exposed to a variety of cases and the strategies and interventions used to improve treatment plans; and

5. Participate once again in the counseling sessions.

Unit Rationale

The problem of the "burn-out" of workers dealing with abusive families has been covered extensively in the literature. Burn-out is certainly a serious potential problem for workers in the field of child sexual abuse since the emotional climate of this field is perhaps more highly charged than in the other areas of child abuse. Regular meetings of the counseling staff have been found to be invaluable in combating burn-out.

The counselors are given the opportunity to air their feelings regarding exceptionally sexually exploitative parents, and the sympathetic reactions of colleagues to their attempts to deal with the families humanistically. This group is in essence a self-help group for the counselors which allows them to express their feelings openly and to expect support and constructive suggestions from their co-workers instead of contemptuous responses or pontifical advice-giving.

Unit Objectives

At the end of this unit, trainees should be able to:

1. Cope more effectively with potential burn-out of people working with extremely troubled families;

2. Assess treatment plans with the help of co-workers and modify them if necessary;

3. Estimate their own strengths and weaknesses in humanistic counseling and resolve to get additional training when they return home; and

4. Begin to formulate plans for the counseling component of their CSATPs and gather all the information they can from the trainers on how to implement those plans.

Module 1: The Staff Counselors' Meeting

Description

The staff counselors meet as a group to discuss difficult cases and to solicit suggestions from one another for improving treatment strategies. Occasionally a counselor may feel that another counselor or intern would be more effective in the treatment of a case. The discussion is not limited to problem cases resisting treatment; successful outcomes are also shared.

The meeting is valuable for trainees since they are exposed to a variety of counseling problems and given the opportunity to ask questions about them. Trainees who already are counseling clients may also use this time to talk about some of their own cases and receive input from the group.

The meetings allow the counselors to explore and discharge feelings of frustration or inadequacy from their work with difficult families. Time is also provided for case analysis; and the history, psychological dynamics, and symptoms of one or two cases are critically examined. The interventions of the counselor are constructively assessed and improvements are suggested.

The trainees are also shown that a counselor may acknowledge incompatibility with a certain client or inadequacy in dealing with a client without fearing that s/he is being judged as incompetent or uncaring.

Goals

To provide trainees the opportunity to:

1. Participate in a CSATP meeting for staff counselors;

2. Understand the value of these meetings as a mechanism for sharing information about unusual or difficult cases, receiving input from other counselors regarding case management and treatment, discharging the negative feelings that inevitably arise, and in general for reducing the stresses of the demanding work;

3. Get a sense of the wide variety of client cases handled by the CSATP counselors and of how the counselors contribute to the team effort for resocialization of the family;

4. Note the various treatment modes employed in the individually-designed treatment program for families;

5. Present cases they themselves are seeing and receive suggestions from the counselors;

6. Observe how counselors deal with their disturbing feelings and attitudes, and how they have developed their own self-help group for this purpose; and

7. Assess how well the counselors have assimilated the humanistic stance by observing how well they help one another.

Rationale

Many of the trainees will soon be saddled with difficult and heavy case loads. The trainees' duties may range far beyond the counseling. They will be involved in the client self-help groups, training and supervising interns, writing evaluations for the court, consulting with law-enforcement personnel, and participating in public awareness programs. In general, they will be responsible for spearheading the development of their CSATPs.

It has been claimed that a CSATP provides clients a regenerative climate, one in which they can learn the attitudes and skills needed for leading productive lives in society. The same climate should be made available to counselors and other staff persons to minimize burn-out and conversely to help them be maximally productive in their CSATP.

Objectives

At the end of this module, trainees should be able to:

1. Be familiar with the therapeutic case-management of a variety of cases;

2. Be more competent in treatment tactics and strategy and apply this ability in the treatment of cases they are working with or will be working with in their own counties;

3. Be more astute concerning their own training needs and more assertive in asking for missing information; and

4. Appreciate the value of the self-help group formed by the counselors and resolve to form one of their own.

Activity 1. Case Presentations by Staff

The counselors present significant or problematical cases to the group. The cases are discussed with the goal of enhancing the group's knowledge about atypical cases, and the treatment plans are assessed in terms of the overall goals of the CSATP. The counselor's successes as well as failures in achieving these goals for a family are scrutinized. Feedback is given by group members concerning interventions that might enhance the resocialization process.

Activity 2. Dealing with Counselors' Feelings

A counselor who is experiencing frustration and/or feelings of inadequacy in dealing with a difficult case may confide, for example, that s/he feels angry and repulsed by the ugly details of a particular offense. The counselor has a chance to vent his or her feelings and is helped to deal with them in a supportive group setting.

Activity 3. Reassignment of Counselors or Interns

A counselor may bring up and admit uneasiness about his or her ability in handling a case, or question the suitability of an intern s/he supervises. If the counselor or intern is patently unable to cope with a particular client, the group assigns another counselor or intern to the case.

Activity 4. Case Presentation by Trainees

Trainees discuss the clients they are currently seeing in their own agencies who are posing problems. Group members discuss the situations and make suitable recommendations. The trainees may also discuss clients they encountered in the co-counseling sessions or in the group session of Parents United or Daughters and Sons United.

Module 2: Co-Counseling Sessions

Description

This is the final co-counseling practicum. In this module, the importance of homework for certain clients in advanced stages of counseling is underscored. The counselor assigns special readings* or exercises to be done at predetermined times during the week; these assignments reflect and elaborate on work done in the sessions. Keeping a daily journal is often recommended and generally worthwhile for the more literate adolescents and adults.

Homework augments the counseling process and therefore may shorten its duration, an important consideration when staff is limited and case loads are heavy.

Goals

Module 2 is designed to provide trainees the opportunity to:

1. Make intimate contact with clients and counselors;

2. Become familiar with different kinds of crisis counseling, methods, and techniques;

3. Observe CSATP counselors using the skills that trainees will need to implement the methods and principles of humanistic counseling with their own clients;

4. Become more self-aware as they attend to the client's process and feelings;

5. Become acquainted with the multifaceted work of the counselor and with its contribution to client growth and productivity; and

6. Ask questions, challenge CSATP counseling methods and their effectiveness, and continue to assess how CSATP methods and counseling styles compare with their own.

*Counselors assign readings on the basis of personal preference. The books most often used are: *Born to Win* by Muriel James and Dorothy Jongeward (Addison-Wesley, 1971); *Women as Winners* by Dorothy Jongeward and Dru Scott (Addison-Wesley, 1976); and *The Intimate Enemy* by George R. Bach and Peter Wyden (William Morrow, 1969).

Rationale

The repeated exposure of trainees to the counseling sessions enables them to make closer contact with the families than would be possible through the group sessions alone. It becomes apparent that incestuous families can become families that develop healthy, autonomous children with coping skills that foster self-actualization and social responsibility.

Initially, when a family comes into the CSATP, the counseling concentrates on the individuals—the mother, the daughter, and the father. But dyad counseling quickly becomes important: first the critical mother–daughter dyad, second the husband–wife dyad, and later the father–daughter dyad. Eventually the siblings and the entire family become involved.

A healthy family system is possible only through nurturing parental guidance, whether by a single parent or two parents. The trainees see the differences between authoritarian or permissive parents and parents that lead democratically: the latter know how to communicate openly and directly and are able to negotiate conflicts fairly between each other and between themselves and their children.

Objectives

At the end of this module, trainees should be able to:

1. Have a good understanding of the CSATP's counseling component, which includes the group counseling sessions of Parents United and Daughters and Sons United;

2. Understand the multifaceted but consistently humanistic treatment approach exercised by all personnel of the CSATP in ministering to the special needs of the sexually abused child and her family;

3. Understand how the individual, dyad, or family counseling sessions foster productive self-management and thereby productive relationships between the clients and spouses, children, and other significant persons;

4. Perceive the positive changes in the life-postures of family members, in particular of the parents, which lead to a strengthening of the family system that precludes chronic dysfunctional behavior; and

5. Understand that a person who is beginning to feel better about him/herself is more apt to court new and/or better interpersonal interactions and therefore is more motivated to improve his or her communications skills.

Family Service Center
Naval Submarine Base New London
P.O. Box 93
Groton, Connecticut 06349

Unit X. Closing Experiential and Didactic Workshop

Unit Description

In the morning, the trainees evaluate the training, report which parts of the training benefitted them most and which were least important, and indicate the parts they would have liked expanded. Since the training concentrates on the inculcation of a humanistic attitude towards incestuous families, the trainees review the concepts and assess the degree to which they have been assimilated. They also state whether the training provided them with at least the preliminary skills for implementing the humanistic concepts. The trainers, some of whom are members of PU/DSU, recapitulate the principal ideas and those the trainees want to be elaborated.

After the trainers and trainees share a potluck lunch, the trainees discuss their specific plans for starting CSATPs and their essential PU/DSU component. They help each other devise strategies for realizing their individual plans. They might choose to do role-playing exercises to "rehearse" how they might cope with potential opponents who may misunderstand their efforts and try to defeat them.

The trainers answer the final questions of the trainees before making their closing remarks. These include assuring the trainees that the CSATP staff will be available to them for consultation by telephone, and that members of PU/DSU and the professional staff will make at least one visit to their localities during the development of their CSATPs. If possible, such visits will occur during the early phases of the organization of their self-help components.

The trainees are also reminded that they can help one another if they work in adjacent areas. This collaboration is especially valuable while the trainees are organizing PU/DSU groups. Clients living in adjacent areas can meet together at first and split up into two groups when they feel they are ready to meet separately.

Unit Content, Module Design, and Activities Requirements

Module	Time	Activity	Time	Materials
1. Assessment and Recapitulation	2.5 hrs.	1. Assessment of the Training Course and filling information gaps	50 min.	Coffee, beverages, and supplies.
		2. Review of the Humanistic Approach	1 hr.	Space requirements: enough room for the group to sit comfortably in a circle and to do role-playing.
		3. Recapitulation of CSATP principles and methods	40 min.	
2. Potluck Lunch	1.5 hrs.			Kitchen, if available. (Trainees supply lunches.)
3. Individual Action Plans	2.5 hrs.	1. Individual action plans for starting CSATPs in trainees' communities	2 hrs. 25 min.	Paper and pencils
		2. Final farewell circle	5 min.	

Unit Goals

To provide trainees the opportunity to:

1. Give trainers constructive criticism about the training and the program;

2. Finish unfinished business and tie up loose ends;

3. Clarify CSATP principles and methods;

4. Identify more explicitly and analyze the problems they anticipate in establishing a CSATP;

5. Brainstorm and devise action plans for establishing a CSATP;

6. Focus on the self-help component and leave with a step-by-step procedure for getting one started;

7. Realize that if they work in the same geographic region they can help one another, especially while forming their self-help groups; and

8. Have adequate closure with each other and their trainers before departing.

Unit Rationale

In this last unit of the training course, the trainees have the opportunity to fill in gaps in their information regarding the professional, self-help, and volunteer components of a CSATP and the methods used for coordinating them. It is hoped that the trainees have internalized sufficiently the humanistic attitude that must be maintained in their dealings with clients and co-workers to develop the caring, educative climate that resociaizes the clients and fosters their own personal and professional growth, as well. It is important also in this wrap-up meeting to convince the trainees that the connections they have made with the CSATP staff and PU/DSU members will not end here.

Unit Objectives

At the end of this unit, trainees should be able to:

1. Leave with the conviction that an incestuous family can recover from its crisis with humanistic assistance and go on to become a productive family;

2. Have the incentive and the preliminary skills to develop a CSATP in their own communities;

3. Be prepared with a specific plan of action for starting a CSATP and its key PU/DSU component, and possess the ability to carry it through;

4. Win the support of key people in their communities;

5. Resolve that they will persevere with their own program of self-management and continue to augment their training in humanistic counseling;

6. Be reassured by the fact that the CSATP staff will maintain its ties with them and will be available to them for continued consultation and on-site assistance;

7. Determine to assist each other, particularly if they live in adjacent regions.

Module 1: Assessment of the Training and Recapitulation of CSATP Principles and Methods

Description

After the usual relaxation exercise, the trainees review the training course. They ask for missing information, assess the training, make constructive suggestions for improving it, and/or express their disappointment if they feel that the training on the whole, or in part, has not been useful to them. The trainees should always be given the opportunity to evaluate the course.

The trainees' needs may differ—some may want more information on coordination and administration, while others may want more information on counseling techniques. During the course, the trainees were repeatedly encouraged to be persistent in their demands for training specific to their needs.

In this module, the trainers attempt to provide supplementary or missing information requested by the trainees and to reassure them that the trainers can be contacted by telephone for further consultation when the need arises.

Goals

To provide trainees the opportunity to:

1. Review and assess the training program;

2. Offer suggestions to the trainers on how the training program might be strengthened;

3. Review once again the principles and methods of the CSATP; and

4. Ask questions about any feature of the CSATP still unclear to them.

Rationale

This is the last day of training, and it is important for the trainees to end the training with confidence in their ability to establish CSATPs in their own communities. This module provides them the last opportunity to discuss and ask their remaining questions regarding the principles and methods of the CSATP, in terms of their personal requirements and the requirements and constraints of their communities.

Objectives

At the end of this module, trainees should be able to:

1. Feel comfortable with the principles of the humanistic approach and be able to start and develop a CSATP;

2. Have a good understanding of the organization and operation of a CSATP; and

3. Know that further help from the trainers will be available to them in the future when they need it.

Activity 1. Assessment of the Training Course and Filling Information Gaps

The trainer informs the trainees he does not want them to leave the course feeling unfinished. He encourages them to assess the course in terms of what they feel was omitted from the two weeks of training and what they would have liked more or less of. The trainees are given ample opportunity to voice critical opinions while the trainers listen carefully.

When a trainee expresses a negative opinion or regret about omissions or redundancies in the training, the trainer does not respond defensively but gives the trainees' opinions full dignity and then requests their suggestions for improving future training courses. Invariably, trainees desire clarification on various aspects of the CSATP, such as the treatment, the administrative, and the legal aspects, and the trainers respond accordingly.

Activity 2. Review of the Humanistic Attitude

The trainees recall their pretraining attitudes towards child sexual abuse and incestuous families and discuss the degree to which those attitudes have been supplanted by humanistic ones. They describe the positive changes in their opinions and stances and the training experiences that stimulated the changes.

The trainers review the philosophy of the humanistic attitude, compare it pragmatically with a judgmental and punitive viewpoint, and urge the trainees to reread the sections on the humanistic approach in Part I.

The trainees test the strength of their abilities to empathize with clients and colleagues they presume will be antagonistic to a CSATP by role-playing exercises with the imagined antagonist.

Activity 3. Recapitulation of CSATP Principles and Methods

The trainer reviews the organizational structure of the CSATP and the general procedures for initiating, developing, and coordinating the professional, self-help, and volunteer components. The case management of a typical family is described once again to demonstrate how the three components are involved in this process.

Module 2: Potluck Lunch

This module is the trainees' last lunch together. The trainees were asked the day before to bring some food to share. The meal usually becomes a festive occasion, with each trainee celebrating his or her accomplishments, the completion of the training, and the new friendships.

Module 3: Individual Action Plans for Starting CSATPs

Description

The trainees are asked to anticipate and ponder the specific problems each of them will encounter in starting their CSATPs. In turn, the trainees are helped to develop start-up plans tailored to the requirements and constraints of their communities. The trainers devote the remaining time to answering questions related to the action plans.

The group members use the last farewell circle to thank each other and to share what they have gained from the training and the bonds they have formed. The trainers inform the trainees that they are available to them in the future. The trainees are at the end of their training but the beginning of their involvement in a widespread effort to replace the neglectful and/or punitive approach in the handling of sexually abused children and their families with one that is caring and productive.

Goals

To provide trainees the opportunity to:

1. Anticipate what they will encounter when they actually start establishing CSATPs;

2. Prepare action plans to suit their individual situations;

3. Get their last questions answered; and

4. Experience sufficient closure with each other.

Rationale

The essential purpose of the training course is to prepare each trainee to start and to develop a CSATP in his or her own community. In this module, the final preparatory training is provided and ends by focusing on the design of start-up plans tailored to the needs of each trainee.

Objectives

At the end of this module, trainees should be able to:

1. Feel prepared to meet the specific problems they foresee when they return to their own communities to establish their own CSATPs;

2. Have their remaining questions answered to their satisfaction; and

3. Know that the trainers will be available to them for help in the future, when they need it.

Activity 1. Individual Action Plans

This time period has been set aside to help each of the trainees to devise a procedure tailored to his or her unique situation. The trainer gives a detailed outline of the steps usually followed in starting a CSATP. S/he acknowledges that situations differ and that some of the trainees may have already completed the initial steps.

Each trainee (or group of trainees from the same community) describes the local conditions and the key people whose support they must enlist in order to get a CSATP under way or to further its development. The group brainstorms the situation and offers ideas and strategies for establishing a CSATP in each particular community.

The trainees are advised to avoid repeated meetings with community decision-makers during the early stages. The most convincing argument for a CSATP is not a verbal one but the PU/DSU self-help component. Thus, the trainees' early efforts should be pointed primarily toward acquiring clients and forming a victims' group and a parents' group.

Activity 2. Final Farewell Circle

The group members stand in a circle with their arms encircling each other's waists. The group members have shared deeply personal experiences and feelings and the farewell circle becomes an occasion for the exchange of warm expressions of appreciation and friendship. Before breaking up the circle, they remain together for a minute or two in quiet reflection.

Epilogue

Dear Swako:

I need to write you this letter because I want you to know how I am feeling at this moment.

I am feeling strong, confident, and I am liking myself. As I feel this all at once, I notice that my feelings for you are also changing. I am no longer feeling threatened by you or angry at you. I am beginning to see the sweet, beautiful, woman that I fell in love with. I can see how my behavior and attitude changed you into the cold and hard person that I have been for so many years. I can see how my insecurity and my immaturity forced you to take charge for the family's sake. As I learn to reach out to others for support, I can see just how much I need others and how I pushed you and your love away.

I am glad I have become aware of just how much hurt and pain I grew up with and how it kept me from being the kind of husband and father that I always wanted to be. I can see now how I failed to provide our son with the kind of love and support that little boys need. Although I may never be a real father to him, I know now that just as others have extended the hand of friendship to me and given me their love and support, I too can provide love and support to him and I can be a good friend to him.

I am happy that you are seeing Penny and that you and the children are attending church. I was touched very deeply when you told me that you and the children pray for me. Thank you all for your prayers.

I am feeling happy because I can now share my feelings openly and because I can let you and others know exactly where I stand without fear of rejection.

I feel happy because I can now accept others for themselves, with their faults and weaknesses just the way you accepted me for myself and provided me with your love and support throughout our marriage.

I feel it important to share these feelings with you because I want you to grow stronger too, and because I want you to see me and yourself through my new eyes. I know now that things will work out for the best.

Your loving husband

Appendices

1. Counseling Methods and Techniques

by Ellie Breslin

Gestalt Therapy

Fritz Perls can take nearly all credit for Gestalt therapy's innovative approach to individual and group counseling. The Gestalt approach usually involves the client actively in what oftentimes appears to be highly theatrical activity in which the client is encouraged to give dramatic expression to the feelings, thoughts, images, and sensations of the immediate moment.

The techniques of Gestalt therapy are at one level a synthesis of many other techniques found in alternative counseling methods, but Gestalt has an essence of its own. The focus, or central point of unification of the alternative methods, is beyond technique, however, and is referred to in Gestalt literature as the experience of actuality–awareness–responsibility. Its aim is to make the client more aware and more responsible for: his feelings, thoughts, and actions; his introjected family; the irrational attitudes and feelings he projects onto others; the myths and illusions by which he has guided his life; and all the undesirable and disowned parts of himself, i.e., the total reality of himself and his existence. The desired attitude for both client and counselor is one of present-centeredness, or the experience of being fully present in the moment and in full contact with one's ongoing experience.

Nearly every technique in Gestalt can be viewed as one that will bring the client into awareness. The broad prescription of Gestalt is "be aware." This means that the client takes responsibility for himself as the doer of his actions, the thinker of his

thoughts, and as the one who feels and senses, so that he begins to experience himself as he is and not as what he thinks he should be, and he begins to experience life as it is and not what it is not. The approach is concerned with the wholeness and uniqueness of the individual and with his resources for having gratifying interactions with the environment. Clients are helped to assume responsibility for themselves, to develop clarity in communicating with others, to develop independence and self-support, to complete the unfinished business in their lives, to explore new more effective ways of satisfying emergent needs, and to foster a high level of self-awareness, excitement in living, self-nurturance, and creative contact with others.

Gestalt techniques are designed to give the clients a moment of true contact, of true experience. They learn there is nothing to fear, and that the reward of real contact with the moment far outweighs the pain of avoidance and withdrawal from experience. The importance of this cannot be underestimated when one looks at the troubled family in which the family members may be experiencing a pervading sense of isolation and aloneness—where they are alienated not only from others but from themselves as well—and where the family's idiosyncratic ways have kept the members isolated from the mainstream of society. Since one of the tasks of resocialization of a family is to reeducate its members in personal and interpersonal skills that will enable them to dissolve the barriers that separate them from others, the clients' experiences with Gestalt techniques seem more helpful than cerebral and discursive talking "about" historical events or probing deeply into one's childhood and family of origin in search of the "whys" of behavior.

Gestalt techniques teach people to observe precisely objects, events, thoughts, sensations, and feelings as they appear. They also teach the ability to acquire and sustain presence so that one can remain in the moment and in a state of awareness that allows one to be "on top of" the situation or experience, rather than being controlled by it. In Gestalt terms this is referred to as "awareness continuum" or "stream of consciousness." Awareness is also a requisite for meaningful contact or encounter; according to Gestalt thought, to be in contact is the natural state of the alert, healthy human being.

Of the many innovative techniques developed by Perls, perhaps the most comprehensive one is the technique that Perls named "experiment." The experiment is an attempt to bring the individual's action system right into the room. In their book, *Gestalt Therapy Integrated* (pp. 234–35), Irving and Miriam Polster write:

> Through experiment the individual is mobilized to confront the emergencies of his life by playing out his aborted feelings and actions in relative safety. A safe emergency is thus created where venturesome exploration can be supported.

Experiments are built around small units of behavior: an expression, a tone of voice, a verbal cue. It is important to build the experiment as soon as possible on the behavioral unit being manifested —that is, to create the experiment based on what the facilitator or counselor has just observed about the client's ongoing experience. The facilitator must take care to make the experiment safe for the client, to make it one he will succeed at. When an experiment has been successfully completed the client will look, act, and feel differently. The experiment will probably start with the client being tentative, cautious, and confused with lack of focus, since the behavior being asked for is new. Tension builds to a climax through several often well-delineated steps, as the client works through the experiment with resulting release of tension and a sense of achievement, peace, and calm.

There are many kinds of experiments, and most Gestalt techniques will fall into one of these categories: (1) enactment; (2) directed behavior; (3) fantasy; (4) dreams; and (5) homework.

Enactment

Enactment is an acting-out, not in the perjorative sense but in the sense that an act is fostered by the timeliness of the action as determined by the facilitator, and its fit into the person's life. The act is structured in a specific way to solve a specific problem. Enactment is the dramatization in the group or counseling session of some aspect of the client's existence. It may start from a statement, a gesture, a feeling, or an image. Perhaps the client is tapping his foot. He is asked to extend this movement, that is, exaggerate it. He says he feels like kicking and that he's feeling angry. He is asked if there is a face or image that goes with the motion and the feeling. He may say his father, or his boss.

At this point, there are several ways to go. The experiment might shift to the mode of directed behavior: the client is directed to place his boss in the chair and talk to him or behave toward him in any way that feels right, which could include screaming at him all the things the client had thought to say but could not allow himself to express heretofore, thus leaving himself feeling powerless and used. Usually by the time the experiment is completed, the client will have discovered a new side of himself—the power side— and will have tapped into his own held-in excitement, realizing that he has expressed violent rage in a controlled situation and that his catastrophic expectations of what might happen if he were to let go with his anger did not materialize. This client is not rehearsing for the future event of confronting the boss but is experiencing in the present what it is like for him to move from awareness to experimental action and feel power that he did not know he had. Although he may not rage at the boss in reality, he might be better able to take a stand with him in the future.

There are several kinds of enactment: enactment of an unfinished situation from the distant past; enactment of a contemporary unfinished situation; enactment of a characteristic; and enactment of a polarity. An example of the first type would be an adult molested as a child who talked about her total passivity during sexual relations with her husband. She recalled how her father had pinned her down as he molested her, and that no matter how hard she protested he would not desist. She had learned that if she were quiet and submissive, he would hurt her less and leave her alone sooner. The facilitator asked if she would be willing to engage in an experiment with one of the men in the group role-playing her father. She asked what she would be expected to do and was told that she would engage in a hand-to-hand pushing contest with the man. She chose a man who was her size, if not somewhat slighter. The man was instructed to feed her lines that would attack her weakness and passivity, such as, "You're a pushover," and "I've got you where I want you."

As they began to push against each other's hands and he fed her the lines, she was very tentative about pushing back and allowed herself to be moved about the room fairly easily; but as the man goaded her, mounting anger soon began to take over and she did indeed begin to push back. As she experienced a mounting excitement, her strength seemed to increase and soon she was pushing the man across the floor with considerable vigor while she continued to express her anger by grimaces and expletives.

She finally exploded, yelling, "Stay away from me, you dirty . . .!" and succeeded in breaking contact with him with a mighty push. Her face was flushed with the exertion and the excitement as she returned to her seat. As she quieted down, she remarked how good she felt and how great she felt in taking control of the situation.

It must be pointed out that the goal of the experiment was not to improve her sexual relationship with her mate, but to put her in touch with old feelings, allow her to experience some new ones, and to create a new ending to an old nightmare. What she may begin to understand is that her husband is not her father, and that she does indeed have an effect on her environment when she can tap her latent powers for action.

Enactment of a contemporary situation occurs when adults molested as children role-play and rehearse for an actual confrontation with their parents. Often these parents are still alive and important in the person's life, but the issue of the molest has never been resolved. Other situations might be a parent who finds his child's behavior intolerable, or a spouse trying to resolve a marital dispute.

Enactment of a characteristic is exemplified by a client who hated the way she looked and wore her hair in long bangs that partially obscured her eyes. Having a poor self-image, the client didn't want to see herself; and she also hid from others behind the hair. Her feelings about herself did not allow her to meet the world positively.

By giving her a mirror and having her speak to her image, the counselor got her to project her feelings outward. The counselor had her focus attention on the eyes behind the bangs and then asked her to push her hair aside, focus on her eyes again, and note if she experienced herself differently.

The counselor had the client become aware that she held her head in a way that did not allow her to meet the eyes of others fully or to see her world straight on and that she maintained a timid, downcast, and fearful expression. Then the counselor had the client shift the angle of her head, thrusting it forward slightly into a position that would be more likely to facilitate encounter with other people. The client began to get a more positive image of herself.

The counselor then had the client return her bangs to their usual position so that she could contrast the two ways of appearing and the different feelings associated with these two appearances. The counselor also had the client accept ownership of those images by attributing them to herself: "I'm alive, I sparkle, I can see clearly, I'm curious, I'm interested, I feel good."

The client was excited by the new experience and decided to cut her bangs. The counselor showed her she could have the same good feelings even with her hair in bangs. The client's perceptions of herself have changed with her new awareness.

The enactment of a polarity is exemplified by a client whose show-off self contrasted sharply with her programmed self (as characterized by a dark cloak). Margie, an adult molested as a child, had been in the group for many weeks. She occasionally commented on the work of others, but chose not to work on herself. Her comments and feedback to others were creative and thoughtful, and the facilitator sensed how much of herself she held back, afraid to become the focus of the group's attention. The counselor did not urge Margie to disclose herself; she had to trust the group and the counselor before revealing herself. In the twelfth week, Margie said she wanted to work on her fear of opening herself to the group. The facilitator asked her to say more about her fear.

Margie: *I feel scared now because everyone is looking at me.*

Counselor: *What do you imagine they are thinking as they look at you? (Note: The counselor avoids premature confrontation by asking the client to assume what the group members are thinking rather than having her ask them directly for their opinions.)*

Margie: *Oh, they're probably thinking, "At last, the timid mouse is going to do something."*

Counselor: *Going to do something?*

Margie: *Oh, yeah. I guess I'm already doing it, aren't I. (Margie looks embarrassed. She swallows and blushes.)*

Counselor: *What did you experience just now as you swallowed. Were you aware that you swallowed?*

Margie: *Yes. I feel embarrassed. Here I am out on the hot seat. I'm afraid I'll make a fool of myself. (As she says this, she pulls her shawl tightly about her shoulder.)*

Counselor: *(Deciding not to pursue the swallow but to go with the shawl.) What are you covering up with your shawl?*

Margie: *(Looks down at herself, then at the counselor with a sheepish smile.) My creative, show-off self. I cover that part of me up with a dark, heavy cloak.*

(Now the parts seem well defined: the show-off who wants the world to see her; and the dark cloak, the programmed self that has learned not to disclose her inner experience.)

Counselor: *So a minute ago you were more or less unconsciously doing something—working, if you will—and as soon as you became aware of that, you shut down, pulled your cloak around you.*

Margie: *Yes. I always do that. I hate it. What I really want to do is get out there and dance and be free and have fun with everyone else, but I'm too timid most of the time, unless I've had a few to loosen up.*

Counselor: *(Taking a really bold step and risk with the client; not at all sure the client will go along, or that the client will feel safe enough to risk acting on the counselor's suggestion.) Can you do a dance that expresses the two parts, the show-off and the dark cloak?*

The counselor has posed a paradox. If Margie does a dance, she sheds the cloak and even in dancing the part of the cloak, she is "showing off." If she does not dance, she is taking a stand in not following the counselor's prescription, using her cloak to keep herself hidden. Perhaps then she can see the power in her timidity.

Margie slowly gets up and moves tentatively, cautiously to the center of the group. She closes her eyes and takes some deep breaths, then begins to move her feet and body in dance. Her movements are awkward and self-conscious. She stays with the movements, mostly swaying, for only a moment, then swoops down on one knee, pulls her shawl up over her head, and hides her face under crossed arms. She remains there for a long moment, rises, and dances a few more steps, more fluid now, less tentative; then she swoops down on one knee, pulling her shawl tightly about her head and shoulders. The process repeats, and again she dances a little more freely; but as self-consciousness takes over, she hides again under the cloak.

Counselor: *What are you experiencing now, Margie?*

Margie: *I feel so self-conscious up there as "show-off," I wish I could really let that part out for all the world to see. I wish I could just throw this old cloak away, get rid of it. Whenever "show-off" wants to come out, I always have the cloak ready to pull over her.*

Counselor: *Like a quick flasher who opens, but closes before anyone can really see.* Put your cloak over here on this pillow, close enough to where you can get it whenever you need it, and let's see what happens when you dance.*

(The cloak was a defense. Asking Margie to put it aside for a moment helped her see what else was there. Roles and feelings can be put aside, too, especially those that are repetitive.)

Margie: *(She folds the cloak and puts in on the pillow.) I feel naked.*

Counselor: *You look beautiful.*

Margie: *(Dances around and around.) Look at me, look at me, I'm dancing, dancing. (She looks radiant and finally stops, breathless.)*

Group: *That was beautiful, you were marvelous. (They are clapping.) Encore!*

Counselor: *Go around the room and talk to each person about yourself without your cloak. (Margie is ready to make contact with each one individually, having successfully completed the experiment and gotten a new sense of herself.)*

Margie: *I'm shiny.*
I'm new.
I can dance.
I can play.
I feel open.
I'm free.

(As she moves around the circle she giggles, grins, squirms, but she has a new excitement about her, a new aliveness. The group rejoices with her and she gets lots of attention for being herself. She is radiant and tearful as she sits down.)

Counselor: *(To the group.) It is important to put people in touch with the positive parts of themselves. When Margie took off the cloak, she showed much more of herself, not just a flash or tantalizing look.*

Directed Behavior

Directed behavior refers to the requirement for stronger direction on the part of the counselor or facilitator. The facilitator often becomes more directive as the client progresses in his growth.

*Counselor's note: "Those were my original wrods. I could also have said something like: 'My experience of you is that you throw something out, then pull it back, like you want to dance, but you don't think anyone here will dance with you.' "

Telling the client what to do is done selectively and for exploratory purposes. For example, the client may discover a certain behavior previously blocked out of awareness; or s/he may try on a new behavior that is just the opposite of his or her usual behavior. A person may be complaining but be unaware of the plaintive quality of her voice and utterances. The facilitator might direct her to exaggerate her dissatisfied state deliberately by complaining directly to each person in the room. The person who speaks in a slow methodical drone may be asked to speak nothing but gibberish, to let meaningless sounds pour and spill out of his mouth.

The directed behavior is not intended get people to do what they don't want to do. It is intended to help them increase their repertoire for contacting their environment. By practicing new behaviors they may have been afraid to try before, they may discover new things about themselves.

Fantasy

Fantasy is used in several ways, including making contact with a repressed event or feeling. One client was resistant to exploring her sense of emptiness in her life, of being a void. She was asked to close her eyes and to let images or a feeling sense of the huge void come to her. She described the void as a huge, empty room with doors around the perimeter. She saw herself as a five-year-old in a red velvet dress and patent-leather shoes, all alone in the room. She was frightened and did not know what to do; she was afraid also to open the doors and discover what was beyond them. When she finally opened one of the doors, a huge white dragon jumped into the room and chased her about, breathing fire and threatening to consume her. The client let out a scream of terror and clutched herself tightly in a ball. The facilitator held her and soothed her until her sense of security returned.

Gradually she began to talk about her father, who molested her, and the angry rages he would fly into as he sent her off to her room alone before he came in to berate or molest her. The relating of these events was a great relief to her, and she broke into convulsive sobbing. When she had composed herself, she looked much younger, her face no longer drawn into a constrained look of anguish. She commented that she felt very peaceful and that the facilitator's caring and attending to her in her moments of terror meant a great deal, as her own mother had not been able to do that for her.

Visualization and fantasy can be used in many ways: "Visualize yourself as a strong lion," "Visualize yourself being born," "Visualize having different parents and what it would be like growing up with them." Requests such as these are made in accordance with the client's on going process, from clues evidenced by the client.

Dreams

Perls assumed that dreams are projections and that all their components are representations of the dreamer. In the enactment, the client is asked to recount a dream in the active voice, as if he were dreaming it presently—a technique that helps him reexperience the dream consciously—and to play parts of the dream that seem particularly significant. One use of dreamwork is given in this example of Molly, a woman molested as a child.

Molly: *I'm so sad. (Her hands are shaking and she's huddled in the pillows.)*

Counselor: *Your body is full of sadness.*

Molly: *I had a dream in which I felt very sad.*

Counselor: *Does your sadness connect with anything specific?*

Molly: *With Julie [a mother who has just finished working] when she was talking to her daughter. I'd like to be that daughter and hear that from my mother.*

Counselor: *What would you like to hear from your mother?*

Molly: *That she loved me. The dream is about my father. (Molly shifts back to dream.)*

Counselor: *You want to tell us about the dream?*

Molly: *Yes. I want to understand it.*

Counselor: *Tell the dream in the active voice as if you were dreaming it right now.*

Molly: *I am in the kitchen. I'm about eight. My father is angry with me. I feel sick to my stomach. He's very angry.*

Counselor: *Can you say to your father, "You make me sick"? (This directive was not the best choice; it was jumping ahead of the client, and not following her process. The client ignores the request.)*

Molly: *I begin to sob. My father says he has to leave permanently because of me. He begins to put on his coat and hat, and I hold onto him and beg him, "Don't leave, please don't leave." Then he hands me the coat and hat, and I think he's telling me it is I who must leave. I* *put the coat on. It's too long and he laughs and jeers and says, "You're a silly clown." I fall down at his feet crying and wake up.*

Counselor: *What feelings in the dream seem most important to you?*

Molly: *I feel abandoned.*

Counselor: *Where is your mother in the dream?*

Molly: *She's in the background watching, doing nothing.*

Counselor: *From what I'm hearing, it sounds like you feel abandoned by both your mother and father. (The counselor is sitting right next to the client and has had her hand resting lightly on the client's back between her shoulders.) What are you experiencing now? Your energy feels different. Did something change in the telling of the dream?*

Molly: *I don't feel so bad.*

Counselor: *Lean back and see if there's anything you want to say either to your mother or father— or the dream.*

Molly: *(Leans back, closes eyes.) Nothing. (Silence.)*

Counselor: *(Not accepting client's "nothing" and sensing there is an intense internal dialogue going on.) Who are you talking to?*

Molly: *Both of them.*

Counselor: *I want you to do something. Become either your mother or your father. Which one?*

Molly: *My father.*

Counselor: *Be your father, assume his posture, get a good image of him—what he looks like, what he's wearing, his facial expression. Describe yourself as him.*

Molly: *I'm solid. I'm a farmer. My body is strong and tan. My beard has two or three days' growth. My hands are large and there's dirt under my nails. I'm wearing Levis and a red shirt that has patches on the elbows. I have five children. I think something is wrong with my wife, but I never say what I think. I don't say much to anyone.*

Counselor: *Where is Molly in birth order?*

Molly: *She's the oldest.*

Counselor: *Do you like her?*

Molly: *Yes. I feel close to her. Closer to her than anyone. My wife does not care about me.*

Counselor: *Does Molly know how you feel about her?*

Molly: *Yes.*

Counselor: *How do you let her know? How do you tell her?*

Molly: *(Long silence.)*

Counselor: *How, as Molly's father, do you tell her how you feel about her?*

Molly: *(Silence.)*

Counselor: *(Shifts focus away from painful area, guessing it may be molestation.) Do you know why Molly is in such pain?*

Molly: *I'm trembling inside. I don't want to talk about it. I don't want to think about it. I want to be quiet inside.*
(Molly's breathing is fast and shallow and the counselor again feels she's pushed the client too fast. The counselor puts her hand lightly on Molly's chest and tells her to breathe deeply. Molly's legs are trembling, her body shaking.)

Counselor: *Let your body tell you what it needs. Let it move the way it wants to, say what it wants to. If there is anything you want from me, let me know.*

Molly: *(Sobs and shakes.)*

Counselor: *(Softly.) Are there any images you're having?*

Molly: *Two. A little white bed; I'm very small. The other is confused. I'm in a hospital, all alone in the corner. I'm holding myself.*

Counselor: *I have an image of you as a very small child, a baby, and you weren't held right. You were the first baby and your mother was only a child herself, and she was afraid of the tiny baby, held you stiffly so you couldn't make contact with her. (The counselor has noticed* *that when she puts her hand on Molly's chest, her trembling wanes; and when she removes her touch, Molly's trembling increases. This observation has helped form the image above.)*

Molly: *I don't think she ever held me. There was always another baby.*

Counselor: *Do you want me to hold you?*

Molly: *Yes, yes.*

Counselor: *Tell me how you want me to hold you. What feels right.*

Molly: *(Settles into counselor's arms and sobs deeply.) I don't know what I'm crying about.*

Counselor: *It doesn't matter. Let yourself be comforted. I feel good holding you as my daughter.*

Dreamwork in the Gestalt mode is extensive and often involved. For a more complete discourse on the Gestalt use of dreams, the reader is referred to Chapter 8 entitled *"Experiments in Gestalt Therapy Integrated"* in the book by Polsters; and "Dream Seminars" by F. S. Perls in *Life Techniques in Gestalt Therapy*, edited by Fagan and Shepherd.

Bioenergetics

Background

Bioenergetics is a way of understanding personality in terms of the body and its energetic processes. These processes are the production of energy through respiration and metabolism and the discharge of energy in movement. These are the basic functions of life. . . . Bioenergetics is also a form of therapy that combines work with the body and the mind to help people resolve their emotional problems and realize more of their potential for pleasure and joy in living. A fundamental thesis of bioenergetics is that body and mind are functionally identical: that is, what goes on in the mind reflects what is happening in the body and vice versa.[1]

Alexander Lowen, the father of bioenergetic analysis, was interested in integrating bodily and emotional states and laid great emphasis on the notion that all neuroses are manifested in the structure and functioning of the body. In his work he looked for the special relationship between emotional states and their physical manifestations, and then employed therapeutic techniques involving integrative physical work on the body with analytical work aimed at giving the client intellectual understanding and insight.

Lowen might have worked in the following manner with a client who as a child experienced great hostility and an urge to hit out at her parents, but was prevented from doing so by guilt and fear of rejection, so that the direct expression of rage was inhibited. Lowen might note that the client complained of back and neck pain, and that she hunched her shoulders and arm muscles as if girding to strike out. He might also note that the client clenched her jaw and pursed her lips as one might do if holding back the expressing of anger. Lowen's approach would be to talk analytically or intellectually about the client's feelings and at the same time have her physically hit out—in a controlled setting—on a couch or pillows either with her fists or with a tennis racquet clenched in both hands and raised above the head and then brought down upon the pillows in repeated motions. He would also ask the client to shout an appropriate word or phrase as she struck out, words that would stimulate the pent-up rage.

If the intervention were successful, the client would probably beat the pillows until exhausted, and perhaps dissolve in convulsive sobbing. The result would be that important childhood material would be brought into consciousness for analytic use; the client would have discharged an enormous amount of tension, leading to the relaxation of the muscles in the neck; and assuming that the tension was chronic, Lowen would expect that with further work on the muscles, and with the original cause of the tension having been dealt with, there would be no further conflict between the emotions and the bodily structure.

Of course, this example is simplistic and incomplete. Indeed, it would be difficult to find a simple but general statement that would adequately define bioenergetics, and counselors and workers interested in the uses of bioenergetics in working with clients would do well to expand their reading to include the books listed at the back of this appendix, as well as to experience some of the exercises that will be described in more detail further on.

---

1. Alexander Lowen, M.D., and Leslie Lowen, *The Way to Vibrant Health.* New York: Harper & Row, 1977.

Theory

A major concept in bioenergetics is the concept of grounding. According to Bellis, the function of grounding is relevant to the development of the ego and its most basic functions. These functions can be described as: the ego's motor functions—how one moves in the environment and copes with the world; the ego's perceptual functions, or what is perceived through the senses leading to conceptualization, self-understanding, and one's relationship to others and the physical environment; and the ego's vocal function, where each person attains his own voice, gains a voice in the community, and is able to actively verbalize thoughts and feelings. Development of the ego also includes the individual's ability to monitor his impulses to a degree that brings about harmonization of his needs, wants, desires, and fantasies with social demands and expectations—without repression, on the one hand, or acting out hostility on the other.[2]

The sensation of contact between the feet and the ground is known as grounding in bioenergetics. It presumes a flow of energy or excitation through the legs into the feet and ground. Metaphorically, one can be said to be connected to the ground rather than "up in the air." A grounded person has his feet "on the ground." He knows where he stands and can take a stand. He has "standing," an identity; he is "somebody." In a broader sense, grounding represents how much the individual is in contact with the realities of his existence. A person who has good motor connection with the ground is most likely well grounded psychologically as well. That is to say that when a person becomes highly charged or excited he need not give in to impulse and, indeed, has mastery over his feelings and is able to discharge them appropriately while still experiencing them fully.

Grounding is closely related to breathing. Most adults tend to have disturbed breathing patterns because of chronic muscular tension that limits their capacity to breathe fully and deeply. When breathing is suppressed due to tension, then it can almost always be assumed that the restricted flow of breath serves a purpose in preventing dreaded emotional conflicts and feelings, usually originating in childhood, from surfacing.

The primary way we ground ourselves with others is through the visual and auditory senses. Bioenergetic theory states that when the auditory and ocular ways of perceiving have been blocked by terror in earlier childhood years, perception is often interfered with. In bioenergetic terms, a person cannot be said to be grounded until his eyes are

2. Olsen, Paul, PhD, ed. *Emotional Flooding*, Vol. 1 Chap. 8, "Emotional Flooding and Bioenergetic Analysis," John M. Bellis, pp. 144–46.

opened both in an optical and a feeling sense. It is believed by many practitioners that distortions of hearing and seeing on an emotional level often result in distortions of the same functions on a mechanical level.

Finally, at some point a person must attain his own voice, for it is through self-disclosure and verbal expression that one knows another and comes to know oneself. When a person can speak for himself, he is self-possessed; he is an individual who cherishes his uniqueness and is not afraid to declare who he is.

Technique

Grounding someone means assisting him in getting in touch with himself through the language of the body, his parts, and introjects. Bioenergetic exercises are designed to help the client get in touch with his body, become keenly aware of it, its sensations, and its tensions. Awareness sharpens the client's knowledge of self, which in turn helps him cope with life's stresses more effectively and enhances his capacity for fully experiencing life. A person who can fully feel and fully express his emotions is an alive human being, vibrant and exciting. According to bioenergetic theory, when tension becomes chronic and acts as a dam to block the experience and full expression of feeling, the result is a deadening of the body and alienation from it. Getting in touch with the body again is a process of learning to sense the tightness and tensions that block the flow of excitation and feeling. Only by sensing a tension can one release it. If one does not learn to sense tension, particularly chronic tension and the underlying causes, he may be forced to use pills, alcohol, or act out symptomatically, as does the child-abuser. If one senses the tension, relaxation can be achieved through appropriate and expressive movement. Hence, exercises (such as kicking a mattress, hitting, shouting and screaming) or emotional releases (such as heartfelt crying) will often relax the inner tensions and lead to a sense of well-being.

Let us say we have a client who is blocking her impulse to cry. She does this by gritting her teeth, reducing her breathing, tightening the throat, getting the customary "lump in the throat." While directing her to keep breathing, the counselor will try to get her to open her teeth, drop her jaw, and make noises upon expiration of the breath. The client may tighten elsewhere to block the feeling, but she may also begin to sob. The crying will have the effect of releasing the tension, deepening the breathing, resulting in a feeling of calm, and she will have learned some of the ways in which she blocks her feelings, divorcing herself from her body.

Every release phenomenon is accompanied by sound and enhanced breathing. If the release is not accompanied by sound, the counselor should encourage the use of sound, suggesting the sound to be used, or sounding with the client until she gets the feel of it. No sound, or partial sound, indicates that the release is not full and is being choked off. The person who can make full resonating sounds from within can be said to have attained his own voice.

CSATP Bioenergetic Training Exercises

The following exercises are used with each group of trainees that come to Santa Clara County for training. They are described here but can be read about in greater detail in Lowen's book, *The Way To Vibrant Health: A Manual of Bioenergetic Exercises.*

1. **Basic vibratory and grounding exercise.** This is one of the most fundamental exercises in bioenergetics and is simple and easy to do. It is used to start the vibrations in the legs and to help the person sense them.

Stand with feet about ten inches apart, toes slightly turned inward so as to create a stretch in the muscles of the buttocks. Bend forward and touch the floor with the fingers of both hands. Knees should be slightly bent. No weight should be put on the hands; all the body weight is in the feet. Drop the head.

Breathe through the mouth deeply and easily.

Let the weight of your body go forward so that it is on the balls of the feet.

Straighten the knees slowly until the hamstrings at the back of the legs are stretched. However, the knees should not be locked or straightened.

Hold the position and experiment with shifting your weight, bending the knees a little and straightening to the original position.

When the muscles have relaxed, they will begin to vibrate. Stay with the vibration and enjoy the sensation of energy traveling down your legs, through your feet to the ground.

2. **The Bow or Arch.** This exercise puts the body under stress to open up the breathing more fully. It also places more strain on the legs. If done correctly, it helps release the tension on the belly.

Stand with the feet about eighteen inches apart, toes slightly turned inward.

Place both fists with knuckles facing upward into the small of your back.

Bend both knees as much as possible without lifting the heels off the floor.

Arch backward over your fists, but keep weight forward on the balls of the feet. Breathe as deeply as you can with the breath going into the belly.

If the exercise is done correctly, the legs will begin to vibrate. If the perfect arch is maintained, energy and sensation will flow fully into the feet.

3. **Working with the Bioenergetic Stool.** A bioenergetic stool is twenty-four inches high; rolled blankets on its top add another six to eight inches. It looks like a kitchen step stool, having a wide and solid base. Lying face up with shoulders over the stool stretches tight back muscles and helps the user breathe deeply and effortlessly. Lying over the stool also creates a physically stressful situation. However, if the person lies over the stool and relaxes into the stressful position, breathing will deepen spontaneously. This exercise will point up tension in many parts of the body: the upper and lower back, the shoulder girdle, the diaphragm, abdominal muscles, and muscles used in breathing. The idea is to submit in a relaxed way to the uncomfortable, perhaps painful position, allowing the tense muscles to relax and become energized.

If the person lying over the stool feels the throat tightening or becoming choked, this is a sign of resisting the natural tendency to breathe deeply. Making sounds on expiration will help to open up the breathing. A choked feeling is often caused by blocking the impulse to cry. If this happens, the person should try to express the feeling and give in to the need to cry or even to sob. Pain experienced in any of the muscles affected by this exercise indicates that these muscles are being held in tension.

The primary exercise with the stool is as follows.

A chair is positioned with its seat toward the stool. Stand with the back to the stool and put both hands on the blanket roll behind you. Then slowly lower the back until the shoulder blades rest on the roll. Let go with the hands so that the stool and your legs support your weight. Now raise the hands and reach backward until you grasp the back of the chair behind you. Bend your knees and keep your feet flat on the floor.

Lie on the stool for as long as you can tolerate the stress, but at first limit your stay on the stool to about one minute.

Try to sense what is going on in your body. Where do you feel tightness, pain, rigidity? Is there tension in the diaphragm, abdominal muscles or the lower back? Do you experience tingling in your extremities denoting an excitement or charge into these parts? Do you have trouble breathing?

Emotionally, do you experience feelings such as anxiety, fear, or an urge to shout or cry?

The important aim of this exercise is to sense your body and become aware of where you hold tension in the musculature.

4. **Expressing Anger.** In this exercise, the client is given the opportunity to express anger physically in a controlled setting. Most people are too frightened of violence to be able to express anger physically unless seriously provoked. This exercise helps people get in touch with their anger and provides the experience of expressing it physically without hurting someone.

Stand in front of a bed or a pile of pillows that is not quite waist high. Stand with your feet about eighteen inches apart, both knees slightly bent so you have a good sense of your feet on the ground. Grasp the handle of a tennis racquet loosely in both hands. If you grip it too tightly you will feel pain in your hands as you make contact with the bed or pillows. Now experiment with the correct distance from the pillows so that when the racquet descends with arms outstretched the racquet will hit the middle of the pillow pile.

Raise your elbows and take the racquet back across the top of your head as far as you can. Keeping the knees slightly flexed, bring the racquet down on the pillows with as much force as you can muster without hurting yourself. Try to stay relaxed, yet hit strongly.

Say any words that express a feeling of anger. The facilitator can act as a goad, feeding you lines to respond to such as,

"Yes, you will!" in various tones and inflections as you hit the pillows while responding, "No!" or, "No I won't!" or "Leave me alone," "Damn you!" or "I hate you!"

Generally, as the person hits the pillows and gets in touch with his unexpressed rage, he may become frightened as he experiences his potential for violence. However, repeated use of the exercise serves to reduce anxiety since no one is hurt, thus giving the person more control over his anger because he's found a safe way of releasing it. He also experiences intense satisfaction, as bound tension in the musculature is relieved. Discharge of rage allows one to gain control over the feeling since the likelihood of releasing that anger in a real life situation is significantly lessened.

Additional Exercises

The following bioenergetic exercises are used by certain CSATP counselors to help clients declare their feelings openly. When the expression of a feeling is inhibited, it leads to loss of that feeling, which in turn results in a loss of vitality. The suppression of feelings, particularly negative feelings, begins in childhood as children learn to hold back the expression of fear, anger, sadness, and frustration because they are afraid that the expression of such feelings may lead to withdrawal of love from the parents—an outcome which children cannot tolerate. Parents may be quite severe in demanding suppression of negative feelings by a child. The expression of these feelings is often interpreted by the parents as indicative of the child's rebellious or unloving nature, as defiance and lack of respect for their authority. The child correctly perceives that the parents won't tolerate his feelings, so s/he learns to keep them under cover. Gradually the ability to feel much about anything is diminished.

The goal of the following exercises is to help the client recontact lost feelings in a safe and supportive atmosphere. Unresolved feelings that go back to childhood are often manifested in adult life by abusive behavior toward self and others. Such is the case with most adult CSATP clients, including the offending parent, his spouse, and adults molested as children. Counseling of the youngsters involved in the molestation must include the active and full expression of feelings of rage, hurt, betrayal, guilt, and shame so that they do not enter adulthood with unresolved feelings that will sabotage them throughout their lives.

Kicking Out Exercise. The client lies on the floor with a rolled towel or blanket under the hips, or on a mattress or pillows, and brings the knees to the chest, one at a time, then kicks out strongly with the heels. The action is repeated with the client being encouraged to express anything s/he feels like saying, like "Get away!" or "Leave me alone!"

Reaching Out Exercise. The client is asked to lie on the floor and to extend both arms upward as if s/he were a baby reaching for its mother and hoping to be picked up. The client may be encouraged to put words to any feelings or images that this gesture evokes. Sometimes pushing out or reaching out with the lips adds another element to the reaching out experience. The client may say "Mommy" or "Daddy." If you as counselor are comfortable enough with the client, you can bend over her and let her reach out for and touch your face. Many persons will spontaneously begin to cry as the suppressed longing surfaces for closeness and touch, particularly for that of the neglectful parent.

Kicking the Bed. This exercise, an extension of the "kicking out" exercise, is best done on a bed or a foam rubber mattress on the floor. The client lies on his back on the mattress and begins kicking alternately with each leg. The leg is raised high so that the entire leg hits the bed on descent. Legs should be straight but not stiff and the kicking should be rhythmic. The client is directed to say "no" with each kick in a loud voice, or a long sustained "No-oooo" as s/he executes several kicks. Often the client will contact anger as well as effectiveness or ineffectiveness in being able to say "no" with conviction. The client can also be instructed to say "why?" as s/he does the kicking, as s/he begins to contact his confusion and rage at the injustices s/he was subjected to. These need not be childhood feelings, although their origins are usually there. They may also be very current feelings relating to things going on in the client's present life. The kicking exercise with the "no" and the "why" may erupt in a scream as a feeling reaches its peak, and then subsides as the client experiences relief.

Banging the Arms. Lying on the mattress as in the previous exercise, but with knees bent, the client makes two fists and raises them overhead. S/he is instructed to bang both fists down alongside the body and say "no" with each blow. Instead of "no," the client can try saying "I won't," which is a more self-assertive expression.

Temper Tantrum. This is an emotionally powerful exercise and should be done with a counselor in attendance. It is usually done with clients who have done some of the prior expressive exercises and who are ready for this opportunity to let go emotionally. The client lies on a mattress and bends the knees so the feet are flat. S/he is instructed to start drumming each foot against the mattress alternately with bent knees. The motion should start from the hip for fullest movement. After experiencing the kicking, the client is asked to start pounding the fists alternately into the mattress so that both arms and legs are being used. The head will almost automatically turn left and right with the blows. The arm and leg movements are coordinated so the right leg and right fist come up, then down together, and then the left leg and fist strike the mattress at the same time. The client is instructed to repeatedly shout or scream "I won't!" as s/he does the movement without restraint, giving in completely to the tantrum.

Demanding. Standing, the client makes two fists and raises them in front. S/he shakes both fists violently and says "why?" "Why weren't you there?" "Why didn't you protect me?" "Why didn't you listen to me?" or other similar expressions. If the person can get real emotion into this exercise, it is a sign that s/he is not holding back. However, exercises that are not appropriate and that fail to meet the client's emotional needs will not evoke strong feelings. The counselor must determine whether the client is holding back but can be urged to let go, or whether the counselor's intervention was poorly timed and must be modified.

Aggression. This means "going for what one wants." It connotes moving toward gratification of one's needs and wants rather than passively waiting for things to happen. The client takes a medium-sized turkish towel, rolls it up, and then twists it as strongly as s/he can with both hands. As s/he twists, s/he says, "Give it to me." S/he keeps twisting the towel and repeating this phrase.

In this exercise, as in all of them, the client and the counselor must remain aware of the feelings evoked by the exercise. In this case, the client becomes aware of the tone and quality in his or her voice as s/he demands, "Give it to me"; s/he notes whether it is a strong, assertive voice or a weak, unsure voice. Also, s/he notes whether s/he can hold on to the towel and continue twisting it or is inclined to loosen the grip and let go, again, as if uncertain as to whether s/he could or has the right to get his or her needs met.

Summary

To be fully self-expressive, the body must be free from disabling tensions, specifically those that block the expression of natural aggression. Aggression, as indicated before, means moving out toward the world and can refer as much to reaching out for love and closeness as to making demands or taking steps to fulfill one's wants. Aggression includes, where appropriate, statements such as, "I'm really angry at you," or even "I hate you." When aggression is blocked from childhood, it requires considerable effort to free it.

All the expressive exercises described here help the clients to be more aware of their bodies, discharge built-up tension and achieve states of calm and relaxation, improve and deepen the breathing, and be in touch with repressed feelings clearly manifested by the chronic tension in the musculature.

A few words of caution are needed here. No technique is therapeutic in itself, and no response to a therapeutic intervention leads to growth unless it occurs in an atmosphere of caring, empathy, and support on the part of the counselor. If the client derives personal awareness and self-management skills from the exercises, they can then be regarded as successful.

The reliving of painful events and feelings can be counterproductive, humiliating, and devastating to the client unless the client has the resources to resolve them. The discharge of tension and the ventilation of ofttimes primitive feelings will be of little use to the client unless s/he can be helped to integrate the experience in a way that will bring about positive changes. In terms of professional ethics, any counselor wishing to use the powerful techniques of bioenergetics must first experience them personally. The counselor must be closely attuned to his or her own bodily sensations so that s/he can be sensitive to the client's experience, giving him or her only as much as s/he can adequately integrate. Release alone solves very little in helping the person to become better grounded in reality. Release may give the client a new and different experience which is an alternative to his or her traditional ways of making contact with the world. But unless s/he can also control and synthesize the experience and integrate all his or her parts and introjects, s/he will remain fragmented, alienated, and ungrounded. Bioenergetic work is a powerful tool in experienced hands but it, too, is only one of the resources of an effective counselor. When employed skillfully, bioenergetics allows a client to acknowledge his or her rage, fear, and terror, the violent self as well as the weak and passive self, his or her irrational feelings, wildest fantasies and dreams, to say nothing of his or her incestuous self. To the degree that a person has assimilated the undesirable as well as the desirable aspects of his or her life process (all acknowledged as "grist for the mill"), s/he has become an integrated, grounded person.

2. Personal Accounts

Personal Account of a Stepdaughter

Once when I was a little girl, while my stepfather sat on the bed, he touched my back and his hand dropped to my bottom. I turned around and looked at him; and he looked at me with a look that I learned later is desire. I got off the bed and ran away and pretended it never happened. Recently my sister said he did the same thing to her when she was little.

When my stepfather started molesting me in third grade, I thought I was the only one this had happened to in the whole world. I felt isolated and was sure none of the other kids would have been able to understand it. I told a few of my friends. One girl, when she got mad at me once, said, "No wonder your parents beat you." So I learned not to trust people with my confidences. Instead of telling me what I could do to help myself, they just razzed me for having it happen. One girl told me I was a liar when I told her my stepfather beat me. She said I would be dead if he hit me as hard as I said he did.

His molesting continued through fourth, fifth, and sixth grades. Between sixth and seventh grade, I realized no one was going to make him stop except me. I didn't want him to do it anymore, but I was mixed up because it felt good and gave me orgasms. I liked it when he had oral sex with me, but I never copulated him. He tried to make me do that, but I refused and moved my head away.

My sister and I were given single beds because we fought too much in a double bed. One night after we had single beds, my stepfather put his hands under the covers, coming for me, rubbing my back. I said, "No," but he said, "Why not? It's supposed to feel good." I said, "Don't. I don't want you to." I cried so he left. I felt so bad saying no to him, but I just couldn't stand for him to keep doing

that. I didn't know what to do. I just wanted him to stop. I could not understand why he did it. He is supposed to love me. Didn't he know what it did to me inside? But I felt bad telling him to stop, because I still wanted closeness with him.

Soon after I told him to stop, I learned that the only way he would stay close to me was if I let him molest me. He was so frustrated around me from then on that he withdrew from me. That left me all by myself again, this time with neither parent to love me. I was twelve then, going into seventh grade. I had such a hard time with boys. I wanted a boyfriend, but I didn't want him touching me the way my stepfather did. My stepfather never had intercourse with me, but he did everything else; and I'm sure he was working his way up to that, too.

I told a babysitter once, and she got in contact with a minister's wife, who talked to my mom. My mom was confronting my stepfather when I walked into the kitchen, so I just heard the tail-end of him saying he had not done it. He left to go to the grocery, and I asked if I could go with him. My mother said that after what I had done, I had to go to my room and stay there.

From then on, I felt really lonely at home. My mom encouraged my sister and me to hate each other. She pawned us against each other as if it were a game, so I didn't have a friend in my sister. My little brother was more spoiled than my sister, and he didn't know what was happening. I loved my brother more than I loved my sister. Later when I had to leave home he was only eleven, and I felt so hurt that I didn't get to be around him as he grew up to go through his hard times with him. He wasn't allowed to see me during those years either, because I had been banned from the family. I didn't exist as a family member any more. I was poisonous, and my mom pretended I wasn't among the living. I think it angers me most to think of all the good times I missed with my brother.

After I told my stepfather to stop molesting me, his beatings increased. When I had been nine years old, my mother had beaten me several times with a belt. She got me in a corner where I couldn't escape and beat me wherever she could reach. I was bruised from my shoulders to my ankles and wore leotards to school, because I was so embarrassed by the marks. One day in school a sore started bleeding. My teacher sent me to the school nurse. When I took down the leotards, the nurse was shocked. She called Children's Protective Services to come and look at me, which was very embarrassing, and they took pictures. They went to my house and told Mom she had better not beat me or they would take me away and press charges against her. After that she had my stepfather beat me instead, which was worse because he beat me like a man. He threw me around and hit me in the stomach. His favorite place to beat me was in my pelvic area near my ovaries.

I never was good in school and never did well, because for me it was just a place to get away from home, so I never really applied myself. Classes were too big, and teachers never could understand why I was such a rowdy and mischievious child. No one took the time to sit down and teach me. Other kids were smarter and were teacher's pets. I couldn't handle life at home or at school.

My parents were interested in camping, and we needed another room since my sister and I couldn't share a bedroom peacefully. My parents bought an Apache folded camper with plastic walls and said to me, "Since you're older, you can have the nicer room in the garage." I bought that bullshit, because I was so glad it was my room and a new room, not realizing that what they were doing was isolating me from the family. I started sleeping there and loved it. I bought an electric heater to heat the room. I was sent to my room more and more often, and watching TV was my escape. I watched people on TV shows so I could forget myself by getting interested in them. It helped me forget I had trouble getting along with real people. Then my mom took the TV from me.

One day my stepfather wore his Hawaiian swimming trunks. He walked around the house with an erection, and he moped around and cried. I took him into my room and said, "What's the matter with you?"

He said, "Nothing is the matter with me," but he didn't look at me, and he started to cry.

I said, "I can tell something is the matter. Why don't you tell me what it is?"

He said, "There are five people in this house, but I'm still a lonely man."

"Doesn't mom have sex with you?"

"She says you kids make her nervous and she can't have sex when she's nervous. She said that when you're at camp everything is fine."

"Do you think she's using that as an excuse?"

He said, "No, because when you're away, everything *is* fine between us." I felt really bad about that, but there wasn't much I could do about it.

One night my mom sent me to my room before she left the house. I guess she could tell my stepfather might molest me. I thought I heard her

telling him, "You'd better not; you'd better be good." I went to my room and did my math homework. Then I was about to lie on my bed to kick back and relax. But my stepfather came to my room with a drink, so I kept doing more math problems. I did math assignments weeks in advance! He sat there and watched me. I knew what was on his mind. He offered me a drink and I said, "No."

After an hour had passed—it seemed like ten hours, it was so awful—he told me I could stop doing homework and could watch TV. Then he said, "Thank you for keeping me honest," and he hugged me. We went inside, and I felt really weird. I got to watch TV—the one thing that was so rare for me to get to do. He treated me well for keeping him honest.

My parents, sister, brother, and I went someplace one time and didn't get home until late. My mom told me to eat chicken noodle soup she had made and to get to bed. I said I didn't want to eat noodles because of my diet (I had grown to 150 pounds and was only five feet, two inches tall). My mom wanted to remind me who was boss, so she started yelling at me. My stepfather came in and said, "What is the problem here?"

"She won't eat her soup and she's making me nervous."

All my mother had to say was the word "nervous" to get my stepdad to come after me. I was sitting on the stool near the counter. He lifted his arm as if to hit me across my face, but when he struck, I blocked it with my arm. I had a calcium deposit bruise on my bone for three months. I'm sure if he had hit me in the head, he would have broken my neck. I flew onto the floor.

I couldn't cry, because I was so pissed and felt so much hate for him. I was only fifteen years old, but I couldn't cry anymore. I tried to force myself to cry, but it didn't work. He kicked me with his shoes and slugged me in the stomach and ovaries. Finally he stopped. When I stood up, he told me to get in the other room. I ran by him because I was afraid he was going to slug me again as I passed him.

That was the final straw for me. When my friend picked me up for church the next day, I didn't talk because I was still so totally pissed. She asked what was wrong with me, and I said, "Nothing." Finally I told her what had happened. She told her mom, who called my school counselor, the same one I had had in junior high. He had gotten me a social worker then since I was in trouble so often and had tried to resolve some problems. I had never told him about my stepfather molesting me. None of the problems he helped me with got resolved, because it was just a cat-and-mouse game to my parents.

Now here I was, going to see the same counselor again. I went to his office before he even had time to call me in, because I had made up my mind that this treatment of me was going to stop and that, no matter what, I was not going home.

A police officer came with a high school senior. (That was part of a school program that sent a peer as an advocate to talk to the student in trouble.) He kept asking me, "Are you sure this is what you want to do?"

I said, "Yes, I'm sure."

He acted as if he wanted to talk me out of carrying through with it. Another police officer called my mom, so she came there. She had been there before about the beatings, so she thought this was another usual bullshit rap. She said, "Quit playing games. Let's go. I have to take your sister for her allergy shots."

I said, "I'm not playing, Mom. This isn't a game and I'm not going home."

The officer said, "She claims she she was kicked and beaten."

Mom said, "Whatever you got, you deserved."

Before she came, I had prayed to the Lord to tell me what to do. I sat in a white room and looked at the place where two walls came together in the corner. A voice in my head asked me, "Do you deserve to be molested?" Hearing that voice from, I believe, the Lord and Holy Ghost, gave me the strength to say aloud to my mother, "Did I deserve to be molested, too?" Her mouth dropped to her knees, the officer swung back in his chair, and I just sat there. He walked into the other room to get more of his men to help him figure out what to do. Obviously, they didn't believe me. I said, "I'm sorry, Mom. It was the only thing I could do."

She said, "You're not sorry. You started something you can't stop." So that was it. She had to bring my sister to the police station to make her statement.

After my mother left to get my sister, the officer brought in two other officers to help him question me. I don't think they believed what I told them. I think they thought I made it up to get out of going home. When they questioned me, it wasn't in a very nice way. One big policeman leaned against a table as he talked and looked down on me as I sat in the chair. The other officer stood by the door on my right; and a third officer stood to my left on the other side of the big man.

The big man asked me all of the damn, fucking questions. I felt so sick and dirty inside when he asked them. He said, "What did your father do to you?"

I said, "He molested me."

"In what way?"

"By touching me and kissing me."

He said, "Did he have an erection? How do you know? Do you know what an erection is? Do you know what a 'hard-on' is? Did he come? Do you know what come is? How do you know he did?" He interrogated me totally, like I was a suspect or a liar. It made me sick. It was so awful to have to sit there and answer to three men, especially one big, fat-looking, piggish man who didn't even care about me or my feelings. He looked at me and said

maybe I enticed my stepfather to do it. I felt he looked at me as if he hoped I would entice *him* to do it. too.

Before my mother brought my sister back to talk to the police, she told her, "You're supposed to tell the truth when they question you." She also told her, "You know, we have to discipline you kids once in a while and spank you when you're bad." My sister didn't understand the situation until she got to the police station and told what had happened to her.

The police let me make a few phone calls, and I called my neighbor who was my best friend. I had told her for years that I was going to do something about the way my parents treated me. But for the past two years, no one listened to me anymore when I said it. I got beaten on in seventh grade because I told my problems to kids at school, and one of the black girls didn't like it.

My neighbor was really shocked at first that I was at the police station and had finally told on my stepfather. After I talked to her, I felt really happy, like I had really stood up for myself and like no one was going to treat me like shit anymore. Now I had rights like adults do. Just because I was a kid didn't mean I could be pushed around and beaten and mentally tormented just because someone wanted to do that to me.

The police sent my sister and me to the Children's Shelter, and my stepfather came down and admitted that night what he had done. I slept like a babe in the shelter. I felt so safe, as if I could never be hurt again. I began to have nightmares that I had to go home again though; and I still have nightmares about my stepfather molesting me and about having to go home and live with my family. My sister and I stayed in the shelter a month and a half together. My sister didn't want to be in the shelter, but my whole world had changed for the better all of a sudden. I was no longer threatened. I didn't have to live filled with fear, and no one could touch me anymore. There was no threat of someone coming through the door to beat me because I didn't perform to their expectations.

Counseling started for my sister and me about two weeks after I reported the situation. The first week we were in the shelter, a man with an attache case came to write down our stories; but I guess they thought I'd feel more comfortable with a female, so they sent me into a room with a Senior Girl counselor. I told her my story, and it was hell to tell it. My stepfather hadn't molested me for three years. But he *had* molested me for three years prior to that.

She wanted times, dates, exact circumstances, amount of times, and the exact acts he committed. She wanted to know everything. And I couldn't remember everything that happened in three fucking years. Especially when it was something I did not want to remember. It made me sick, totally sick. We were in that room one and a half or two and a half hours. I told the counselor everything I could remember.

Then I went back to my unit and was sick. I couldn't eat. I felt totally nauseated from having to relive every minute of what had happened. It made me feel dirty and guilty and brought back very old memories. When my father left my room after molesting me, I always felt so guilty if I had had an orgasm or had "gotten off" on any pleasurable feelings. I would become physically ill and lie on my bed and want to die. A sick feeling would start from my stomach and go all the way up to my throat. I put my arms around my stomach and rolled on the bed during those times.

I didn't understand at the time that we are made to have good feelings when someone touches our body, that it is natural to feel pleasurable feelings. I couldn't find these things out from other people, because I felt too awful to tell anybody. Later, when I did tell people, they didn't understand and didn't do anything to help me. I don't think anybody wanted to do anything about it.

After my sister and I both gave our statements, we started seeing Hank Giarretto for counseling. I don't remember if I met Hank alone or with my sister, but I remember thinking: "They want me to talk to a man about what another man did to me? There's no way I can ever open up to that guy. I would be too embarrassed to tell him, and for all I know, he'll act the same way the cops did to me." I was really scared, and by that time I didn't trust *any* men. I decided not to tell Hank anything.

I did want to see a counselor, though. I had wanted to see one for many years. My mother used to tell me, "I'll take you to the state mental hospital to see what crazy people look like and show you what you're turning me into."

I jumped at the opportunity and said, "Take me there. Let me see."

She said, "I'll take you to the doctor, and he'll cut your head open and see what makes your brain work and what's the matter with you."

I'd think: "I hope she does take me, because maybe there is something wrong with me and I want to find out." So by the time I met Hank I was at the point of really wanting counseling—but not with a man.

Hank and I talked, and slowly I started trusting him. He showed me that he really understood and cared. He helped break a lot of my barriers by telling me I was not to blame, that I was the victim, which really blew me away after hearing from my family for years that everything was my fault. And he explained so much, and I learned so much about myself and about life. Finally I had answers, and I learned other people in the world were confused, too. Hank arranged the first meeting between my mother, sister, and me.

We had our meeting in a large room with a long table. My mom arrived and immediately rushed to my sister and started sobbing. She kissed and hugged her, told her how much she loved her, how much she wanted her back home, and how things were going to work out between them. My mother had her back to me, and my sister and I faced each other. By the time my mom turned around to me, it was because Hank had said, "Now, go hug (me)." She was going to do it because he had told her to do it. For years before this moment I had worked hard trying to get my mother to give me some love, trying to get close to her, to do what she wanted, to be her daughter, her girl. I wanted a special kiss and hug and to have her tell me she loved me; but she never had.

I remember when my mother dropped me off at a friend's house when I still lived at home. Mom had locked her car door, and when she saw me coming toward her to give her a kiss, she went for her door to open it as if her life depended on it. Before she even tried the door handle, she was already moving her body away from me. The door wouldn't open, so she ran into the door and was trapped. I planted a kiss on her cheek anyway, and it really hurt me that I couldn't even kiss my mother without her acting like I was poison or like a bomb was going to blow her cheek off. The only reason I could kiss her is that she couldn't get away from me.

Now she was in the same position in the room with Hank. Whenever I tried to get love from her on my own merits, I got rejection instead. When she came toward me to kiss and hug me in front of Hank—the kiss and hug I had been working toward since I was six years old—her tears had dried and she wore an expression of sheer hate. I could see in her face that she still blamed everything on me. To have to give me that kiss must have been worse than having to eat liver for her! I didn't want if it was forced. I wanted it only if it was sincere, not if it was to save her ass because a counselor with authority told her to do it. I told her not to bother, not to force herself. It hurt. It hurt so much, because I wanted it so much and she couldn't give it and she didn't feel it. I felt a lump in my throat, but I wouldn't cry for her.

Personal Account of a Daughter

I am a special person, but my story is not unique. At my age, my story should be short and sweet; but it is not short and it definitely is not sweet. Sometimes it is so hard to find words to express my pain and fears and anger. Until I found Parents United, I didn't know it was okay for me to have any of those feelings. After being in Parents United I realized: I'm a real human being, and I make mistakes like everyone else; and I deserve to be loved appropriately. I do not deserve to be sexually abused!

I was molested by two men. I loved and respected and looked up to these two men—until I realized that what they were doing to me was violating me and confusing my values. I put aside my anger toward them and my fear and pain. These emotions were all there, however, on a shelf, until I decided later to stand up and start cleaning and dusting myself off.

My father started molesting me when I entered puberty. Shortly after fifth grade, he talked more and more about sex to me. I was afraid of him at that point in my life. He behaved neurotically and had since I was a little girl. I liked living with my dad until he started whipping me. He would whip me for no reason and hit me if I came home late from visiting a friend. One strange thing I remember is that my father never drank when he molested me or whipped me.

When I was nine, he and I and my new stepmother moved to another state. My stepmother's son was the same age as my older brother, and they had the same type of personality. They competed with each other constantly, especially for my father's attention and approval. Later in my life, I had a difficult time coping with that macho attitude in males.

Whenever I visited my mother, she was always so honest with me. She remarried soon after my father remarried. The man she married was totally different from my father. He was funny, nice, and treated Mother with respect. Even more important to me, he treated me the same way, something my father did not do for me. I liked being with my mother and her new husband. I was safe, and I was with my mother. My father favored my brothers more than he favored me, which he showed by buying them motorcycles and giving them extra money. So I was happier to be with my mother.

I trusted my father; I trusted my stepfather. Then they both put their trusted, funny-father, good-guy arms around me and broke the golden rules . . . as thousands of other fathers have. There really is no reason to go into detail about the sexual abuse. As I said before, my story is not unique. I will tell you what happened at the end for them and for me: nothing happened for them! No psychiatric help at all. They have never suffered through one day of jail or one hour of counseling. Everyone felt sorry for them, so they were able to remain free. It is more complicated than I can explain, and I have since found out there were reasons and good intentions involved; but I still feel sad. Neither of them has even heard of Parents United. And they are not even concerned with what has become of me. I just am not important to them. I am the one who caused all of this mess in their opinion. They think it is my fault.

The abuse did not stop until my mother said it was wrong. Really! (That was about the only word I could find to express my relief.) I found myself on an airplane with my mother, and suddenly we were walking through the door of Parents United and Daughters and Sons United. We met honest people here, people who share the same pain and fears and anger that we do. These people saved my mother's sanity.

What have I learned from all that happened to me? That what happened to me did happen, and there is nothing I can do to change that. But I learned that it was not my fault. What happened is not an okay thing; it is wrong. But those who break this rule should not necessarily have to go to jail. They should have to get help. If I had known what I know now about child molesting, my father might be getting help back in the other state where I lived.

Because I know now that it was not my fault, I am not ashamed to tell anyone my story. If I tell my story, and if by chance I can save someone the pain I had, and that someone can overcome the fear of standing up and getting help, it is a story worth telling.

I am okay now. I would like to thank one special person who makes my life worth living more and more, and that's my mom. Her warmth, her understanding, her trust and faith are what help make me the strong person I am now. I am proud to be her daughter. Also, I would not even be telling this story if it weren't for those people who took the effort to help me and gave me love with simple hugs and strong, giving arms: Hank, Anna, Bernice (my counselors), and *all* my Wednesday night fathers. Each week, all of you make me feel I'm worth more. Parents United and Daughters and Sons United gave my mother and me the chance to start dusting that shelf off and to keep the shelf clean. Hopefully now, my story will become shorter. And I am happy to be alive.

Personal Account of a Stepdaughter

I was about eight or nine years old when my stepfather started molesting me. I had been really happy to have my stepfather in the family—my parents were divorced when I was six years old, and I really missed having a father around. They had been divorced about two and a half years, I guess, when my stepfather married my mother. I was very anxious to have him in the family. I really wanted a daddy around to fix the bicycles—just the whole trip of being a father. I really wanted that—it was very welcome. I think I was very open; I remember a lot of times of jumping on my father's lap (my stepfather's lap) and just being very affectionate and very open.

What I remember about the initial time that he molested me was that it was either right before or right after their wedding—within about six months. It's hard for me to place exactly when it happened or when it ended or how often—they are hard memories to go back to, but the first time was probably the most distinct. He took me on a camping trip with him. I guess it was an effort to get to know me. He molested me that night that we were camping. We weren't at a campsite—we were really far away from people or places and I felt so very frightened, very isolated. There was no place for me to run to if I had the courage to run.

I remember being very confused. I didn't know if it was right or wrong. I didn't know if my mom knew this was going to happen and that's why she allowed me to go. I think I assumed that it must have been all right, but I was still very frightened.

Ever since the molest started, I think confusion has been the thing that's gone on the most, the feeling that I've had the most. I wondered a lot whether or not it was all right—whether or not my mom knew about it, whether or not my mom thought it was okay. It took me a long time to figure those things out.

I didn't tell my mom when I came back from the camping trip, and I wonder a lot about that now—why I didn't tell her, especially then. He probably told me not to tell; I remember him telling me that later. I don't remember so much that particular night.

I don't remember anything of coming home. It's a memory that's really lost to me. I remember going out on a camping trip and riding on the back of his motorcycle and watching the scenery, and I remember the night that he molested me. He would fondle me and perform oral sex on me and that's

all very vivid, very distinct; but I don't remember anything about coming home and seeing my mom or what was going through my head when I saw her or why I didn't tell her.

I felt guilty for not telling her. I think later on, when I realized that it was wrong, then I should have told her. I should have. I think as it progressed and I realized that it was something that my stepfather was wanting to keep from my mother and keep me from telling anybody else, I realized that it must be wrong. Most of the time when it happened, though, it would be at night when both of my parents were in bed. He would come into my room and I always wondered how he could leave and mom not know or not be suspicious, or why she didn't look any further.

When I was in fifth grade, I told some friends at school. Several friends knew what was going on. We were talking about sex and different people's experience—have you kissed a boy or whatever—and so I told them what I had been involved in and they all looked kind of surprised and asked me who with. I said my stepfather. Boy, I got a really strange reaction. I really got the message that I really wasn't supposed to talk about it. My stepfather had been telling me not to tell and then I did tell somebody and they all looked shocked and surprised. I guess I felt very odd and out of place. A freak. So after that I really kept my mouth shut and didn't tell anybody else.

When I was in sixth grade, the next year, I assume what happened was that some of the friends I had told told their parents, and the parents called the school. The vice-principal of my sixth-grade class (at junior high school) pulled me out of class and asked me if I had been telling stories. At the time, there were a lot of things going on with my brother that I was talking about; when he asked me if I had been telling stories, I said, "You mean about my brother?"

He said, "No—it's something much worse than that."

I got the idea that he was talking about the molest and I became very frightened that he was thinking that I was lying. I became frightened that I wouldn't be believed, or just the whole idea that telling somebody wasn't a good idea, and here I was about to have to tell somebody. So, I told him, no, I hadn't been telling any stories. He said, "Okay, you can go back to class." So, I went back to class and never heard anything about it again.

Somewhere at the time of about seventh or eighth grade, my stepfather was arrested for child molesting outside of the family. I guess I was probably about thirteen then. When he was arrested, I found out some of his past that caused me a lot more confusion. I found out that he had served time at Atascadero for child molest before he married my mother, and that my mom knew this before she married him. It really shocked and confused me more. I realized that she knew that he had done this with somebody before and I thought that she should have known anyway that he was molesting me. She'd had that information and hadn't known or suspected or asked. So, it confused me even more as to whether she knew. About that time I was thinking she knew and that it was all right with her, so I didn't say anything about it then.

It was really a crisis point for the family when he was arrested. The thing that I find really ironic is that after that arrest he was sentenced out at Elmwood and was on a work-furlough program. He couldn't have contact with the rest of the family, but I had contact with him because I worked with him. I find it ironic that I, who needed protection at that time, was the only person that he could have contact with. I really felt unprotected at that time. With the knowledge of what my mom had known— I really felt unprotected with that, too, and let down, confused.

So I remember after he got out of Elmwood he was in a local county counseling group. At the same time, my mom was in a different counseling group for herself. I knew that my stepfather was in a group with other sex offenders for different kinds of sex crimes. Mom would always come home and talk about what happened to her in group and what was going on with her, and my stepfather never talked about what was going on for him.

My stepfather and I never talked about the molest. Nothing was ever said outside of when it was going on, and so I didn't really know what to look for to see if things were going to change or not. Now I feel that I was really unprotected in that, too. I found out later that he had told the people in his group that he had molested me prior to his being arrested. They never came back to me or my mother to find out if I was all right or if it was still going on. In looking back on that, I see a lot of places where people could have intervened. It would have been so easy for somebody to reach out and just ask me about it. I think if I had been asked, I would have told. I never had the courage to go up and tell somebody just on my own.

What was going on about that time with me outside of the family? When I was about thirteen or fourteen, I didn't start becoming promiscuous so much as I remember being real interested in boys at that time. I was pretty flirtatious outside of home. I remember being very careful around home to not wear sexy clothes around my stepfather or do anything that I thought might attract him. I felt real guilty about that, that somehow I must have brought it on, somehow I must have done something to lead him on.

I remember at the time that he started molesting me, it was about the time that I started masturbating. I remember thinking that that might have been one way that I led him on—that somehow he knew that I was doing that, in some way that was asking for it.

So I remember being pretty flirtatious and later becoming pretty promiscuous outside of the home, but really keeping that away. I lost my virginity just after I turned fourteen and became interested in a whole string of boys after that. I remember even with my first sexual experience, except for the molest, feeling that this guy was there only for sex and not out of any caring for me. I remember telling him that—I didn't believe that he loved me. That's always been a confusing point for me, trying to reconcile love and sex. I remember my stepfather would tell me that he loved me when he was molesting me—that he was doing this because he loved me. It was very confusing because here he was saying that he loved me and yet what he was doing didn't feel right or comfortable. It felt bad and I felt bad.

Later, as it became more obvious to me that it was wrong, even aside from whether or not I got it on, I just felt that because it was wrong and I was there, no matter who started it, that I was wrong or bad for being involved in it. Later, in being involved in sex I felt used a lot. I had sexual desires and I would act on that a lot of times, even while believing that this other person didn't really care about me and was just after sex.

The first time that I told anybody later on was just because of that. I told a boyfriend (he'd been my boyfriend for two years at that time). I had had a child by him which I placed up for adoption and I remember being real confused about what love was and how it fit in with sex. I was just trying to make the two of them work together to where I could feel sexual and feel love at the same time. In the middle of the conversation about it, I broke down and started crying because I realized that the problems that I was having with him were the same kind of confusion that I had with the molest. I just felt real lost and helpless—like I had to tell him. So I cried for several hours and finally I told him.

One of the things that was hard for him was a previous conversation with him about rape. He had told me that if I were ever raped, he didn't think that he could physically touch me again—that he would feel revulsion at my having been abused and touched by somebody else. So that made it really hard for me to tell him about my stepfather. I was also afraid that he would be very angry and want to beat him up, and I didn't want my stepfather beaten up. I didn't want him to go to jail; I didn't want him hurt.

I remember another reason I didn't tell anybody was I didn't want them to not like my stepfather. I didn't want them to be uncomfortable being around him or being around my family or being around me. The one reaction that I had gotten was that I was some kind of freak. I didn't want somebody thinking that my whole family were freaks. So, when I told my boyfriend, he did become angry and wanted to go over and punch him. I talked him out of that.

I think later on that night or the next day, I went home. About a week after that, I remember hearing noises outside my bedroom door. By this time, the molest had stopped for nearly two years—I was seventeen—and just hearing noises at my door and window like someone was trying to get in, I became very frightened. Now I don't think that that was my stepfather; I think it was a friend of my brother who was staying in the house. But at the time, I was too frightened to even face my stepfather with it. When I heard a noise, I didn't want to open the door and confront him—I just wanted him to go away, or for me to go away.

So, after the noises outside my window stopped, I put on a robe and got in my car and drove over to my boyfriend's. It was the first time that I had someplace to run to—somebody who already knew about it, somebody I could talk to without having to tell the whole story from the beginning when I was so upset. So I stayed over there a couple of days. I had him call my parents and let them know I was all right. I wanted him to talk to my mom and tell her what was going on. She wouldn't go for that—she wanted to talk to me. So he gave her a clue that it was about my stepfather and his past. So my mother asked him about it. I guess he first said, no it never happened; then he said it happened once a long time ago and asked her not to leave him.

She came and talked to me, and I told her everything that had been going on. I remember when waiting to talk to her I felt real scared at having to face her and tell her this really big thing that had been going on and that I had been keeping from her. But then also a lot of relief. I had told my boyfriend and now I was pretty sure that I was going to tell her.

It was a relief to get that out. When I told her, she listened and was supportive. She asked me if I wanted her to get divorced. At the time, I was about six months away from being eighteen and moving out. I didn't want to split up their marriage; during the whole time, I didn't want to disrupt the family. I felt very protective of my mom and her marriage. It was her second one and the first divorce was pretty hard on her and I think I felt real protective of her.

So I told her I didn't want that to be my decision. I didn't want them to get divorced. She said that I could stay away until I was ready to come back. So I stayed away for a few more days. Then I came back to the house, and my mom and I talked about it a lot after that. My stepfather and I still never talked about it—it was kind of decided on by everyone, you know. It was two years done with and it wasn't going to happen again. I was safe and I felt that it wasn't going to happen again now that it was out in the open. But at the same time, it was really comfortable to have it be out in the open but yet not talk about it with him. I got the impression that he didn't talk about it with my mom, either.

So that went on for another six months while I was living at home. I became increasingly uncomfortable with my family. I broke up with my boyfriend after that and started dating, and there were just a lot of struggles about my wanting my independence and being ready to move out and feeling that I was taking care of myself, and not feeling like I was getting a lot of recognition for that. So I moved out when I was eighteen and supported myself and lived on my own.

All during that time, from about eighteen to nineteen, I started becoming increasingly alienated from my family. I started really being uncomfortable around them a lot of times—even my brothers and sisters. It was just that they really didn't understand where I was at, and I couldn't relate to them and be close to them. My friends were taking a greater place of importance and there was a real feeling of loss, a feeling that that wasn't how it was supposed to be. An uncomfortableness —that I was supposed to want to be with my family and yet when I was with them I was uncomfortable.

I think I was really most comfortable with my mom. We talked about the molest, but I didn't talk about it with anybody else. My brothers didn't even know about it at that time. My sister knew a little bit—I had told her when I was in about fifth grade. She never heard anything about it after that. Now she has shared with me that she thought that it had stopped after that and that she didn't know what to do with that information. I guess she felt pretty helpless.

But after I moved out, my parents started having a lot more marital problems. My father, who had always drank a lot, was starting to drink more heavily. There was a lot of bickering and things going back and forth for them. They separated and went into marriage counseling. I guess somewhere in the course of marriage counseling, they told a counselor about the incest. He recommended that they should go to Parents United. My mom called and told me a little bit about it and set it up for one of their interns to come out and talk to us one night.

So I went over there. It was a real tense situation. I remember feeling very protective of my family—that this person was going to come in, a stranger, and not so much criticize as just see all the faults in the family.

The thing that was really neat about it was the four of us sat down and it was the first time that I had even talked about the molest in front of my father, much less talked to him about it. That was really a lot more comfortable. I was really feeling that there was going to be room for some progress.

So we came down to Parents United a couple weeks after that. Everybody was in agreement to go. I think we were all kind of nervous—I was nervous about what I was going to find there or what was going to happen. I remember the night that we got there: it was a small group—it was a holiday—and it was just real close and real warm and people just started talking about their own experiences with molest and incest. It was the first time that I had ever been with people who were maybe not comfortable with it but who could talk about it.

I always felt that I was the only one that it had happened to, that I was alone, that nobody could understand what I was going through. I really felt that the kids around me were very shallow because they didn't know the experiences that I was going through, and that their problems were very trivial compared to mine. So it was really hard for me to get close to people.

Then when we got to Parents United, there were people there who understood, who had been through it, who knew all those things that I felt, and who could talk about it and help me talk about it. I remember being very happy to be there, being very enthusiastic, realizing how big the problem was, and wanting to go out and help others—trying to keep somebody else from going through what I went through.

I've been in the program now for about ten months, and I feel like I have grown a lot. I've done a lot there—had a lot of things come out—and I feel like a valuable person there. I've made a lot of important steps for myself, and I've had a lot of people to help me in making those steps. I've experienced a closeness and a sharing there that I've never experienced anywhere else, and that closeness and sharing extended into being able to be close and sharing with my stepfather and my mother and also my sister and my brother and my father.

Both my brother and my natural father never knew about the molest until after we had been in the program. My stepfather told my brother, and we still haven't been able to talk about it that much but it's nice having him know and to be a little more comfortable about the things that I'm doing now.

I told my natural father after I had been in the program about seven months. It was a really hard thing for me to do—to tell him one of the really crummy things that had happened in my life. I think with all of my parents' families I always felt under a lot of pressure to have a wonderful life, to be a good person, to get good grades, and to achieve in life. And part of that was just to not have crummy experiences. It was hard to tell my father that—to let him know that I had been through something like that—and I was really surprised when I told him that he was angry with my stepfather, but he was mostly concerned about me and sorry that he hadn't been able to help me at that time. I think that's what I really wanted out of telling him—that opportunity for closeness and just to know that he would have protected me if he had known, and that my mom would have protected me if she had known.

Since that time with my natural father, I have been able to be really close with him—much closer than I think we've ever been—and to be able to share the important things that are going on with me now and let him know how I'm feeling about things in my life without him. My father and I could very rarely tell each other that we loved each other; and now I can do that, and he's able to do that.

I just feel that the closeness and warmth is extending out from what I'm getting at Parents United to my family and other relationships. It's just like warmth seeping into all the corners of my life. Some of the things that I'm feeling now feel really good and positive and different. I'm feeling really good about myself. I'm learning that I have qualities as a person that I value and that other people value and that I don't need to use sex to get attention—I don't need to buy it that way anymore. That feels real positive—that I can be loved by somebody for myself.

I feel that I have things to offer myself. I think a real important one is recognizing that people have a lot to offer me. I think that was a hard thing for me to realize, that I felt very alone and isolated. I think in a lot of ways I felt very superior; now I'm learning how much I have to learn and how much other people have to give me. I'm very glad that I have people there to help me learn that. About the program itself: the closeness and the sharing there is something that I haven't found anywhere else. Not like that, not with that many people and happening that often. It's really special.

Personal Account of a Woman Molested as a Child

I had just remembered that I *loved* him, that there *were* good times with him when I was a child, that he was my best friend. And now it is all in ruins.

I loved him when I called him at Christmas. I wished him well, I *felt* love for him. Now it is all disgusting and he is unreal.

What can I do?

The neighbors can't help me. Mama isn't home. L. and T. lay there in their downstairs bedroom sweetly sleeping. They don't have to go through this.

Daddy, put your pants on.

All the things I used to feel during intercourse with S.: "I've felt this way before. Your hands feel too big. I'm afraid."

Hold tight, don't feel anything, it's a sin, it is IMPURITY and my holy daddy is doing it. What can I do? I can't run away, no one is here to help me. Just close myself up, just be tight and turn away my face to the neighbor Pricer's house next door. Think of them, think of the lilac bush in their yard, think of anything but what is happening.

He is weaker than any man, he is the weakest of all. God, that's what I was thinking when I looked in our basement window—I can't tell Grandma, I can't tell Mama. The shadow across the wall was his, not Kenny's. *He* was the perverted one.

And above all this I am saying: none of this is true, I will not think about it, I will not let it touch me, he is the same strong, pure, holy daddy.

I cannot read, I cannot concentrate, the day is beautiful and I want to just be a part of it and forget this bad thing.

He was drunk.

Saint Maria Goretti. She tried to fight off her attacker. I didn't. I couldn't. He could have killed me. No wonder I would look at that martini shaker and hate it.

No wonder I complain and complain, disaster, *god,* something bad *has* happened, something irreparable. The spot, the black spot on your soul.

The smells, the bad smells, the toilet dreams, the fear, the disgust. Ten years of nightmares.

Sexual stirrings. No. No.

No wonder I hated my uncles leering and hugging and breathing their whiskey breaths on me. No wonder I had to forget that daddy used to play with me. He not only took me to the circus and the park, he "played" with me in that bad way.

Here is how I remembered: last night in the middle of making love because S. wanted to (I was tired but I felt I should oblige him), things got difficult. A dark shadow kept passing in front of me; it was nothing distinguishable, it was *almost* something, almost a different person, a different place. Perversions. Where am I? What is happening? He is forcing and forcing me, he pulls my hands. Don't touch. My hands are numb. He keeps insisting. He pulls me toward him, wanting me to do strange things to him, and finally, after the tension mounts and mounts, I think: "I didn't know I had a place inside me like that—a space, air, a hollow." Trying to remember, trying to remember, I look toward Pricer's house and burst into tears, sobbing: "Mr. Pricer, help me!" This is disaster, but I cannot think that thought. I close myself and think instead: "This is the last straw. I wanted my daddy to love me and hug me and hold me as his little girl and instead *this* is how he gets 'close' to me."

I am on his bed. How did I get here? Is it night and are there candles? Did he carry me up the stairs as he did when I'd fall asleep in the car coming home from Grandma's? Why am I in his bed? Why did this occur? I look to the right and I see my father's face. It *is* his face. Finally I see that it is him. He has been drinking, he has a weak pleading smile on his face. God, *this* is my father.

Once when I was twelve, I was invited to spend the night with my girlfriend. Her father was blind. Another friend laughed when I told her and said: "Mr. ___ will come in, in the middle of the night and he will feel your face, he will touch you to see what you look like." I spent the night awake, listening for his footsteps.

Ten years ago, S. waking me in the night—wanting sex, and I, hating him, wanting to push him away, to slam him against the wall.

My boyfriend saying: "Prove you love me." I couldn't fight him off any longer. I had no feeling about the matter any longer, I just wanted to finish it so he would go away.

Whatever it is is here, has surfaced after all these years; all the signs make sense now. I feel in a state of shock as in the middle of a catastrophe or after the death of someone close. I am numb and unable to feel. I want to forget about it again and go about my business and be happy in the world.

When I was that child and it was happening to me, I made myself pretend that it was not happening. I forced myself to forget. I erased what I knew: that my own father was a liar and a sneak and a child molestor.

When he touched me I felt the cringe of: "Oh, god, no, I don't *want* to, please don't make me, oh no, oh *no!*"

I didn't do anything. I was disgusted and revolted and sickened as any good Catholic little girl would be. I had just made my first Holy Communion. I knew what "impurity" meant what "sin" meant, what "evil" meant.

It is true. I know from how terrible I feel that it is true. I have to talk about it to someone who knows about these things. I must feel the pain. Then will I finally be free?

I feel it for a moment. It is him, it could be no one else *but* him, I can see his face, I know it is my own father. I think of words like sleaze and sludge and filth and slime. This is my FATHER!

Was I awake in the kitchen once in the middle of the night? In the harsh kitchen light after coming out of a dark room, was someone giving me warm milk? Who is with me? I stand looking down at the baby's high chair, I see the black dark outside the kitchen door; it's scary. Who stands next to me? Is someone comforting me? I do not look at them.

It's not bad like war, it's not suffering like being blind or crippled, it's not like that. You didn't get hurt so bad. It's just another thing he did, like the rages and the ridicule. Who says these things to me?

But Christ, its so *personal*, my body is so personal. Don't touch it any way you want.

Her baring of my breasts in front of him when I got my first bra. My feeling of being exposed when he would pull my covers off me mornings when it was time to get up for school.

Wanting to lock my door, wanting to keep him out.

When I read, at fifteen, in the *Reader's Digest* about sex, I think: "Oh, so that's how its done."

At twenty, seeing my brother's furry penis and being shocked by its ugliness.

My father has a tiny penis.

How do I know this?

My father pacing the floor at night when I am a teenager. I tense up when I hear him, I tell myself I'm worried he's sick. I hear him turn the pages of magazines, trying to relax so he can go back to sleep. I don't sleep until after he returns to his bed.

How can I have loved a father who would do such a terrible thing?

Every time I look to the right side of that bedroom I see his slimy, whimpering face. Then I know it is true. When and how and what and how often are unanswered questions. But I know now that it really happened.

Last night I was seeing his black-rimmed glasses, the words in the book seemed written in his hand, it was his wallet on the dresser this morning.

No wonder I blocked so badly when the therapist asked: "Can you picture your mother and father in bed together?"

Sigh-sobbing.

I have been up in mama's and daddy's bedroom for my nap. It is quiet up there. I get bored.

The revulsion I felt when he put his arm around me. No. You're not supposed to be doing that.

He never kissed me. He used his hands to touch me, to hold me close when I wanted to get away. No, this is *not* true, it is impossible. It could not be true ever of him.

I am unsure of it as I move away from it. I'm all right, nothing's wrong. Everything's okay.

Who is giving me warm milk?

I play outside in the soft summer air with Ralph, the neighbor boy. Suddenly grinning, he lunges for me: "I'm gonna kiss you." I pull away, terrified, and run into the kitchen where she is ironing. "What's wrong?" Nothing, I say.

Don't tell her. Don't tell anyone. I am lost.

The look on his face, when he caught me in the bathroom, masturbating at thirteen—a conspiratorial, sexual look. I hated that look. And when he told me to go to confession for it, that I couldn't receive Holy Communion without doing so, I must have forgotten the thought: "He wants me to go for this little thing when he can do all he does and pretend he is whitely pure and holy."

Blues in the Night.

Immaculate Mary, our hearts are on fire.

She must have known, if what I remember is true. It is murky, I must have been sleeping. I pull the covers close up around my neck. Safety. Is he asleep there on the sofa with no shirt on? Is it the hot summer? Am I beside him? Why? Where is she?

Fire. Fear of fire.

I remember fear of their bed when we lived on R. Street. I was afraid of his black shoes. Looking at our bed one day last year, I became afraid and thought of being in bed for a nap with Grandpa. I was two or three. And I went into deep feelings about going upstairs to go "home" and I felt the suicidal impulse of that child on the stairs as Grandpa slept soundly, and I knew then that "No one cares" and "No one protects me."

Daddy's curly head, I see the top of it as he tickles my tummy with his mouth. I lay in the upstairs bedroom on Topeka on a white-sheeted unmade huge expanse of bed. Where is my mother? I am very young.

I sit in his lap in the rocker upstairs in the bedroom. I am only a year old. I love my daddy.

In the past, thinking: "I have never, since the age of one, been truly virginal."

Saint Tarcisius? He allowed himself to be murdered rather than profane his temple of the Holy Ghost.

Shock at seeing S.'s erect penis for the first time: do they really do that, do they really do that?

And during intercourse, in those nights of ten years ago, when the thing was trying to rise in my mind: the object between my legs is a furry animal-like thing. What is it?

Asleep on the couch at Grandma's, afraid of a man coming in through the french doors in the dark. How old was I? Five? Seven? Three?

No wonder he goes to confession every week.

Bad smells. Filthy brown diarrhea water. Him. Bathroom.

God, Jesus, I cannot face the fact that she knew. On Sayles Street she knew. If it happened. Maybe she stood in the doorway and shouted, "C.!" for another reason. No. I know better.

Being revolted by an uncle-in-law, the leering look on his face as he poured the catsup. It made me shudder. It was only a symbol.

Fear of the boys, my schoolmates, fear of them when they threatened to kiss me or hug me or rub my face with snow.

One woman wrote: "I had intercourse with my father when I was eleven." I think of my bedroom as a twenty-year-old when I read that.

How can I get free of it? If this is true, how can I get free of it by remembering? It seems I will be dragging it along after me forever.

In the middle of the night, in the midst of the pain of knowing this is true, is the feeling that comes and goes: "I'm getting free." I feel an elation and a soaring that only lasts a second, but it is happening.

The snake dream. The painting of the lizard falling into the fire. I had to cover it up, it was too frightening.

There's no use telling her, she won't do anything. It's not such a big deal. There's a lot worse suffering that goes on. You don't have it so bad.

Christ God, I just last month remembered a good daddy doing happy fun things like taking me to the park and the zoo and the lake and going fishing and now I must *lose him again!*

Just a foul place with me in it and him in it.

The shit-filled dreams. Absolutely unexplainable unless he molested me. That filth-filled and violated feeling in my dreams.

Almost all the other dreams have fallen into place.

This is so much work, so much effort and agony, I do wish I was already dead and happy in heaven, like Tarcisius.

Dreams of long black hairs in my throat and of spitting out an ugly yellowish substance in the form of ducks.

God, I don't want to get involved in this. I want to live in the present and love my people.

N. talked about him putting on mom's nightgown. "Clowning around," she called it.

The smell of fresh body odor is safe, it equals the men I trust and love. The unsafe smells are male shit, semen, old body odor.

Two days ago I actually thought I was finished with feelings about my father. I loved him, I felt love for him, I had remembered the good times. And there were, I thought, female symbols arising. I thought I was about to begin on feeling about my mother.

Listening to Bach and trying to forget as I paint. But it keeps coming.

The personality type. He fits it.

That boy I dated, whining and squirming and saying, "You know what to do to make a guy feel good." And my inward vehement denial and disgust at how he rubbed up against me.

Something terrible has happened and I cannot believe it. Try to forget.

January 1. After the telephone rang at 3 A.M., I lay in bed terrified someone was trying to break in. I had no protection. My back and shoulders felt vulnerable, I couldn't feel S. next to me. My covers weren't enough to protect me, the door wasn't enough, S. wasn't enough. I was totally vulnerable and doomed. In the dream after I finally fell asleep, an eight-year-old child tells me she tried to commit suicide when she was four months old. As I relate the dream to S., I am crying and sobbing, it is too sad.

Please, I don't want to do it. It seems an eternity of ugliness and pain stretches before me. I want to run away from it; instead, I must dig through all the old nightmares and dreams and feel this awful thing that I wish and hope is not true. It is too long and hard and torturous.

In May of last year I dreamed: "I am in the closet. At the back is an octopus/snake shape moving, hanging from the shelf or a nail in the very back of the closet. I always knew it was there, I had just forgotten."

I don't want to do this painful work. It is sunny and beautiful and I am at the bottom of a pit of filth. Please make it go quickly so I can be free.

I feel relief at knowing the mystery is solved even though it will mean pain. At least I have not been crazy all these years.

Telling S. last night how I, for a second only, could feel: "Yes, this is the way he was with me—not touching me in a loving, nurturing way, but in this manipulative, using, sly, weak, revolting way that makes me a prisoner in my own bed." And at the same time that I am saying this and thinking, "That's exactly what happened," I am denying it and feeling sexual arousal—which I understand intellectually and know emotionally is just an accident of physiology, a by-product, as in a rape, but which shames me in my child soul.

We made love last night. He is my safety, my friend, I trust only him. I love him. And at the same time I know I am feeling the safety I used to feel with my Grandpa, because I loved my Grandpa and trusted him and he was good to me. Thank you, Grandpa, for all the hugs you gave me that didn't hurt me. I am so happy I could trust you to love me without harm. Thank you for that, Grandpa. And I feel cynical that, instead of believing it is normal that your male relatives don't hurt you, I feel deep gratitude that he did not harm me.

In the middle of making love (even my confusion over the term makes sense now—with my father, what was it? It was not screwing, it was not . . .

etc.), I remember a fifth-grade fantasy: I go down the inkwell and I must lie on the table while the hard, mean, cold evil doctor who is in power does things to me sexually. I cannot resist.

I feel such great relief that this is all making sense even as I do not feel the main terrible feelings.

Blacking out, blanking out, going inward years ago when S. pressured me about putting his hand up my dress. Blacking out his face when my father raged at me.

In July, I wrote: "My secret is I don't trust you."

Pinocchio—he lied and his nose grew long and ugly. He was with evil men who did bad, leering things. It was scary. No one was there to help him.

When you wish upon a star
Makes no difference who you are
When you wish upon a star
Your dreams come true.

Jiminy Cricket was a liar. Just like my evil daddy. I knew that song was a lie.

Near the water, near the ocean, near the river on Pierce, the muddy flood water.

I saw a black spot on a wall downtown. I'm soiled! I'm soiled!

Last night fear, I am unprotected, by the locked door, by my bedroom door, by S.—in my mind he is not even here—, by my pajamas, by my being here in California, 1,500 miles away from him. And in the hall, blackness, terror that a man will close in on me and touch me, I must run into my room and slam the door quickly. It is real. He is there in the dark and I must get away from him.

That day at the ocean, I felt in danger, my back was vulnerable to an attack, I heard myself saying: "This is the day I am going to be raped." I scanned the beach constantly to be certain no one could approach without my knowing.

In August: "The secret is: I cannot trust my own father." I cannot trust the person I love most.

His dirty look, his slimy laugh. He whispered to me in the night, I know it. That is why I have always hated the priest's dark whispering in the confessional.

All the men I've loved are dead.

In April of last year: is it a fantasy or an imagining? "He made me, he stinks. I don't want to, Daddy, don't make me do that, Daddy. No, daddy. I want Mama." The bathroom. How did it happen? Did it happen? Or did I see him—his limp white penis while he sat on the toilet? He smelled, and did I think sex was dirty and smelly because . . . I don't know, I don't know.

In September of 1973: "I hate all this talk of sex and defecation. It's all mixed together.

If he molested me, why would he bring me a statue of the Virgin Mary from his St. Louis trip?

In May of last year: "Fellatio to me is being attacked and hurt and punished and spat upon all over again by my father. It is being invaded in my most sensitive parts—my vagina in real sex, my mouth in oral sex." My God and Jesus, no wonder I could barely restrain myself all those times with S., I could barely keep from screaming at *daddy* "No, no, don't do this to me. Get away from me! Don't touch me! It only leads to hurt and pain." Now as I say this I get heavily sleepy. I cannot face it yet. Sleep, sleep, shut down, shut out.

Am I trying and trying to make it come out right this time: to fight him off, through S., to fight off his sexual advances, to *make* him just hold me and hug me as a good father should?

In November 1974 I wrote: "Sex equals: nasty, grunt, animal, guilty, suffer, punish."

May 1980: "The feathery soft peachy pink penis of my husband vs. the white hideous maggots and evil doings and bad smells in feces filled bathrooms. What does this mean? What am I saying?"

It is no wonder I'm afraid to be open and loving and expressive and sensual with S. Every time I did be my sweet self, joyful, with a person, I immediately lost them. I never had anyone for over a few months at a time. The ones I was open with all abandoned me.

January 1981. Last night I was able to love him as himself, as a desirable, good-feeling lover of mine. Even what he asked—"You're saying you want to make love?"—seemed finally right. I am happy.

The next night, after I waited all day to make love with him, it all turned bad. We began and I wanted to love him. Suddenly it changed, someone else—an older man—was holding me. I don't know who it is. I rear back and feel disoriented. I look and look at his face trying to change it back into S.'s. I can't, I can't, who is it? I am afraid.

Yesterday I felt great relief and happiness that I *do* love *him,* he *is* my love. When I know firmly that it is him, I am attracted to him. It's when he changes into someone else . . .

Oh, Jesus, I was trying to tell somebody, when I lay awake in the middle of the night at Girl Scout camp. I was twelve years old. I lay there terrified that a man was trying to cut the screen and get in, and finally I unfroze from my rigid, sacrificial bed long enough to walk through that great exposed hall, through all those sleeping bodies to the scout leader, to shake her awake and tell her someone was trying to cut the screen, a man was trying to get in, a *killer.* She said it was just the wind, and told me to go back to sleep. I lay there listening, on that hard bench, until sunrise.

We had seen a man walking behind us in the camp park. Every one pretended fear and shrieked to each other that the man was following them. I was genuinely afraid as they talked about him.

The man, I know now, was harmless. It was the forgotten vision of my father that terrorized me, it was my own father stalking me.

Today I feel, for only a moment before I shut down: disgusted, revolted, saddened, trapped, mute, numb, confused, disabled, soiled, sinned against, scared of the dark, in despair.

NOTE: This account was written immediately after its author finally remembered being molested as a child. She is now active in Parents United, and part of her treatment involves art therapy. Three of her sketches follow and are described in her own words.

Her mother is throwing her away into the killing jaws. the monster-father will pull her under, he will rip her into shreds, she cannot survive. A part of her cries out to be rescued and weeps and howls with sadness, her present strong self is watching, and the wasted child falls helplessly toward the pit.

He is in the room with her. His penis is attacking her. She runs away while another part of her cries in desolation. She is caught between the attacking penis and the monster symbol. Or is there a way out.

The little child in me is trying to get away from the monster-father out of the past. Someone kind is helping me —she is part Hazel and partly my own strong self. My friend is waiting for me on the other side as soon as I can get away from the father.

The Personal Account of a Daughter

When I married, it took me almost two years and an emotional breakdown to tell my husband I had been sexually abused from ages nine to twelve by my father. I took another two years and a second breakdown before I quit refusing psychiatric help. It took two years after that just to build enough trust in my "doctor of the mind" to tell him what I had fearfully told my husband. That's because he was a booming-voiced, big-bodied, bearded, pipe-smoking, frightening authority figure to me. It takes me longer to trust what I'm afraid of.

By that time I was twenty-seven years old but still feeling nine years old emotionally. I had uttered THE UNUTTERABLE SECRET to only two people. Why? Because I had never heard human beings say one word about child sexual abuse; I had never seen one brochure or one warning poster about it (like the ones warning us about polio or crime). I hadn't come across anything about it in books or magazines, and it wasn't mentioned on any Marcus Welby–type TV programs or in any films.

Once the doctor knew that I had been abused, he said in later sessions, "Until you talk to your parents directly about this, neither you nor your family will find any peace." That made no sense to me; it was an outrageous idea. My reply each time he guided me toward that end was, "Doctor, I could *never* do that. I'd be too terrified ever to talk about it with them." I felt that, while it might be best for other families to confront the problem openly, *my* family was different.

My father's sexual behavior with me (which evolved into partial intercourse and ejaculation) seemed to me to be part of a romanticized love affair that he envisioned between us. The effects of that notion and his deep, troubled feelings for me were harder to deal with, in the long run, than any threat of violence or physical coercion could have been. I felt I belonged to him and should be careful not to feel too much emotion for my boyfriends. I did allow myself to have feelings for them; in fact, I was extremely emotional, but I stayed within the boundaries that my father permitted. I was afraid to go beyond that point.

The first time I fell in love, I was away at college. The boy more than met any parents' requirements for being the ideal boy. I told my parents about him when I was home on vacation. My father fell into a deeply depressed state, but I didn't associate his depression with me or my new love. I returned to college, and, two weeks later, my mother wrote

to tell me that my father had been committed to a mental hospital. At the time, I didn't know that he had attempted suicide. My mother tried to keep it from me, but my parents' friends eventually told me. (Years later, my father told me himself, bursting into my bedroom during a visit I made to their house following separation from my husband.) Although I was uneasy at the time, I still didn't directly connect his behavior with the incest.

During my senior year in college, I fell in love a second time—again, with the kind of young man who would delight parents. This time I had a premonition that my parents would not be pleased to see me get so serious about anyone, even though I was twenty-one years old. On my graduation day, while my parents were in a pleased mood, I asked if I could have my young man visit us for a weekend. My father reluctantly acquiesced. My mother wrote my friend a formal note, telling him when to arrive and when the visit would end.

The night before the young man was to arrive, my father took my mother and me out for a lovely evening. He was always very proud of us both, and he said several times that evening, "I'm so happy to be with my two girls." We all said goodnight affectionately.

The next morning when I awoke, my mother was standing over my bed looking stricken. Our family doctor was there. I learned that my father had taken the car into the woods before dawn and tried to kill himself with carbon monoxide poisoning. A groundskeeper found him or he would have died. He was flown on a stretcher to the psychiatric ward of a clinic in another city. My mother and I spent months in that strange city, just so we could visit him for an hour each day.

I had to tell my young man that I could never see him again, let alone become his fiancee. I couldn't bear the thought that my father might harm himself again. Although my friend continued to write and call me for the next five years, hoping I'd be free to come back to him, I didn't dare respond because I'd risk upsetting my father again. I had all the guilt I could stand during those days. To add to my feelings of powerlessness, I had to stand by, helplessly, while my father underwent electro-shock treatments, which permanently impaired part of his memory.

The first evening my father was out of the hospital I asked him if he liked the new dress Mother had bought me for this special occasion. He said no, that it was far too risque for me (in fact, it was a very demure dress). I knew that it was just his imagination, and I also began to realize that he would continue to try to control my life, even though I was almost twenty-two years old. I moved away to another city in order to establish my own life.

Eventually I fell in love a third time with a fine man who asked me to marry him. When it was settled in our minds, I told my parents that I wanted to be married. My father was very reluctant and unhappy about my upcoming marriage, which put a damper on my whole engagement. Since I lived in a different city, I wasn't planning to see my parents until two days before the wedding. However, shortly before the wedding, in my parents' home, my father went into my old bedroom and shot himself next to the heart. As he fell, he fell onto my bed. For months, we didn't know whether he would live or die. My mother got me to go ahead with the wedding by not telling me that my father would not be out of the hospital in time to walk me down the aisle. When I found that out, I was completely devastated. I began deteriorating from that point on, obsessed with the belief that my actions had harmed my father. It is hard to describe the enormous guilt and confusion that his behavior (both sexual and self-destructive) instilled in me as a child and as an adult. Those feelings, coupled with my terror that my husband would someday discover I was an incest victim and would stop loving and respecting me, led to the first of my three breakdowns and three suicide attempts. The first occurred two years after my wedding, when I was twenty-five years old.

My psychiatrist's recommendation that I talk to my parents about the incest filled me with the fear that, if I confronted my father, he would try to kill himself again. In addition, I told myself that my mother couldn't handle any kind of discussion about sex, that she'd fall apart if forced to deal with the subject of incest in our family. My doctor didn't waiver from his position, however. He continued to say, "As long as you and your father try to bury this secret, it will continue to make both of you as sad and as mad as you are now. It will keep eating at both of you; it won't go away. If you can bring yourself to talk to your parents, it may free you and free them, too."

I respected and trusted this man, but I didn't believe this line of thinking. I continued to sit on the secret and work on straightening myself out with his guidance and support. I improved in many ways, but the anger and sadness stemming from the incest still spent each day and night with me. I didn't understand yet that until I lanced and cleansed the "sore," it wouldn't heal. I just kept putting fresh bandaids on it to keep it from getting more infected.

Three years after therapy began, my doctor moved away. Therapy stopped. I tried to "go it alone." A year later, I had another breakdown. I needed more counseling. My new therapist didn't have a beard or a pipe, a booming voice, or a body bigger than mine. She was my size, my sex, my age, my equal. I trusted her immensely and immediately. My transferred medical records told her about the incest, so I didn't have to. I was ready to face it and work on it once again.

You can imagine how jolted I was, just as I was easing into a comfortable and workable

relationship, when what did she do? She said the same words my former doctor had said, "You keep taking out your anger and hurt on everyone . . . except your parents . . . and they're the ones who caused you that anger and hurt. Try to deal directly with them, get to that source of the anger and hurt, or it won't stop." Astonishing. I sensed some conspiracy among professional mental health helpers. I mean, where do they learn the same words? At the annual mental health conferences? These two people had never met, worked in different clinics, and were giving me the same idea. At first, it made me suspicious of both of them. Later, that sameness became the key that unlocked my disbelief and let me believe both of them. These two had helped me most; they were the two I trusted most. They hadn't steered me in any wrong directions in the past, and now they were steering me toward the same end. Could they possibly be right?

During the next four years, I studied everything I could about incest. Therapy was strengthening me so much that I finally found the confidence to say to my lady therapist, "I'm going to help other families who are trying to deal with incest." I set up my own service to help families like mine. This meant doing frightening things I had never before felt capable of—driving on the freeway and contacting people in authority (district attorneys, county supervisors, physicians, etc.). I didn't stop being scared, but I started taking action. For the first time, I believed I had something to offer, and I offered it. Counseling had helped me stop being a victim and start being a whole person. I wanted to share that with other incestuous families. I began having hopes high as chandeliers for myself and them.

One afternoon, I heard myself repeating the words of my two therapists to an incest victim who had phoned me anonymously: "The best way you could help yourself and your family is to talk with them about the sexual abuse." I believed those words. My studying and work had convinced me this was best for families whenever it's possible to do it. Now that I believed this, I knew I had to confront my own family.

I began to prepare for the confrontation. I wrote out what I would say to them, I read books about how to confront difficult situations, I talked into a tape recorder, I had imaginary conversations with them in the shower or while driving. I flew to my childhood home to talk to my parents. Within hours, I lost the courage to do what I had come for, had planned so long for. I was on their territory, became their little girl again, felt subservient to them, couldn't stand up to their united front. I became distraught. I couldn't even function normally. I had failed. I felt desolate.

That disaster was exactly one year ago. Shortly after that day, I was invited into the Parents United program, a group formed by family members who have experienced child sexual abuse. With their help, I started from Step One to prepare again for a confrontation. It took months of weekly sessions. We worked as a group, discussing it and role-playing. I also talked individually to mothers and fathers in the group and to victims who had already confronted their parents. The feedback they gave me was invaluable. The fathers reiterated what I was now convinced of: "My daughter was the only one who could forgive me. Until she was able to talk about it, we couldn't rebuild the relationship we both wanted and needed." From daughters, I heard an equally important message: "Despite what other people had told me, it was only my father who could really absolve me of my guilt. It wasn't until I actually heard him take full responsibility for what had happened that I knew I wasn't to blame." I knew that I was hearing two of the most powerful concepts in the resolution of the incest secret.

I went to my parents. I did it. This time I wasn't alone: I had brought the encouragement of Parents United with me, and I had them to return to afterward. I could sit close to my parents and lay aside my old anger while I talked. I could talk calmly except for the few times I had to stop and wait for my voice to steady. I had prepared so long and so thoroughly that my thoughts came clearly. I was now assertive enough that they listened respectfully.

It was a devastating, exhausting day for all of us; but that's a crucial point to remember: Confrontation takes only one part of one day. It's worth it to make all the days from then on better ones. Secrets are hard on families. Opening the SECRET opens other doors, too. For instance, I was now free to tell them that I had formed my own incest help service and that I was a member of Parents United. My hope is that in the future they'll become members, too, and get help and emotional support. Now we can talk to each other without the SECRET filling the space between us like a huge air pocket, pushing us away from each other. My last words to them as we got in our separate cars were, "Now I know what the word *family* really means." We'll never be as far from each other again.

The Personal Account of a Mother

We were not married, but we lived together for five years. I was drawn to him because of his love for children. He was the epitome of my ideal, my dream. But the dream gradually faded. We tried talking about our differences. It always ended up the same way: he stood his ground that children need to be chastised. This chastising ultimately ended up in child beating. I find it very difficult to forgive myself the pain I caused my son by staying with this man.

This situation and constant conflict started before my son was born and became a bigger and bigger wall between us as the years went on. I was always thankful and at the same time confused as to why he never hit my daughter. I guess I rationalized that his son was his son and that he didn't feel he could or should hit my daughter. I always thought the reason she was crying when I came home was he had been "chastising" her. I would ask her if he'd hit her. I would always make the mistake of asking her when I found the two of them together. He would come back with something like, "I was just talking to her."

My daughter finally told me about the molest when she was thirteen. It had been going on for four years, which means it started only one year after we started living together. I remember how she would always follow me around when she thought I was going somewhere. Sometimes she would ask if she could go too, and sometimes not. Just that look in her eyes. I wish I had understood. I knew she was pleading with me, but it never entered my head why. I thought she was just clinging to me, wanting always to be with mommy. I was feeling very pressured and a lot of times would tell her no, I'm going by myself.

Toward the end of my relationship with him, I started going to night school. This seemed to be an answer for me. A new way to go. I also started going to a lot of Tupperware parties.

It was on a Saturday morning. I had gone to deliver some Tupperware. When I got home my husband met me at the car. He said he had to talk to me. I said, "Okay, what about?" He told me my daughter had gotten very mad at him because he had told her to do the dishes. And she was going to tell me she wanted to talk to me. He said he just wanted me to know that she was really going to do something bad. I was scared. I had such a surge of fear run over me.

I fiddled around for a while, trying to work up the courage to face her and find out what it was that had happened. I kept asking him what it was. He told me it was something that she hoped would get him out of the house. Finally, I abruptly said to my daughter that I had been told she wanted to tell me something. She was very angry and said yes.

My daughter and I went into my bedroom and sat on the bed. I asked her what it was. What did she want to tell me? She couldn't get it out. It was very hard for her. I asked her, "Did he rape you?" She said yes. I was so stunned and terrified I didn't know what to do. She asked me not to leave her alone with him any more. I promised her I wouldn't. And I never did leave her with him again. My heart was broken. Broken for her, broken for me, broken for the family.

I just didn't want it to be real. Didn't want to be the one who did this to her. I was panicked, but I knew I needed help. Knew we all needed help. I raced through the house looking for a phone book. The only thing I could think of was to call Family Service. I talked to a lady on the other end. She listened to me. I did a lot of crying. The more I talked, the more I cried. I told her what my daughter had just told me. I also told her that my husband had totally denied it. I didn't know what to believe. My husband tried to convince me that she had said it out of anger. He said she had told him she was going to tell me that so she could get rid of him once and for all. At the time, it seemed possible: she was mortified and angered to the point of sticking up for me and her brother when he went on one of his rampages of chastising. My daughter's a very brave and loving girl.

On Monday we went to see a counselor at Family Service. This really got us nowhere. The counselor didn't know how to deal with this problem. First I would talk; then he asked my husband how he felt about what I had just said. My husband didn't say much. He just tried to keep from upsetting anyone further as well as trying to keep up the charade. The counselor asked my daughter how she felt. He asked her if she loved him. She said yes. He asked her if she hated him, too. She said yes. She said she just wished he'd stop "bugging" her. At that point, I felt as though I were living a nightmare. It was so real. It couldn't be real. In my heart, I knew my daughter wasn't lying. I wanted to change everything—to take all the pain away from her.

It's so hard to say all of this. I talked to my babysitter about it. She, being a nun for eight years, seemed to be the one person who could help me do what was right. I trusted her judgment. She had taken care of my daughter for twelve years. I told her that I just couldn't believe it. It couldn't be true.

I guess she tried her best. She told me, "Just tell her that you know it's a lie, and she'll probably admit to the truth."

Well, I did this and have never been sorrier. My daughter said it was true. "Now you don't believe me. I've loved you all this time." I love my daughter very much and am feeling a lot of pain and regret.

Well, I then confronted my husband again and asked him to tell me the truth, thinking maybe we could find help and work this out. He continued to deny it. The next day I called a friend of mine who was an attorney. He advised me to set up an appointment for my husband to take a lie-detector test. He told me that if he hesitated in any way to take the test, I could be pretty sure he was lying. Well, it's all history now but he agreed to take the lie detector test. I got the $175 from the bank and gave it to him.

A few days later when the results were to be in, I called the agency. They said he hadn't come in for the test. I asked them, "Are you sure?" Yes, they had no record of him coming in.

In the meantime, my mother got involved. I'm not really sure at what point in time, but her husband picked my daughter up from school and asked her if anything was wrong. She told him no. He asked her if my husband had gotten fresh with her. She told him, "Yes."

My mother then called the San Jose Police Department and was referred to the County. The County sent an investigator to my daughter's school. My daughter denied what had been going on. At the same time, it was becoming more and more urgent that this be taken care of. I was contacted by a juvenile intake officer. She talked to my daughter after school. My daughter told her what had been going on.

The juvenile probation officer called me at work from my babysitter's house and said, "You're going to have to make a choice between your daughter or staying with him. Otherwise, she will be taken to the Children's Shelter."

I said, "Of course, I'll choose my daughter." She asked where we would go. I told her we would stay with my babysitter. She said that was fine and she'd call me later in the day and set up an appointment. When she called, she told me she really didn't believe my daughter, but had to treat the case as being true.

It was a few days later that my daughter and I went down to the police department. It was very scary for her. The officer talked to us together and took her statement. He told us my daughter would have to be examined by a County doctor. I had already taken her to my own doctor but we had to go anyway. The examination resulted in no clear-cut evidence. The police officer told me at that time that he didn't believe her, either. He then proceeded to tell my daughter that he didn't believe her.

When she came back to the car, she was very angry, very sullen, very alone. I told her that I believed her. She said, "No, you don't. You didn't believe me when I told you." I tried to explain to her that I was very frightened and hurt and scared at the time and I just wanted it not to be true—and that I did believe her. I told her I hadn't acted as a very good mother and I was sorry I had hurt her.

The days during this police and juvenile department involvement, before my husband was arrested, are not clear. The next thing that happened was an appointment was set up with a counselor. The juvenile officer took us over to see Bee Mitchell.

She saw us separately. She told me about a meeting on Wednesday night. She walked me out to the lobby and introduced me to one of the mothers. She asked the mother to show me around that night and told me to look for her.

I'll never forget that first night. I walked in and there were women and men laughing and talking to one another. It seemed so strange. How could they be so happy? I figured the happy ones must be counselors or visitors. It didn't sink in until orientation that the men in the group were the child molesters. I was afraid to look at them. I kept kind of sneaking a peek when I thought they weren't looking.

No one spoke for quite a while. Once the ice was broken and I had listened to the people for a while, I began to feel safe. They were human beings, too, not monsters. The meeting finally ended with one huge group hug. I didn't know how much I needed that. The feeling of love and caring for me and me for them.

My daughter began going to Daughters & Sons United meetings. She would come home from the meetings, as I saw it, feeling much more free. More at peace with herself. She told me she had thought she was the only one this had happened to and now she knew she wasn't.

We went through the court system. My daughter didn't have to take the stand. My husband finally decided to plead guilty. He didn't want her to go through that. I thank him for that.

In the following months, we made an effort to communicate. I found that I really didn't want to continue our relationship. As of right now, he is still angry with me and there is no communication. He just would not take the help available. He still clings to "not needing anyone."

I have been with Parents United for twenty-one months now. I am now the Chapter Secretary and look forward to working on chapter development in other counties. I want to see our program grow and grow. Parents United is my family; without everyone I've come to know, I would not have made it. I've found a lot of strength—strength through love and support, strength through honesty. I know when I started in the program I was terrified of being honest with another person. Parents United has offered me so much love and caring and support that I trust myself and can be honest. Parents United helped me save my life.

The Personal Account of a Father

Hello, Me!

"Hello, me" seems like a strange thing to be saying, especially when you're saying it for the first time to the person that's lived inside you for almost thirty-eight years. As far back as I can remember, I've felt dislike, disgust, and displeasure. Hell, I downright hated myself most of the time.

Oh, I managed to project a desirable image of myself which I considered socially acceptable—self-confident, dependable, understanding, honest, brave—a lily-white pillar of respectability. That was me.

Suddenly, out of nowhere, I had been discovered. My protective covering had been penetrated. The world would know who and what I really was. I would be destroyed. There I stood, naked and ugly, the likeness of a Dorian Grey. I wanted to hide, to run, to somehow disintegrate.

The phone rang. "Hello, I'm with Parents United. I'm a member of a group of people who've been through the same thing you're going through."

"My god," I thought, "not only am I not the only one this has ever happened to—hell, they've got their own club."

The voice on the phone continued. "We understand your pain. We share your pain with you. We want to help you." I didn't believe any of this was possible. How could anyone understand my pain? How could anyone want to help *me*?

What I could have easily believed was that this Parents United was a colony on an island off the coast somewhat like a leper colony where they sent people like me so we wouldn't be able to contaminate the rest of the people in the world.

Well, I came to Parents United's Wednesday night meeting. What I found was a room full of normal, everyday-looking people—hugging and kissing, smiling and greeting each other as if they were all family and hadn't seen each other for years. What I discovered that first night was that they *were* a family, a very special family held together by a common bond of unconditional love and understanding, of honest truth and caring. I began to feel warm inside. I felt alive again. I began to feel that "I, too" might be a worthwhile person.

Before I attempt to recreate for you the events that led up to the molesting of my daughters, I would like to make a few things very clear to you. First and most important, I accept without reservation the complete and total responsibility for my actions. I am deeply ashamed and heartbroken over those actions, and for the pain and heartache I've caused my wife and children.

Second, I want to make it equally clear that any statement that I make in this story is to enable you to understand my criminal acts and the events that led up to them. I do not intend to cloud the issue of my guilt, discredit the police report, nor in any way diminish the severity of my actions, but to perhaps enable you to understand why I committed the crimes I did.

It would be impossible to compress a lifetime of confusion and dismay into a few handwritten pages. There are so many factors that contributed to my state of mind at the time of the molests. For over thirty years (since I was about six years old), I've been thoroughly confused about love, about trust and understanding, about myself—who and what I am.

I was raised by my mother, a stepmother, two stepfathers, my grandmother, and my father. I've been bounced from person to person, and place to place. I've lived in so many places I used to stammer when asked where I was from. During one period of my life, I went to eleven schools in one and one-half terms in three states. I was lied to and coerced into sharing lies by my mother, beaten by my stepfathers, and sexually molested by my own father.

When I was 6 years old, my mother left me with my grandmother and said she would get a job and find us a place to live. Over two years later she returned; she had been married for over a year. She explained to me that the man she had married had never been married before nor had he ever had children of his own, and that things would be okay if I would be a good boy and mind. I was also told to call him "Dad," as was the case when she married my second stepfather.

So, they took me to live with them. I don't believe he was an alcoholic at the time, but he and my mother would party and drink heavily on weekends. When they came home, they would fight, and I would lie in my room in fear, listening to them beating each other. On a couple of occasions, I tried to help my mother and was beaten severely for my efforts.

After about a year or so, my mother thought it best to send me to my father, who was in California. I spent the next six or seven years going from parent to parent. It seemed whoever needed me the most for whatever reason could have me. As far as love, my mother would tell me that she loved me, then she would leave me or send me away. There was always a condition attached to her love: if I would not cause trouble, I could stay. If I would lie for her or support her in one of her own lies, she wouldn't send me away.

My father and I had no father–son relationship at all. He had been confined to a wheelchair since before I could walk. Because of his illness and his inability to do father-and-son type things, we had nothing in common to talk about. His way of showing love was to smile or say "Thanks, son" when I would clean and dress the pressure sores on his buttocks, or help him get dressed, or bathe him. Sometimes I would even have to strip and remake the bed and bathe him in the middle of the night (he had no control over his bodily functions). Love and security for me was like the little boy looking through the candy store window—I could never quite reach it.

I finally did receive affection of a sort from him at the age of twelve. I had to sleep with him because of his frequent needs at night. I began to wake up with his penis in my mouth. He would use a hand mirror to watch my face for a sign of wakefulness. I didn't know what to do, so I would just pretend to be asleep still and roll over. I couldn't stand what was happening but I had no place to turn. You see, I couldn't go to his church where he was the minister, and tell anyone there that the man who was their spiritual leader was engaging in homosexual acts with his son. Besides which, I did not know the word homosexual at that time. According to my friends, they were just queers, fruits, people to stay away from.

I didn't know if they could tell what was going on but I felt unclean and I was afraid they might be able to detect something was happening. So, I began to withdraw from my peers. I had found an old basement in the rooming house where we lived which no one knew existed and after telling my friends that I had something to do or chores to perform, I would go there and play alone. After awhile I played with no one. I would just go to my basement to be alone. I was almost twenty before I could feel comfortable in close contact with other men. When I was in the service, I remember many occasions when I was asked why I would flinch or pull away when a guy would put his arm around my shoulder or touch me in a friendly way.

At the age of eighteen, I met a girl, Sharon. We had a sexual relationship and she became pregnant. I was notified by my commanding officer and was given a three-day pass to go home and rectify the situation. We were married in April 1959.

Our first child, a son, was born that same year. By 1963 we also had three daughters. We were deeply in debt and I was working almost constantly to survive; it seems we were always just one step ahead of the bill collectors. My wife was alone with the children most of the time. She was very unhappy. When she couldn't take it anymore, she began to go out. She met a man and left me and the children. I was very frightened at the prospect of raising four children alone, but I loved them and they were all I had.

During our separation, I had met and had been dating my present wife. She was a sweet and wonderfully kind woman. I knew that she loved my children and would make them a good mother. In 1967 we were married. Things went along well for a while; we were happy.

My mother had come to live with us. At that time, it wasn't too bad: my wife and I were both working, and she helped with the children. She lived with us for a little less than a year before she met a man and married him. When her marriage collapsed after about two and a half years, she came back to live with us, as she had no way of supporting herself. My wife resented her being there but accepted the fact that we had no choice.

I believe it was sometime in 1970 that my wife began having difficulty with the side-effects of the Pill. I don't remember where the idea of a vasectomy came from, but we decided that it would be the best thing to do. I was afraid of the idea and I had some strange belief that somehow this would remove my manhood. However, I never expressed it to anyone. After all, I had burdened this lady with enough—this one I could handle alone.

Well, as luck would have it, I developed a cyst that made intercourse quite painful. The longer I let it go, the more painful it became, until the majority of the time I could not achieve an erection. Even after corrective surgery, the emotional damage I had sustained continued in our sexual life. Now I had failed as a lover, too.

You must be asking yourself now, "Doesn't this couple ever talk? Do they just blindly go along not dealing with or solving any of their problems?" My wife would try to talk to me about this problem as well as others we were having, but I always put them down as minor problems: "Don't worry, I can handle them. It's just a phase." I would try to see that my mother didn't upset my wife, that my wife didn't upset my mother, and that my children didn't upset anyone. I took on the role of peace-maker, of father-confessor, so no one would have any reason to be unhappy. You see, all my life, that which represented love, home, and security to me only existed as long as I performed as expected. As long as I didn't cause trouble, as long as I could handle any situation without complaining, everything would be all right. For fear of rocking the boat, I therefore accepted whatever came my way, made no demands on anyone, and didn't share my problems.

Now we come to the period of the molests. My wife and I had almost completely excluded sex from our lives. Being aware of the mental anguish I was experiencing, my wife would avoid contact. She would retire early or read. For the same reason, I would stay up late and watch TV. I lived under the constant fear that any day she would just pick up and leave. It was a pattern I had become accustomed to.

I was in an almost constant state of depression. I disliked myself very much. I had very little self-esteem and very little self-respect. All I wanted was for my family to be happy, and it seems I had no idea what to do about it. I needed affection and the my daughters were removed from school and placed in the Children's Shelter.

The events of the next three days were like a horrible nightmare. I couldn't sleep or eat. I couldn't stop crying. I cannot begin to tell you of the pain and suffering I went through, the shame and utter disgust I felt. I wanted to run away. I contemplated killing myself. I wanted to hide, to cease to exist.

Then I received that telephone call from a member of Parents United. She explained that her husband had been through the same thing and that they wanted to help. I accepted that help. Since that time I have been a member of Parents United and CSATP. I have been receiving an average of five hours per week of counseling.

I cannot begin to tell you all the things that I have learned through their help. I have been made to look deep into myself—to pierce the shell that I had formed over the years to protect myself from further hurt; to reconstruct the events of my life and to look at them objectively, to understand their meanings and the effects they have had on my life. I now have an understanding of myself I never thought possible. Even though I have a lot more to learn, I now have an understanding of love, trusting, sharing of one's self, and parenting I never thought I could achieve. I know now that I am loved and I know how to return that love in a proper way. I have regained my self-image, my self-esteem, and my self-respect. And beyond that, I know that I will never lose it again.

As to punishment, I have been punished severely. I have been physically separated from my family, I have deeply hurt and wounded my wife, I have caused unknown and immeasurable emotional damage to my children, and I have caused myself great personal anguish and despair. I will continue to be punished every day for the rest of my life for the shame and heartache I have caused.

I am particularly concerned for my daughter, even though I have at every opportunity reassured her that I love her deeply, and even more for having the courage to seek help when I had none. It was because of her that our family will be saved —and for that I will be forever grateful. It was I, and I alone, who was responsible for these terrible things. She felt responsible because it was through her that the molests were discovered. Knowing that her father was in jail because of this was detrimental to her therapy. When I assured her that she bears no guilt in any way, her only response to me was, "When can you come home, Dad, so we can all be happy again?"

Enough time has passed now that I am at home. Once again, we are together as a family. A very special family held together by a common bond of unconditional love and understanding, of honest truth and caring. I am feeling warm inside. I feel alive again. I feel that "I, too" am a worthwhile person.

The Personal Account of an Intern Counselor

About three years ago, I was in a class at the University of Santa Clara in psychosocial development of school-age children. During one of my classes, Ellie and a member of Parents United came to talk to the class on molest in families. As I listened, I thought how could Ellie (a counselor) work with these families, especially the fathers. I too had a little girl at that time who was six years old. I had been divorced about six months.

When Ellie spoke about those with whom she counseled, my stomach turned. My feelings of anger surfaced: those horrible men—I would castrate them and throw them in jail. How dare they violate a young female child. How sick they must be. And to allow them to forfeit prison time and attend counseling . . . totally beyond my comprehension!

Internship was offered. No, I did not want anything to do with such a heinous crime. The seed, however, was planted. I heard how from great tragedy and pain, good would occur. The closed communication pattern would be broken, and open communication would replace it. Human beings were assisted in discovering a variety of alternatives in dealing with feelings rather than in inappropriate behaviorial patterns, i.e., molest. The seed was planted. I chose to set all of my prejudices aside.

About six months later, I began counseling at a local high school with a probation officer for dependent children. He was working with men who had molested their children. As I worked with this beautiful, dedicated man, I looked at my own feelings and began to evaluate what I felt and heard. A growing desire was gnawing at me to explore the possibility of an internship with CSATP.

I remember walking in, afraid and insecure. What was I doing here at the Juvenile Probation Department? I'd never interacted with the criminal justice system, nor did I know much other than what the probation officer had shared about dependency intake, etc.

I was welcomed with warmth and respect by the program administrator and program coordinator. I felt such acceptance from them that somehow I felt I belonged. I freely chose to be there and *I felt scared.* They shared their expectations with me. I shared mine with them.

I was invited to the interns' meeting and the Parents United meeting. Slowly, I began to hear the experience of human beings who chose to help others grow and change. I felt excitement and enthusiasm and love, and I wanted to work in this environment. I went to Parents United meetings and listened to people sharing their experiences, hopes, and strength. I watched the loving, caring interaction that took place. I wanted to be a part of this.

I began to work in counseling with women and men to unravel what had occurred in their lives. Although I felt frightened by the magnitude of dealing with their problems, I received a tremendous amount of support from the CSATP and other interns. I felt trusted and loved. My self-confidence as well as my wisdom, knowledge, and skills increased due to the trust of others. I began to see my role as a teacher and model, and I realized that I am a student in life. Each person whom I instruct brings a gift of self to me that teaches me.

I am learning that from great pain comes beauty, love, goodness, and self-acceptance. I believe in what I am doing. I am learning about myself. I realize that my values and attitudes are changing. I have discovered that I chose to limit myself in the past. Now these beautiful people with whom I interact are assisting me in the process of discovering who I am. Through dealing with the mothers who are experiencing tremendous pain, I am reminded of my pain. As I work with my families, I am reinforced in the positive changes in my life, in honest communication, in being open.

The Personal Account of a Grandmother

On a Friday afternoon two years ago when my husband did not return from work, I discovered he had been arrested for molesting our two granddaughters, ages ten and eleven. That was the beginning of the worst hell any human being can experience. I did not believe my son when he told me that my husband had molested the girls. A few days later I was allowed to hear portions of the girls' tapes from their interview with the police. Then I had to believe it, and I knew I could not go to sleep and wake up to find it was just a nightmare. It was a reality. The numbness began to wear off, and my real hell began.

I had so many questions: What can I do? Where can I go to get away from this terrible pain? There was no one for me to talk to about it. I knew there wasn't anyone in the entire world who could or would understand our secret, so we chose not to share our pain with anyone. We kept the secret from our neighbors, our friends, and the people in the church we had attended and been very active in for twenty-five years.

Every time I looked at my husband, I felt an explosive reaction rise up inside me. During the first week of agonizing, ten thousand thoughts ran through my mind: Why? I've lived with this man for all of these years, and I know him so well; so how could he have done this? When did it happen? Where could it have happened? I've been right here in our house every time our granddaughters have visited for a weekend or a whole week.

I thought, "A big hole has opened up and swallowed six of the most important people in my world. And here I am all alone again." My father had molested me years before for two years following my mother's death, when he and I lived alone. I ran away from home and got married. My marriage ended very soon, and I was all alone with a son to raise. Here I am again with that same feeling of loss that will not go away. (At this point, I had not left our house since our crisis had begun.)

My husband got the name of an attorney who represented men and families who experienced child sexual abuse. After his appointments with her, my husband would come home to my questions. But the attorney had told him not to talk to anyone, so he would not even tell me what his charges were, what he had actually done, or whether he had indeed done anything. All I knew was what my son had told me—and that was very little, because my son was trying to protect me and save me from knowing the details. My husband's evasive answers just added fuel to the already explosive fire inside of me, though, because I wanted to know what was happening.

My husband got the name and phone number of a woman counselor who worked for CSATP. All I knew about the organization was that it was a program for people who needed help dealing with child sexual abuse. He saw her once and told me she wanted to see me, too. I said, "I didn't do anything. Why should I see a counselor? Anyway, no one can help me. You go ahead and keep seeing her. You're the one who needs help."

The next day, my husband pulled himself together enough to go to work (after calling in sick for several days). After he left, the counselor called me and asked me to come talk to her. I said, "No. No one can help me with my pain." She did not pressure me, nor did she try to convince me that I should come. She left the invitation open and said she would stay in touch with me; and she told me to feel free to call her if I felt the need.

My husband had an appointment with his counselor one Wednesday afternoon. The counselor called me that morning, and I agreed to see her. At that point my face and eyes were still so swollen from my daily crying that I could hardly see to drive my car to her office. When I arrived, this beautiful lady named Anna came up to me and put her arms around me and said, "Come with me. Let's just talk." She took me into her office, sat beside me, and just let me cry.

I was so surprised that she didn't demand answers of me or ask questions like, "Why did you allow your husband to molest your granddaughters right under your nose?" Instead she said, "I really feel your pain," and she had tears in her eyes, too. She explained that this program had helped over a thousand families in the past six years—people caught in a situation just like ours. I heard that sentence more clearly than I had heard any words since my husband's arrest. She told me about a meeting that many parents and grandparents would attend that evening. She said they met weekly to talk and support each other. I agreed to come.

My husband and I walked into a huge room at 7:30 that evening. Most of the people there laughed and talked; and some of them hugged and kissed like long lost friends being reunited. I had never experienced any group like this before. I could not understand how they could be so happy and cheerful while I was hurting so badly. I felt really strange for the next two hours. Finally, I couldn't take being there any longer and walked out before the meeting ended.

But I went back the next Wednesday night. It didn't seem so strange the second time, because during the week one of the members had called me. She told me she and her husband were surviving their crisis and had been in the program almost a year. I was beginning to understand what she was trying to tell me. She just allowed me to talk for the most part. I felt safe confiding in her since she and her husband had been through the same experience we were now living.

A turning point came when our counselor called me one day and said, "Some members are meeting on Tuesday to form a steering committee. They really need help. Can you join them?" I joined them, and the meeting went very well. We discussed how to help incoming families in a more effective way. That was the beginning of a very involved life for me. There was a great need for our help, and I did have something to contribute. Every time a CSATP counselor called me to say, "Please call this lady," I would set aside my pain and reach out to the woman I called. Often I would drive to their house to visit as a way of being supportive.

I went to the CSATP office just to look around, and I realized how understaffed they were. I didn't know what function I could serve, but I stayed there answering phone calls. A typical phone call would be a mother calling to say that she had just discovered that her husband had molested their daughter. I soon realized I was very effective just talking to and giving these people support during their initial crises. Also, it gave me an opportunity to talk about Parents United and to invite them to a Wednesday night meeting. On Wednesday nights I would greet the new members I had talked to on the phone and introduce them to other members who had been there for a while, people who were ready and willing to reach out to someone else in pain.

I believe this program is the most important one in existence today, because it handles such a taboo subject. I tell others how it saved my life. I also tell them how frightening it was for me to expose my feelings to people I didn't know and how worried I was that I would be recognized by someone who knew me, who would then realize I had this problem.

When this problem first hit our family, it was hard for me to realize I was still an important element in our society. I was afraid to go to the grocery because I assumed anyone who saw me could tell what my problem was. I thought only my husband had a problem—not me. Parents United helped me to see that I, too, must accept some responsibility for what happened and that I needed help. I realized that our marriage was not good and that we both needed to learn more about ourselves.

Before, I had bottled up my hurts and stayed busy, ignoring my husband and his problems. I was unable to see that he needed support and understanding from me. I know now I did the only thing I knew to do at the time. Because we didn't know how to cope better than we did, we got into the situation that led us to Parents United. Since being in Parents United, my life is fuller and has much more meaning. Being a member means learning to live and hear and see life in a much more meaningful way. I have grown and learned more about myself than I ever thought possible.

The Personal Account of a Father

In April 1972, I was arrested for sexually molesting my daughter. It was one of the loneliest and most devastating experiences of my life. My daughter was taken from our home and placed in a children's shelter for her protection. I spent the weekend in jail and our entire family suffered. I was released from jail on my own recognizance with orders to have no contact with my daughter. I readily agreed to comply with the order and stayed with my sister-in-law, thinking my daughter would be returned home immediately. This was not the case; it was two weeks before she could come home. It took approximately four months for the entire court process to be completed.

During this time I received individual, marriage, and family counseling with Hank Giarretto. I met Hank through my daughter's probation officer, with whom my wife was in contact. Before I saw Hank, I saw a psychiatrist who was not associated with Hank; afterward, I really wondered what was happening to my state of mind adn whether I was crazy. That is because talking to the psychiatrist was like talking to a wall and left me feeling desperate. So when I found out there was a person like Hank to talk to I couldn't believe my good luck.

When I first met him, he looked like a hippie to me, because I was a bank examiner with short hair and conservative suits. Hank wore a tweed sportcoat. He didn't look like I expected a counselor, psychologist, or psychiatrist to look. He looked strange to me at first, but it didn't take long for me to relate to him or for him to relate to me. In him I had finally found someone who really cared about what I felt and who I was. He was able to listen to me, and he was able to *hear* me and restate my feelings. I could tell him anything and he truly seemed to understand it.

More than that, he could put into words my feelings about myself: words and pieces of myself that I had blocked off for years. Here was someone in my life who really cared about how I felt. I couldn't get over my amazement. Then I took a hard look at myself and my relationships, not only with my wife and children, but with my friends. I opened up more and began to feel safe.

I spent nine months in jail, and it was during that period that Hank told me about a meeting that took place in the evening once a week. He said a few of the women married to incest offenders met together regularly to talk about their problems and what was happening to their lives. I said I wanted to go. It was what I needed: a place where I could talk about my feelings, make a connection with other people who knew how I felt, and be with people who could hear my words.

Helped by Hank, Anna (his wife), and my daughter's probation officer, this group was eventually named Parents United. I was the first male member. By the time I left jail, the group had grown from the three women and me to fifteen or twenty members. We sat and talked about what was going on in our lives. Sometimes Hank would lead us through a meditation exercise. I didn't always like that, and for a while it seemed like bullshit. But everything else about the group seemed okay, so I thought I'd go along with meditation.

When I had first entered jail, my rehabilitation officer wanted to rehabilitate me. After two weeks of talking to me several times, he decided I should not be in jail, that I had no business being there. His thinking changed really fast. That made me feel good about myself; consequently, I got him involved in the group that would eventually become Parents United. I invited him to it while I was in jail. Then I remained in contact with him, and he and I were able to get permission for other men on work-furlough to attend the group.

In some ways I was fortunate. I was the first sex offender I know of who was put on work-furlough immediately and allowed to go to work. I was able to go to school two nights a week, and I was treated fairly. But I laugh at the word "rehabilitation." There was no rehabilitation involved in my treatment by the law. It was strictly punitive. They wanted their pound of flesh and they took it. I would rather have heard them say candidly that that was what they intended than to hear the bullshit they told me.

I lost my job, sold our home, and was without my family; so I had to reconstruct my life all over again. Before I left jail, my No-Contact order was lifted; so when I left jail, I could have gone home to live with my children so far as the law was concerned. I did take them on a vacation, and we spent time together making a connection with each other. My wife and I could not communicate well, though; every time she and I tried to make contact, it didn't work.

Things Hank had said were now finally sinking into my brain and being integrated. They were, for the most part, thoughts about being open and saying what was happening in the present, and being able to say how I felt. I was finding out that it was okay to do that. Some people may not like it, but what was important was that I liked myself when I did that. I kept learning more about myself.

Parents United kept growing. We moved from one small room to a bigger room and then to the biggest room of the Juvenile Probation Department. By 1974, Parents United had grown to thirty or forty people. Hank decided we needed to add another group since we were growing at such a phenomenal rate, so he talked to us about it. He suggested that another member and I co-lead the new group. We called it the Mixed Group, meaning the members attending the group did not have to be parents or part of a couple or married. I co-facilitated that group for two years, and it amazed me how much I learned about myself doing that.

I began speaking on radio talk shows. Listeners called in and asked me questions. The first two times I did it I was too afraid to use my own first name, so I used George or John or whatever name came to mind. Then it struck me that there are so many people with my first name in this country that using my own name did not threaten my family's privacy or my own. Listeners were really interested to hear how I felt and to talk to *me.* So it made more sense to use my own name and it became a lot easier. Each time I felt good about being interviewed. I was interviewed for some films about child sexual abuse. For instance, my ex-wife and I were interviewed by a TV channel in St. Louis. They did not show our faces in a way that we could be identified, but we were there; and doing it was a contribution we could make that was worthwhile.

Parents United grew to the point where we added a Men's Group and Couples' Group. I led the Men's Group. My life kept progressing positively. I had no problems making or keeping relationships with men or women. I had never had much difficulty talking to people anyway; but now I could do so even better than in my past relationships. I could talk about feelings and ask and answer personal questions, and make real connections with the people around me. I met my present wife in one of the groups I led.

I stayed active in Parents United, kept attending different workshops, and kept meeting new people. At this time every aspect of my life was functioning. Everyone respected me, and I knew some answers. I connected well wth my daughter and knew why I had molested her. I listened to other people and helped them.

My two sons lived with me. My younger son was 10 at the time. I had an adult male friend who did not have any friends except for an occasional woman to relate to sexually. He could not keep a relationship going. He and I had been friends for a couple of years. When the Center for Human Communications offered a group facilitator's course that my wife and I attended, I invited my friend to take it with us. He did and spent weekends at our house during that time.

One morning I walked by my younger son's bedroom and caught my friend molesting him. I could not believe my eyes. After all I knew about child sexual abuse, and after everything that had happened, everything I was doing presently in my life, I should have been aware that something was happening. I was *not* aware it was happening. I make this point because people often say that a mother always knows when her child is being sexually abused. I did not know; I had no idea. My friend had been molesting my son for quite some time, too, before that morning when I discovered it.

I confronted my friend, and at first he denied it. A half hour later he told me everything. I contacted an officer in the sex detail unit of the San Jose Police Department and an attorney. I went with my friend when he turned himself in because, even though I hated his guts for what he did, I still cared about the man.

Also, I realized how my ex-wife must have felt about me when she found out that I was molesting our daughter. It was quite a blow, quite an experience, and it triggered so many thoughts. This was my chance to practice everything I preached and talked about to everyone else about child sexual abuse. Once again I had an opportunity to find out about myself. I believe I used it in the best possible way.

I know one thing for sure: it helped my son much more that I was just there with him than if I had asked him questions like, "Why didn't you tell me?" He felt good about the way I handled the situation. If he wanted to talk about it to me, he knew he could. We did talk about it; and I told him what was happening to his friend, because they *were* still friends. The secret was broken, and we don't want secrets like that. Everyone in the family has to know the truth.

Offenders do not need to go to jail, and I hope we can keep them out. Some changes can be made in the system, but I am not on a bandwagon to try to keep people in jail or out of jail, to keep them married or unmarried. What I do want is to be present for people when they are hurting and to have a group available for them. Primarily, I just want to be in contact with the people who need us, and to keep doing this work.

The Personal Account of a Father

In the children's home where I grew up, I learned to hate: social workers, school, almost everything and everyone. Next I learned to destroy what I hated. I played some very sad and heavy games. It became easier to hate than to love. I stuffed inside myself any feelings of being hurt and didn't let myself hurt. I never let a tear come out of either eye, because the guys I lived with at the home wouldn't have tolerated that. I learned not to discuss or share any emotion about being physically hurt or sad.

I didn't ever think I had a meaning or purpose or sense of flow about my life. I just pointed myself in a certain direction and tried to conquer and destroy. I had no sense of belonging to a family or to society. Once a priest came to the home and cornered me to get inside my thoughts. I wasn't a Catholic and didn't want him to know my thoughts. To get back at him, I let the air out of his tires. My faulty reasoning was that it would keep him from coming back. I was seventeen years old then but operating with a ten-year-old's reasoning. I wasn't close to males at any time in my life on any kind of a feeling level. I didn't know how to deal with the fact that the males I know kept all their feelings repressed and pushed down. They couldn't do anything for me that I needed, so I just let them do their own thing.

I was ready to give but not receive, even when I was very young. I could give and give and give . . . but I didn't know how to let anyone else give. As a result, lots of people rejected me because I didn't accept anything from them. They needed to give, too, but I didn't let them. I learned not to attach myself to anything or anyone.

I liked being rejected because then I knew how to react. I knew my ground and what to do next each time that happened. I thought I knew what other people thought and that I could guess when they didn't want me around anymore. Then I'd say, "Okay, I don't have to be around anymore." And I'd hurry and detach myself, even if it was someone I really was drawn to. I learned that very young and kept that pattern as an adult. I learned to fantasize about relationships, about being close to people. Of course, it was always on *my* terms. At night lying down, I'd fantasize in a dream state about having relationships where people accepted me. The only place I could have relationships was in my dreams —not in real life.

As an adolescent, I had several girlfriends. I'd make each one reject me and make them go on to someone else. I kept repeating that pattern. I kept all of them from being able to harm me or get into my "garbage can." By garbage can I mean all my repressed or angry feelings that I kept stuffing inside myself and keeping a lid on.

What I learned in the children's home about stuffing feelings inside myself and denying them followed me into adulthood. I was very, very negative about everyone and everything. I was angry most of the time. That really affected my outlook on life. I didn't share my feelings with anyone. I didn't want to be touched or to be close to anyone, because they could reject me by surprise. I pushed people to reject me so that I could maintain control of any rejecting that resulted. I was used to being in a rejected state. Any other state was unfamiliar and left me feeling I didn't know what ground I was on. Being rejected was ground I knew, so I could handle that.

I kept my thoughts to myself in that garbage can I started filling as a boy. That can was never empty, because I kept filling it every day. I also held on to everything that I had ever put in there, so it got more and more full every day. I had a very low opinion of myself. I wasn't accomplishing much success or adding much to the world. I never tried suicide, but I often thought that if I snuffed out the light on my life that it would be better for the people around me.

I had very little self-control and let myself be very violent. I got frustrated a lot; and when I did, I wanted to throw or bang or destroy something. One time I got a bolt started right but couldn't make it fit back in my car. I threw my wrench neatly through the windshield and blew the glass apart. That just caused me more problems and more frustration. Another time, when I was in business for myself, I designed and drafted some drawings. After spending seven hours on an overlay drawing, which was $140 worth of work several years ago, I ruined it with one sweep of my knife. I did it because it didn't fit precisely the way I wanted. I did that even though it looked acceptable enough and the people I did it for had approved and accepted it. It wasn't what I wanted, so I destroyed it. And when I had to do it over, I got angry with the people and blamed them instead of myself. When I was finished, I destroyed the plates because I didn't want any reminders around of that experience.

I was destructive to others and to myself. I didn't eat much or eat right. I'm six feet tall and was three hundred pounds and looked like a bloated hunk. Even if I got hungry at work, I wouldn't eat. I'd get the shakes and be nervous from hunger, but I'd use will power to deny that it was happening and try not to let it bother me.

I was a real loner. I thought I liked being alone. I wallowed in my garbage of thoughts by myself. I tried to keep thoughts straightened out in my head enough to satisfy myself. I didn't try to straighten out matters with anyone else. I avoided any place where there were crowds, like parks. I didn't want people staring at me, so I stared at them instead. I liked being the silent observer, so I'd sit in a corner and watch people. I'd try to figure out what was going with them and try not to let them see what was going on with me. I watched a lot of football on TV and tried to be knowledgeable about it, because the guys at work related to that. I wanted to sound knowledgeable.

I deceived others about how much I drank. I thought it was manly to sit down and drink a case of beer. Sometimes, I'd follow the beer up with a quart or a couple of six-packs. I won approval from my fellow employees and other acquaintances by doing that. Right before I came to Parents United, I drank a fifth each day and drank all day long.

I convinced myself that drinking helped me cope with my wife's health problems. In reality, all it did was help me repress those problems. I kidded myself that if I lived alone, I could lick my drinking problem easily. When I drank, I could talk more easily, hold a conversation better (I thought), be a different person that I couldn't be when sober. When I was drunk, I related to other people's stories better and forgot some of my "garbage." Drinking helped me get into a comfortable "gray field." It made me feel more successful and stronger than I felt at any other time. In recent years, when I couldn't reach that level and just got sick, I felt helpless that booze couldn't do for me what it had done for me earlier in my life.

I became a Boy Scout leader. I learned about boys' problems and about counseling them. I didn't drink when I was with those boys, which was one weekend a month. I had to give up being a scout leader after I molested my stepdaughter. I couldn't risk that they'd find out about me. I still regret that so much and it still hurts. I can't take the chance, though, that someone would call them to say they had a child molestor as a leader. I contribute to them now in a more indirect way. Scouting seemed to be the one place where I really started to get in touch with myself. That happened on campouts when I had time to myself late in the evenings and would do some sober thinking.

I had met my first wife while I was still in the Marines. We lived together before marriage, then just took off one night and got married. We had two children. At first the marriage was very secure and we shared a lot of thoughts and feelings. I felt enlightened and enthused about the marriage. Then my drinking interfered. I became depressed and began visualizing us separated and divorced. That fantasy became a reality. I let both of my children go completely. That was very frightening then and still is today.

After my first wife and I became alienated from each other, I became aware of a warm feeling inside myself that I'll call love. I thought maybe I could be capable of love, but I didn't deal with it beyond being aware of it. Then I jumped out of my first marriage into my second one. I was single for only thirty days when I married my second wife. Our communication level was great before marriage but slipped right after we married. My drinking interfered, and she chose not to talk about some things anymore.

I let my wife pay all the bills and take care of all the household needs, because I had no interest in the house or in my family. I was interested in one thing: drinking! I had a cocky, arrogant attitude at home. Everything had to be my way or no way at all. If I didn't like what my wife cooked for dinner, I didn't go to the table to eat. I didn't always win with my family; but at least when I lost, I knew where I stood. I knew the actions I could take about losing, because I was used to losing.

I didn't understand my wife. I was confused and I didn't know the reasons why I had married a woman with many physical illnesses. I resented her being sick because I hadn't asked to have those problems, and they were very hard to cope with. I was angry with my wife all of the time, mostly because she was physically sick a lot of the time. One of the times was from a hysterectomy that caused her trouble afterwards. Our physical action certainly wasn't great. In sex, she made me feel like her partner didn't count. She seemed just to want to get herself taken care of. It took me longer to climax because of my heavy drinking, I think. My mind wanted to perform, but my body wouldn't. She didn't know how much I was drinking because I always denied it. It was at this point in my life that I began to get so close to my stepdaughter.

I never felt I was a natural, functioning part of my family. I was the strong arm, the heavy, in the relationship with my wife. I was the disciplinarian. My kids were used to my wife saying, "Wait 'til your dad gets home." Sometimes I'd come unglued when I punished the kids: I'd lose control and I didn't know when to quit punishing. I wouldn't let things drop even after I had punished them. Whatever they had done wrong, I might bring it up over and over again for three weeks. I was mentally abusive about the way I did it, too, because I'd ride the hell out of one of my stepsons.

I acted differently to my stepdaughter. I let her get away with a lot of shit. The interaction between us was very different. She knew how to twist me around to get what she needed, and I let her do that. I started to get close to my stepdaughter when I started helping her with her homework, and that's when I started molesting her. She started touching me first, and I really liked that. I started touching her back. It happened over a period of most of a year. I drove her to school and back every day, and that brought us even closer together. I was the one who took her clothes shopping for her gym clothes and uniforms that she needed for the private school

she attended. My wife decided that it was more practical for me to be the one to shop with her since it was on my way home from work and since I was the one who picked her up from school.

I had set up in my own mind a plan, a fantasy, of making my wife reject and divorce me. That is what I wanted. I envisioned living alone in a trailer safe and sound, surrounded by my possessions and being only with myself. Then all of a sudden there was this young person loving me without question (my stepdaughter). She'd put her arms around me and depend on me to do things, which my wife did not do. She'd stand beside me while I watched football games just to be near me. She'd pressure me in a nice way to do things I couldn't do on my own—like put on a swimsuit, which I was very self-conscious about. She'd make me feel it was okay to do. She had a special way of bringing me out of myself and she did it in a way no one else could. She got me to take her and other kids places —like a fair or somewhere—where there were those crowds I hated. She'd hold my hand and help me through those situations. I was still uncomfortable but at least I could bear it with her at my side.

We became very close. Then the touching became closer. One evening I was showing her how to operate a calculator, and she started to rub my neck and shoulders. I returned her touches. This touching was the wrong message for me to give her.

The sexual abuse got progressively worse from that evening. I never had conscious intentions of having intercourse with her. I just wanted some self-gratification, I think. I don't really know. The amount I was drinking made me unable to get an erection or ejaculate, anyway. I had desire, but my body wouldn't respond physically. Because of that, I don't see how I could have done some of the things I was accused of doing. I remember touching her back and buttocks frequently and probably her private parts. (I say "probably" because my drinking made my memory hazy. I've accepted the responsibility of it, though. If it happened, then it did. All I can do about it is never do it again.)

My stepdaughter told my wife I was patting her on the butt. Moments before she told her mother, I was patting her on the butt and rubbing her back with her in my lap. She told her mother afterwards she didn't like that and didn't want that much closeness. At the time, I thought her idea of closeness and mine were the same because she'd often start rubbing my neck or back before I touched her.

I denied it and refused to admit I had been drinking. Immediately afterwards, I had a six-day drinking binge. During that time, I had a motorcycle accident but didn't get hurt badly. My wife has since told me that during those six days, I was extremely violent and ran all of my family out of our house. My wife told our relatives that I had molested my stepdaughter. Soon there were several people coming down on me for what I had done. I knew how to have enemies one at a time; but I couldn't handle this whole group.

My family left me. Then my wife called to tell me a police sergeant wanted to talk to me in a few days. I kept drinking until I got sicker and sicker and wasn't even high. On the third day, I contacted AA (Alcoholics Anonymous). I had listened to an employee of mine talk about it. My police interview was to be in two days, and I knew I needed help pulling myself together for it. AA sent a member over to my house. He didn't try to stop me from drinking. He said, "You said you wanted to kill yourself drinking. While you're doing that, I'd like to sit here and tell you part of my life." I could really relate to him. Pretty soon he was making coffee with honey and orange juice with honey, and I was drinking it.

Guilt feelings started to surface. I confided to him that, in a rage, I had run off my family. I didn't tell him I had molested my stepdaughter, because I didn't think he or anyone else in AA would understand that. The AA people stayed with me for the next two days until my appointment with the sergeant. My wife and daughter had already seen the sergeant by that time. The sergeant cut some tapes about my case and had written a report. What he wrote was not the truth. He later admitted that the facts were a combination of my case and someone else's case.

I spent seven days in jail. I began feeling that I didn't want my family to reject me and that I wanted us all to be back together. I didn't know it at the time, but my wish would never come true. Two guys who were in jail with me for the same charge told me about all the frightening possibilities I was facing. I tried to deal with all the different people involved by myself: the public defender, the OR (own recognizance) program people, etc. A lady from the OR program was the one who told me about Parents United and its list of attorneys that I should consult. Since the public defender wanted me to plead guilty and told me to expect five to fifty years, I decided to try a private attorney.

At that point I had been sober several days. I thought I should be able to go on and live my own life and have this problem dealt with and over with. But I had no goals and no place to go. I didn't know whether I would work or go on welfare. I was very confused, and I'd start crying inwardly over little things. I didn't want to be in jail, yet I wanted to be away from people. I was caught up in feeling guilty.

I contacted an attorney through Parents United, and a beautiful relationship developed with him. When he talked to me, I still had the shakes from days before and felt very uncertain of myself. I was going to be released on OR, but first I had to be arraigned. My attorney advised me to plead guilty, which switched my case from municipal to superior court. I was allowed to live in a Halfway House for alcoholics when I had been sober for nine days.

I went to several AA meetings that week. And I met Hank Giarretto and Ellie Breslin, who was to be my individual counselor at Parents United.

I did not know what to expect from the court system, and I was afraid. I had a woman judge in superior court, a woman counselor in Parents United, and a woman group leader. Women seemed to be in charge of my life at that point, and that was frightening. I also felt terror about not knowing what tomorrow would bring. The lawyer I had found through Parents United prepared me for what might happen in Superior Court. He spent time with me and put me at ease. Almost everything he prepared me for *did* happen. Now Parents United has a chart to offer members telling them about the court system and the possible sequence of events and explaining legal terminology like "arraignment" to those who have never been through the system. I'm one of the sources of that paper.

My case was postponed many times and dragged out for nine and one-half months. My attorney assured me that meant that the people in the court system were taking a thorough look at my case. The court system was not very humane. I felt I was locked up like an insane person. I do not think I should have been slapped into a brown uniform and forbidden to communicate with other prisoners. The system really did stink.

I was forced to have a Mentally Disordered Sex Offender hearing, which scared the hell out of me. Someone else was going to make a value judgment about me, and they might see nothing else about me except that I was an alcoholic and child molestor. The first doctor gave me a clean record. The other doctor decided I needed to see my mother. They gave me a clean report and stated that I was not mentally disordered. It was a frightening experience.

My sentencing was postponed four times, and each time was very frightening because it left me hanging, not knowing what was going to happen. Some Parents United members were in court with me. My shaking nerves may not have shown outside, but inside I was torn up. I didn't even hear my sentence when I finally got it; I just heard the woman judge say, "I am now sentencing Jim to five years." She paused before she said, " . . . proba-tion," so I missed that word. I thought I was going to jail. I was also sentenced to do 500 hours of community service. The probation department allowed me to give all my community service time to Parents United work. That was really nice. Even as simple a thing as setting up chairs for the weekly meetings was a reward for me and let me contribute to the group and feel I belonged to that group.

I don't think being in jail would have helped me to grow at all. It would have made me clam up and not learn anything about myself or my problem. It probably would have taught me more about being a criminal. The adult probation department put my sentence up for modification now.

The week I came to Parents United and met Hank and Ellie (my individual counselor), emotions were cropping up from everywhere and driving me crazy. When I met Dorothy Ross at CSATP, I resented her because she was an authority figure and I was the slave. I felt I no longer had control over my body or mind, that these people could decree what I had to do.

I began individual counseling with Ellie, disliking her at first because she was trying to pry information out of me and get into my head and into my garbage can of stuffed feelings, I thought. I didn't think she could get in, though, because my garbage can was the long-lasting chrome kind, not just the galvanized kind that's easier to break through. She was making me deal with what I didn't want to deal with. By looking at the situation, though, I did start to deal with it. My wife and I went to the Parents United group session the second week I was out of jail. For a month I didn't say anything in those sessions in the Orientation group. I didn't know what I was supposed to say. I didn't understand what purpose it served for all of these members to stir up the thoughts that made them feel bad. So my concept was that people in this group make everyone feel bad.

After finishing Orientation, we went through the Couple's Communication Group. Two fantastic people led that group and let me be silent for a couple of weeks. Then they made me interact by throwing questions and statements to me. I was scared and told them so. One of them asked me if I could tell why I was so scared. I said, "Because no one else has ever felt the pain and guilt I'm feeling, and no one else could share it with me." I discovered that the other guys in the group felt exactly as I did. I talked to those guys and worked with them in the sessions. Things started opening up. Then my wife and I started to communicate. She told me she had filed for divorce. I didn't want to lose her and tried to hang on to her. I was afraid of being alone. Ellie recommended a book on loneliness. I was more aware of my loneliness than I had ever been in my life.

I underwent a big change after being a member for a while: For the first time, I wanted to take care of myself physically. I watched what I ate and drank. I took vitamins. I got enough sleep, brushed my teeth, kept my hair combed. I thought, "Hey, I ain't such a bad guy, but I'm going to be in a real bad place if I don't take care of myself." After taking care of what was physically wrong, I could deal with my emotional problems better. Ellie showed me a couple of meditation exercises in our counseling sessions that really put me in touch with my life. I'd sit quietly and count breaths. It taught me to let problems and feelings be there. It made me alert to the fact that I was hurting and crying.

After being in Parents United two months, I cried for the first time. I sat under a tree one day, and my whole life fell in on me. I felt very sad about who I was and what I had done. I still drive by that tree sometimes and remind myself that that is where my life turned around. I felt relieved after crying and after talking to Hank and Ellie about my stepdaughter. I told them I couldn't remember doing all the things she said I had done, but I knew she had no reason to lie.

After that, I grew very rapidly in the program and kept seeing Ellie every week for counseling. I participated more in the groups and learned a lot about myself: What make me tick, what I like and don't like, how I feel, whether I'm afraid. I got in contact with all the feelings I had suppressed for years. I learned that I could feel good if I wanted to feel good. I learned even from the things that went wrong. After I had been in Parents United for six months, I set goals for myself, and I have met all of them. My newest goal is to co-lead an Alcoholic Group for Parents United.

I have gotten more support from Parents United than from any other people in my life. I remember once one of the women members sat on one side of me and held my hand while my wife held my other hand. It helped me realize the kinds of love that aren't sexual at all but are just a way of caring about one another. But before that when any of the women members put their arms around me to give me a friendly hug, I would stiffen and pull away from them. What they did scared me and I'd think, "What do they want of me?" I hadn't realized yet that they just wanted to be my friend.

I learned to realize something else, too. Through Parents United, I learned to talk about incest outside of PU—like through the Speakers Bureau when I went on speaking engagements. I was surprised to realize that there were people out in the community who would relate to me personally and didn't think I was the most disgusting person in the world. I learned that they could talk about the problem. So all of a sudden I had a new worth I hadn't known I had.

I kept educating myself in many ways. Every time Ellie said a word I didn't understand, I looked it up in the dictionary. I read books that covered the topics she talked about. Now I have three shelves of paperback books about self-esteem, humanistic psychology, etc. Being in Parents United made me look at myself, see how I had put it together, see how much garbage I was carrying. It's sad that I had to fall so near the bottom before I could get turned around, but now I'm on an uphill climb. I sometimes slip downhill, of course, but my worst day now doesn't compare with how bad my past days were.

This program saved my life. When I was first released from jail and lived in the Halfway House, I thought, "Why don't they just castrate me? They should just throw me in a box, close the lid, and throw dirt on it." They didn't. And what I learned is that human beings don't always destroy other human beings. That was really a revelation. That let me start thinking, "Maybe there is something worthwhile in me." I found the worthwhile parts, and now I can love life, and through that I can love other people.

I can't relive the past, but now that I know I have choices, I can choose not to live the same way I did. Now that I'm more aware of how and why I let my daughter twist me around to get what she wanted, I probably would never let myself slide into that situation again with anyone—the situation of letting someone control my behavior because they have some kind of hold on me. It's great to know I can be responsible for not getting back into the space where I would molest my stepdaughter.

I haven't lived in my make-believe world for a long time. Now I want to remember about the molest. I want to find out where things first went wrong. That knowledge may push me back down and make me take several steps backward in progress. Eventually, I'll look at more of what actually happened. When I do take that look, I'll have the wisdom that Alcoholics Anonymous taught me with it slogan: I know what I can change and what I can't. And I can accept things that I can't change.

Now I know how to let people into my life. I still have difficulty having a concept of God. But some higher power within me allows me to watch myself develop now and to watch what I do turn into accomplishments. Until after I molested my daughter, the only feelings I dealt with were anger and superiority over others.

My biggest concern now is love—whether I have enough of it and whether I'm giving enough of it. My main goal is to love everyone even if I can't like them. In my opinion, love means you keep trying to understand the other person and really listen to their words. I'm entering a new relationship with a woman, and I'm scared about it. I've never felt a natural or functional part of any family. I want to be able to do that now. I'm looking forward to marrying the beautiful woman so that we can share our lives. I want her to walk beside me—not under me. I do not want us to clip each other's wings. I want her to look ahead, behind, and to the side with me. She and I can enjoy the journey together.

3. Parents United Newsletter

Official Newsletter of the Santa Clara County Chapter of Parents and Daughters and Sons United

August 1, 1981
PARENTS UNITED, INC.
Post Office Box 952
San Jose, California 95108
(408) 280-5055
a non-profit organization

PRESIDENT'S MESSAGE

As a newly-elected officer of Parents United, the vote of confidence I received from the membership feels wonderful; I'm awed as well as challenged, intimidated as well as honored. For weeks I've known I have a publication deadline to meet for my first "President's Message" (which coincidentally is also our conference issue) and I've been putting off writing ('just one more day') for weeks—mostly because of expectations from myself that this article has to be the best, longest, most inspired, most inspiring, etc.

I've been getting a lot of input from chapter members and staff as to what's the best way to do this job of being "fearless leader,"—and that's contributing to my feelings of being stuck. Not only do I have my own expectations to manage, but those of all these *important* people! Many of you felt I could and would do the best job—it appears now that how I go about doing that job may not be what each of you had in mind. Therein is the catch; I can, at best, please myself only a part of the time and do the "right" thing only a part of the time. Never in a million years could I please all of you, even part of the time.

Each person who has assumed this job and the responsibilities which go with it has had to find his or her own style or method of accomplishing all there is to do. I expect to work into my own style, too, and I realize I work differently than those who have held this office before me. It's taking courage I didn't know I had to say out loud, "I want to do it *my* way."

Recently I shared my feelings and concerns regarding the above with my friend, Anita—a wise woman who also happens to be a past-president of our chapter. She told me that she had not been sure she could do this job either. Knowing that she was very successful (while doubting her abilities) was reassuring—I'm not the only person who has felt somewhat overwhelmed by the responsibilities. Anita spoke of Parents United as being a place where we learn, and I liked that idea. I know that as I've faced challenges before, I've learned and grown, and I expect to keep doing so.

To all of our conference attendees, welcome, and my personal thanks for attending "Ten Years of Treatment of Child Sexual Abuse—Looking Back/Looking Ahead." I am gratified that so many of you have decided to join us this year in our process of sharing, learning, and growing.

Sue

PU/DSU-AN EXTENDED FAMILY

An Interview with Hank and Anna Giarretto

SANDI: I've been with Parents United for three years and this period has been one of the most important in my life. Both of you have been parenting the program for over ten years and I can only imagine what these ten years have meant to you. We can't cover much ground in a short interview but I'd like to discuss the key events or milestones which stand out in your minds.

HANK: I can't think of any *one* single key event or breakthrough . . . there are many. What immediately comes to mind is a typical current experience, one which gives me the greatest satisfaction—one which tells me that maybe we're accomplishing our major objective. The experience that I value the most happens when I'm visited by one of our DSU graduates, a young person whom we treated for several years and haven't seen for a while. After the traditional PU/DSU embrace, we sit down and I try to be very casual as I listen and question her, looking her over very carefully to see if she is *really* doing as well as she says she is or appears to be. I see and hear a bright, articulate young woman who

" . . . this awful pain and dispair is always there at the beginning . . ."

seems to be coping with life very well. I'm filled with great pride and pleasure, the kind I would feel for my own child when she says she wants to come back not only to visit old friends but to try to help the new kids and their families.

I invite her to the orientation group and as I watch her interact with the group members I get a still better understanding of her ability to cope in a social setting. Although I can tell that remnants of the old hurts are still active, they no longer dominate her but in fact may be sharpening her sensitivity to the feelings of the other members. She knows how to listen, how to empathize and to reveal her own feelings. To me she is the star of the group drama for that evening. And she rises to her role when she, at eighteen, is able to comfort the woman across the way who is twice her age—a woman who was molested as a child and who is just beginning to deal with the terrible pain that she has carried all those years. *(continued on page 2)*

HAPPINESS IS . . . A LETTER FROM TUCSON . . .

Happiness is . . . something different, surely, for everyone . . .

Happiness for me, today, specifically . . . is pride. Contented, fulfilled, rewarding pride that I am a contributor to an occasion that is a landmark in our lives . . . with the positive conviction that we, individually and collectively—United—are capable of changing the lives of most of the people we come into contact with . . . for the rest of our lives.

On behalf of the Santa Clara Chapter of Parents United, I wish to welcome all of you—sister chapter members, law enforcement officials, social services representatives, state and county department heads, non-profit organization representatives . . . former trainees, future trainees—all of you—to this special conference. This will be a place for us to spend time, in retrospect, evaluating the past ten years—and time for us, in a super-group, to work on our future.

It is important for each of you to know that this time and place is for you—it is important that you recognize that it is your voice that needs to be heard, in the smaller workshops and in our large, conference group. It is important that you make your individual, unique, mark on this program that was created so that each of us could learn that our individual happiness is truly in our own hands, and that we can control our own lives.

As the exceptionally proud editor of this publication, I would like to express my sincere gratitude to the members and staff of the Santa

Clara Chapter and to those chapter members from Tucson, Portland, Humboldt, Shasta, Olathe, San Antonio . . . for their response to my call for contributions to enhance this special issue to reflect the feelings and growth of our members, far and wide.

We have also obtained permission to print additional responses to the Reader's Digest article, which was published in January of this year—and is reprinted herein . . .

In particular, I am pleased that we can keynote our very own, beloved DSU Program Coordinator, Cindy—and attempt to give her a token of our appreciation for her dedication and her years of exceptional service . . . my thanks to her co-workers and to our DSU members for their participation in this effort.

I need to call your attention to the statement of a DSU member from Tucson . . . who wrote to me and said, "I saved my family." In many ways, this represents the entire focus of the Parents United program—and, in particular, this Conference—the restoration of the faith of a child in her family.

On behalf of every mother and father in this program, everywhere—I dedicate this issue to that little girl in Tucson, and all of her fellow members . . . across the country. As Dorothy Ross wrote of Cindy . . . "She made us remember why we are here . . ." That little girl reminded me, again, why I am here.

I love you all. Welcome.

Sandi

PU/DSU — AN EXTENDED FAMILY
(continued from front page)

The contrast between our DSU graduate and our new PU member is vivid. To know that somehow we have at least reduced and cut short the effect of the molestation in this one child, that she doesn't have to be burdened by the trauma all her life, and that—in addition—she is now able to help our new members all add up to the experience I value most. This is what our program is all about. This is the only true measure of its success.

ANNA: Amen. I see the good changes happening in the DSU groups. When a new member starts to talk I agonize with her. I guess I'll never be able to stop those feelings no matter how firmly I say to myself, "this awful pain and despair is always there at the beginning, she'll feel much better in a few weeks." My sympathy pains are reduced a little when the older members start to chime in with caring and reassuring words of support. And then in a few weeks you can start to see the changes taking place. You can see them in her face and body set and you hear them as she speaks.

Of course, this doesn't happen in every case. A few girls seem to be paralyzed by he pain. These are the girls who feel their mothers and families have deserted them. Even after all these years I want to do something desperate to such a mother. To shake her up violently. To tell her she is not only betraying her child but herself and family. My

"The way our kids and adults worked together moved me to tears . . ."

brain tells me that probably she, too, was abused and deserted as a child. That she, too, has a hurt child within her. But until I meet her and see for myself that my hunches were correct, I know she needs a lot of help and bolstering herself. I must confess that my initial feelings are not loving but hateful. I think we are wise in having both DSU and Parents United and that we work hard towards getting the mother and her child together first. It's amazing how the father and the rest of the family falls into place once we can establish a caring relationship between the mother and her child.

But I do want to say that I remember a milestone in the history of PU and especially DSU that I'll never forget. I'm always filled with great joy when I remember how Terry, Joanna and Cletus handled themselves at the national conference. Not only during their presentation but in the ways they made contact with the other DSU kids that attended. Of course, their presentation was a highlight. They did themselves proud. Cindy, Leona, Anita, Art and John Dean, the counselor from Boulder, Colorado program, were wonderful also. The way our kids and the adults worked together moved me to tears. I looked at Hank and he, too, was teary.

We were all so proud when DSU received an invitation from the conference officials. The first invitation given to a children's group. We were all a little nervous, I know I was, both during the trip to Milwaukee and while we were waiting for the time assigned to our workshop. When the time of reckoning arrived the room was filled to overflowing. And the kids—our *young people* ("Sorry, Terry") rose to the occasion. Later, many of the conferees told us that the DSU workshop was more rewarding to them than any of the other events at the conference.

SANDI: Okay, I think you've made it crystal clear that you're proud of DSU. What about Parents United? We need a few strokes too.

HANK: Well, Sandi, I don't have to tell you that DSU goes as does PU. Of course, I get enormous satisfaction over the growth of Parents United. Not only the local group that has grown both in size and quality. None of us guessed during the early stages at the San Jose group that in a few years there would be over sixty groups all over the country meeting the way we were. But I've got to go back to the bottom line. To me the essential significance of the new chapter is reduced to one fact.

(continued on page 8)

SANTA CLARA OFFICERS

President
SUE — 280-5055

First Vice President	Second Vice President
DONNA	GLENN
Executive Secretary	**Assistant Secretary**
DEBBIE	CATHY
Treasurer	**Assistant Treasurer**
VIRGINIA	FLORA

A VICE PRESIDENT GROWS

I am Donna from the Santa Clara County Chapter. I came to PU September 1979 seeking help for myself because I was molested by my father. I was asked to write an article for the Parents United newsletter, and I will tell you some of the reasons I came to Parents United and what this organization has done for me.

While I was growing up I had bad feelings about myself. I lacked self-confidence and felt I did not measure up to my mother's expectations . . . but, I did not realize that she was resentful and jealous of me because she knew my father was molesting me. As a consequence of the molest, there was a wall between my mother and myself. I found it easier to talk to my father because he accepted me better.

It never occured to me that one of the reasons my father molested me is that my parents were not able to communicate with each other. My mother has always been critical of my father. I feel she wears the pants in my family and my father goes along with it. About 15 years ago I moved from back East to California because my dad worked nights and my mother was stuck raising three kids by herself. She felt trapped and she blames all three kids for staying home for eighteen years. When I was four years old, she almost had a nervous breakdown. She had few friends and few interests to occupy some of her life.

I hardly knew my father until I moved to California. He is an intelligent man who never got the opportunity to realize his full potential. He has worked as a service station manager for 30 years, but I feel he could have been an engineer or a professor. My mother keeps throwing this up to him, and this causes friction between them. My father is also a loner because he feels people will use him. It is interesting that he has been used and he was not able to say no to someone. He does not speak up for his rights and everyone walks on him. When things went bad between my mother and him, he would tell me his problems instead of confronting her.

I was surprised when I came that first night because I did not realize that there were other people in similar circumstances as myself. I was very scared to attend Parents United because it was the unknown. I was reached out to by some dear people when I needed it most. There were fathers of such a vast age group and occupational status who crossed different socio-economic groups and nationalities. In the same room there were mothers whose children were molested and mothers who had never dealt with being molested yet trying to help their children at the same time.

I found out that not all mothers knew that their children were being molested as in my case. My mother tried to look the other way even after I had told her. She made the choice to ignore it rather than losing the security of my father. My mother comes across as a very strong

"It's better for me to deal with some heavy shit, than run—like I used to."

person but under all that facade she is very insecure. It was reassuring to me to see that other mothers did, in fact, care about the welfare of their children. Many left their husbands in order to protect their children. Some mothers stayed with their husbands to work on why the molest occured and to change that behavior through therapy. I have seen families even closer because they all had to deal with each other.

Parents United was one of the best things that has ever happened to me. I learned the skills of caring for other people—an ability we are not born with, and if their are no role models for us, that skill is not learned. I have also gained the skill to care for myself. I gained self confidence as I became involved with the organization a little at a time. I started to grow as the agenda secretary and was able to give of myself and was respected for my achievements. I was not given recognition as a child even though I graduated part of the California Scholarship Federation—to my parents this was not important, but I have received recognition from this chapter by being voted First Vice-President. I am confident I shall handle this position well. My parents never gave me responsibility and I feel I was taken advantage of by my father. I was not as strong a person as I am now.

In this chapter there are many people who think highly of me. I have learned the skills of open communication and can realize that the whole world may not accept how I feel but that's OK. Parents United is a big family that I never had before, caring about each other. When one of us is down, we reach out, rather than keeping the feelings bundled up inside. Otherwise, we could explode and hurt the ones we love most. It is better for me to deal with some heavy shit than to run from it like I used to do.

Sure, it isn't easy to take a risk, but I am glad I did when I joined this chapter. My life is much more fulfilling to me, I feel good about myself and I can reach out and help people—whether they are PU members or

(continued on page 7)

READER'S DIGEST REPRINT

INCEST: FACING THE ULTIMATE TABOO

The problem has long been with us, and long ignored as an abhorrent but mercifully rare phenomenon. Abhorrent, yes. Rare, no. Under a veil of shame and secrecy, incest has been one of our most under-reported crimes; it may infect over half a million American families. Now the veil is lifting, and help is finally on the way for both victim and offender.

It started innocently enough. Jim's 10-year-old daughter, Debbie,* had long been "Daddy's little girl." She'd snuggle up to him in the evening and they'd watch television while her mother was out. As things began to sour in Jim's job and marital relations, Debbie remained the one sweet spot in his life. She was warm, loving and trusting.

When Debbie was 12, her body began to mature, and Jim teased her about it. Soon teasing turned to touching, then fondling, and eventually, as Debbie entered her teens, to intercourse. Jim was paralyzed with guilt, but powerless to stop. The situation changed when Debbie's school counselor, noting her falling grades, talked with her. The conversation turned to boys, and Debbie, then 15, admitted she had a problem. She did not mean to reveal what was going on at home, but

---

"Has anyone touched you? You can tell me and it'll stop." The girl was silent; then she said: "Daddy did."

---

when asked if she minded when boys touched her, she blurted, "I don't even like my father to do it!" That opened the floodgates. Soon the counselor had the whole story and, several hours later, so did the police.

Debbie was taken to the Children's Shelter, and the police called her mother, explaining what had happened and suggesting that Jim come in the next morning. Confronted by his wife when he arrived home, Jim admitted everything. That evening, he drove off with a loaded pistol, planning to commit suicide. But he couldn't do it, and the next morning he walked into the police station. After Jim's confession was taped, he felt as if a tremendous weight had been lifted. At that point, he didn't know—or care—what penalty society had in store for him.

Incest has been a taboo in all ages and cultures. But so much shame attaches to this abhorrent crime that society has drawn a veil of secrecy around it. This conspiracy of silence has served both to protect the offender and to conceal the victim.

As recently as 15 years ago, experts claimed that incest—broadly defined as sexually arousing physical contact between family members who are not married—occurred in only one out of a million families. Now some professionals believe the actual incidence could be as high as one in a hundred. Although only 6000 cases were reported nationwide in 1978, the lowest estimated total, according to the National Center on Child Abuse and Neglect, and the figure is rising each year as it is finally beginning to be discovered, reported and dealt with.

In most states, incest is still a crime, with penalties that range from 90 days to life imprisonment. But a man who commits incest (90 percent of all reported cases involve father, or father figure, and daughter) is rarely convicted, since there is usually little physical evidence of abuse, no eye witnesses, and the credibility of children is often questioned in court. In those rare instances when the man *is* convicted, the burden of his punishment falls on both offender and victim. With the household head in prison, often other family members must go on relief. The daughter, frequently blamed by the mother for causing the trouble, may be put in a foster home. Separated from her siblings, guilt-ridden, she can become bitter and self-destructive.

Cathy is typical of the 1600 women who have received therapy at Christopher Street, a rehabilitation center in Minneapolis with an incest and family-abuse program. A minister's daughter, Cathy was first molested by her mother when she was seven, and a few years later by her father. "I'd always been taught to trust my parents," she says, "and I didn't know how to make it stop." Finally, on her 15th birthday, Cathy tried to commit suicide, and ended up in the hospital. The incest ceased, but not the emotional trauma. Laden with guilt, she overate, burned herself with cigarettes, tried drugs, became promiscuous.

At 18, she sought escape in marriage, but couldn't cope with the intimacy involved. After her marriage failed, she drifted through jobs and attempted suicide several more times. Today, after a year in therapy, she is just beginning to climb out of her abyss. "I think the best thing was to learn that there are others like me," she says. "I've faced up to my problem and I've talked it over with my family—something I thought I

(continued on page 4)

DEAR PARENTS UNITED

I'm getting desperate! My husband and I need your help. The judge refuses to make an appointment to see me and our pastor to talk about my husband's case. We are trying to persuade him that my husband is not a menace to society and his family needs him home.

We have gotten a dozen or so friends to write to the judge but we need more people to write. He gave him 12 years, and wants him to serve every day of it! He stated he would oppose probation when my husband was eligible. He needs to know that there is another way than putting these men behind bars for years and splitting up families. Please also mention the chapters of Parents United in this state. It could be that he would allow my husband to be on probation near one of those cities while he works and goes to counseling.

Of course, the way that that would help us would be only financial, unless we moved to the area and were able to go for the counseling also. That would be a little more difficult because of my going to college. The best solution would be to start a chapter and get counseling here.

All that I am asking is that some of the judges and counselors who are involved in Parents United write to the Judge. There is counseling available for my husband at the V.A. Hospital but he has to be free to go to them. With a ten year probation, he could be working, supporting his family and also getting counseling. He wants the counseling and so do I. We will go for the counseling as a family if they will let us.

My husband will not live another year in there. He is losing weight and is now down to 130 pounds. He is only 5'4" which is to his disadvantage because without the Lord's protection the other inmates could try to abuse him. So far this has not happened. The reason that he is losing weight is we are vegetarians who do not eat anything seasoned with pork. Most of the vegetables there are seasoned with pork. We are Seventh Day Adventists who believe in the dietary laws set up in Deuteronomy and Leviticus.

Please write to the Judge explaining to him about the effectiveness of counseling and the need for the families to be reunited—not split up. I don't know if you can do this but please try. Our time is running out. The judge can recall my husband up to his 120th day incarcerated but after that it would involve a lot of red tape and expense. I am presently out of work and limited on funds. If anyone can write to the judge, please send me a copy so I can keep a record of all letters sent to him.

We would greatly appreciate any help that can be given. In helping us it could help to influence the outcome of other troubled families. Thank you.   **From Texas**

I CAN'T STAND HER

I read your article in the January Issue of Reader's Digest—on abused children and sexually molested children. I was stunned about how the father was molesting his daughter, but yet she forgave him.

How could she forgive him? I just can't understand how she forgave him. I was touched by your article, mainly because I was a child who grew up abused and raped by my mother when I was thirteen years old and sixteen years old. I have never forgiven her for it. In fact, I wish she were dead. I've found it hard to deal with most of my life.

Now at the age of thirty I still can't let go of my past. I've grown up NOT respecting women and hating them. I am now in my second marriage and still find it hard to adjust in a relationship with my wife. I've grown up being treated like a dog, therefore, I treat women the same way. I'm in therapy now, but I still can't relate in a women's world. I grew up dominated by women and the funny thing of this whole issue is that I love women, but I can't understand how I can be expected to forgive my mother if I can't stand her.

She has in a large way ruined my life—how could I forgive her? I'm interested in your responses.   **A Confused Man**

I'M TOO ASHAMED

I read the article on incest in the January issue of Reader's Digest and for the first time in my entire life I am realizing that this is more common a problem than I thought all my life. I am 18 years old, have been through two alcohol detoxes and am full of guilt over what has happened. My mom died in 197_ and my dad has taken things out on me. When I sixteen he raped me and several times afterwards. It has become a series of beatings and sex. I finally got away from him and live alone but I'm not handling the guilt about this. There's no one to tell about this because my dad is a pretty well-known doctor and they'd act like I was burnt out and I would just be too ashamed anyway. If there's any information you can send, I'd sure appreciate it.   **from New Jersey**

READER'S DIGEST REPRINT ON INCEST
(continued from page 3)

could never do. They're facing up to it, too. I've even started a relationship with someone which is working for the first time. I like myself better."

One of the first communities to try a new approach to incest was Santa Clara County, California. In the last ten years, Santa Clara's program has provided help to more incest victims—2500—than any other single organization in the country. To understand how the program works, consider Jim and Debbie again.

After his confession, Jim was released on his own recognizance, pending a court appearance a month later. Meanwhile, he was ordered out of his house, so Debbie could live with her mother and the other children, and forbidden any contact with his family. He was able to continue his job so he could go on supporting them. He also joined Parents United, a group of offenders and their wives who meet regularly to discuss their problems. Debbie joined an affiliate group called Daughters and Sons United. Because of his willingness to cooperate and the fact that he had used no force with Debbie, Jim was put on probation for five years and assigned 600 hours of community service, in lieu of prison. He chose to work for Parents United, doing office chores and helping to organize discussion groups. Soon he was permitted to communicate with his family, and then visit them.

Ten months after his arrest, Jim moved back home. "When I drove up, I was filled with both fear and joy," he says, "I wondered what my daughter would do. Then, when I crossed the threshold, I saw her standing there—shyly, awkwardly. After some agonizing moments, she came over and put her arms around me. I cried. Today, we have a wonderfully healthy relationship."

While Jim spent no time in jail, 48 percent of Santa Clara offenders do—anywhere from a few days up to a year. But even those incarcerated are usually allowed to go to their jobs during the day and return to jail at night. Eventually, the majority of the families are reunited. Does the approach work: Apparently so. Re-molestations are reported in less than five percent of its incest cases, compared with an estimated national rate as high as 85 percent for untreated offenders. Also, because help and support are available, Santa Clara's confession ¬ate is extraordinarily high—90 percent. In areas that lack such programs, denials remain the paramount problem. And a confession, of course, is a crucial first step toward rehabilitation.

The effectiveness of the Santa Clara Approach was evident at a recent national meeting of Parents United, which now has 46 chapters in 15 states. Someone started off by asking a man who'd been attending for

"...Yes, I did molest my stepdaughter. I feel like the scum of the earth."

several months if he was ready to talk about his "problem." There was a heavy silence. Finally, in a strangled voice, the man spoke: "It's hard for me to get the words out, but ... yes ... I did molest my stepdaughter. Maybe you won't believe me, but I do love her. I didn't want to hurt her ... I just wanted to be close ... I feel like the scum of the earth." He sat back, emotionally drained. It had taken months to get that far. More silence; then, after a minute or so, a woman next to him leaned over and hugged him. "I know what you're going through," she said. "You'll be all right."

Because of its success, the Santa Clara program became the first national training center for the treatment of child sexual abuse. There are now 28 similar programs in California and 18 in other states. Altogether, there are 200 rehabilitation programs around the country, compared with only three in 1971. And more are on the way.

The new openness about incest is clearly having a beneficial effect. A young mother in Seattle, for example, turned on television's Phil Donahue Show" one recent morning. The subject was incest. Her husband became so outraged that the woman grew suspicious. Their three-year-old daughter had repeatedly complained about her genitals hurting. After her husband left, the woman asked the little girl: "Has anyone touched you? You can tell me and it'll stop." The girl was silent; then she said: "Daddy did."

The mother and daughter went immediately to Harborview Medical Center, where there is a sexual assault center. Help was found for both of them, and the husband was reported to the police. Dr. Shirley Anderson, Harborview's pediatrician, sees 300 such cases a year. "For too long," she says, "victims have felt betrayed, shamed and rejected. So they kept silent—and remained victims." She stresses that communities should get across this message: "Don't hide it! You are not alone and you *can* be helped."   **January, 1981**

I WANT MY FAMILY TOGETHER

Dear Parents United:

I am the 30 year old mother of a daughter who was a victim of incest. I came upon an article on Incest: Facing the Ultimate Taboo, in the January Reader's Digest. I am writing because for the first time I feel I can reach out to someone who can help our family.

Is there help for the victim and the offender, can a family reunite, I sure would like to be able to talk to someone who would help.

My husband was sentenced to an active prison sentence, and I can't believe it was the best thing to happen. I want to explain more of what happened but I would like to be able to talk in person. The case was not handled for the kids benefit. There are three children all in school and believe me when you aren't prepared for supporting a family it can be hard. I have felt all these things you talk about in that article.

I feel that I am not doing something right, I feel guilty because I still love my husband and want our family together. Our daughter loves her father and maybe if we hadn't hurt so much last year things could have been better, we'd have a place to live. Sometimes I feel this has taken all my pride, I've had to beg for myself and the kids, I know being in prison is no party for my husband, but he's all the kids and I have. If I had family of my own who cared it would be so much easier.

Please send me as much information as possible, and if I can get someone to counsel and talk to me, maybe I can understand the feelings I have, I can help my daughter know this nightmare can end, our family can be helped   **Thank you.**

I'M A PARENT NOW!

The initial trauma of learning that incest occurred is devastating! No one who has experienced this, knows it better. However, such a crisis instigates an unbelievable new and exciting turn-about in the emotional and psychological personal being of every member of the family unit. The growth and development of new relationships among each member of the family are so rewarding, even overwhelming!

I can only speak of my own experience as a parent and my family's growth with utmost pride. Fortunately, we had a firm foundation of love to work from and the desire to hold everything together from the beginning. I'd like to share with you some new skills I've learned and used.

I remember how I used to make demands and give orders to my children, expecting no static because "I was their mother." How many times I would get so frustrated, even angry! Now when they need guidance or protection, or direction, my positive attitude and encouragement creates a cooperative or accepted response. Such as, "When you clean your room, I feel good. You are showing me you care as much as I do about your room."

Mom is always busy. Right? Times have changed! I choose not to put off listening to the children when one of them expresses a need for my ears and/or support or encouragement. When this is really not convenient for me, I arrange a specific time as soon as possible. I also set aside time for individual attention for each one. The other day, my daughter and I went out for coffee so that we could be alone together and share feelings and experiences. She is now 16. Sharing like this, with each other, is new to us. We enjoy and care about one another so much more now. Really listening, I've learned so much about each one as well as learning more about myself. Children are so keen and can even be intelligent. When I listen I learn a lot.

Children are not always willing to use verbal communication and often use body language. This is one way my children have used to find out if I really do care or if I'm alert. I think they want recognition and wait for my response for assurance of my love or caring. I love it! My nine-year-old son uses this more often than my daughter.

My husband and I both share with the children together as often as possible. "Daddy" is still not living in the home yet ... and the children and I are anxiously awaiting permission to be given for him to return home. He is allowed frequent visits with us ... mostly for meals and some evenings.

One of the most important factors, I think, in parenting is awareness, both of self and of others in the family. Sharing and caring too, of course ... and keeping the lines of communication open. The willingness to learn and a desire to change and create a more comfortable and amiable family has enriched each and every one of us.

All this and more did not happen overnight. It has taken a year and a half for me to come this far and I'm still growing.

Jane, Tucson Chapter

ACTIVE PARENTS GROUPS

PRE-ORIENTATION GROUP
This group is organized especially for new Parents United members, the emphasis being the introduction to the program, its objectives and goals. The group meets *during* the regular Wednesday evening business meeting, for two or three weeks, until individual members feel comfortable about joining the orientation group.

ORIENTATION GROUP I AND II
These groups are a cross-section representation of our membership—old and new—a total sharing group, facilitating orientation into the program and further information about our development.

RE-CONTACT GROUP
A unique group, developed in recognition of the need for individdiuals to have a safe, supportive place to deal directly and effectively with the anxieties of communicating with parent, victim, or spouse.

SPANISH GROUP
This group is specifically oriented toward removing and relieving the pressures of any language barriers and concentrates on constructive help and understanding.

COUPLES GROUP I AND II
These groups focus on effective communication on both verbal and non-verbal levels. Developing skills to keep the channels open, dealing with the exploration of what went wrong and how to correct it.

WOMEN'S GROUP I AND II
In a caring and understanding atmosphere, wives and mothers have an opportunity to air their frustrations, attempting to understand and deal with their anger. One group is designed specifically for women new to the program, while the other group concentrates on dealing with the problems and exercising support techniques, with constructive feedback for older members.

MEN'S GROUP I AND II
Here, fathers learn to recognize and handle their problems, make social contacts, express personal objectives and concentrate on constructive personal growth.

WOMEN MOLESTED AS CHILDREN
In this mutually supportive group, women share whatever are issues in their lives—how these experiences have affected their lives, working to clearly express these feelings and deal effectively with them.

OPEN GROUP I AND II
These groups are open to everyone: singles, couples. women and men—sharing specific problems to gain insight via group feedback—a safe place for everyone, any subject or problem.

PARENTING GROUP
Open to all parents, singles and couples, custodial and non-custodial, this group focuses on improving parenting skills through teaching, role playing and feedback—sharing experiences and problems.

MOTHER-DAUGHTER GROUP
A group where daughters can hear from mothers and how they feel—about the molest, about anything—and vice versa. An opportunity to explore mother/daughter relationships.

SHARING AND CARING GROUP
A unique group for Parents United members only—films and related materials—extensive rap sessions provide members with insight into the physical and mental problems which plague those who drink.

SPONSORSHIP/SPEAKER'S BUREAU
An inter-related group where a portion of the session is spent on methods of developing sponsorship training—and the remainder concentrates on the skills for Speaker's Bureau.

HUMAN SEXUALITY CLASS
In association with De Anza College, a qualified human sexuality representative leads and guides intensive discussion on this subject. This class is made available to Parents United membership only.

MOTHERS AND DAUGHTERS

Most all of us—the daughters who have been in this program for some time—are now able to talk openly about our hostility, our hurt, our confusion and our pain. At first, most of us were not convinced of the need for counseling. A lot of us were afraid to risk losing close ties. Many of us were afraid of recidivism. In the beginning, we couldn't really be honest . . . it was important to continue to hold back feelings—and facts—to protect our Mother, and shield her from more pain. But, we grew . . . and our mothers grew. We were exposed to other women and other truths in this organization, and it has opened up ways for us to communicate and talk openly.

This is not a magic program. It takes work . . . meaningful, intense, hard work.

Starting in orientation, many of us have attended the human sexuality class with our mothers. Together, and individually, we have learned communication skills and parenting techniques that we are able to use in all parts of our lives. This program has helped us build a bridge across a generation gap and explore feelings together. We've been able to talk about jealousy, and hostility . . . all kinds of feelings, including sexual feelings.

One of the most important parts of Parents United, for most of us, has been our friendship and interaction with other daughters, especially those who are working with their mothers. We have so much in common—not just the molest—we have so many of the same things happening to us . . . with our moms. I have been able to talk with my friends about what our mothers are going through, what they're really like—and I believe we sometimes understand these older women more

"... it won't work for everyone, every time; but it has worked for me."

than they think. In Parents United, I can talk to other mothers and I can see my own mother in nearly every woman here. I think my mom sees me too, in the other girls.

Many of us did not know how much we hurt, how much pain we really felt, until it became OK to recognize it. Our mothers were feeling their own pain, and dealing with it at the same time, and we were able to be supportive of each other. We have learned that it is OK for us to switch roles, to comfort each other. It's OK for her to feel comfortable when I hold her. We have learned how to recognize many of the games we used to play with each other . . . they aren't necessary anymore. They don't fit anymore.

An important thing has occurred for many daughters—those of us who thought we had been sending loud "help" signals to our mothers—we've been able to recognize that the hints we thought were obvious were not so obvious after all. One of the strongest feelings many of us have is a need to know why this happened to us? Why did he do what he did? The parent relationship broke down—but that's *not* answer enough. We need to know the reasons, so we can look for the signs of the problems in our own relationships, in our own future.

All of the girls I know are not working with their mothers. Some daughters are here without their families. But, this program is full of mothers and their hearts are full of love. Parents United has a way of filling the needs of members that are alone. Some of the daughters did not feel comfortable in this program. Some felt the pressure to reconstruct the family was too strong and they wanted no part of it. It is not possible for this program to satisfy the needs of every single individual. This is not a magic program. It won't work for everyone, every time.

But it has worked for me. And it has worked for my mom. Right now, for me, in my life . . . my mother is one of my best friends.

As a representative of the young woman in this program . . . I, your daughter, hereby say to you, Roberta, my mom . . . and you Sandi, my mom . . . and you, Anita, my mom . . . Peggy, and Anna, . . . all my moms . . . Thank you for Parents United and the love and sharing and help through this part of my life. I love you.   **Julie**

This is excerpted from a speech Julie presented in December, 1980 at the Women's Ninth Night Program.

THOSE WE LOVE

They say the world is round—and yet I often think it square.
  So many little hurts we get from corners here and there.
But there's one truth in life I've found while journeying East and West,
  The only folks we really wound are those we love the best.
We flatter those we scarcely know, we please the fleeting guest,
  And deal full many a thoughtless blow to those we love the best.

From Julie's Mommy

WOMEN'S VENTURE WEEKEND

If you've never been to Venture—a whole exciting experience awaits you. Nestled in the Santa Cruz mountains, among the smells of Redwoods and the quiet sounds of nature sits the Venture Lodge. Driving that winding road during the daylight hours is a beautiful leisurely drive, but after dusk it can be nerve-wracking. When I arrived that evening at Venture, I was aware of being very tense. After all, I had just escaped the side of a mountain at least twice, saw a deer staring from the side of the road and was sure that I was lost when I turned off onto a dirt road. My neck hurt . . . my back hurt . . . I was tired . . . I was scared.

What was I doing here—a whole weekend committed to spending with a group of women, some of whom I had never met, some I knew on sight and only two who I felt acquainted with? What did I expect? What did I want from this *retreat*? I expected to meet some new people and to exchange feelings and ideas. I wanted to reach out, but I wanted someone to reach out to me and help me to feel cared about. I knew one thing, this was my weekend to escape, if you will, being "Mother," being all the things I think I am expected to be. Just for me, I wanted to be selfish and *be just me*.

I was very bound up, physically and emotionally. There are many things that I have wanted to experience, but for many reasons I never felt safe enough to reach out for those things. I mean, after all, I was raised with certain expectations of what was the right thing to do, the right thing to say, the right thing to wear—all those "right" things—my mother's "right" things. I was feeling like a child who had suddenly escaped from her mother's watchful eye and I felt free to experience. My daughter wasn't there, and my mother certainly wasn't there to watch me, so I could risk doing something I wanted to do or feel how I wanted to feel.

You may wonder, what was it that was a risk? A Hot Tub! Yes, a Hot Tub. One of my fantasies. I wanted to go down to that Hot Tub, but I was afraid. Someone knew why I was afraid and reminded me, "it is dark—nobody can see you—why don't you go . . . it will help your back and neck to relax." That, and someone saying "I'll go with you," was all it took!

Stepping into that hot tub was symbolic of that weekend. I stepped out of my isolation—into the warmth and sharing and caring of that weekend. I was with people who really cared and who accepted me as I am . . . I felt all the tenseness and aloneness draining away. That venture into that weekend has changed what I want for me life to be. I am me, and I can love and share that part of me that was hidden. I am really thankful for the "sisterhood" that I found, because of those special 10 women who were there at Venture Lodge, I was able to reach out and share and grow. Thank you "SSCGS."

Editors Note: This article was presented anonymously.

"WHICH CAME FIRST . . .

Once upon a time, a thousand tears ago, I found myself screaming into the 'phone, "Why! How could it happen . . . why?"

"I was drunk . . ." my stranger-husband told me.

"Oh, great!" I hoped my voice dripped with the disgust and the bitterness that made me want to vomit: "I should have known there was a good reason!"

We've never been able to really 'talk about it,'—he has not had the benefit of facing the judicial court system, or of attending this program—so I have nothing more that I can really say to him . . . but my pain and confusion is still sharp and clear and there are still a thousand unanswered questions. Many of them come to mind, bringing back the bitter taste of bile, when I hear another father say, "I was drunk . . . the next morning I realized what had happened . . ." Inside I scream at him—through him—"Which came first . . .

THE BOOZE OR THE INCEST?"

I know there are a lot of women who wonder . . . just what part did (and does) the demon drink play in the ugly game called incest. I had originally intended to dedicate this little space to the gentlemen who promised me they would respond to my questions before presstime—weeks ago . . . now, however, I would like to ask any and all members, everywhere, to respond: write me, please, let me compile your statements; tell me . . . which came first?

Sandi

ICEF TRAINING PROGRAM

A training grant to help establish treatment programs to deal with the increasing number of child sexual abuse cases reported across the nation was awarded to the Institute for the Community as Extended Family (ICEF) early in 1980 by the HEW National Center on Child Abuse and Neglect.

Training of eligible applications is based on the model developed by the Santa Clara County Child Sexual Abuse Treatment Program (CSATP) and Parents United, Inc. The principal trainers for this national project were also the trainers in the state demonstration project which resulted in the establishment of 25 similar programs in California, and those across the country.

Developed to enhance the coordination between agencies who become involved with the discovery, reporting, investigation, legal protection and treatment services of sexually abused children, the objective of the training is to foster the development of this program in communities to deal effective with parent-child incest as well as related forms of intra- and extra-familial child molestation.

Each training course is two weeks in duration and designed mainly for the personnel from child protective and mental health agencies who work directly with families. The course provides an overview of the CSATP model and stresses the learning-by-doing approach. Trainees will be actively involved in the on-going functions of a CSATP—participating in individual, marriage and family counseling session, in meetings of the Parents United and Daughters and Sons United self-help groups, as well as in the resolutions of problems in case management administration, interagency coordination, and the recruitment and supervision of volunteers.

Approximately 30 trainees are enrolled for each session. Ten of them will be "living" with us for two weeks. Then they'll go back to their home states and begin their own Child Sexual Abuse Training Program, Parents United and Daughters & Sons United groups. The remaining 20 trainees will only participate in the first three days of the session. The full two-week course is for counselors and case workers who will work directly with PU/DSU family members over an extended period. The three-day session is an orientation seminar for the two-week trainees as well as for their supervisors, law enforcement and crisis intervention workers.

The areas covered in the training are:
- Dynamics of incestuous behavior and its social ramifications
- Laws and reporting procedures
- Crisis intervention and referral procedures
- Roles of involved agencies and interagency coordination
- Services provided by the Child Sexual Abuse Treatment Program and the self-help program: Parents United/Daughters & Sons United.

During the final days of the course, the trainees are assisted in the preparation of a start-up procedure for a child sexual abuse treatment program in their own communities. Not all of the three-day attendees will be from out of state. Some are PU/DSU members. Local police, probation, sheriff, nursing and crisis line personnel will also be in the training, as well as counselors new to the program.

A total of nine training courses will be conducted through the year. Trainees can apply for university credits upon completion of classes. No tuition fee will be charged to trainees from governmental agencies or trainees approved by such agencies.

For information regarding the Child Sexual Abuse Treatment Training Project, please contact:

Training Coordinator
Institute for the Community as Extended Family, Inc.
P.O.Box 952
San Jose, California 95108

ICEF/PU/DSU CHILD SEXUAL ABUSE TREATMENT TRAINING DATES REMAINING FOR 1981

August 17 - August 28
October 5 - October 16
November 2 - November 13
November 30 - December 11

ONE-ON-ONE SPONSORSHIP

A couple of issues ago, I wrote an editorial called *It's A Small World, Isn't It?*, about running into Parents United members in the strangest places—where I work, on bus trips . . . and about people walking into this program from the outside world—people I have known from another time and place in my life.

It hasn't stopped for me. I feel that I have developed my own personal sponsorship program: my world seems to be full of *my kind of people.* I hope it's started for you—it is hasn't yet, it will. It's remarkable . . . and rewarding.

In my case, it isn't difficult for me to meet people who should know about Parents United, primarily because I have no problem in opening up the subject of who I am and where my feelings are. I am constantly not available for one thing or another because I'm on my way to a meeting, or proofing up an article, or working on a newsletter mechanical. When I'm asked what I'm up to, I open up . . . and because I have consolidated my personal presentation, I can deliver a three minute thumbnail of what this program is and what it means to me before I light another cigarette . . . or before the next traffic signal.

I have found (another mini-survey) that most men are initially offended, astounded and defensive, something that used to disturb me . . . something that amuses me often. I have also found that they usually stay offended and defensive. That has become *(finally!)* for me, *their* problem, and not mine.

The most rewarding, meaningful responses have come from women. Most listen carefully, asking questions, responding with a look in their eyes that tells me they really do identify with the problem of sexual advances from men in family situations. Then, there are some women who don't say much at first; they just look at me, there's a feeling, maybe a special chemistry—and I know that they *need* to know about this program.

That's how Honey reacted . . . she looked at me, really quiet, like she was thinking about something far away. I knew who she was right at that moment. And she knew that I knew: a silent, aware togetherness, across the table at the local watering hole. It gives me shivers to write this when I think about that exchange—and it makes me feel whole and worthwhile to see her an immediately active, loving and important part of our membership . . . perhaps the ugly chain of events that finally brought me and my daughter to this program was programmed by a higher-up . . so that I would meet Honey, and she would subsequently change the life of someone else.

Two years ago, my daughter casually announced that our roommate was coming to group with us, one Wednesday. Laura had been sharing with Nancy about her group . . . she had a strange feeling, she said, and encouraged Nancy to talk; we were a threesome for over a year at meetings. Later, there were times, in my home, when we would have mini-groups . . . Dee and Debbie, Laura and myself, my son Michael, Nancy and David (roommate #4½), who wrote for the PUN about his roommates, and later took some learning from our household to help a girl that he worked with. Michael, who had personal counseling from Peggie about being a son and a brother, called recently from Arkansas to ask his sister to talk to a girl he had met who ''. . . needs to know about you guys . . .''

It keeps spreading . . . this good word.

Three months ago, a 28 year old woman, molested by her grandfather, came to room with me. She has private counseling and she works evenings and cannot attend groups, but she reads the newsletter, talks with Donna and Laura and I. She's a member of Parents United, even if you don't see her name on the sign-in sheet every week.

When I was taking my famous mini-survey for my Ninth Night Presentation I gave questioneers to the women I work with, I discovered that four had been molested themselves, one suspected that her daughter had been molested by an uncle, and one divorced mother had been a member of PU three years ago. The man I worked with who recognized Hank's picture on the November issue . . . he later revealed to me that his involvement in this program was *not* because the natural father had sexually abused his step-daughter—but that he, himself, had.

On a bus trip to Reno, I met and talked at great length to Lockheed employees, men and women alike—and I know they'll spread the word about that mouthy lady with the fuzzy hair (it was blond then, not green!)—and the word will keep on going: there *is* a safe, comfortable place to discover a workable resolution to the ugliest problem that can erupt within a family.   **Sandi**

not. I am able to speak up to may parents when I feel they are wrong whereas I used to feel threatened by my mother's power. I can speak up and be assertive when someone tries to screw me over. I am more respected in my job than I ever was before because of the changes in me. My parents know that I am a person with feelings just as they are now. They have revealed to me that they are proud of my ability to take care of my needs. My value system used to be similar to theirs, but now I would rather take care of me than to own a fancy car. I chose to go through years of braces and settle for an older car. It was one of the best things I ever did. You cannot put a price tag on personal self-worth.

One of the most important things I feel as people we need to do is to spread the word of this organization. People need to know that there is a place to get help for this problem. Many of our chapters are forming because of our reaching out to police, courts, schools . . . in newspaper articles, on television appearances, radio spots, through friends . . . people need to take a risk in order to reach out.

Where would we all be if Parents United did not exist. Yet, there are many people who have not heard of our organization and spend wasted years of feeling bad about themselves, allowing the cycle of molest to

I feel we must spread the word . . . of PU

continue. The men who are convicted sometimes spend 20 years in prison, and are never rehabilitated. The children have no way of dealing with the guilt of sending a father-figure to prison. No one has a way of trying to put the pieces of their life back together. It would be more beneficial if the entire family could get help, and if the marriage is a good one, that the family come together again. I find it said that many people I know had to wait half their life to find a place to deal with their childhood.

In the circle of my life I tell people what Parents United is about and the need for it. My hope is that if someone else talks to someone I have shared with, that they can tell them about our group. It is a shame it took incest for people to start caring for each other and to learn how to openly communicate with the people in their life. Maybe someday we will reach those countless people who were molested and prevent it from happening to future generations of children. But we all need to work together.   **Donna, Santa Clara Vice President**

SAGA OF A SUPT. ON SAT.

I awakened early *that* Saturday morning . . . nervous and full of fears. I knew what had to be down at the house, *I had my list.*—however, I knew my limitations. Over the years, I have painted, scraped, and performed other various maintenances on my own home, but I knew if they were held to inspection, that all the flaws would show. I didn't want to be laughed at or ridiculed for my ignorance.

How, I thought to myself, am I going to supervise these volunteers . . . it will become very apparent that I don't know a heck of a lot about construction and repairs . . . oh well, I thought, as I put on my levis and tee-shirt . . . I will have to face the "firing squad" sooner or later. As I drove to the house, I formulated a "plan of action." Upon arriving, two people were waiting for me. I decided to wait until more showed up before "doing my thing."

Finally, others showed up and I decided it was time. All of us gathered in the kitchen—all eyes were upon me. Gulping, my heart pounding, I blurted out "I have a list of things we're supposed to work on. . . but, to be quite honest, I don't know a lot about construction, so . . . I would like all of you to use your expertise and skills and teach me as we go along." Everybody stood there, for what seemed eternity, then one of the guys said "well, what are we supposed to do?" That broke the ice and we got started on scraping the paint on the house.

I have learned a lot about construction and repairs. *Most Importantly,* I have learned that I just have to be me. Of course, I am teased and there is a lot of joking, but it is with love and caring. We all work hard in between squirt-gun water fights and taking time out to talk when one of us is hurting. The house is becoming beautiful, but the real *beauty* is in the sharing and caring between all of us.

From all of Parents United and especially from me, thank you: Eddie M, Jim, Jim H, Brenda H. Geneva, Peter B, Jeannie L, Bill M, Bill H, Sam, Arthur, Frank R, Louie, Ted, Carlos, Pancho, Honey, Dennis, Glenn C, Tom S, Ben T. Mary M, Ron M, Gary F, Joe F, Willie S, Donna, Fran, Michael S, Art T, Larry T, Mary T, Victor, Dianna, Frank S, Cheryl D.   **Sharon**

Editor's Note: For all those Saturday's . . . for your love and caring. Sharon . . . we at PU thank you . . . Sandi

7

TASK FORCE COMMITTEES

NEWSLETTER   Sandi
The Santa Clara Chapter Newsletter is printed regularly in an effort to inform and to educate, and to develop a close, self-supporting internal membership—as well as an extended relationship with Parents United chapters throughout the state and across the country.

OFFICERS ADVISORY   Past Officers
This committee was created to provide comprehensive opinion and suggestions to assist the officers when non-bias information is necessary in order to make chapter decisions that reflect a complete, informed evaluation; these valued committee members are requested to express viewpoints in areas of concern, at the request of the officers.

'PHONES/RECEPTION   Maria
This committee coordinates the personnel available to provide telephone coverage and the reception of the Parents United business office and counseling quarters

FUNDING   Brenda
These members are responsible for raising funds for our organization: coordinating fund-raising events—such as raffles, auctions, inter-membership collections, recycling of cans and newspapers, and coordination of the joint PU/DSU Flea Market.

SPONSORSHIP   Peggie/Sharon
This important committee coordinates new and continuing member sponsor programs, serves as a welcoming committee for regular meetings and coordinates the recontact of absent members with the Attendance Committee.

COMMUNITY AWARENESS   Dick
Members handle public awareness/publicity of Parents United and communication with the public through the media.

SPEAKERS BUREAU   Sandie/Roberta
Working closely with the Community Awareness Committee and with the Sponsorship coordinators, these chapter members present our program goals at speaking engagements before the public.

NINTH NIGHT SOCIAL   Michael
Members handle coordination of various activities with regard to the Ninth Night break between groups, which entails refreshments, entertainment and the structuring of the proposed adjenda for the social evening, which occurs every nine weeks.

ATTENDANCE RECORDS   Maria
The function of this committee is to maintain the records of mandatory attendence at groups, and to contact members who are absent—and to maintain contact with counselors and facilitators and CSATP representatives regarding absentees.

VOLUNTEER LIST   Sharon
Working in coordination with the members of the Task Force Committees, this group prepares and distributes the Volunteer List, coordinates the results, and determines the availability of help for various projects and activities necessary for our self-support system.

GROUP REPRESENTATIVES   Michael
This committee coordinates the various types of input and output generated within the individual groups to the officers during their meetings, representing the feelings of the membership. In turn, the representatives report back to their groups.

SPECIAL PROJECTS COMMITTEES
When it is necessary to form a Task Force Committee for a special purpurpose for for a special project, the Officers of the Chapter will takesuch steps and authorize a special committee. The Conference Committee is such a committee, as has been the one formed for the relocation of the Parents United house and for repairs and renovation.

All Parents United officers and Task Force Committee leaders can be contacted through the receptionist office at Parents United Office: call 280-5055. Committee meetings and locations will be announced during the General Business Meeting.

BETH AND ME

I was asked to write about mother/daughter relationships. In truth, the only mother/daughter relationship I can write about is the relationship I have with my daughters. To me, each child of mine is unique in all the world and the relationship with each of them is also unique.

Beth's personality has been influenced by her father, her step-father, her brother, her sister, her teachers, aunts, uncles, grand-parents, friends and me, —not necessarily in that order. The way I raised Beth, including the way I responded to the molest situation, came from the experiences I have had—from my mother, my father and all the others who have influenced my life, therefore, the relationship we have is special and unique. It is different from the relationship I have with each of my other children because they, too, have had unique experiences. It is different from the way other mothers and daughters relate to each other. It is not the "right" way and it is not the "wrong way—it is just our way and it fits for us. If it doesn't fit we talk about it.

Some differences between our relationship and that of other mother/daughters in the program seem to be more obvious than others. Beth was nearly 18, out of high school, attending college and holding down a job by the time I knew about the molest. I can see where there could have been a great deal more conflict if we had been living together. I am aware that when two people are living under the same roof and each struggling with their own growth that there can be many difficult moments. I really feel there is little I can share with other mothers except to say that what Beth and I have, we worked hard to get and it was worth every struggle. I am sure it was hard for Beth to talk to me about her feelings—it was hard for me to hear and share my feelings. I am glad we were in a place to hear each other.

I would like to conclude with a letter Beth wrote to me while she was living in Seattle, a letter I treasure with all my heart.

My Dear Mother:

I'm in a slightly poetic mood tonight and am thinking of you and mostly wanting to share how I feel about you. I feel like you've invested 22 years in me. Twenty-two years of making decisions—major and minor, consciously and out of habit, out of plan and foresight and out of involuntary response—decisions that have shaped my life. I want you to know that I'm pleased with the Beth we've shaped together and with the character you've built in me. I'm happy with who and where I am and I'm grateful for your efforts. I feel that I am coming into woman-hood. It feels glorious and noble. I feel that the possibilities are endless. . . and exciting.

Mostly I feel I can be proud of myself and whatever I do. I feel that I have earned the things I have and my happiness has a sweet taste of victory. You have taught me honor and justice, compassion, kindness,

(continued on page 12)

PU/DSU — AN EXTENDED FAMILY
(continued from page 2)

A new chapter means that a treatment program is forming that will help molested kids whom otherwise would not be getting that help.

All right, Sandi, I'll come back to Parents United and the adult members. My most personal, direct rewards come from the adults, the so-called clients who are now my friends. I think the main distingui-shing factor between Parents United and other self-help groups is that Parents United is a self-help group that includes not only people with a special problem but the people who have helped them to cope with this problem. The difference between the clients and the professionals dissolves and we all become people helping one another. I think that this is why we have so little burn out among the professionals. I know that I probably would have burnt out long ago if it weren't for my new found friends—Tom, Marge, Sharon, Peggie, Art, Anita, Vickie and on and on. They give me back much more than I ever gave them. No matter how exhausted I am . . . I get recharged every Wednesday night and by my daily contacts with the veteran members of PU/DSU.

Another remarkable feature of PU/DSU is that the atmosphere generated by the San Jose group can be found at any of the other chapters. When I go to visit them I feel the same warm environment. I hear the same thing, the same expressions. And when I start up a conversation with one of them it's like continuing the conversation I recently had with one of the local members.

ANNA: I also have the same impression. It's really nice and comforting to know that when we travel around the country, there is likely to be a PU/DSU group nearby which we can visit and renew ourselves.

HANK: PU/DSU is like an extended family. We have "relatives" all over the country.

SANDI: Thank you both . . . I'd love to keep talking, but our newsletter is only so big. Congratulations on your tenth "Anniversary" . . . As the *Parents* of Parents United.

WHO IS CINDY DENOYER-GREER?

I really think she is a really neat person to talk to. She's given me a lot of strength. I have noticed she only says what she feels—nothing more nothing less—none of that what you want to hear." Myself and my two foster sisters who go to group also have enjoyed Cindy's encouragement. She really makes us feel that we are someone special. If I have any problems, she tries to help . . . she never promises us that she will do something if she's not sure she can.

I am really glad that I'm involved with DSU. I first got involved while in the Children's Shelter. They made me feel really comfortable about myself. They made me feel like it was not my fault for what my dad did.

I feel like I'm not the only one in the world. I always felt that I was the only one . . . my first night at DSU I was scared . . . but, the counselors there have really helped me. Now they help me think about the things that I say that I think are right—and they set me on the right track and I can find out if it's been right or wrong.

If it wasn't for DSU, I don't think I would be able to control myself. DSU has really helped me. Thank you.   **Cyndi M**

Who is she? A person who helps us sort out our minds . . .
A person so sweet, lovely and kind . . . who helps out with DSU.
A person who will tell you, "I care about you."
A person who willingly takes time to listen and helps us with our important decisions . . .
That person is Cindy—who helps with our problems, big or small.
She's the most perfect, beautiful person of all!   **Mary B**

Cindy is very nice. She cares about how you feel and she worries when you're feeling depressed. I don't really know how to say what Cindy is because there are a lot of words to describe her. Cindy brightens up the day with her smile and just being there when you need her. She is like a big sister I never had. I don't think I've ever met anyone as sweet or as nice as Cindy is. I'll never forget this special person.   **Denise S**

There are a lot of words that describe Cindy . . . nice and kind, caring and loving . . . she is one lady who cares if you are depressed and tries to help. She is also like a big sister to me because she sets aside time to talk to me. She's kind and loving and she really brightens up the day . . . just by saying hello—and the glow of her beautiful smile. I really want to say, "Cindy, I love you and I care about you."   **Debbie R**

WE LOVE YOU CINDY

Cindy DeNoyer Greer was a shy non-assuming person when she applied for a supportive services internship four years ago. She was a senior at San Jose State University majoring in Administration of Justice and was interested in becoming a probation officer. From the beginning, she realized that the program was providing only minimum group counseling services to child victims and siblings. At that time there were only two groups (preadolescents and adolescents).

The primary reasons for the lack of participation of child victims and siblings was due to a lack of coordination of victims services and lack of transportation services. Cindy immediately saw the serious gap in victim services and subsequently decided to focus on improving self help/counseling and support services to victims.

She is very organized and was able to provide more consistency and structure to the then named Daughters United. Cindy was able to plan and implement a more organized transportation system to the degree that approximately 400 youth are being transported to the 13 groups in DSU. Cindy, in unity with the members, developed the DSU Task Force which is now the organized body which provides the leadership and decision making for DSU. As a resource to the Task Force, Cindy has acted as a guiding force towards the overall significant improvement in DSU. The groups grew to 13 weekly groups under Cindy's assistance. The business meeting, sponsorship and child advocacy in court have all been enriched under her leadership.

As if she did not have enough to do, she helped in the planning and implementation of the cultural enrichment program for the youth. After the State Funds ran out, Cindy organized various fund raisers in order to continue to keep the cultural enrichment program alive.

Due to her total dedication and commitment, Cindy was hired as the first DSU coordinator about three years ago. Since her involvement, DSU has become nationally recognized as a *very* important part of the overall national program for dealing with sexual abuse.

Cindy is a person who naturally exhibits a great deal of warmth, compassion and empathy towards the youth in this program. She is a true advocate for children's protection and rights. I am very proud and honored to have her as a colleague and a close friend.

Cindy, thank you—for touching the hearts and minds of us all and making this a better world in which to live.
                                                  Bob Carroll
                                    Supervisor, Child Abuse Unit

Cindy is essential to Daughters and Sons United. She spends her own time making sure that everything gets done. She transports at least four hours on Wednesdays and organizes the groups. At the same time, she may sit down with a couple of girls who are very upset and gently help them work out their problems. She believes in the members and they trust her.

Cindy is someone very special to me. She has taken the time to be my friend. She will listen to me talk and encourages me to do my best. We are a lot alike in many ways. This is important to me because it helps me look at myself. She serves as a positive role model for me.

By watching Cindy, I can learn to be gentle, work hard and believe in myself. Cindy really believes in me. She cares about me. It is hard for me to write how much she means to me . . . I need to say, "Thank you, Cindy; I love you."   **Terry F**

Who is Cindy? Cindy is a very special person.

I have been working with Cindy for nearly four years . . . when I first met her, she was a reserved person who didn't really share herself; but, she has come a very long way since her involvement with DSU.

She listens to the kids and when there is a problem she follows it through. The kids realize this and they trust her because they know she is there for them. It is rewarding to see the respect that the kids have for Cindy.

I feel very lucky to be working with her. She has taught me so much. When I have a problem with one of the kids that needs special treatment, she helps me to help them talk about it. I have a lot of respect and love for Cindy.

Cindy does more than just talk to the kids . . . she plans activities for them and spends a lot of time getting the information or whatever is needed to be done. She puts a lot of time and effort in making the event go well.

Who is Cindy? My friend; a very special person.   **Anita S.**

Cindy is a very warm and wonderful person. She has helped me out a lot. She knows how to relate with the kids in group. Cindy is a super person; I love her.

Group is wonderful for me. I get in touch with a lot of feelings here. When I first came to group I was in the shelter and I felt I was the only one this had happened to. Group helped me to realize that I'm not alone. I'm home with mom and dad now.   **Lana Z**

I like Cindy. She is a nice person. She helps you to relate to problems and to deal with them . . . she's helpful. I think group is helpful, too; I felt scared my first time in group. I feel now that I'm wanted, loved . . . and I have someone to talk to.   **Tamara S**

Little did I know . . . the day I interviewed a pretty, quiet blond undergraduate student from San Jose State University for a role as a support services intern . . . that she would do what no staff person had been able to do up to that time—develop Daughters and Sons United into a strong, essentially self-directing service provider and advocacy for the child victims in our program.

During the years prior to Cindy coming to work with us—the staff had repeatedly stated that we existed for the welfare of the child, but that our level of service did not reflect this concern. Cindy saw this and she quietly, efficiently—with incredible dedication, strength and organizational ability—set about to change that situation. It was not always easy for her and as obstacles would occur, she would seek the support she needed to overcome them.

Cindy is wonderful to work with . . . even in the most hectic, harassing situations, she is like the calm in the eye of a storm; posed, confident—dealing with each need as it arises with due concern, without getting upset—maintaining complete control of the situation. She inspires the staff and children alike with her modeling of care and responsibility and her ability to hear and reflect . . . and to be right there in any given situation.

Her vision is miraculous . . . her judgment is tremendous; she has brought about the impossible: transportation of four hundred children to group each month . . . cultural enrichment activities that boggle the senses (such as Christmas parties for several hundred children and their families . . . a field trip to Great America for ninety-five children . . .) as well as participation by a record number of children in the summer-school-work-program, SPEDY.

Cindy has truly helped make the kids the reason we are here! She has invited all components of the program to participate in this process so that they know, too, why they are here.

Cindy DeNoyer Greer . . . we all owe you a huge thank you. In your beautiful, efficient, effective manner you have clarified and expanded our reason for being. With deep admiration and respect, I thank you for coming to us over four years ago . . . and sharing your vision and skills and yourself . . .   **Dorothy Ross**

FROM DSU, TUCSON

I have really enjoyed being here because I know that I am not the only one that has been abused in some way. The counselors have been real nice to me and they have tried to convince me that I am somebody special. When I first came to DSU I was scared to say anything; but, in time, I finally realized that if I speak up and tell them about myself and my problems . . . maybe they can help me. I am sure that DSU will not solve all my problems, but as long as some of them are solved . . . it makes me happy.

Linda, Tucson DSU

Our feelings at DSU . . .
Hurt—hurt not only because of the pain of losing families . . . but even physical hurt . . .
Pain—mental anguish and pain from a molestation within the family.
Fear—fear of losing your mother and siblings.
Anger—anger for what your father, grandfather, stepfather, uncle . . . did to you, causing all of these pains . . . But most of all . . .
Love—love for what everyone is doing for you to help you through your ordeal.
This love must come from you . . .

DSU, Tucson

I attended DSU in April, 1981, because my father molested me. It was the very saddest moment of my life. I thought the world would end because my father was in jail for one night. I was so happy when there was somebody to help him and our family.

At DSU, I learned to cope with my anger and regained my love for my father. I always loved him . . . but I love him more for letting us help him. I saved our family.

My father isn't a bad guy . . . nor is our family. We all love each other and help each other with our problems. That's what my mom and I did. So did DSU . . . they really helped.

Now it's been a month and I get to help others at DSU and I can be with my dad more . . . with my mom there.

a daughter, DSU, Tucson

My life is a sea—tossing, rolling, swirling . . .
    The waves go up and down and crash against the shore.
My life is settled now, peaceful and calm.
    My sea is just smooth sailing . . . with small storms.

Angela, DSU, Tucson

DSU is a great program . . . we have a lot of committees and workshops that are of benefit to everyone who attends our program. Kids can go to DSU knowing they will get support in dealing with the molest . . . and any other problem they may have at the time. I enjoy helping people just like everybody does at DSU. I've seen girls and guys come a long way since they first started. Thank you very much for funding our program.

Ron, DSU President, Tucson

I'm supposed to tell you about DSU. Well, when I first came in . . . I felt scared, insecure . . . and very guilty. But, the kids there met me with open arms. I really needed a lot of support and they were there to give it. I've grown very close to a lot of the people there . . . I guess you could say, friends forever.

That's what DSU is all about: people *there* to help you through the crisis . . . and a whole lot more. Thanks for reading this letter. I am a DSU fundraiser and a very close member to everyone.

Val, DSU, Tucson

Sadness—like a damp blanket—covers me. As I snuggle down, the smell of mildewing guilt fills my nostrils.
Shame, like a pesky fly, refuses to be shooed—and when I start to doze, fear abruptly wakes me.
Regret and remorse join me for breakfast . . . but, after sausage, eggs, toast and coffee—I'm empty.
Throughout the day, pain and sorrow are my co-workers . . .
Evening: Loneliness.
    Then, once again, I try to hide under
    that damp, smelly blanket.
And so . . . I slowly moved, android-like, from day to day, unaware that I was being just like those Rubberneckers I so disliked . . . who would slow to a near-stop to stare with morbid curiosity at an accident— becoming hazards themselves.
Now . . . I'm concentrating more on the road ahead and resisting the temptation to dwell on the accident of my past.
I'm even beginning to believe that happiness and self-forgiveness may—with a little luck—be 'round the next corner.
It sure would be nice to get out from under that damp, smelly blanket . . .

Mm, Tucson DSU

AN AWFUL DREAM

Sometimes I wonder where I've been, who I am, do I fit in? When I'm down and feeling low, I just close my eyes and try to find a clue. Sometimes I feel some people know me better than I know myself. They know what I'm thinking, they know what I have done. When it comes down to not knowing things, I'm the only one.

I don't know who I am and it makes me feel like a lost grain of sand. I am a drifter who comes in and goes out, always with a lot of doubt. I think if a thousand things all at once . . . they have me so confused and not knowing which end is up. It starts out like a tide and grows until it surrounds me. I try to hide my fear by striking out in anger. It keeps building and it scares me—then I don't know what to do or where to go.

My emotions are the strangest ones around. I find myself crying for no reason at all, laughing at heartache—crying over victories. I keep a lot inside, trying to hide the feelings I shouldn't and trying to express the ones I shouldn't . . . inside. I find myself in a world only knowing my name. Seeing faces I don't recognize and others I wish I'd forget. Places and faces unpleasant for me which brought me pain and misery. Sometimes I find myself living in dreams and fantasy so I won't have to know what's going on in reality.

They tell me my teen-aged years are the best time of my life . . . no bills and no responsibility. They say my problems are only minor and I'll look back and laugh in years to come . . . and don't worry because I'm not the only problemed one . . . I feel like I am in a burning fire—having an awful dream, not knowing what happiness really means.

I thought hell was for years to come, but because of the places I've been and the things I've been and done, I wonder if *this* is hell. Does anyone know what tomorrow will bring and what will become of me? If so, please let me know.

a teen in Portland

WILL YOU HOLD MY HAND?

I reached out to touch but could not find a hand—
    Lonely in my world so blue
    I cried and prayed that life would end.
Living revolved around drugs, alcohol and abuse
    Which I could no longer handle . . . not that . . . and
        life too.
    So I drank
    Used drugs
    And was abused
    Now Who am I?
        What am I?
        And what should I do?

Sandy, Portland DSU

HELL IS FOR CHILDREN

They cry in the dark so you can't see their tears.
They hide in the light so you can't see their fears.
Forgive and forget, all the while.
Love and pain become one and the same
    in the eyes of a wounded child—because, hell . . .
    Hell is for children, you know.
You know their little lives have become such a mess.
They shouldn't have to pay for your love
    with their bones and their flesh . . .
    But, hell . . . Hell is for children, you know.
It's all so confusing, this brutal abusing.
They blacken your eyes, and then apologize.
    You're Daddy's little girl
    (don't tell mommy a thing).
    Be a good little boy and you'll get a new toy
    (tell Grandma you fell off the swing).
Because, hell . . . Hell is for children.
You know their little lives have become such a mess.
They shouldn't have to pay for your love
    with their bones and their flesh . . .

Pat B.

DAUGHTERS & SONS UNITED

Daughters and Sons United, the children's component of the Santa Clara County Chapter of Parents United was formed in 1972. DSU is closely coordinated with the Child Sexual Abuse Treatment Program (CSATP) and receives supportive direction, practical assistance and supervision by CSATP staff. This is an indispensable component in the county's effort to deal with Child Sexual Abuse.

GOALS

Daughters and Sons United's primary goals are to:
1. Alleviate trauma experienced by the child though intensive emotional support during the initial crisis.
2. Facilitate children's awareness of his or hers individual feelings
3. Promote personal growth and communication skills.
4. Alleviate any guilt the child may be feeling. as a result of the sexual abuse
5. Prevent subsequent self-destructive behavior
6. Prevent subsequent reoccurance by increasing the childs independance, assertiveness and self-esteem.
7. Prevent subsequent dysfunctional in pattern relationships.
8. Break the multi-generational abusive and dysfunctional pattern which is evident in many of our families

PROGRAM DESCRIPTION

Daughters and Sons United membership currently ranges from five to eighteen in age with over 200 active participants and another 50 or more sporadic members.

Daughters and Sons United decision-making body is the Task Force Committee. The Committee is presently composed of members who meet weekly with a Parents United representative and the Daughters and Sons United Coordinaters. The Committee establishes goals, objectives and projects geared to enhance the development organization and unity of the Daughters and Sons program. The Program coordinators and the cadre of interns under their supervision implement the decisions of the Task Force Committee.

The following services have been developed:
1. **Childrens Shelter and Juvenile Hall Liasons:**
   Makes initial contact within one or two days after admission for crises intervention, provides an introduction to the Daughters and Sons United program and the groups. Provides continued support and councling throughout protective custody, 2 to 3 times weekly.
2. **Home Liasons:**
   Daughters and Sons United Coordinaters make initial contact during crises period with those children who remain in the home and introduces them to group involvement.
3. **Sponsorship Program:**
   Longer term members serve as sponsors to facilitate new member entry into group.
4. **Time Out Corner:**
   Area designed specifically for program members. Resource and reading materials are available to enhance their educational awareness of such things as drug abuse and communication skills.
5. **Police and Juvenile Investigation, Medical Exam and Court Hearing Support System:**
   Children are accompanied by a supportive person through the above steps in the criminal justice system process.
6. **Big Sisters and Big Brothers Program:**
   A one-to-one relationship for those children demonstrating the need for additional support.
7. **Transportation:**
   Coordination and Organization of transportation for children to weekly groups and counseling sessions. This service is for hardship cases. Over 150 children are transported per month.
8. **Self Help Groups:**
   Task Force Committee screens all new groups proposals. Groups range from play therapy to young adults groups. Within the older age groups, groups are objective/goal oriented, i.e., orientation, social skills, self-awareness/sensitivity, communication, etc. All group facilitators are systematically trained and/or screened.

The following groups are in session:

Play Therapy I	Adolescent Girls Group II
Play Therapy II	Communication Group
Preadolescent Girls Group	Human Sexuality Group
Preadolescent Boys Group	Adolescent Boys Group
Adolescent Girls Orientation Group	Young Womens Transitional Group
Adolescent Girls Group I	Young Male Offenders Group

WHO WAS SHE?

Who was I? Better to ask *What* was I like when I was a little girl .. because I was very confused about who I was. My role as a child was warped and distorted.

If there are such things as 5-year-old bitches, that's what I was. I was my step-father's little bitch—a specially-trained, home-grown, pleasure object; a co-conspirator in an ugly game that eroded my mother's marriage and destroyed all the little-girl potential I might have had. I was argumentative, narrow-minded, conniving, judgemental before my time, uncooperative . . . I was a sneak, a thief, I destroyed things. I attempted to kill my mother and her husband when I was twelve. I nearly destroyed myself when I was thirty

I was never really a little girl.

Because there was no opportunity for me to get help . . . because I carried the stain of what I was as a child . . . because I buried who I was, hid it from everyone . . . I believe that I denied my own daughter the ammunition to protect herself, and the man who impregnated me

As a . . . 5-year-old, I was instructed to perform acts that I was not aware were unspeakable . . .

with her taught her the same ugly game I had been taught to play. Then, later, my second husband took advantage of her confusion . . . her vulnerability. I know what it was like for me as a child; I want to vomit when I realize that my daughter knows, too.

Because of those early lessons that destroyed my childhood and distorted my values, I have carried misconceptions and the fine art of manipulation into my adulthood, running from one marriage and participating in the destruction of another. My daughter is a woman now, and I am watching her attempt to overcome the very same confusions and frustrations that I am. The men who have attemped to love us honestly cannot understand. It may be that that they never will. It's almost like having an indelible stain on your soul.

When Hank and I were talking about subject matter for this issue—that the focus would be on DSU members and adults molested as children—he mentioned that a comments from adults that had *not* been able to get help would be valuable, as a comparison to those who have been able to work on the problems generated inside an individual who was sexually abused as a child . . . I thought about myself.

Sometimes, for me, working primarily in the program as the mother of a molested child . . . I put to the back of my brain my own experiences as a child. My daughter's experiences, and my association with other mothers has seemed primary . . . but I often feel internal pressures building inside me that can only come from the fears and frustrations of that period of my life.

(continued on page 16)

PARENTS UNITED CREED

To extend the hand of friendship, understanding and compassion—*not* to judge or condemn.

To better our understanding of ourselves and our children through the aid of other members and professional guidance.

To reconstruct and channel our anger and frustration in other d rections, *not* on or at our children.

To realize that we *are* human and have hang-ups and frustrations—they are normal.

To recognize that we do need help, we are all in the same boat, we have all been there many times.

To remember that there is no miracle answer or rapid change; it has taken years to get this way.

To have patience with ourselves, again and again, taking each day as it comes.

To start each day with a feeling of promise, for we take only one day at a time.

To remember that we *all* are human; we will backslide at times, but that there is always someone willing to listen and help.

To become *loving, constructive* and *giving* parents.—become the *person* that we really wish to be.

MY PU FAMILY

I came to Parents United two years ago as a supportive agent, accompanying a friend who had a similar problem. What she had told me earlier about his group is a blur now . . . but I remember that she said "I am not alone, now . . . there is a place to help me."

I found the same support and caring as she did . . . I believe we all find it here. I joined the program for *myself*, and have been able to develop the self-sufficiency that enabled me to tell my family and my father what had happened to me, years past, when I was molested by my sister's husband.

Until this program, I was by myself, unable to deal with my past. When my family members turned away from me . . . no one here turned away. Except for my friends in this program, I have been alone.

Through other mothers and daughters, I now know some of their pain is just like mine . . . and I have grown because they have shared with me. I have a better knowledge of how deeply this has hurt my sister. I now have a better understanding of how she is feeling about what happened to me. I have learned this understanding right here, in this program.

I have discovered that I am not the only molested woman in the world. I have found a place for my own pain to be understood. I have become more assured, and my actions now are right. Even if some of my past actions were not right . . . I can accept them. It seemed that most of my male relationships were often built upon my doing things for them . . . instead of my just being me. I see that now. I am working on being a better person—for others and for myself. I am working on caring for myself as well as for others.

I have challenged my past roles and I am working on them. In acknowledging these past roles, with the self-help principles(?), and with counseling help—I can see things I couldn't see before. Now I can work to change the parts of me that I want to change . . . since *all* of me, back then, was not *all* bad . . . and even some of the bad parts had some good parts.

I have shared a lot with my close friends here, and now want to share something important with all of you who read this: Parents United is my *family*. Just as if I was born again to you. I am growing up, and I like myself. I am going to grow up and go away, someday . . . just like your own children will.

But, I will always come back home.

Debbie

BETH AND ME
(continued from page 8)

strength, endurance, spirituality and so much more. Often it seems these qualities are rare and precious and I feel honored to have them.

What we share is special and precious and I so rarely take the time to tell you what it means to me. You have been with me for 22 years. You've taken me from total dependency to self-sufficiency. Everything that I am and have had its beginnings with you.

And I want you to know that I'm happy, that I revel in life. One day it thunderstormed after a long, dry spell and it was so intense. I ran outside and danced in the park and ran and got wet and laughed. I felt joyous. Another day I felt my heart to out to my friend and felt care and concern and cherished her. Some days the sun shines on me and fills my face with light and brightness. Some days I notice people noticing me and I feel attractive. I feel that my days and experiences are in closer harmony with who I am than ever before I feel that I'm finally living a me that I've never fully let out.

It's 22 years of investment, earning interest in the happiness of a full and well-rounded life. Part of it is my investment. But anything that I've nurtured and developed was first planted by you. Well-rounded is a good and accurate term. I often felt that different sides of me were mutually exclusive. Now I feel that I can be any and all things that I feel in me.

I like and respect myself and have found that others do, too. The words love and respect have a very real and true meaning for me. I think you've taught me that meaning. I wish to use them of you now. I love and respect you—as my mother, as my friend and as a person. Those two words hold all the qualities that I most value in others and in myself.

Thank you mom. For being you, for being my mother and for helping me become someone that I enjoy being and can be proud of. You have given yourself to me and in doing so have given me myself too. Thank you. I love you.

I have asked Jo and Beth for permission to reprint this letter in future issues . . . I have read only a few others that inspire me the way this does—to work for such a relationship with my own daughter. This is truly a unique, remarkable family . . . thank you, ladies, for sharing your love with all of us.

Sandi

PU CHAPTER LISTING
CALIFORNIA CHAPTERS

Alameda County (C)	**San Diego County**
Contra Costa County (C)	San Diego (C)
Humboldt County (C)	Encinitas (I)
Kern County (I)	**San Francisco County (I)**
Los Angeles County	**San Mateo County (C)**
Los Angeles (C)	**Santa Barbara County**
Long Beach (I)	Santa Barbara (I)
San Fernanco (I)	Lompoc (I)
UCLA (P)	**Santa Clara County (C)**
Marin County (C)	**Santa Cruz County (P)**
Mendocino County (P)	**Shasta County (P)**
Monterey County (P)	**Solano County (P)**
Napa County (I)	**Sonoma County (P)**
Nevada County (I)	**Stanislaus County (I)**
Orange County (C)	**Placer County (I)**
Riverside County	**Tulare County**
Riverside (P)	Tulare (I)
Indio (I)	Visalia (I)
San Bernardino County	**Ventura County (P)**
San Bernardino (P)	
Victorville (I)	

OUT-OF-STATE

Anchorage, Alaska	**Trenton, New Jersey**
Tucson, Arizona	**Bismarck, North Dakota**
Little Rock, Arkansas	**Tulsa, Oklahoma**
Coolidge, Arizona	**Eugene, Oregon**
Boulder, Colorado	**Grants Pass, Oregon**
Denver, Colorado	**Hillsboro, Oregon**
Wilmington, Deleware	**Portland, Oregon**
Miami, Florida	**Roseburg, Oregon**
Honolulu, Hawaii	**Pittsburg, Pennsylvania**
Bolingbrook, Illinois	**Amarillo, Texas**
West Branch, Iowa	**Houston, Texas**
Olathe, Kansas	**San Antonio, Texas**
Metaire, Louisiana	**Norfolk, Virginia**
Bay City, Michigan	**Virginia Beach, Virginia**
Kearney, Nebraska	**Madison Wisconsin**
Reno, Nevada	

SYNDICATED HOTLINE

Reprinted with permission from Ann Landers, May 1981

Dear Ann Landers

I've read your column for years. I must admit that I thought a lot of the stories were made up by you and your staff, but now after what has happened to me, I would believe anything.

My husband had been molesting our daughter for several years. She told a close relative, who then told me. It was a terrific shock. At first I refused to believe it. We were a middle-class family, my husband a professional with good morals and well-respected in the community.

When I confronted him, he said he was sick in the head and would do anything to get well. A friend gave us the answer. We are now in a therapy program called Parents United. My daughter is in the same program, only it's called Daughters/Sons United. I'm so grateful for this group of people who have suffered through the same problem. These folks saved our marriage and kept me from going crazy.

We are now a family in the process of working together on a day-to-day basis. I urge all young people who read this letter, if it is happening to you please tell your mother, your teacher, your doctor, the mother of a girlfriend—*someone*. And I urge all you mothers to please listen to your children. Believe them and do something about it. Only 1 percent of the children are not telling the truth! Fathers, men, women, if you will only seek help, the problem can be put in the past. Contact a Parents United group in your area.

Child sexual abuse is a terrible tragedy. People need to know that they have to talk about it and there are groups to which they can go for help. Please print our hotline number— (213) 325-8368—which I'm sorry to say is not toll free. Urge your readers to write. The address is: Parents United Inc., P.O. Box 84353, Los Angeles, Calif. 90073. Enclose a self-addressed stamped envelope if you wish a response.

PU/DSU HOUSE . . .

Then and Now . . .

Think back for a moment . . . do you remember what the Parents United/Daughters & Sons United house looked like last summer? Yes, it was a mess. The roof was leaking, walls and ceilings were cracking, all the rooms were dark and dingy, wallpaper and paint were peeling off the walls, the hallways were dirty and noisy, the exterior was shabby and badly in need of paint. We didn't have a parking lot or paved driveways . . . and there wasn't a DSU room or playground.

Look at our house now. What a transformation! DSU has their room which was built out of an old shack. The exterior and interior of the house is freshly painted, and we have a new roof. There is new carpeting in the halls and most offices and counseling rooms. A fantastic playground, donated by Southern Lumber and the San Jose Rotary Club, designed by Sam and Rita Eisenstat, is nearing completion. The house and grounds look wonderful. Thanks is due to *all* the DSU and PU member volunteers for their hard work and to local business and industry for donating all the materials we have needed.

How did we do it? Last summer, DSU decided they wanted to have a room of their own built out of an old shack in the backyard. They agreed to gather the building materials and to repair the main counseling house. PU agreed to supply the volunteer labor to repair and remodel. DSU members and support service interns Anita S, Terry F, Joanna R, Cheryl D, Jose C, MaryAnne K, and I pulled our resources together and formed a fund raising team. We coordinated our efforts with PU, reseached the companies in our area that sold the materials we needed, wrote letters describing who we are and what we needed, and followed our letter with telephone calls. By the end of the summer, not only was the DSU room built but major repairs were started on the main house.

The DSU fund raising effort was so successful that we utilize the same method—with a few variations and refinements—for other fund raising endeavors. PU has recently formed a committee that continues to invite the community to donate needed items which includes Chairperson Brenda H, Gwen K, and Geneva R.

We approach the community for donations by first sharing what PU/DSU is and how it helps children and families. We then invite them to help us treat and prevent child sexual abuse by donating tax deductible items that will enhance our program. Volunteer participation is essential for successful fund raising activities. Many long dedicated hours have been given by PU and DSU members on both the fund raising teams and in providing the labor necessary to repair and remodel. I hope everyone who has participated in transforming the PU/DSU house is proud of the fruits of their labor. I am.

The following companies have donated materials and/or services that have made the PU/DSU house what it is today:

1980-81 IN-KIND DONATIONS
SOUTHERN LUMBER COMPANY

Calhoun Brothers ● Neu Brothers

Reed & Graham, Inc. ● Hillsdale Rock Company

Gagliasso Trucking ● K-Mart/Fruitdale ● The O'Brien Corp.

Owens Corning Fiberglass ● Ameritone Color Key Paint Store

Pittsburgh Paint Center ● Special Products Co.

Lisa

THOUGHTS FROM INSIDE

My wife and I are learning some of the most beautiful lessons of our lives now. I wish we could have the opportunity to put them to practice now, but we must be patient. While I am at the "Graystone College", our separation is causing a love and appreciation for each other we never had before. I'm also learning to appreciate our children as never before.

I wanted to share with all of you some thoughts I was just now writing to my wife. If our relationship had been what it should have been five years ago, I wouldn't have started loving my niece the wrong way. I'm not blaming my wife. I was at fault in our marriage relationship in not keeping faithful.

The thing I see, looking back, is my feelings from childhood that love, tenderness, sharing, romance and all those things were sissy, un-manly things. Oh what a fallacy! The real man realizes his wife is a gift from the creator for him and him alone. No one else in all the world has the privilege of calling her "My wife." For that privilege I should do my best to become the best lover in the world to her, and keep my thoughts and actions faithful to her. We must always remember that our nieces and daughters have been created for another generation and keep our thoughts and hands off them. **Harold, Oregon State Prison**

HOW DID WE DO IT?

The following is a step-by-step procedure on how we accomplished our goals . . .

1. *We identified what we needed.* We asked ourselves: What specifically is our goal?
2. We identified what we needed to accomplish our goal. For the DSU project we found out *exactly* what materials was required, i.e., exact measurements, trade/professional names, what we needed first, second, third, etc.
3. We researched all possible resources to get what we needed. The yellow pages of the telephone book proved an excellent resource.
4. We made lists, from the phone book, of all companies in our area that carried the materials we needed.
5. We called every company and asked for the name of the manager, owner or person in charge of donations to non-profit organizations. In that call we got the mailing address and ZIP code. (See Script #'s 1, 2 and/or 3.)
6. We wrote a letter describing who we are, what we do, and what we needed. Enclosed with the letter was a more detailed description of the program, a list of exactly what we needed, and a copy of our non-profit status letter from the IRS.
7. We addressed the envelopes directly to the person who could authorize the donation (We learned, that if possible, every letter should be written in business form, including the persons' name, title, business name, address, etc., and begun with a proper salutation.
8. We waited one week—then we called them back and spoke directly to the authorized people. (See script #4.)

SCRIPT 1

"Hello, may I have the name of the manager, owner or person in charge of donations to non-profit organizations? (Be sure of the correct spelling of the name.) Thank you. Also, may I have your *mailing address and ZIP code? Thank you.*"

SCRIPT 2

If the person on the phone questions you about why you want this person's name or if you want to talk directly to the owner/manager:

"Let me tell you why I am calling. My name is _____. I am a volunteer with Parents United/Daughters & Sons United—the self-help groups for the victims and families of child sexual abuse. We serve families and children in crisis. We offer professional counseling and self-help support for our members."

"I would like the name of the manager, owner, or whomever is in charge of donations to non-profit organizations so I can send him or her a letter describing our program and an invitation to support us in _____ (the project you are fundraising for, i.e., supply materials to paint the interior of our counseling facilities). Thank you. May I also have your mailing address and ZIP code? Thank you."

SCRIPT 3

If the owner, manager or person in charge of donations answers the phone . . . "Hello, my name is _____. I am a volunteer with PU/DSU, the self-help groups for the victims and families of child sexual abuse. We serve families and children in crisis. We provide professional counseling and offer self-help support to both the abused child and their families. I would like to know if I can send you a letter describing our program and an invitation requesting your participation by donating _____ (the project you are fund raising for).

"A major source of support for our community based programs comes from people like you. All donations are tax deductible under California and Federal regulations. Would it be okay if I sent you this letter? Thank you. Also, may I have your mailing address and ZIP code?"

SCRIPT 4

Note: I prepare for each call by: re-reading the letter and information sent to every potential donor, I remind myself why we need the donation and how the donation will be used, I remind myself that I am inviting the community to help us treat and prevent child abuse. I then dial the number and ask to speak to the authorized person.

"Hello. My name is _____. I'm a volunteer with PU/DSU. Did you receive your letter describing our programs and inviting you to donate _____?"

Response: Yes, I read it but it's buried under papers on my desk. What was it you wanted?

Answer: Review the letter—use Script 3.

Response: Yes, I looked at it briefly. I haven't had a chance to read it thoroughly. What's the name of your group?"

(continued on page 14)

13

FUND RAISING GUIDELINES

This article is written to share with you some fund raising techniques that we have found successful. A more comprehensive fund raising pamphlet is being prepared. If you are interested, please contact Peggie or Art at 408/280-5055.

1. Know exactly what you are asking for and know exactly why you are asking for it.
2. Know you will get what you are asking for—coordinate all efforts with the volunteers that will provide the labor. Know who will pick up the donations.
3. Be positive in every verbal and written communication and be *knowledgeable* about the program. Answer the questions you are asked.
4. Emphasize that we are a *non-profit organization*. All donations are tax deductible.
5. Be convinced that a community based program which serves the people in your community must also be supported by people in your community.
6. Invite donors to support the program and invite them to visit the program.
7. If you don't know, admit it, then ask or find out the answer.
8. Be sure to thank everyone. Send written thank you letters to all donors immediately.
9. **Remember:** You are asking. You are the receiver. The potential donor is the giver. Show you are proud of the program. Fund raising takes a gentle combination of humbleness, trust, politeness, and a firm knowledge that you will get what you are asking for. Invite a resource person to support the program. You are giving an opportunity for the community to help us treat and prevent child sexual abuse.
10. **Remember:** Chapters must submit a report of all donations over $25 to Parents United, Inc., on your quarterly or semi-annual reports. We need to report all donations to the IRS.

Lise

HOW DID WE DO IT?
(continued from page 13)

Answer: PU/DSU. Review letter.

Response: We have given all our funds to another organization.

Answer: Ah, yes, I understand . . . There are so many worthy organizations that deserve community support. As you know, we serve children and families involved in a sexually abusive situation. We are inviting the community to support our programs. If you can't work with us right now, is there another time we can contact you?

Response: All donations are given out of our main office.

Answer: May I have the name of the person I should contact? And the mailing address and ZIP code?

Response: We don't carry exactly what you are looking for but can you use _____?

Answer: (If we can use it.) Yes. Then arrange a time to pick it up.

Response: I have _____ that you can have.

Answer: You do. Thank you so much. When would it be convenient for you to have us pick it up? When we do pick it up, would you please give the driver a receipt so we can send you a thank you letter that includes a retail amount for your donation. We both need it for tax deductions under California and Federal regulations. I will send a letter of introduction with the driver.

Response: It sounds like a worthy organization, but I will have to talk with _____.

Answer: I can understand that. I would be more than happy to come and speak with both of you to answer any questions you may have concerning our programs. You are also more than welcome to come and see for yourself how we treat and prevent child sexual abuse. Also, if you would like any more information I would be more than happy to send it or bring it to you."

If you are asked to call back for any reason, make a telephone date at the donor's convenience. Keep calling him back until you get a definite answer. Don't be discouraged with evasive answers . . . give people a chance to say YES. Only a NO is a NO. Be persistent . . . be polite. It will prove rewarding.

Lise

PARENTS UNITED 408-280-5055
14

SAN ANTONIO SPEAKS

Sandi:
Here are some messages from San Antonio Parents United . . . it makes us feel good to know you think about us "down here." We find the Newsletter important to keep a link with you. We think you do a wonderful job in organizing the newsletter.
John Daver, Coordinator, Family Sex Abuse Counseling Program

When I found out about the incest it was by anonymous letter. As I read the letter I felt sicker than I have ever been in my life. I thought I was going to die. My whole world was crumbling right before my eyes. I was scared, ashamed and angry all at the same time. I was scared because I did not know how to handle it. I was ashamed because I saw the scandal coming and I was angry at both my husband and my daughter . . . later, I found out all three of my daughters were involved. But, most of all I was angry at myself for not having been aware of what was happening right under my nose.
Lupe

I have been a member of Parents United for three years now. I am a different person from the time I walked in to Family Services. I have learned to understand myself, my children and my husband. I met my present husband there at Family Service. We have been together for three years. He, too, sexually abused his daughter. It was very hard for us at first—me dealing with myself, and him dealing with getting himself together. We tried to deal with both families as best as we could. Together we've learned to love ourselves as individuals and most of all respect for each other. We too learned to understand the wrong doings and mistakes that lead to incest in our past marriages, and now with help from Family Service, we have help to practice in changing our lives for incest never to happen again.

My husband helped me with my 15 year old daughter. She was abused by her father. It took almost 2½ years to reach her. My daughter became rebellious when her father had to face court. She turned away from us, she refused at first to accept her step-father, but now they are the best of friends and she has learned to love him and respect him as a father. She respects him for his work and participation and effort he puts in at Parents United. She wishes her father would attend but he refuses.
Mary

Family Service is a safe place to deal with the problem of incest. I have seen people come and go to our Parents United meetings. I strongly believe the ones that stay are the ones that want to help themselves and their families. Some men have tried and some have beat the system, they get away from facing what they have done.

What we feel so effective is the Fish Bowl. It is successful with couples who don't really communicate with one another, plus it helps daughters when they are in fish bowl to let their parents know what they feel and never say. We look forward to our open meetings every nine weeks. We have met people from DHR, policemen and policewomen, attorneys, probation officers.

We, the members, sponsor each other—we contact a new member, some of us even visit each other and work with each other. Work is not the only thing we do, we have a Parents United picnic every nine weeks and boy are they fun!
Mary

Yo soy la Senora Andrea. Soy miembro del grupo Parents United de Family Service Association. Les agradesco a los consejeros de nosotros toda la ayuda que nos dan tanto a mi como a mi familia. Cuando yo vine aqui por primer vez, yo me sentia muy sola, tenia a mis hijos pero yo necesitaba ayuda para mi y para mis hijos. Entonces yo estoy muy contenta con los consejeros que tanto nos han ayudado. Le doy gracias a Dios por mi hija tambien que yo se que ella se sienta mas contenta y a recibido igual que yo de estos personas bastante ayuda. Gracias atentamente
Andrea

It is so difficult for me to write what has happened these past four months. I came to Parents United about three months ago when I found out about the incest. Our daughter, 18, had talked with the parish priest . . . my husband had been sexually abusing her since she was a child. The pain was unbearable. What kind of a monster was he? How could he have done such a horrible thing? I wanted to tear him apart with my bare hands.

Where was I when all this was going on? Trish and I are very close. Why couldn't she confide in me? Mike had been hospitalized about two weeks before with a back injury. I thank God for that because I know that if he had been home I could've killed him.

Ever since joining Parents United, I have had private counseling and have participated in the group meetings. I am learning to cope with my problem. Being able to talk about it with people who understand has given me some of the answers. I still have a very long way to go. My
(continued on page 15)

TO WHOM IT MAY CONCERN

Six days after my husband was arrested for molesting our thirteen-year-old daughter, I attended Parents United for the first time. Tears continually welled up in my eyes. My heart was broken beyond repair. Never before had I felt more frightened, confused, disoriented, helpless and angry. My ilusion of having a happy, productive home provided by two loving, caring parents was totally destroyed. The trust I felt for the man with whom I shared my life was shattered.

I wept for our lovely, bright, energetic daughter. What had this done to her? I wept for my husband, an honest, gentle man, now labeled a criminal and burdened with guilt and shame. What was to become of us all? The feeling of shame was beyond description. That, coupled with the strong desire to protect our girl from being branded "molested" and my husband from being branded "child molester" made it impossible to seek help from family and friends We had no support system to help us cope with a tragedy   such immensity.

When that initial meeting ended, I knew we were no longer without a support system. Parents Un ted is that and much, much more. At times, the collective heartbreak in our discussion circles is overwhelming, but out of it comes a strength and support that must be experienced to be understood. Tears still flow, but less and less frequently, the heart is mending, and the head is beginning to understand. One begins to understand the concept of compulsion, reasons for in-family molestation, the damage it does, but more importantly, how it can be cured and what needs to be done to rebuild our family into a healthy whole again. Much is expected of us as we struggle to understand and communicate that understanding. Without the bonding that occurs among all of us involved in Parents United and the hand we extend to others who share our common problem, the tragedy of in-family molestation will be compounded by shattered lives.

from a mother in Tucson

SAN ANTONIO CHAPTER
(continued from page 14)

daughter has joined Daughters United, and she has my love and support. Mike and I have divorced. He had a nervous breakdown after everything came out into the open. He also has joined Parents United and I am able to talk to him now.

I still hurt a lot, but I have strength that I never knew I had. And I know with time and the help of God, the counselors and Parents United, I will accept it and learn to live with it.   **Carmen**

The San Antonio Light (a reprint April 1981)

A gangly young man in corduroy jeans strode up to the stage in the basement of the San Antonio Police Department, cleared his throat, took the microphone tentatively in his hand and introduced himself to the audience as a victim of incest. For what seemed an interminable half hour, he unraveled his family's grim history. When he was 13, his mother and stepfather taught him "the ropes of sex."

"I thought it was a dream," he said softly. "But when they came to apologize to me the next morning, I knew it wasn't. They were apologizing more for their own relief than because they were really sorry."

It was several years before he learned that his two sisters also had been sexually abused—one for eight years, the other for five. Although he had vague suspicions that "something was going on," until the truth came to light, he said, he believed he was alone. He is far from alone, representatives of the Parents United and Family Sex Abuse Counseling programs say. Sexual abuse of children is a serious and widespread problem. Only in the past few years, however, have parents and children had anywhere to turn for help, other than the police or religious institutions.

Parents United, organized in Santa Clara County, Calif., was the first program designed specifically to help victims of sexual abuse. The San Antonio chapter has grown steadily in the two years since it was established, coordinator John Duer said. Twenty-five fathers, mothers and adult victims—people who were abused as children and are just now seeking help—attend meetings weekly. Two local chapters of Daughters United provide 15 young girls with professional counseling, support and compassion. Although an estimated 20 percent of sexual abuse victims are boys, Dauer said, a program for them has not yet been organized in San Antonio.

Incest is so unspeakable a humiliation for both children and parents that it is kept a dark secret in many homes. As a result, an enormous number of cases remain "untapped," he said. "But if we as social service and criminal justice agencies strt looking—the cases will be there."

He emphasized that many parents who commit incest were victims of incest as children.

THANK YOU, VICKI

I remember the first time I saw Vicki Imabori. It was a Thursday evening in 1973 when I was interviewed by Parent's United—about 20 members strong—for the position of Program Coordinator.

It was the beginning of a professional association with a lovely, talented person that would span the next eight years—an association from which I would learn and grow to the point that I would come to consider her a dear personal friend and a co-worker for whom I have tremendous respect and in whose integrity and judgment I have complete trust.

In knowing and work g with Vicki, I have experienced her as one of those persons who seldom asks for anything for herself. Yet, she is willing to give of herself to others even in times when she is in need. Because she works so quietly, diligently and effectively, people are often unaware of the incredible contributions she has made and continues to make to Parent's United, the Child Abuse Unit and Daughter's and Sons United.

She touches the lives of our clients and the staff members alike with her generous giving and sharing of herself and her skills. Her courage and charm and sense of humor have brought inspiration to us all. All three components of our program are indebted to her for her essential part in their development. She has literally been known to work around the clock to accomplish a task.

Vicki brought to the original Parents United team her ability to organize and develop, her rational persepctive, her energy—and her dedication. To have received a written tribute from such a wonderful person and co-worker is indeed an honor that I will treasure always.

Thank you, Vicki . . . for putting out your time and energy and effort for me. I feeling of humility came over me when I first read your article in our June newsletter . . . then I realized that no greater accomplishment could be mine than to receive a written tribute from a peer whose opinion I value so much and of whom I think so highly. Thank you for all the times you've been there.

Thank you, dear Vicki, from me, for all you do and all you are.

Dorothy Ross

FROM SHASTA COUNTY

I would like to thank Peggie, Art, Hank, Peter, Rudy and all those I had a chance to meet on my visit to Santa Clara County Parents United in June. My appreciation to all the members, staff and support people that have made Santa Clara County Parents United what it is and for extending that support program to Shasta County.

In January of 1980 a pilot program of Parents United was started by a few Shasta County Welfare and Mental Health workers. Thanks to these concerned individuals and the willingness and enthusiasm of a few families Shasta County Parents United was started. In the first six months the group grew to 28 regular members and more than eight volunteer professional counselors from various community sources. At this time the members elected officers, drew up by-laws and applied for a Parents United charter.

Our Shasta County Chapter received its Provisional Charter in March, 1981, and now has grown to about 40 regular members. Recently we have printed a Shasta County Parents United pamphlet explaining what incest is, how it affects the whole family and what can be done. Also the Parents United program of self-help and group support is explained. On the back of the brochure are phone numbers of the local HELP line and county agencies through which our referrals are received. At a recent Shasta County Parents United rummage sale these pamphlets were available to the public and the response from all was very good. Pamphlets were also distributed to city and county agencies concerned, lawyers, and other community groups to promote more public awareness.

Now, starting our second year and our membership growing, we are looking forward to further accomplishments. As the new president, I shall do my best to continue in the professional manner that has been the trademark of Mel, our past president.

My thanks to Mel, David, Audrey, Ken, Pat, Don and all the members of Shasta County Parents United for their work and support. Also a special thanks to Virginia, Dave, Bev, Randi, Gary, Phil and all professional people that have made it possible for our chapter to help so many families in Shasta County.

Shasta County Parents United is still having growing pains but I do believe that with continued work we will all arrive at the common goal: to ease the trauma of families, promote public awareness, education, and prevention programs. If, through our efforts, *one man* stops just for a minute to think . . . and it saves one family from the heartache caused from incest . . . all our work is well worth it.   **Jim, President**
Shasta County

WRITE IT DOWN!

As I look around, after the newsletter has been published for the month, I see people reading the issue with interest. This brings a tremendous amount of satisfaction to the people who have put their time into it. We have the opportunity to see the fruits of our labor.

I am going to bring up an old subject again that you will probably say, "Well, there goes Bob again!" It is hard to put together an interesting paper when you do not have any contributions to make a newsletter with. This is a problem that is not unique to just this chapter, San Jose has it also. Everyone should be well aware that we welcome any items that you would like to put in the newsletter. I have had people come to me and say that what happened to them nobody wants to know about. all I can say is "Try me."

The purpose of Parents United is to learn how to deal with our personal problems. Maybe you, like others who have done it, will find that after you have written out some of your feelings, you can actually deal with them a lot more effectively. I know that after I wrote the article about my story this month, I was able to see several things differently than I had before. Also, I had found some answers to what had happened in a round about way.

Give it a try! Let us know what you feel. Writing it down is one you can do it. It is called "sharing."

Bob
Editor, Portland

JUST FOR TODAY I will exercise my soul in three ways: I will do somebody a good turn, and not get found out; if anyone knows of it, it will not count. I will do at least two things I don't want to do—just for exercise. I will not show anyone that my feelings are hurt: they may be hurt, but today I will not show it.
AA

WHO WAS SHE? (WHO AM I?)
(continued from page 11)

I am one of those adults who did not have any help at all—until I joined this program with the total intent being to help my daughter and I cope with *now*. The *then* in my life was completely covered up. I had the best, most capable counselor this program can offer, and she was the one that opened the doors to down deep inside of me. Much to my amazement (not amusement, believe me) I have discovered that probably *all* of the problems that I have had as an woman attempting to develop a meaningful relationship . . . a total, trusting feeling with one man . . . have been directly linked to my experiences with my step-father, and now compounded by the deeds of the men I married. I know my relationships with other women has been colored by the judgments I formed of my mother when I was a child.

As a bewildered, obedient 5-year-old, I was regularly instructed to perform acts that I was not aware were unspeakable . . . later, somehow, I was aware that the *secrecy* that could have been a fun thing was a "bad" thing. Perhaps it was the tone of my step-fathers voice, when he would remind me not *ever* to tell my mother what he was doing . . . perhaps it was the times that I would feel a funny power over him, when his face would look scared—maybe I was eight or ten when something told me that this particular he and I had was really not right, even if what he was doing often felt good.

There's another subject: how can you possibly acknowledge that something as odious as *that* actually felt physically OK? One of the most difficult climbs that Laura and I had was that barrier . . . it was *bad*, therefore there should not have been any good feelings But, what about the feeling of power, the feeling of being special . . . how can we admit those truths out loud?

He treated me differently than his own children, my little sisters. I believe my mother noticed this; I don't know for sure if she wondered. I am aware of a strained relationship with my mother for most of my childhood; she and I were nearly constantly at odds, and I believe it was because there were underlying vibrations that disturbed her. We have never truly been close. I also believe that I was aware of my special status and that in my own way I was waving flags in front of my Mom. I was a bitch; a horrible child. I hated myself then and I am only starting to be able to acknowledge my lack of control over who I was trained to be. Sometimes, I still feel responsible.

But, I wasn't responsible; I know it and you know it. He was—they were

Thank God thank Hank—for Parents United for me now—and for my daughter — right now I am going to enjoy watching her grow through this in a healthy way
Sandi

WELCOME TO PU/DSU

Remember, you only need to use your first name.

Group participation is encouraged—but not unless you feel comfortable about joining our discussions. If you would rather talk to someone individually, either in person or by telephone, that is okay too. At times you may need to do both.

Remember, we cannot give a *sure cure* for any problem. Everyone is unique and will need to find their own solutions, according to what is right for them.

> *We can share what we have learned to help ourselves.*
> *We can share our own insights.*
> *We can understand what you are going through—*
> *We have been through it too!*

Parents United, Incorporated, is a non-profit and non-sectarian volunteer organization open to all who have experienced intrafamilial and child sexual molestation. The Santa Clara County Chapter is the original founding chapter.

Every member of a family involved in a child molest situation is a victim. The present lack of knowledge and understanding by the community increases the difficulty in working to understand, cope and deal with the problems and to find satisfying fulfillment in the lives of every one of us.

Through programs of discussion, with professional leaders, in study groups and through local chapter newsletters—real help is provided to find oneself and to reshape our lives to meet the unique and unpredictable conditions of families with this problem. Parents United can help you.

You will find sympathetic and understanding people with whom you can share your experience, problems and hopes. You can gain new perspective as you discover that you are not alone, and that others have triumphed over the same difficulties that you are facing.

Never forget the basic fact about yourself—you are greater and finer than you think you are! *Norman Vincent Peale*

LOW-RISK ALTERNATIVE

Parents United has helped me start to realize that my problem is one of self-destruction, not one of sexual need. Parents United has helped me understand that there is a very good person in me, and when accepted, I have deep within me a very productive and useful member to society. I realize that I can be cured . . . that I can be strong and that I can live the rest of my life without fear of molesting again and destroying myself and my family. I have every hope that my family will someday be reunited and be stronger than ever before.

Parents United is also helping my wife and daughter so that they can have strong healthy normal lives . . . it offers an alternative to complete self-destruction, repeat molests, and most important it returns to society strong, healthy productive people.

Parents United is not a short term high risk project; it is a long-term, extremely low-risk, alternative to more child molesting, and to no prevention . . . and no help.

Child molesting is a curable sick compulsion, caused not by a need for sex—but for self destruction. The pain of hurting or destroying someone you love is far more intense and greater than just inverted destruction. The reason is to destroy any love, warmth, or understanding that anyone may feel for you, therefore denying that there is any within for yourself. Parents United helps cure these problems, and it is playing a vital role in society by teaching people about child molesting, how to recognize it, and most important how to prevent it.

Child molesting has been going on since the beginning of time. Parents United offers a beginning of an end to it. I have within me more good than bad, Parents United is helping by reinforcing the good and by understanding and displacing the bad. As production groups know best how to do and improve their jobs (they are the experts) so do a group of child molesters know best how to cure and prevent child molesting the cure comes from within Parents United has two primary functions, the understanding and cure of child molesting, and the understanding and prevention of child molesting. Both of these are long term

Parents United has been and will continue to be successful in achieving it's duty.   **from a child molester, Tucson Chapter**

16
AUGUST 1981

BUBBYLONIAN ENCOUNTER

Dear Sandi,

I enclose our contribution to your special Conference newsletter. We are excited about this play and have found it very effective in the initial testing we have done with children. We are planning to show the presentation to our DSU groups.   **Helen Swan, Project Director,**
Tolenson County Child Sexual Abuse Program
Olathe, Kansas

Bubbylonian Encounter is a child sexual abuse prevention play designed specifically for elementary school age children. The 30 minute production involves three characters who use humor, drama, and audience participation to communicate various types and effects of human touching. The drama covers the range of positive and negative touching, giving specific information to children about the steps to take if "forced sexual touching" should occur.

Bubbylonian Encounter is an effective primary prevention program in that its purpose is to teach children that:

1. Touching can be positive, negative, and "forced sexual."
2. They have the right to protect their own bodies and seek help when touching feels bad or confusing.
3. Sexual abuse can be harmful and is against the law.
4. Sexual abuse can happen by someone you know, even a family member.

These objectives are accomplished by giving children a vocabulary that helps them to discriminate between various touching experiences. In addition, a leading character models the process for seeking help when a child feels helpless to protect himself/herself.

Bubbylonian Encounter is the result of a collaboration between Johnson County Mental Health Center, Theatre for Young America, and the Kansas Committee for the Prevention of Child Abuse. Currently the play is available in two mediums, a live production and a videotape. For more information about obtaining a videotape or any of the other services described above, please contact:

Kansas Committee for the Prevention of Child Abuse
214 W. 6th, Suite 301, Topeka, Kansas 66603

*You are never
given a wish without also being
given the power to make it true.*

You may have to work for it, however.

from ILLUSIONS, by Richard Bach

PLATE PASSING

Mention the word money to someone and watch the many different responses that you get. Especially if it is going out of instead of into your pocket. Some people at Parents United have asked me where the money goes that is collected every week. That is a very fair question and an answer is coming at you.

First, and foremost, is the rent that is paid to the Church for the use of their rooms. At the present time we are paying them $25.00 a week. This amount of money is very minimal considering the number of rooms that we are using. The potential use of the church is fantastic. We are using only two floors of the East Wing at the present time and we have room for expansion if it becomes necessary. Of course, if we do expand further, $25.00 a week is nowhere near enough. That amount now pays for the heat and electricity.

Then, we use the fund for coffee, sugar, and creamer. The box by the coffee pot doesn't pay for all that is used every week. Also, the fund is used as an emergency fund for needy families. The loan of any money for emergency has to be approved by the board.

We eventually are going to have to pay for the printing of the newsletter. Parents United, Inc. is now paying for the printing of the newsletter and it is costing them over $30.00 a month. Also, we have the opportunity to rent films from Portland University Film Library. These films are about incest and other family problems that confront us and how to deal with them. Rental fees go as high as $20.00

As you can see, there are many places that the collection money goes. I don't like to pass the plate every week, but it is necessary. If we are to continue, we need the finances to do so. The only regret I have is that I have to be the SOB that has to be the asking.   **Bob**
Portland Treasurer

ON BEING HUMAN

Most of us unconsciously use certain mechanisms of personality to avoid being fully alive. The reasons for this are many. Perhaps chaotic qualities in our pre-natal environment evoked anti-life feelings we have never resolved. Or a traumatic birth could have convinced us that being alive is terrifying. Or perhaps we were trained from infancy to believe that sexual energies should be suppressed, at whatever cost. Or maybe our early failures at self-expression caused us to compensate by being irrationally aggressive or withdrawn. Perhaps we believe ourselves to be basically inadequate, unlovable, or loathesome.

Such anti-life attitudes, upon being solidified into patterns of personality, often persist into our adult experience. And thus it is that a discerning observer of human interaction is likely to note that much of what passes for adult activity is actually the interplay of overgrown children trying desperately to be loved or validated. Since such behavior has been a part of human functioning as far back as histories were written, our implicit assumption is likely to be, "that's just how people are."

But what if people don't have to be that way? What if a person brought to consciousness and resolved pre-natal conflicts? Or the trauma of birth? Or was able to be freely expressive of the entire spectrum of human energies, governed in that expression not be decades-old fears, but by present appraisals of truth and appropriateness? What if a person trusted life without question, knowing that being human meant being whole, lovable, and creatively spontaneous?

We might call such a person *self-realized*. We would witness in his behavior an absence of infantile survival-anxieties. Rather than his personality's being an accumulation of mechanisms designed to clutch onto love, to defend against fear, and to be constantly anxious that a threat to his survival might materialize . . . his personality would simply be the way he freely expressed life, moment-by-moment.

This raises an interesting question: how would we deal with someone who lovingly and politely declined to connect with us through the network of fears, anxieties, apologies, defenses, and manipulations which are ordinarily prominent in everyday personal relationships? Because most of us are so accustomed to dealing with each other on the basis of unconscious mutual childishness, an honest, unapologetic, confidently self-assertive, loving man or woman might seem to be less than human.

But, what *is* human? Does it mean feeling habitual fear, eternally questing after basic security, being frightened by genuine intimacy, and constantly struggling for supremacy over our fellows? Or does it mean being loving and joyful, relating to one another honestly, and manifesting the full potential of our true nature in each moment? Which of these alternatives, after all, is less than human?
Science of Mind magazine

JUST FOR TODAY I will be unafraid. Especially I will not be afraid to enjoy what is beautiful, and to believe that as I give to the world, so the world will give to me.   **AA**

A FATHER . . . A TRAINEE

I suppose I was frightened of the unknown . . . but, there I was, an hour early, waiting to face those interns and professional people interested in what was happening here in the city where it all started.

My fears were still gripping me, even after helping at whatever needed to be done—hoping never to sit still long enough to be asked the fatal question . . . why . . . how could you . . . (you snake, you good-for-nothing . . .) You don't know?

The question never came, so I did not volunteer . . . (good thinking—I won't need to reveal myself . . .)

My biggest problem has always been my big mouth. The most out-of-control part of my body. Before I could control myself, I was telling the whole trainee group where I came from and where I expect to go because of the self-help program in Parents United.

I revealed myself and to my surprise and delight, I was accepted and from that point until now . . . and forever—I have been growing inwardly into a better person. It's almost as if after the third day in the training program, all my defense walls came down and I have a new peace in my body; a renewed soul to have better fulfillment in my life.

Thanks, Hank; thanks, Dino . . . and Laura. Thanks, Marji, Thanks to everyone . . . in no set order.

I'm a better person. I am Peter B—and I'm proud of it.

CHAPTER NOTES

Thanks to the 167 people who attended the **Santa Clara** Sponsorship and Speakers Bureau Workshop on April 25. Please keep coming. *Everyone* from all chapters are welcome to join us. The remaining dates for '81 are: August 22, October 10, November 7 and December 5.

The Department of Mental Health, in **Nevada County, California** sponsored an all day workshop on February 6. The workshop panel participating from Santa Clara County were: Laura Costello, Staff Counselor; Elizabeth Cobey, PU Attorney; Peggie and Art, PU Reps; Cletus, DSU Rep; Vickie, Spouse Violence Coordinator. Subsequently PU/DSU program was started for their area 2 weeks later. Congratulations, Nevada County!

On April 14, 1981, a group of Parents United and Daughters & Sons United got together for the first time in **Ontario, Oregon.** After the meeting was over they asked, "Now, how can we start a Parents United here?" Good work, and smooth sailing.

Santa Clara County, Parents United. Inc., has received a grant from the California Office of Criminal Justice Planning (OCJP) to aid in outreach services to California. Chapters under the grant, professionals and members are offered workshops in a variety of topics and skills to help build fully-functioning Child Sexual Abuse Treatment Programs in communities throughout the state. For information call Art and Peggie at 408/280-5055.

The 1981 Southern California in **Orange County** Conference was a great success! The basic needs in outreach efforts, in addition to factual information and consultation on specific problems, is always to inspire others to replicate a successful approach; to let them see for themselves that it is possible in their community; that resources are available when help is needed; and to know that personal contacts help to form a mutual support system. In short, show that a program is possible and that people do care about each other when they find they are not alone anymore.

Solano County has been granted Chartered Chapter status. Congratulations Solano!

A half day workshop was conducted in Visalia, **Tulare County** for County agency people. It went very well. Santa Clara people present were Carroll Blackstock, San Jose Police Dept.; Nancy Tadlock and Leona Tockey from the Child Abuse Unit; Peggie and Art from Parents United. Keep up the gooooood work Linda and Shirley

Our chapter in **Anchorage, Alaska,** has applied for Chartered Chapter Status. Good luck, Anchorage. Keep up the good work. ("Brrrrrrrrrr.")

A new chapter in **"Reno, Nevada."** See Art or Peggie for the bus schedules to "Reno!"

We all loved doing the workshop in **Madison, Wyoming.** My love goes to all of you and the "Safe House." (Art)

We've a good chapter in **Bolingbrook, Illinois!** Keep up the good work, Shirley and staff.

Special message to the **Indianapolis, Indiana** Chapter: "It's hard work but stay with it, Linda and Susan! Special thoughts to Alda, with all my love." (Guess Who)

Bay City, Michigan is a new chapter. Congratulations!

Three new chapters in the **Los Angeles** and **San Bernardino** area in the Long Beach, Victorville and San Fernando. Good show!

Milwaukee, Minnesota! Guess who was at the National Conference on Child Abuse and Neglect? Hank, Anna, Leona, Anita, Terry, Joanna, Cletus, Art and 2300 other people. Wow! Was it good to see some of our past trainees there—and the staff from other projects . . . like **Boulder, Colorado!**

For the first time in the history of Josephine County, **Grants Pass, Oregon,** representatives from county and private agencies joined forces to address a particular problem in their community. That issue was Child Sexual Abuse and there were 35 participants in the three full-day workshop held June 22-24 presented by Parents United Staff Counselors Annie Riley and Don Hadlock and Parents United Representative, Anita M. The outreach team returned with an application for Interim Status for a Parents United/Daughters and Sons United Chapter in Grants Pass, our 64th Chapter!!!

Special thanks to Peggie—unique, complete, total-outreach-woman. *Santa Clara Chapter* (tho' we fear *most* chapters feel she belongs to *them!)* for guiding the creation of this new column in our newsletter . . . with able assistance from Art & Anita. We need this sharing. Sandi

CALENDAR OF EVENTS

FLEA MARKET   TBA
The Flea Market, 12000 Berryessa Rd—all day Sunday
The PU Funding Committee, working with DSU representatives, collects all *useable* items, facilitates their restoration and repair, and hauls them out to the biggest Flea Market in Northern California—for additional membership funds. Please support this important effort: **Contribute!** Or, visit our booth, and **Buy!** *Contact Brenda.*

SPONSORSHIP WORKSHOP   Aug. 22 & Oct. 10
Saturday, 10:00 a.m. to 1:00 p.m.
Committee members bag up their meals or organize a pot luck, create a warm and comfortable atmosphere—and settle in tof the most important aspects of our program—giving of ourselves, to ourselves. The effectiveness of our goals, the comforting support for new members is the major foundation on which we build our program. Come, join and share. This workshop meets in coordination with the Speakers Bureau, see below. *Contact Peggie or Sharon.*

SPEAKERS WORKSHOP   Aug. 22 & Oct. 10
Saturday, 1:00 p.m. to 5:00 p.m.
The bureau workshop concentrates on training and instruction to develop techniques for effectively communicating the program and it's goals to various community groups. *See Roberta or Sandie.*

NEWSLETTER   October 1
Article evaluation and preparation of the PUN runs throughout the month prior to the issue. Actual production of the newsletter is one week before the issue date. The next issue will be printed October 1. Deadline for final copy is September 2. *Contact Sandi.*

THE NINTH NIGHT SOCIAL   September 23
For eight consecutive weeks, Parents United Members, Santa Clara Chapter, concentrate their collective and united efforts on restoration and repair and intensive self-support. On the ninth week, we rest and enjoy an evening in a casual and informal sharing atmosphere. Particulars will be announced at the business meeting. *See Michael*

OFFICERS MEETING   Aug 11 & 25, Sept 8 & 22
Parents United House, promptly at 6:30
The elected officers of the membership meet regularly the second Tuesday and fourth of every month, in open session, to discuss general business. Any member of Parents United who has business to discuss should contact *Woody or Donna, at the PU office, 280-5055.*

BOARD OF DIRECTORS MEETING
The monthly meetings of the board of Directors are not open to the membership. Mike attends these meetings as our duly elected representative, speaking and acting in our behalf, reporting back at the next business meeting. Any information regarding the Board, any suggestions or clarification, should be directed to *Mike, 280-5055.*

CHILD ABUSE TREATMENT PROGRAM
The Child Sexual Abuse Treatment Training Program (CSATTP) has been renamed to indicate that it deals with *all* forms of child abuse and its function is *treatment.* JPD, ICEF, and PU/DSU representatives and staff participate in the training sessions. For details and further information, contact Chuck Juliano, 280-5055.

PU NATIONAL CONFERENCE   July 31, Aug. 1
Parents United National Child Sexual Abuse Conference, a comprehensive two-day workshop, will be held in San Jose. Over 500 attendees are anticipated. Contact the Business Office for additional information and particulars.

THE FRIEND YOU ARE TODAY

Friendship never happens unless you do your part
    You have to cultivate the soil to help the garden start
You have to keep the petty weeds of jealousy pulled out
    And prune the weakest branches of timidity and doubt
You have to nourish friendship with a smile along the way
    For the friend you have tomorrow is the friend you are today

4. The Criminal Justice System

A. Dealing with Parent and Child in Serious Abuse Cases: A Judge's Viewpoint

by Leonard Edwards*

The legal response to cases of serious intrafamily child abuse presents a number of complicated and difficult issues. Among them are: Should the family be separated at the time of the discovery of the abuse, and if so, which members of the family should be removed from the home and for how long? Should the legal system be concerned with developing a plan to reunite the family? Should the offending parent be prosecuted by the criminal justice system, and if so, to what extent should the needs of the child and the family be considered by the criminal courts in dealing with the offending parent?

There are conflicting legal and social goals in any attempt to resolve these questions. In some respects, the conflicting goals are reflected in the fact that a child abuse case typically is handled by two different courts, the juvenile and the criminal. In juvenile court the judge and other participants in the legal process attempt to structure a program that will be in the best interests of the child. The child is the subject matter of the proceeding, not the parents. In the criminal court, the judge, prosecutor, and other participants are focusing on the offending parent and determining the degree to which the aims of the criminal law should be applicable to him. To the extent that the best interests of the child involve continued contact with the offending parent and the restructuring of the family, there may be a conflict between the juvenile court order and judgment by the criminal courts in sentencing the parent to long periods of incarceration.

The remainder of this paper focuses on five propositions which I believe should be guiding principles for those persons charged with administering cases of serious child abuse. Within the discussion that follows the five propositions, I attempt to outline certain approaches to serious child abuse cases which will in part resolve the conflict inherent in dealing with the parent and child in these cases. Although the propositions may appear to be somewhat abstract, each is based on the experience of professionals involved in the handling of child abuse cases in Santa Clara County, California.

A few introductory words are in order. Child abuse cases, as referred to in this paper, include only intrafamily occurrences. Those cases involving strangers who abuse children are excluded because there is no preexisting relationship between the offender and the child. There are some abuse situations involving family friends or relatives other than parents, but whether they should be included in the category of cases will depend on the relationship between the offender and the child and the specific needs of the minor.

---

*The author is a Superior Court judge in Santa Clara County, California. As a practicing attorney in that county for over ten years, he has written extensively in the area of juvenile law. This partricular paper was presented at the National Conference on Child Sexual Abuse sponsored by the American Bar Association, in San Francisco in July 1981.

"Serious child abuse" in this paper refers to conduct that has caused serious physical or emotional harm to a child. More specifically, "serious" refers to those incidents of battery and sexual molestation upon a child which are punishable as felonies in the criminal courts.

"The best interest of the child" in this paper means the alternative that most closely meets and satisfies the child's needs. As defined by Goldstein, Freud, and Solnit in *Beyond the Best Interests of the Child* it means "the least detrimental available alternative for safeguarding the child's growth and development."[1]

The Five Propositions

(1) After discovery of an abuse, the child should be placed in as familiar a setting as possible (preferably her own home) consistent with her protection from future harm.

(2) The child's best interests are served if she is permitted to continue her family life with as little interruption as possible even if this means reuniting her, after appropriate intervention, with the offending parent.

(3) Before and during any reconstruction of the family, therapy is necessary for both parents, the child, and often for other family members.

(4) It is necessary to have coordination and communication between the various decision-makers in the juvenile and criminal courts concerning the disposition of child abuse cases.

(5) Therapy must be available in each community for families involved in child abuse. There should be widespread publicity in the community that therapy programs exist, that their purpose is to rehabilitate the families involved, and that the legal system is utilizing them and is supportive of them.

Discussion

(1) After discovery of an abuse, the child should be placed in as familiar a setting as possible (preferably her own home) consistent with her protection from future harm.

Perhaps the most traumatic period for the child is at the time the abuse is first reported. Her life is suddenly interrupted by a number of professionals including police, protective workers, and probation

officers. Statements are taken (often repeatedly), family members question her, and some may even attempt to persuade her to deny the truth of what she had reported. The family turmoil is often blamed on her.

While in many cases it is necessary for the protection of the child to remove her from the family home immediately, it is recognized that for the child, the isolation from her family often results in feelings of depression and of being punished.[2] One approach preferable to removal is to exclude the offending parent from the family home, thus permitting the child to remain with the family. This procedure is regularly followed by police departments in Santa Clara County and particularly the San Jose Police Department working in conjunction with the Juvenile Probation Officers in Santa Clara County.[3] The offending spouse is told to leave immediately, find another place to live, and avoid all contact with the family home and the family members.

Critical to this approach is the ability of the police agency or probation officer to talk with the entire family and explain how such a no-contact situation will work and what the alternatives would be (incarceration for the parent, emergency foster care for the child), and to receive assurances that all parties will abide by the rules set down by the investigating officers. The officers must be satisfied that if there is a violation of the rules, it will be reported immediately to the proper authorities. The police and juvenile probation officers in Santa Clara County are so skilled at dealing with these family situations that such removals are the rule rather than the exception.[4]

One of the reasons for the success of the police and other workers at this stage is the existence of the Juvenile Probation Department's Child Sexual Abuse Treatment Program (CSATP) in Santa Clara County and the related groups, Parents United and Daughters and Sons United. In sexual abuse cases, after the initial police investigation is completed, and often simultaneously with the investigation, the officer will invariably refer the case to the CSATP

[1]Goldstein, Freud, and Solnit, *Beyond the Best Interests of the Child* (New York: Free Press, 1973), p. 53.

[2]Henry Giarretto, "A Comprehensive Child Sexual Abuse Treatment Program," in P. Mrazek and H. Kempe, eds., *Sexually Abused Children and Their Families* (Oxford: Pergamo Press, 1981).
[3]In Santa Clara County, the juvenile probation officers fill the role of child protective service workers. In other California counties, these workers may come from the Department of Social Services.
[4]The San Jose Police Department, in conjunction with the juvenile probation officers and CSATP workers, are so successful in their investigations of sexual abuse situations that they have an estimated 90 percent rate of confessions from the abusing parent prior to filing of a criminal complaint (interview with Earl McClure, San Jose Police Department, May 5, 1981). Compare this with similar sexual abuse cases in Los Angeles County, where the percentage of confessions at the investigative stage is less than 5 percent (interview with Deputy District Attorney Jean Matusinka, District Attorney's Office, 1601 Eastlake Avenue, Room 131A, Los Angeles, CA 90033, by telephone on May 12, 1981).

or Parents United group, (if, in fact the referral did not come from one of these groups at the outset),[5] and the staff and volunteers in these programs can begin to give the various family members the support and therapy that is so necessary at this critical time in their lives. Having contact with these groups exposes the family members to others who have been through similar situations. Members of these groups, in turn, will strengthen the notion that the no-contact arrangement should be strictly followed. They will also encourage each family member to begin therapy immediately and hopefully thereby considerably reduce the trauma for each family member.

(2) The child's best interests are served if she is permitted to continue her family life with as little interruption as possible even if this means reuniting her, after appropriate intervention, with the offending parent.

This proposition is consistent with the principles stated in *Beyond the Best Interests of the Child* and the *Standards Relating to Abuse and Neglect*.[6] If the offending parent can be rehabilitated through therapy so that the family can be safely reunited, then that effort should be the highest priority for the legal system. The alternatives of removal of the child for foster home placement or permanent removal of the offending parent should be utilized only if rehabilitative efforts have been tried and failed.

In Santa Clara County, reuniting families which have experienced serious child abuse has been accomplished in the great majority of cases. In sexual abuse cases, more than 92 percent of the children return home, and more than 75 percent of the marriages remain intact.[7] In physical abuse cases, both the number of children returning home and the number of families remaining together after therapy is over 90 percent.[8] Moreover, all of this has been accomplished with a remarkably low rate of reported recidivism. In the sexual abuse cases, for example, the recidivism rate is 0.6 percent for those families who have completed the program.[9]

With such a high percentage of families being reunited successfully, even after serious abuse has occurred, any efforts by the legal system to support similar rehabilitative programs would seem to be well placed.

(3) Before and during any reconstruction of the family, therapy is necessary for both parents, the child, and for other family members.

A family in which a parent has been involved in child abuse can, in most cases, be rehabilitated. However, mere separation of family members and incarceration of the offender, or even individual therapy for him, may not be sufficient. In most cases, the entire family must be involved in therapy.[10]

This point has been demonstrated by each of the two therapy groups in Santa Clara County, the CSATP (combined with Parents United and Daughters and Sons United) and the couples' physical-abuse therapy group directed by Judith Siegel, MSW. From the considerable experience of each of these groups, it is evident that child abuse is a family problem, the solution to which involves the entire family.

In the physical abuse cases, Ms. Siegel began experimenting with a couples group in 1967. The child was generally not a part of the therapy because in so many of these cases s/he was too young. Therapy typically lasted nine months and involved the revelation of interpersonal problems between the parents. Of the more than seventy-five couples Ms. Siegel has treated during these fourteen years, there have been only two reoccurrences. Moreover, as noted above, more than 90 percent of the marriages continued after completion of the therapy.[11]

The CSATP and the related groups have received national attention and are recognized as innovative, effective therapy groups utilizing creative techniques for the rehabilitation of families involved in sexual abuse. In over ten years, more than 3,000 families have been provided services. The recidivism rate of 0.6 percent is much lower than any figures in the literature on incest and child abuse.[12]

These programs can be duplicated in other areas of the United States. In fact, currently there are sixty areas in the country which follow the CSATP model as a result of an ongoing training project conducted by the CSATP staff. Training and materials are available for interested communities. (Refer to the list at the end of this appendix for persons and agencies to contact.)

---

[5]Forty percent of the referrals to the CSATP come from the clients directly. Giarretto, *op. cit.,* footnote 2 at p. 3.

[6]Goldstein et al., *op. cit.;* Juvenile Justice Standards Project, Institute of Judicial Administration, American Bar Association, *Standards Relating to Abuse and Neglect* (Cambridge, MA: Ballinger Company, 1977, tentative draft), part VI, pp. 114–35.

[7]Jerome Kroth, "Evaluation of the Child Sexual Abuse Demonstration and Treatment Project" (Sacramento, CA: Office of Child Abuse Prevention, California Department of Health, 1978), pp. 26–27.

[8]Interview with Judith Siegel, MSW, on May 11, 1981.

[9]Henry Giarretto, "The Treatment of Father–Daughter Incest: A Psycho-Social Approach," in *Children Today,* vol. 5, no. 4 (July–August 1976), p. 4.

[10]Giarretto, *op. cit.,* footnote 2 at pp. 7–9.

[11]Siegel, *op. cit.,* footnote 8.

[12]Kroth, *op. cit.,* footnote 6 at p. 294.

(4) It is necessary to have coordination and communication between the various decision-makers in the juvenile and criminal courts concerning the disposition of child abuse cases.

In order for the goals outlined in the first three propositions to be realized, there must be communication between the decision-makers in the juvenile and criminal courts. The juvenile court may propose a program for the victim child and her siblings. The parents may be involved in therapy as a part of the plan. The juvenile court judge, the attorneys, and the social and probation workers may all be in agreement with the program. However, the actions of the judge and prosecutor in the criminal court may make much of the juvenile court program unworkable.

For the best interests of the child to be fully served, it is necessary for the decision-makers in the criminal courts to be aware of what has happened in the juvenile court so they can coordinate with that program if they believe that is appropriate. In smaller counties, it is likely that the same judge or prosecutor may be involved in both parts of an abuse case. However, the larger the county, the more difficult such coordination may be and the more likely that one court will act in a manner contrary to the goals of the other.

For example, the judge who hears the offending parent's motion for bail reduction or for release on his own recognizance should be aware of the agreements reached between the police, the CPS workers, the juvenile court, and the family regarding placement of the child pending disposition of the case. If the juvenile court is satisfied with the family placement, and if the criminal court is otherwise satisfied that release is appropriate, that court can be helpful to the entire case by releasing the parent with specific restrictions, such as a no-contact order.

The prosecutor who reviews the request for a complaint or who discusses a case for possible settlement or who appears at the time of sentencing should be fully apprised of what has happened in juvenile court.

The most critical stage at which communication between the two courts should be maximized is at the sentencing stage of the criminal process. This typically occurs after the juvenile court has completed its hearings. In California the dependency process takes from three to five weeks, while the felony child-abuse prosecution takes from three to four months. The sentencing judge must decide what is to be done with the offending parent after the juvenile court judge has decided on a program for the child.

At this stage, the criminal judge should have a complete report on the juvenile court proceedings, including an update on the progress of any therapy programs undertaken. Without suggesting what judgment should be pronounced in these cases, I would like to make three observations. First, removal of the offending parent to a state institution (prison) generally means that he will be unable to participate in the therapy program structured by the juvenile court. Such a commitment, in most cases, is tantamount to preventing the family from being reunited.[13] Incarceration in a local facility is generally consistent with participation in such a therapy program. In Santa Clara County, the Sheriff's Department permits furlough time for therapy programs.

Second, the fear of incarceration can be effectively used to ensure compliance with rehabilitative orders. A recent study has shown that court-ordered therapy is much more effective than therapy voluntarily undertaken.[14] The reasons seem clear. Therapy involves the in-depth examination of why a particular person engaged in child abuse. It requires a great deal of time and is often difficult and painful. Yet when undertaken and completed, its results are remarkable. Whatever else they do, the criminal courts should order therapy over a long period of probation and should thereafter monitor and review it.

Third, it may be proper, as a part of any sentence, to order the offending spouse to serve a number of uncompensated hours working for one of the therapy programs in the community. Such an order should be cleared with the particular group so that the need and the supervision are identified. This type of work may be critical to the survival of these much needed but often underfunded programs.

(5) Therapy must be available in each community for families involved in child abuse. There should be widespread publicity in the community that therapy programs exist, that their purpose is to rehabilitate the families involved, and that the legal system is utilizing them and is supportive of them.

The most remarkable development, after the creation of the CSATP and its related programs, was the increase in reported sexual abuse cases in Santa Clara County. The programs became widely publicized, both in the press and on television. As more people heard about them, more sexual abuse cases were reported, particularly when family members learned they would be helped by the program.

[13]The CSATP experience has been that when the attending parent is released from prison, the family reunites without therapy and the risk of recidisivm is high (interview with Robert Carroll, supervising probation officer, Santa Clara County, in June 1981).
[14]Inger Sagatun, "The Effects of Court-Ordered Therapy on Incest Offenders," in *In Brief* (Santa Clara County Bar Association, 111 North Market Street, San Jose, CA 95110), vol. 17, no. 3 (1980), pp. 28–39.

Along with the therapy that is provided to dysfunctional families, the increased reporting of sexual abuse cases is the most important result of the creation of the CSATP. It is clear that families who would have otherwise not reported sexual abuse problems in their homes did so in the hope that the program could assist them. Santa Clara County does not have more sexual abuse per capita than any other place in the United States—it has more reported sexual abuse. As a result, it has more treatment for abused children and for abusing parents.

By utilizing child abuse therapy programs, the criminal courts do not have to indicate that there will be no punishment for child abuse. Santa Clara County judges have continued to render what they believe to be proper judgments (including jail sentences) for child abusers.[15] It is also true that the judges recognize the importance of the therapy programs and often tailor their sentencing decisions to fit the program ordered by the juvenile court.

Summary

There is a great deal of serious child abuse in our society today. Adoption of the principles outlined in this paper will, I believe, result in more of these cases being reported, more therapy being provided for all family members, and a greater likelihood that the legal system will be serving the best interests of the children in these families.

Resources

Agencies and persons to be contacted regarding the policies and programs discussed in this paper.

(1) San Jose Police Department
Sgt. Eugene Brown or
Sgt. Earl McClure
230 West Mission
San Jose, California 95110
(408) 277-4102

(2) Child Sexual Abuse Treatment Program
c/o Juvenile Probation Department
840 Guadalupe Parkway
San Jose, California 95110
(408) 299-2475
(Attn: Robert Carroll or Dorothy Ross)
Re: Reprints of Articles—Attn: Henry Giarretto

(3) Parents United/Daughters and Sons United
P. O. Box 952
San Jose, California 95108
(408) 280-5055
Re: Training—Attn: Chuck Juliano
Re: Legal Matters—Elizabeth Cobey, Esq.

(4) Judith Siegel, MSW
Guidance Unit
c/o Juvenile Probation Department
840 Guadalupe Parkway
San Jose, California 95110
(408) 299-2680

[15]Kroth, *op. cit.*, note 6 at pp. 125, 224, and 291.

B. Sample Letter to a Probation Officer for Court Review

June 1, 1981

Mr. ■
Deputy Probation Officer
Juvenile Probation Department
840 Guadalupe Parkway
San Jose, CA 95110

Re: ■ ■

Dear Mr. ■

B■, age 3 years, was referred to me for evaluation by Steve Baron, CAU counselor. We were interested in determining: 1) Had the child been sexually molested, 2) if so, who was the perpetrator, and 3) what was her emotional status at the time I was seeing her. The child had been complaining to both her mother and grandmother that her father had been sexually molesting her on the occasions of her visitations with him, and a doctor's examination confirmed that B■ had some discharge and irritation at the vaginal opening as well as what appeared to be a tear in the hymen. When the matter was investigated, however, the mother's boyfriend, ■, was introduced as the possible perpetrator. ■ eventually passed the polygraph and was cleared. The child's father, ■, maintains his innocence and is fighting for B■ to return to him in New York. Throughout my sessions with B■, never once did she refer to ■ as the one who hurt her. It was always Daddy ■ who picked her up, and she went to his house.

Briefly stated my own credentials are an M.A. in Marriage, Family and Child Counseling, and I hold California license to practice # 12123. I have been a counselor with the CSATP and/or Parents United since 1978, and was a volunteer in the same from 1972 to 1978. I have worked with latency age sexually abused children for about four years both individually with seriously disturbed youngsters, and in groups. In the course of this work I have also seen a fairly large number of pre-school children.

I saw B■ three times for approximately forty-five minutes to an hour each. My observations of her were that she was a bright, verbal, outgoing, friendly, normal three year old, who related well to me and who used the play materials appropriately for one of her age. She quickly overcame any shyness in the new situation and exhibited a normal curiosity about the objects in the room and was soon playing productively with them. Her mother accompanied her on this first visit to help put B■ at ease with me, and we three spent the hour mostly in play and having fun together. I felt a sense of trust in B■ that allowed me to suggest we go right ahead and schedule the next appointment a week later for B■ by herself.

B■ came alone to the playroom the second visit. When I felt she was at ease I introduced the book *Where Do Babies Come From* by Margaret Sheffield. This delightfully illustrated book shows gently, yet directly how babies come to be babies and are born. Some of the illustrations show frontal nudes of both male and female adults, and children. We looked at the pictures together and commented on them. I asked her to name parts, "And what do you call this," pointing to the little girl nude's vaginal area. "Tooshy," she replied. "And this," I ask pointing to the male genital. "Penis," she said, correctly naming the organ. In this way I knew what her words for these parts were. At no time did B■ during this phase express any shame or embarrassment. We talked about Daddy's house, Mommy's and B■'s house, grandma's house, and her cousins and friend's houses. My doll house has 8 sections and I attempted to set up Daddy's, Mommy's and Grandma's houses in three of the sections. She seemed confused however, with all three houses under one roof so I moved the furniture out into the room and had the three domiciles in different parts of the room. B■ decided one house would be in the west sand and another in the dry sand, and the third on the floor. I then named the dolls as Mommy, Grandma, Daddy, and B■ and she put them in the proper houses. Daddy's house was in the wet sand, Grandma's in the dry and Mommy's and B■'s on the floor between them. She arranged the furniture awhile and then I said, "Let's pretend you're at Grandma's house and you're going to visit Daddy. What happens next?" She moves the girl doll to Daddy's house and then covers the father doll with wet sand. She also returns to the grandma house and covers the grandma. I asked her what she was doing to them and she replied simply that she was covering them up. I didn't pursue this. I said, "What do Daddy and B■ do together when B■ is at Daddy's house?"
"Play."
"Is it fun to go to Daddy's?"
"Hmm." (not a yes, not a no)
"O.K. This dollie is B■ and Daddy G■ is here in

the sand, and B■ is visiting Daddy. Let's pretend something happens. What happens?"

"He jumps on me and hits me."

"Show me what Daddy does."

She takes the doll out from the cover of sand and brushes him off. She puts B doll on one of the beds. She lays father doll, face down on top of girl doll and bangs it up and down on the girl doll.

"Like that," she says.

"Like that," I repeat. "Is that what happened to you at Daddy's house?"

"Yes."

"And he hit you?"

"Yes."

"Where did he hit you?" She takes her hand and hits a fist against her forehead.

"Anyplace else?" She puts her fist into her stomach. I decide not to follow this.

"When Daddy is hurting you does he have his clothes on?" She nods. I hand her the girl doll which is fully clothed. "Does the girl have clothes on when he hurts her?" She pulls up her own pinafore and shows me her panties. "Does the girl have panties on when he hurts her?" She shakes her head, no. "Who takes her panties off?" She points to the father doll.

"Does the father take the girl's panties off?"

"Sometimes he wants to," she answers.

"Does Daddy take his pants off too?" (Nods yes)

"What do you see when he takes his pants off?"

"His penis."

"You see his penis. Does he want B■ to touch it?" She nods. She is also getting restless, so we stop awhile and she moves around the room arranging the furniture and the dolls, covering them with sand, covering other toys with sand, digging them out, putting them away, getting other toys, burying them, mounding the sand high. It seems to soothe her to play this way. I now get the big baby doll dressed in pajamas and ask her to sit down with me again. "B■, show me on this baby doll where Daddy touched you." She removes the p.j. bottoms and points to doll's vagina. "Where down there did he touch you, B■?"

"On my tooshy."

"On your tooshy. What does he touch you with?" She puts her hand up to show me and wiggles her fingers around. "Show me on the dolly." She puts her fingers on the doll's vagina.

"Does he touch you with anything else? Let's look at the picture in the book and you tell me." I show her the adult nude male. "He touches you with his fingers and what else?" She points to his penis.

"What is that?"

"Penis."

"That's right. Daddy touches you with his penis. Show me where he touches you?" She lifts her pinafore and points to her vagina.

"He puts his penis on your tooshy?" She nods affirmatively and says, "He shouldn't do that."

"No, he shouldn't do that. Did Daddy ever touch you anyplace else on your body with his penis besides your tooshy?" She opens her mouth and points her index finger right inside.

"Tell me what Daddy did there?" She just opens her mouth and points her finger inside again.

"O.K. B■."

The final session was in most respects a repeat of the second. It was to confirm the information garnered in the first. However, I did ask her if Daddy told her not to tell, to which she replied affirmatively. I asked her what he had told her and she said, "It's a secret."

In this counselor's opinion there is no doubt that this child was molested. I tried not to lead the client in my questioning, although that is not always easy to do, because at her age I have to also make sure she understands the question. I also do not doubt that it was the father and not the boyfriend. Sometimes she would refer to her father by name, sometimes just daddy. It was Daddy's house she went to. Historically, although the molests may have started prior to May, 1980, B■ continued to complain about her vaginal discomfort and her father touching her, for the remainder of 1980 and up until the mother fled with her, long after the boyfriend, P■, was no longer living with the mother.

B▪'s emotional status I thought was quite stable. She had been having some problems shortly after arriving here, but the circumstances of being uprooted and moving may have accounted for a large portion of her instability, and when I saw her I thought she was doing quite well. Shortly after my first interview with B▪ her mother reported to me that she was in pre-school and doing much much better, seemed cheerful and happy, and much less anxious and angry. Mother reports she continues to do well, so my guess is she feels secure and protected in this environment. Mother also reports that B▪ regresses and wets the bed only when grandmother calls and B▪ has talked to her. It woudl seem that these conversations with the grandmother evoke anxiety reactions in B▪, as it was usually from the grandmother's house that the father would pick up and return the child to at visitation time. B▪ hears her grandmother's voice and she seems very close indeed, since a 3 year old has no concept of time or space. Perhaps if Grandma is so close, then her father might also be. This is a supposition only.

Children of B▪'s age and at her intellectual stage of development have little consistent objectivity, however, in order to speak in any details about anything in their experience they must have experienced it. A three year old's thinking is dominated by her perceptions. She is greatly influenced by what she hears, feels, sees at each given moment. She believes implicitly that what she perceives is exactly as it is. The experience is static and remains so without going through changes or transformations. What she perceives is her reality and there can be no other. If she had not had the experiences she describes, she could not verbally describe. Ask a 3 year old who has never ridden on, seen, or heard about a roller coaster to tell you about one. If it is totally out of any experience she will not be able to tell you. It has to be remembered that B▪ volunteered the information about her molestation to both her mother and her grandmother. She could not have fabricated it out of nothing, she cannot at her age willfully lie or practice deceit, and if the traumatizing event contains strong personal significance for the child, she may be able to recall events with considerable detail for her age. The molestation was a major issue for her as she experienced pain, anxiety, and enough discomfort to break the injunction of "don't tell" and tell those to whom she looked for protection. Older children up to at least age 8 or so may practice deception around adults, but they will seldom try to deceive about major issues that contain strong personal significance. It is important to understand that B▪ at age 3 is incapable of lies or deception. She can imagine and fantasize at age 3, but the materials for fantasy must be in the realm of her *sensory* experience. It stretches the imagination of this counselor beyond belief that B▪ was fed the information she used to describe the molestation by some other person(s), since she is herself adequately knowledgeable about what happened and has symbolized her subjective experience of having been molested into relatively detailed thought and accompanying affect. It is time we believe the utterances of these very young witnesses. They cannot practice deceit and would have no investment in making up stories of molestation, even if they could.

Sincerely,   Read and approved by

Eleanor Breslin   *Steve Baron*   *Robert Carroll*
M.A., M.F.C.C.   *Staff Counselor*   *Program Supervisor*

EB:SB:RC:dg

C. The Gathering of Physical Evidence

Most of the children referred to the Santa Clara County CSATP do not show physical signs of sexual abuse. This is primarily because such a small percentage of the cases referred actually involve sexual intercourse. If penetration has occured, it has seldom been within seventy-two hours of the report to the police or the probation department; and unless semen specimens are collected within the first seventy-two hours, they cannot be succesfully compared to the specimen submitted by the alleged perpetrator. The police officer may try to obtain the clothing worn the day of the last alleged penetration, for fluid on the clothes can be successfully tested for a longer period of time than the seventy-two hours.

If the child alleges anal or vaginal penetration within the seventy-two-hour time limit, she is examined for seminal fluid, torn hymen, and trauma to the vaginal or anal areas. She is also examined for venereal disease. Normally, unless the child is very young and indicates she is having pain in the vaginal or anal areas, and if it is more than seventy-two hours after the occurrence of the alleged incident, she is not examined at the county medical facility; but the mother is advised to take the child to her pediatrician or family doctor for a VD test.

If the child is in the Children's Shelter, the attending nurse tries to do whatever tests or examinations are necessary so the child will not have to undergo the trauma of being examined at the county hospital. Often these emergency staff personnel are not trained to deal with sexual assault cases, and a pelvic examination done insensitively can become a terrifying experience for the child who is already confused and fearful. For this reason, the police do not automatically send the child to the hospital for examinations. If one is required, a Juvenile Probation Officer or support person from the CSATP makes every effort to go with the child so that the experience can be made as painless as possible.

The officers on the Sexual Assault Investigation Unit in Santa Clara County have become so proficient in gathering evidence that it is seldom necessary to subject children to vaginal examinations. When it is done, it is because there is reasonable cause to believe there has been intercourse; and whether or not the alleged occurrence of the incident was within the past seventy-two hours, a VD test should be done. Officers proficient in gathering evidence are usually able to select the few victims who should be examined immediately and to avoid subjecting those others to a potentially humiliating examination.

In many jurisdictions, the police tend to put a large number of their victims on the polygraph to determine the validity of their statements. Even though a polygraph examination is not admissible in court as evidence, it often satisfies the police and the district attorney that a crime really has occurred and should be prosecuted. Subjecting children to polygraph tests can also be a frightening experience and should be avoided if possible. Again, as the police become experienced in interviewing the victims, they realize that children do not fabricate these stories of molestation and that administering the polygraph is therefore an unnecessary trauma to the child as well as a waste of time.

Most jurisdictions are reluctant to prosecute without physical evidence or a confession from the perpetrator, because traditionally the district attorneys have trouble getting convictions in sex cases with only the word of the victim against the word of the alleged perpetrator. This failure to convict appears to be more a failure of the police to use effective interviewing techniques (such as those developed by the Santa Clara County Sexual Assault Investigation Unit) in questioning the victim and obtaining a subsequent confession from the perpetrator.

The telling evidence usually is not the result of physical, gynecological examinations, but that which is obtained in taped interviews with the victim and other witnesses. Taping interviews is important. The failure to tape the child's interview not only means the loss of an excellent device for obtaining a confession from the perpetrator but also means that the victim will need to be interviewed more than once, and that chances of her having to testify at the preliminary are greater. The more times she must talk about the molestation, the more likely is she to be a reluctant, uncooperative witness, and the less likely are the chances of a conviction.

Another problem is getting convictions lies with the district attorney's office: failure to use appropriate trial techniques. The problem lies partly with the prosecution if it does not fully use Parents United groups where they exist to convince the offender to take responsibility for his act and to plead out prior to the preliminary hearing or trial. Even in Santa Clara County, Parents United is not used often enough by the smaller jurisdictions as a resource to obtain a confession.

D. Parents United Guidelines to Confidentiality

by Elizabeth Cobey

The Parents United policy of confidentiality is based on both California law and the underlying operating principles of our program. The California law regarding privileged communications stems from four distinct and often consistent sources: the Evidence Code, the Penal Code, the Welfare and Institutions Code, and case law.

Psychotherapist–Patient Privilege under the Evidence Code and Case Law

The term psychotherapist–patient privilege means the privilege of the client to have nothing he reveals to a counselor in the course of their professional relationship repeated to a third party (Evidence Code section 1012). This privilege holds so long as the client intended his communications to the therapist to be held in confidence. In California the term psychotherapist includes marriage, family, and child counselors, and clinical social workers as well as clinical psychologists and psychiatrists.

The rationale underlying this privilege was best expressed by the California Supreme Court as follows:

The psychiatric patient confides more utterly than anyone else in the world. He exposes to the therapist not only what his words directly express; he lays bare his entire self, his dreams, his fantasies, his sins and his shame. Most patients who undergo psychotherapy know that this is what will be expected of them, and that they cannot get help except on that condition. . . . It would be too much to expect them to do so if they knew all they say—and all that the

psychiatrist learns from what they say—may be revealed to the whole world from a witness stand.
—*In re Lifschutz* 2 Cal.3d at p. 431

Clearly, a patient is more likely to withhold information essential to effective treatment from his psychotherapist than from his physician, and the least threat to confidentiality may be sufficient to inhibit the relationship. Since full disclosure is essential to the success of the psychotherapeutic treatment, the need to encourage an atmosphere of trust and openness is great. In *Lifschutz* the court also strengthened this privilege by declaring it part of an individual's right to privacy under the Ninth Amendment to the U.S. Constitution. [*In re Lifshutz supra* at p. 433.]

A patient may voluntarily waive this privilege by a number of actions including executing a verbal or written waiver.[1] Without such a waiver, the counselor is obliged to remain silent, even if that silence results in a jail term for contempt of court. [*In re Lifshultz supra.*[2]]

The psychotherapist–patient privilege rarely applies to child sexual abuse victims since THERE IS NO PRIVILEGE if the patient is under sixteen years of age, *and/or the counselor has reasonable cause to believe that the patient has been the victim of a crime* and that disclosure is in the child's best interest. [Evidence Code section 1027.] This section of the Evidence Code is consistent with Penal Code section 11161.5.

Under the Evidence Code there is also no privilege of confidentiality when the "psychotherapist has reasonable cause to believe that the patient is in such mental or emotional condition as to be dangerous to himself or to the person or property of another and that disclosure of the communication is necessary to prevent the threatened danger." [Evidence Code section 1024.]

---

[1]The patient also waives the privilege by placing his mental condition in issue, as in filing suit for a neurosis allegedly caused by an accident. Evidence Code section 1017 reads as follows:
There is no privilege under this article if the therapist is appointed by order of a court to examine the patient, but this exception does not apply where the psychotherapist is appointed by order of the court upon the request of the lawyer for the defendant in a criminal proceeding in order to provide the lawyer with information needed so that he may advise the defendant whether to enter or withdraw a plea based on insanity or to present a defense based on his mental or emotional condition.
[2]The counselor is entitled to reveal confidential communications in private to other therapists in the course of consultation on the case.

The California Supreme Court in *Tarasoff* v. *Regents of University California* [17 Cal.3d 425, pp. 440–41] went even further and held that not only may a psychotherapist reveal his patient's information, but also that the psychotherapist *must* do so if there is a danger to others. The court held that:

> . . . the public policy favoring protection of the confidential character of patient–psychotherapist communications must yield to the extent to which disclosure is essential to avert danger to others. The protective privilege ends where the public peril begins.
>
> —*Tarasoff supra* at p. 442

The underlying facts in *Tarasoff* make it clear that a counselor's failure to warn a subsequent victim will in almost any case be actionable. The psychologist who counseled the patient discussed the case with a colleague, decided that the patient was so disturbed that he should be placed on a seventy-two-hour hold, and instructed police officers to bring him in. The patient appeared rational to the police officers and they consequently let him go instead of following the therapist's orders. Also, at that time, the therapist's superior revoked the therapist's orders to have the killer incarcerated and had the notes on the case destroyed. (The victim was away in Brazil and did not return to Berkeley for another two months.) The point to note is that the psychologist clearly invested considerable time and effort in attempting to do something about his potentially dangerous patient, was thwarted in so doing by powers beyond his control, and yet *he* and not the police officers or his superior was held liable.

Practically speaking, applying *Tarasoff* requires that all active child molestation cases be reported to the victim's mother and/or guardian and to the police. Since the child victims are not presumed able to protect themselves, their legal guardian or parent must be warned promptly. So must the police, as the mothers cannot always be counted on to protect the child victim.

Second, the court has stated that a counselor must err on the side of warning rather than on that of keeping patient communications confidential.

Finally, a counselor trained to deal with child molesters can be expected to know that unless something far more drastic than a mere counseling session is done to protect the victim, there is a distinct likelihood that the patient will remolest the child victim.

The interpretation is also consistent with the legislative intent expressed in the above-mentioned Evidence Code section 1027 and in Penal Code section 11161.5. It must be remembered that the Evidence Code forbids a violation of the psychotherapist–patient privilege *unless* there is a danger to a third party. Thus, if a child molester is involuntarily committed or incarcerated and therefore incapable of harming the child, no reporting of his molestation is required or allowed.[3]

Sometimes the counselor may feel she is in legal danger no matter which path she elects to follow. If she feels her client is likely to molest again, she is under an obligation to report the danger. On the other hand, if she does report a danger and nothing happens, she may be deemed to have breached the privilege without due cause. As a general rule, the prudent action is to err on the side of over-reporting. A court would be hard pressed to condemn a counselor for speaking out too quickly and very likely to condemn one who kept quiet only to have the victim molested or remolested.

---

[3]That is, no reporting is allowed unless the patient has agreed ahead of time on a more restrictive scope of the privilege than enumerated in the evidence code.

In terms of the PU/CSATP, the rule of confidentiality applies to all licensed counselors, all clinical social workers, all counseling interns working under the direction of the licensed counselors, the administrative and support staff (including secretaries, clerks, and receptionists who make appointments, type reports and file for the counselors), and all other persons acting as agents or under the direction of the counselors. This means that all the above-mentioned people may be allowed access to the confidential records, all client files, and appointment books, and may discuss cases with each other without violating a client's privileged confidentiality. The privilege applies whether or not a particular individual is in therapy and regardless of how often or when she or he has sessions with a counselor. All remains confidential and may be shared with no one but the staff without the express prior authorization of the client.

The only limitation on the patient's privilege comes from a court order that the individual or family is to attend the program. With such an order, the attendance and dates thereof are not privileged, but the content of those meetings attended still remains confidential.

A violation of the privilege by any staff member could easily result in a financially disastrous law suit against the staff member and the whole program and in revocation of counseling licenses by the state. For this reason it is critical that staff members at all times act as if client–counselor communications are confidential and not discuss cases in the presence of third parties or leave case files or notes lying around the office. Besides the legal dangers entailed, the practical effect of breaching this rule could also be an end to the trust relationship between the staff and the clients. Regardless of the source of a counselor's income, her responsibility is only and solely to the people she is seeing in therapy and society at large. The standard is the same for privately funded and publicly funded counselors.

Mandatory Reporting Law under the Penal Code and Case Law

Penal Code section 11161.5 requires almost everyone in a helping profession relating to children, including physicians, teachers, marriage, family, and child counselors, clinical social workers, psychologists, probation officers, and peace officers to report any suspected cases of child sexual abuse to local law enforcement and juvenile probation departments within thirty-six hours. This mandatory reporting law was originally written to deal only with child physical abuse and neglect. Child sexual abuse was hastily and not very skillfully inserted later by amendment.

The poor wording of this statute has created much confusion. For example, the statute states that when a physician, etc., observes a child and "it appears" to that person that the minor has been molested, the person must report the suspected abuse within thirty-six hours. Some have erroneously agreed that unless there is visible physical trauma personally "observed," they need not report.

Others have not realized that section 11161.5 applies only when one of the enumerated adults hears and/or observes evidence of molestation directly from the victim herself and not from the offender or other third party. Still others have incorrectly interpreted the statute to mean that when a suspected molestation case is reported to the county welfare or health departments, these departments need not report the suspected incident to the police and juvenile authorities unless the suspected molestation case has been brought to the attention of the health or welfare department's director.

In this way, Penal Code section 11161.5 goes even further than Evidence Code section 1027. The Evidence Code merely permits the counselor to breach her confidential relationship with the victim, while the Penal Code section *requires* the counselor to report the suspected molestation. This Penal Code section also overrides Welfare and Institutions Code section 5328 which forbids mental health workers under Short-Doyle from breaching patient–confidentiality even where the Evidence Code permits it.

Failure to abide by this mandatory reporting law renders the nonreporting person open to suit. In *Landeros* v. *Flood* [17 Cal. 3d at p. 399], a 1976 case out of Santa Clara County, the California Supreme Court held the physician who had not properly reported the child abuse responsible for the child victim's subsequent injuries. The same liability will accrue to professionals enumerated in Penal Code section 11161.5 who fail to report suspected cases of child sexual abuse.

The public policy favoring protection of the child is so strong that Penal Code section 11161.5 allows any private citizen to report a suspected case of child molestation without the risk of incurring liability if the report turns out to be unfounded, so long as the report was made in good faith.[4]

The Psychotherapist–Patient Privilege under the Welfare and Institutions Code and Supporting Law

Welfare and Institutions Code section 5328 provides for the confidentiality of all communications obtained in the course of providing community mental health services under the Lanterman–Petris–Short (LPS) Act. Provision for payment by the counselor to the patient whose confidentiality was breached is provided in this code. Section 5328 applies to almost all if not all community mental health workers, as the state under the LPS Act and the Short–Doyle Act provides the salaries of these workers.

It is the task of the courts to interpret apparently conflicting statutes in a harmonious manner if at all possible. For this reason the mandatory reporting requirement of Penal Code section 11161.5 has been interpreted as prevailing over W&I section 5328 in light of the legislative intent to value protection of the child over the child's confidentiality [58 Ops. Atty. Gen. 824, 11-21-75]. That is, if a child victim confides that she has been molested to a counselor employed under the Short–Doyle Act, the counselor must obey the mandate of Penal Code section 11161.5 and promptly contact the appropriate authorities. Reasoning by analogy, Evidence Code section 1027, which places the protection of the child under sixteen above the child's right to confidentiality, must also prevail over W&I section 5328.

There is also an area of possible conflict between the Evidence Code section 1024 and the Tarasoff decision on the one hand, and the W&I Code requirement of strict confidentiality of confessions of a child molester to his counselor at the community mental health center on the other.

[4]Penal Code section 11161.6: "In any case in which a minor is observed by a probation officer or any person other than a person described in section 11161.5 and it appears to the probation officer or person from observation of the minor that the minor has a physical injury or injuries which appear to have been inflicted upon him by other than accidental means by any person, that the minor has been sexually molested, or that any injury prohibited by the terms of section 273a has been inflicted upon the minor, he may report such injury to the agencies designated in section 11161.5.

"No probation officer or person shall incur any civil or criminal liability as a result of making any report authorized by this section unless it can be proven that a false report was made . . . and the probation officer or person knew or should have known that the report was false."

In Tarasoff, the California supreme court was asked to resolve this conflict between the Evidence and W&I codes. Instead, the court neatly avoided requestion on the grounds of immateriality in as much as the therapist in Tarasoff was not employed under the LPS Act or the Short–Doyle Act [*Tarasoff supra* at pp. 442–43].

It is clear that when forced to speak on this issue, the court must hold that the Evidence Code's dangerous patient exception applies to therapists covered by divisions 5, 6, or 7 of the W&I Code as well as to those therapists who are not. To hold private therapists to a standard different from that required of community mental health therapists would be a denial of equal protection guaranteed by the Fourteenth Amendment to the U.S. Constitution. Practically speaking, any community mental health worker who acts as if the dangerous patient exception does not yet apply to her is inviting a law suit which she will not win.

Children's Right to Confidentiality

As stated above, under both Evidence Code section 1027 and Penal Code sections 11161.5 and 11161.6, the public interest in the protection of children (at least those under the age of sixteen) overrides its interest in protecting their rights to confidentiality. However, once a suspected case of child sexual abuse has been reported, all subsequent communications between the child victim and their treating counselor should be privileged as those between adult patients and psychotherapists.

In a 1978 Santa Clara County case where the allegedly molesting father sought to discover the communications between his child and a staff counselor, the court recognized that despite Evidence Code 1027, the three-year-old child had a patient–psychotherapist privilege of confidentiality. It further noted that since the child's interest may diverge from those of her parents in this type of case, counsel should be appointed solely to represent the child.

This obviously is an area in which the law has not caught up with the times. Recognizing a child's privilege of confidentiality is essential for the same reasons as obtain to her parents' psychotherapist–patient privilege. [See *Lifshutz, supra.*]

The troublesome area is not that of spelling out the child's privilege of confidentiality in relation to her parents, but rather her privilege in relation to the court and professional personnel such as teachers and social workers assigned to "help" her. Should the school psychologist be able to tell the teacher what the child confided to her? Should one of our program staff counselors be able to tell all to a Juvenile Probation or CPS worker? Clearly not if a patient–psychotherapist trust relationship is to develop.

Parents United's Policy of Confidentiality

In order to encourage the necessary trust relationship between the counselors and all program clients, the following policies regarding confidentiality have been adopted by the PU/CSATP staff.

1. Any information indicating that one of the program clients has committed an act of child sexual abuse subsequent to the client's admission to the program must be promptly reported to law enforcement.

2. Any information indicating that a program client has committed an act of child sexual abuse on a victim not yet reported to the authorities must be reported promptly to law enforcement.

3. All violations of court orders by program clients must be promptly reported to the authorities.

These policies have been adopted not only because of the legal constraints placed upon the program staff, but also because of the program's realization that the criminal justice process plays a vital role in the family's resocialization process.

In order to restrict the right of confidentiality in the above manner, the counselor or other staff member must inform the potential client of the program-induced limitations on the privilege and obtain his agreement thereto prior to his entering into a formal relationship with the program. The potential client must expressly agree to the limitations set by our program; if he does not and a subsequent revelation of the client is reported to the police, the counselor and the program are open to suit. Ideally, a document setting forth the program's terms and conditions should be signed by both the potential client and the counselor prior to admission into the program.

Additionally, before speaking with any third party about a particular client, the counselor must obtain a signed release from the client which specifies the person to be consulted and the substance of the intended communication. Once a client has signed an authorization permitting the counselor to speak to a particular individual, any release of further information to that same third party can usually be adequately handled by an oral waiver duly mentioned in the counselor's notes. It is also advisable to obtain a written waiver before sending out any letters or written reports on the client.

If our program is to survive, we need to ensure that we can never be forced to reveal confidential information. It is a harsh reality that we must assume the burden of proof at all times that we have acted in a manner appropriate to maintain our client's right of confidentiality, and that we have fully informed our clients of the express terms under which we will enter into a therapeutic relationship, and that our client has expressly given consent to our divulging information to others.

CHILD SEXUAL ABUSE TREATMENT PROGRAM
LETTER OF EVALUATION

DATE SUBMITTED:_____   <u>COPIES TO:</u>

DATE DUE TO P.O.: _____   NAME: _____
                                            ADDRESS: _____

NAME OF P.O.: _____
AGENCY: _____   NAME: _____
ADDRESS: _____   ADDRESS: _____

Re: (Name of client)_____

This letter is in regard to / response to (circle one)_____
_____
_____

The family of Mr. & Mrs._____ was/were referred to the Child Sexual

Abuse Treatment Program on (date)_____ by _____
_____

due to _____
_____

COMPLETE LETTER ON SEPARATE SHEET USING THE FORMAT BELOW

1. Documentation of participation in program, who has been seen for how long, by whom, who is the supervising staff counselor, and PU/D&SU participation.
2. Some history and background that may include events in the parents' childhoods, as well as how the marriage has evolved, and always, if situational, what the situational events or dynamics are that led to the molest.
3. List the family strengths and weaknesses, i.e. an assessment of strengths, etc.
4. Where is each individual and the family now—particularly include the victim even in letters to the Adult Court.
5. Documenting changes in the family system through counseling that is leading to the resolution of the dynamics that led to the molest.
6. Family and individual goals as stated by them.
7. Counselor's present and future goals for working with the individuals and the family.
8. What is happening in the counseling process that furthers these goals.
9. Counselor's present and projected prognosis.

NOTE: Discussion of CSATP/PU/D&SU and the resources offered for all members of the family is especially important for *out-of-county* letters.

Bibliography

Books

American Humane Association, Children's Division. *National Symposium on Child Abuse.* Denver, CO, 1972.

————. *Sexual Abuse of Children: Implications for Case Work.* Denver, CO, 1972.

Armstrong, Louise. *Kiss Daddy Goodnight: A Speak-out on Incest.* New York: Hawthorn, 1978.

Assagioli, Roberto. *Psychosynthesis.* New York: Hobbs, Dorman, 1965.

Baisden, M. J. *The World of Rosaphrenia: The Sexual Psychology of the Female.* Sacramento, CA: Allied Research Society, 1971.

Bernard, Jean, and Densen-Gerber, J. *Incest as a Causative Factor in Antisocial Behavior: An Exploratory Study.* New York: Odyssey Institute, 1975.

Berne, Eric. *Transactional Analysis in Psychotherapy.* New York: Grove Press, 1961.

Brownmiller, Susan. *Against Our Will: Men, Women and Rape.* New York: Simon & Schuster, 1975.

Burgess, Ann W. et al. *Sexual Assault of Children and Adolescents.* Lexington, MA: Lexington Books, 1978.

Burton, L. *Vulnerable Children.* New York: Schocker, 1968.

Butler, Sandra. *Conspiracy of Silence: Trauma of Incest.* San Francisco: New Glide Publications, 1978.

Chaudhuri, Haridas. *Integral Yoga.* San Francisco: California Institute of Asian Studies, 1965.

Connell, N. and Wilson, C. *Rape: The First Sourcebook for Women.* New York: New American Library, 1974.

DeFrancis, Vincent. *Protecting the Child Victim of Sex Crimes Committed by Adults.* Denver, CO: The American Humane Assoc., Children's Division, 1969.

deRiver, J. P. *Crime and the Sexual Psychopath.* Springfield, IL: Charles C. Thomas, 1958.

DeRopp, Robert S. *The Master Game.* New York: Delta Books, 1968.

Ellis, A. *The Origins and Development of the Incest Taboo.* New York: Lyle Stuart, 1963.

————. and Arbanel, A., eds. *Encyclopedia of Sexual Behavior.* New York: 1961.

Fagan, Joan, and Shepherd, Irma Lee. *Life Techniques in Gestalt Therapy.* New York: Harper & Row, 1970.

Fontana, Vincent J. *The Maltreated Child.* Springfield, IL: Charles C. Thomas, 1964.

————. *Somewhere a Child Is Crying: Maltreatment—Causes and Prevention.* New York: Macmillan, 1973.

Forward, Susan, and Buck, Craig. *Betrayal of Innocence: Incest and Its Devastations.* Los Angeles: J. P. Tarcher, 1978.

Freedman, A. *Therapy of Sexually Acting Out Girls.* Palo Alto, CA: Science & Behavior Books, 1970.

Freud, Sigmund. *Totem and Taboo.* New York: W. W. Norton, 1950.

Fox, Robin. *The Red Lamp of Incest.* New York: Dutton, 1980.

Gagnon, John H., and Simon, William, eds. *Sexual Deviance.* New York: Harper & Row, 1967.

Garbarino, James, and Gillian, Gwen. *Understanding Abusive Families.* Toronto: Lexington Books, 1980.

Gebhard, P. H.; Gagnon, H. H.; Pomeroy, W. B.; and Christenson, C. V. *Sex Offenders: An Analysis of Types.* New York: Harper & Row, 1965.

Geiser, Robert L. *Hidden Victims: The Sexual Abuse of Children.* Boston: Beacon Press, 1979.

Gibbens, T. C., and Prince, J. *Child Victims of Sex Offenses.* London: Institute for the Study and Treatment of Delinquency, 1963.

Gil, D. *Violence Against Children.* Cambridge, MA: Harvard University Press, 1970.

Guttmacher, M. *Sex Offenses: The Problem, Causes and Prevention.* New York: Norton, 1951.

Guyon, Rene. *Studies in Sexual Ethics.* New York: Knopf, 1934.

Hall, C. S., and Lindsey, G. *Theories of Personality.* New York: John Wiley and Sons, 1957.

Hentig, Hans von. *The Criminal and His Victim.* New Haven: Yale University Press, 1948.

James, Muriel, and Jongeward, Dorothy. *Born to Win: Transactional Analysis with Gestalt Experiments.* Reading, MA: Addison-Wesley, 1971.

Jongeward, Dorothy, and Scott, Dru. *Women as Winners.* Reading, MA: Addison-Wesley, 1976.

Karpman, G. *The Sexual Offender and His Offense.* Washington, DC: Julian Press.

Kinsey, A. C. *Sex Offenders.* New York: Harper & Row, 1965.

————; Pomeroy, W. B.; Martin, C. E.; and Gebhard, P. *Sexual Behavior in the Human Female.* Philadelphia: Saunders, 1953.

Kling, Samuel G. *Sexual Behavior and the Law.* New York: Bernard Geis Assoc., 1965.

Kroth, Jerome A. *Evaluation of the Child Sexual Abuse Demonstration and Treatment Project.* Sacramento, CA: Office of Child Abuse Prevention, California Department of Health, 1978.

————. *Child Sexual Abuse: Analysis of a Family Therapy Approach.* Springfield, IL: Charles C. Thomas, 1979.

Lilly, John. *Center of the Cyclone.* New York: Julian Press, 1972.

Lowen, Alexander. *The Betrayal of the Body.* New York: Macmillan, 1967.

————. *Bioenergetics.* New York: Penguin Books, 1975.

————, and Lowen, Leslie. *The Way to Vibrant Health: A Manual of Bioenergetic Exercises.* New York: Harper & Row, 1977.

MacFarlane, Kee. "Sexual Abuse of Children," in *The Victimization of Children,* ed. J. R. Chapman and M. Gates. Beverly Hills: Sage Publications, 1978.

MacNamara, Donald E. J., and Sagarin, Edward. *Sex, Crime and the Law.* New York: The Free Press, 1977.

Maich, H. *Incest.* New York: Stein & Day, 1972.

Maslow, Abraham. *The Farther Reaches of Human Nature.* New York: Viking, 1971.

————. *Toward a Psychology of Being,* 2nd ed. New York: Van Nostrand Reinhold Co., 1968.

Masters, R. E. L. *Forbidden Sexual Behavior and Morality.* New York: Matrix House, 1966.

————. *Patterns of Incest.* New York: Julian Press, 1963.

————. *Sex-Driven People: An Autobiographical Approach to the Problem of the Sex-Dominated Personality.* Los Angeles: Sherbourne Press, 1966.

McCaghy, C. H. "Child Molesters: A Study of Their Careers as Deviants," in *Criminal Behavior Systems: A Typology,* ed. M. B. Clinard and R. Quinney. New York: Holt, Rhinehart and Winston, 1967.

Mohr, J. W.; Turner, R. E.; and Jerry, M. B. *Pedophelia and Exhibitionism.* Toronto: University of Toronto Press, 1964.

Mrazek, B. M., and Kempe, Henry C. *Sexually Abused Children and Their Families.* Oxford: Pergamon Press, 1981.

Murdock, G. P. *Social Structures.* New York: Macmillan, 1949.

Oliven, John R. *Sexual Hygiene and Pathology: A Manual for the Physician and the Professions,* 2nd ed. Philadelphia: J. P. Lippincott, 1965.

Parsons, Talcott. *Social Structure and Personality.* New York: Macmillan, 1964.

Perls, Frederick. *In and Out of the Garbage Pail.* New York: Bantam Books, 1979.

————; Hefferline, Ralph F.; and Goodman, Paul. *Gestalt Therapy.* New York: Dell Publishing Co., 1951.

Phelan, P. *The Process of Incest: A Cultural Analysis* (unpublished dissertation). Ann Arbor, MI: University Microfilm Institute, 1981.

Pol, Otto, and Friendman, Alfred S. *Family Dynamics and Female Sexual Delinquency.* Palo Alto, CA: Science & Behavior Books, 1969.

Polster, Irving, and Polster, Miriam. *Gestalt Therapy Integrated.* New York: Brunner/Mazel, 1973.

Reich, Wilhelm. *Character Analysis.* New York: Orgone Institute Press, 1949.

Remalk, M. L., and Wolfgang, M. R. *Sexual Behaviors: Social, Clinical and Legal Aspects.* Boston: Little, Brown, 1972.

Richett, L. *The Throwaway Children.* New York: Dell, 1970.

Rogers, C. R. "The Concept of the Fully Functioning Person," (unpublished manuscript) quoted in *Theories of Personality* by C. S. Hall and G. Lindsey. New York: John Wiley & Sons, 1957.

Rubin, Isadore, and Kirkendall, Lester, eds. *Sex in the Childhood Years.* Association Press, 1970.

Rush, Florence. *The Best Kept Secret: Sexual Abuse of Children.* Englewood Cliffs, NJ: Prentice-Hall, 1980.

Stein, Robert. *Incest and Human Love.* New York: Third Press, 1973.

Stoenner, H. *Plain Talk about Child Abuse.* Denver, CO: American Humane Society, 1972.

Trainer, Russell. *The Lolita Complex.* New York: Citadel Press, 1966.

Walters, D. R. *Physical and Sexual Abuse of Children: Causes and Treatment.* Bloomington, IN: Indiana University Press, 1975.

Weinberg, S. Kirson. *Incest Behavior.* New York: Citadel Press, 1955.

Zinker, Joseph. *Creative Process in Gestalt Therapy.* New York: Brunner/Mazel, 1977.

Articles

Adams, M. S., and Neel, James V. "Children of Incest." *Pediatrics* 40 (1967): 55–62.

Alvy, Kerby T. "On Child Abuse: Values and Analytic Approaches." *Journal of Clinical Child Psychology* 4/1 (1975): 36–37.

Anastasiow, Nicholas J. "Educating the Culturally Different Child." *Viewpoints* 48 (1972): 21–41.

Anderson, Lorna M., and Shafer, Gretchen. "The Character-Disordered Family: A Community Treatment Model for Family Sexual Abuse." *American Journal of Orthopsychiatry* 49 (1979): 436–45.

Arntzen. "Can Children Be Harmed by Police Interrogation?" *Our Youth* 23 (1971): 66–68.

Bagley, Christopher. "Incest Behavior and Incest Taboo." *Social Problems* 16 (1969): 505–19.

Bender, L., and Grugett, A. E., Jr. "Follow-Up Report on Children Who Had Atypical Sexual Experiences." *American Journal of Orthopsychiatry* 22 (1952): 825–37.

Berry, Gail. "Incest: Some Clinical Variations on a Classical Theme." *Journal of the American Academy of Psychoanalysis* 3/2 (1975): 151–61.

Blumberg, M. "Child Sexual Abuse: Ultimate in Maltreatment Syndromes." *New York State Journal of Medicine,* March 1978, pp. 612–16.

Breen, James L., et al. "The Molested Young Female." *Symposium on Pediatric and Adolescent Gynecology,* 1972.

DeFrancis, Vincent. "Protecting the Child Victim of Sex Crimes Committed by Adults." *Federal Probation,* September 1971, pp. 15–20.

Eaton, A., and Vastbinder, E. "The Sexually Molested Child: A Plan of Management." *Clinical Pediatrics* 8 (1969): 438–41.

Finch, Stuart M. "Adult Seduction of the Child: Effects on the Child." *Medical Aspects of Human Sexuality* 7 (1973): 170–87.

Finkelhor, David. "Sex Among Siblings: A Survey of Prevalence, Variety, and Effects." *Archives of Sexual Behavior* 9 (1980): 171–93.

Gerson, A. "Promiscuity as Function of Father-Daughter Relationships." *Psychological Reports* 34 (1974): 1013–14.

Giarretto, Henry. "A Comprehensive Child Sexual Abuse Treatment Program," in *Sexually Abused Children and their Families* by P. B. Mrazek and C. H. Kempe, eds. London: Pergamon Press, 1981.

———. "Humanistic Treatment of Father-Daughter Incest," in *Child Abuse and Neglect: The Family and the Community* by R. E. Helfer and C. H. Kempe, eds. Cambridge, MA: Bollinger Publishing, 1976.

———. "Humanistic Treatment of Father-Daughter Incest" (revised). *Journal of Humanistic Psychology* 18 (1978): 4.

———. "Illicit Sex in the Immediate Family," in *The Ann Landers Encyclopedia*. Garden City, NY: Doubleday, 1978.

———. "Treating Sexual Abuse: Working Together." Proceedings of the Missouri statewide conference on child abuse and neglect, March 1977 (available from the author).

———. "The Treatment of Incest: A Pscyhosocial Approach." *Children Today*, July-August 1976.

———; Giarretto, Anna; and Groi, Suzanne. "Coordinated Community Treatment of Incest," in *Sexual Assault of Children and Adolescents* by A. W. Burgess et al. Lexington, MA: Lexington Books/D. C. Heath, 1978.

Goldberg, G. "Breaking the Communication Barrier: The Initial Interview with an Abusive Parent." *Child Welfare* 54/4 (April 1975).

Greenland, Cyril. "Incest." *British Journal of Delinquency* 9 (1958): 566–614.

Gutheil, T., and Avery, N. "Multiple Overt Incest as Family Defense Against Loss." *Family Process* 16 (1977): 105–116.

Harbart, Terry L.; Harlow, David H.; Hersen, Michel; and Austin, James B. "Measurement and Modification of Incestuous Behavior: A Case Study." *Psychological Reports* 34/1 (1974): 79–86.

Hawkins, R. "Who Calls the Cops? Decisions to Report Criminal Victimization." *Law and Social Review,* Spring 1973, p. 427.

Henderson, P. "Incest: A Synthesis of Data." *Canadian Psychiatric Assoc.* 17 (1972): 299–313.

Hogan, Walter L. "Brief Guide to Office Counseling: The Raped Child." *Medical Aspects of Human Sexuality* 8/11 (1974): 129–30.

Jaffe, Arthur C., et al. "Sexual Abuse of Children: An Epidemiological Study." *American Journal of Diseases of Children* 129/6 (1975): 689–92.

Justice, B. "The Shocking Facts behind Incest in American Families." *US,* October 30, 1979, p. 38.

Katan, Amy. "Children Who Were Raped." *Psychoanalytic Study of the Child* 28 (1974): 208–24.

Katzman, M. "Early Sexual Trauma." *Sexual Behavior,* February 1972, p. 13.

Kiefer, C. R. "Brief Guide to Office Counseling: Sexual Molestation of a Child." *Medical Aspects of Human Sexuality* 7/12 (1973): 117–28.

Koch, Michel. "Sexual Abuse of Children." *Adolescence* 15 (1980): 643–48.

Laymen, William A. "Pseudo Incest." *Comprehensive Psychiatry* 13/4 (1972): 385–89.

Lester, David. "Incest." *Journal of Sex Research* 8/4 (1972): 268–85.

Lewis, M., and Sorrel, P. "Some Psychological Aspects of Seduction, Incest, and Rape in Childhood." *Journal of American Academy of Child Psychology* 8 (1969): 606–19.

Lovens, H., and Rako, J. "A Community Approach to the Prevention of Child Abuse." *Child Welfare* 54/2 (1975): 83–87.

Lukianowicz, N. "Paternal Incest." *British Journal of Psychiatry* 120 (1972): 301–13.

Lustig, M.; Dresser, J. W.; Spellman, S. W.; and Murray, T. B. "Incest: A Family Group Survival Pattern." *Archives of General Psychiatry* 14/1 (1966): 31–40.

Masters, William H., and Johnson, Virginia E. "Incest: The Ultimate Sexual Taboo." *Redbook,* April 1976.

O'Neal, P.; Schaefer, J.; Bermann, J.; and Robins, L. N. "A Psychiatric Evaluation of Adults Who Had Sexual Problems as Children: A Thirty-Year Follow-Up Study." *Human Organization* 19 (1960): 32–39.

Pacht, Halleck. "Diagnosis and Treatment of the Sexual Offender: A Nine-Year Study." *American Journal of Psychiatry* 118 (1967): 9.

Paulson, Morris J. "Incest and Sexual Molestation: Clinical and Legal Issues." *Journal of Clinical Child Psychology* 7/3 (1978): 177–80.

Peters, J. J. "Children Who Are Victims of Sexual Assault and the Psychology of Offenders." *American Journal of Psychotherapy,* July 1976.

———. "Child Rape: Defusing a Psychological Time Bomb." *Hospital Physician,* February 1973, pp. 46–49.

Pirnay, D. R. "Incestuous Relations in a Large Family." *Acta Psychiatrica Belgica* 73/6 (1973): 713–24.

Polakow, Robert L., and Peabody, Dixie L. "Behavioral Treatment of Child Abuse." *International Journal of Offender Therapy and Comparative Criminology* 19/1 (1975): 100–103.

Rascovsky, Arnaldo, and Rascovsky, Matilda. "The Prohibition of Incest, Filicide, and the Sociocultural Process." *International Journal of Psychoanalysis* 53 (1972): 271–76.

Raybin, J. B. "Homosexual Incest: Report of a Case of Homosexual Incest Involving Three Generations of a Family." *Journal of Nervous and Mental Disorders* 148/2 (1969): 105–10.

Roberts, R. W. "A Comparative Study of Social Caseworkers' Judgments of Child Abuse Cases." *Dissertation Abstracts,* Columbia University, vol. 31 (09-A) (1970): p. 4894.

Robinson, H. "Review of Child Molestation and Alleged Rape Cases." *American Journal of Obstetrics and Gynecology* 110/3 (1971): 405–406.

Sarlis, R. M. "Incest." *Pediatric Clinics of North America* 22/3 (1975): 633–42.

Schechner, Richard. "Incest and Culture: A Reflection on Claude Levi-Straus." *Psychoanalytic Review* 58 (1972): 563–72.

Schultz, Leroy G. "Child Sex Victim: Social, Psychological, and Legal Perspectives." *Child Welfare* 52 (1973): 147–57.

———. "The Sexual Abuse of Children and Minors: A Bibliography." *Child Welfare* 53 (1979): 147–63.

Schwartzman, John. "The Individual, Incest and Exogomy." *Psychiatry* 37/2 (1974): 171–80.

Sgroi, S. "Sexual Molestation of Children." *Children Today* 68 (1975): 18–21.

Shamroy, Jerelyn A. "A Perspective on Childhood Sexual Abuse." *Social Work* 25 (1980): 128–31.

Shelton, William R. "A Study of Incest." *International Journal of Offender Therapy and Comparative Criminology* (London) 19/2 (1975): 139–53.

Smith, Howard, and Van der Horst, Brian. "Innovations on Incest." *Playboy,* September 1976.

Swanson, D. W. "Who Violates Children Sexually?" *Medical Aspects of Human Sexuality* 5 (1971): 184–97.

Tsai, Mavis, and Wagner, Nathaniel N. "Therapy Groups for Women Sexually Molested as Children." *Archives of Sexual Behavior* 7 (1978): 417–527.

Van Gijsehem, Hubert. "Father–Daughter Incest." *Vie Medicale au Canada Francais* (Quebec) 4/3 (1975): 263–70.

Virkkunen, M. "Incest Offenders and Alcoholism." *Medicine, Science and the Law* 14 (1974): 124–28.

Weber, Ellen. "Incest: Sexual Abuse Begins at Home." *Ms.,* April 1977.

Weeks, R. "Counseling Parents of Sexually Abused Children." *Medical Aspects of Human Sexuality,* 1976, pp. 43–44.

Williams, J. E. Hall. "The Neglect of Incest: A Criminologist's View." *Medicine, Science and the Law* 14/1 (1974).

Wolf, A. P. "Childhood Association and Sexual Attraction: A Further Test of Westermarck Hypothesis." *American Anthropologist* 72 (1972): 503–15.

Family Service Center
Naval Submarine Base New London
P.O. Box 93
Groton ,Connecticut 06349